P9-ARS-559

Maya Archaeology and Ethnohistory

The Texas Pan American Series

Maya Archaeology and Ethnohistory

Edited by Norman Hammond and
Gordon R. Willey

*Cambridge symposium on recent research in
Mesoamerican archaeology, 2d, 1976*

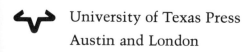 University of Texas Press
Austin and London

FERNALD LIBRARY
COLBY-SAWYER COLLEGE
NEW LONDON, N.H. 03257

F
1435
C3

The Texas Pan American Series is published
with the assistance of a revolving publication fund
established by the Pan American Sulphur Company.

Library of Congress Cataloging in Publication Data

Cambridge Symposium on Recent Research in Mesoamerican Archaeology, 2d, 1976.

(The Texas Pan American series)
Papers presented at the Second Cambridge Symposium on Recent
Research in Mesoamerican Archaeology, Aug. 29–31, 1976, which was
held under the auspices of the Centre of Latin American Studies,
Cambridge University.
1. Mayas—Congresses. 2. Mayas—Antiquities—Congresses. 3.
Mexico—Antiquities—Congresses. 4. Central America—Antiquities—
Congresses. I. Hammond, Norman. II. Willey, Gordon Randolph,
1913– III. Cambridge. University. Centre of Latin American Studies.
IV. Title.
F1435.C3 1976 972 78-19088
ISBN 0-292-75040-4

Copyright © 1979 by the University of Texas Press

All rights reserved

Printed in the United States of America

Grateful acknowledgment is made to the College of Fine Arts, University
of New Mexico, for permission to reprint material previously published
in *New Mexico Studies in the Fine Arts*, copyright The Regents of the
University of New Mexico.

E 015

Contributors

MARSHALL JOSEPH BECKER, West Chester State College

GORDON BROTHERSTON, University of Essex

CLEMENCY COGGINS, Harvard University

GEORGE L. COWGILL, Brandeis University

BRUCE H. DAHLIN, Catholic University

SUSANNA M. EKHOLM, Harvard University and
New World Archaeological Foundation

NANCY M. FARRISS, University of Pennsylvania

MERLE GREENE ROBERTSON, Middle American Research
Institute, Tulane University

NORMAN HAMMOND, Rutgers University and Cambridge University

PETER D. HARRISON, Middle American Research
Institute, Tulane University

THOMAS A. LEE, JR., Brigham Young University and
New World Archaeological Foundation

RICHARD M. LEVENTHAL, Harvard University

ARTHUR G. MILLER, University Museum,
University of Pennsylvania

DENNIS E. PULESTON, University of Minnesota

JACINTO QUIRARTE, University of Texas at San Antonio

B. L. TURNER II, University of Oklahoma

GORDON R. WILLEY, Harvard University

To Geoffrey H. S. Bushnell, distinguished Americanist

Contents

Preface

The fourteen papers in this volume have been selected from the forty presented on August 29–31, 1976, at the Second Cambridge Symposium on Recent Research in Mesoamerican Archaeology, held in Corpus Christi College and King's College. Economic stringency made it impossible to publish a synoptic volume similar to that resulting from the First Symposium in 1972 (*Mesoamerican Archaeology: New Approaches*, edited by Norman Hammond [London: Duckworth, and Austin: University of Texas Press, 1974]), and since more than half of the papers presented were on Maya topics in general or particular we felt that a volume emphasizing this aspect of recent research would be of value. Some of the Maya papers presented at the symposium are not published here, for various reasons: some authors required more time for revision or had already promised publication elsewhere, while others, among them the senior editor, felt that the subject matter in their papers was already receiving publication elsewhere in a manner that would make another published version redundant.

The papers in the volume do, however, present a fair conspectus of the research presently being carried on in the Maya field, in both excavation and library research, and in the Introduction we have attempted to show how these particular approaches fit into the general advance of Maya studies. (Maya-Christian dates are rendered using the Goodman-Martinez-Thompson correlation.)

For the holding of the symposium we acknowledge the help of the Centre of Latin American Studies of Cambridge University and its Director, Dr. David Brading, under whose auspices the meeting took place, and the financial assistance of the University of Cambridge for hospitality. Professor Glyn Daniel, Disney Professor of Archaeology in the University, gave an opening address to the symposium. Much of the administrative load was borne by the long-suffering Secretary of the Centre, Melanie Hall, who also dealt sympathetically with a variety of personal problems during the meeting. The Master, Fellows, and Staff of Corpus Christi College made the members of the symposium welcome guests, and the Provost and Fellows of King's College kindly placed the Keynes Hall at our disposal for the formal sessions.

N.H.
G.R.W.

Introduction
by Gordon R. Willey and Norman Hammond

In a sense, this collection of essays on Maya archaeology and ethno-history is a random sample from the range of current scholarship. The essays are addressed to topics of the authors' own choosing in the for-mat of the Cambridge Symposium, with no restrictions other than quality and limitation to some aspect of Maya studies. We make no apologies for this "randomness" or "scatter." The specialized sympo-sium with its proceedings confined to a narrow theme has its proven value, but so, in our opinion, has the assembly and discussion of heter-odox interests. In the present case, these examples of various lines of current Maya research do tend to cohere around a central theme, albeit a broad one, that of the nature of ancient Maya social and political structure and the degree to which Maya culture approximated those conditions of civilization and urbanism which, in the larger compara-tive perspective, are of interest to most anthropologists and historical scholars.

Marshall Becker's essay, with which we open the volume, is directly concerned with this theme. It treats with the way Maya archaeologists, for over a century and a half, have conceived of the great Maya Pre-Columbian sites, of the model of the "city" as opposed to that of the "ceremonial center," and of the implications of this for our interpreta-tions of the larger fabric of Maya society. The four articles which fol-low, those by Bruce Dahlin, Clemency Coggins, George Cowgill, and Dennis Puleston, all, in their quite different ways, face this same set of problems. We have grouped these first five essays under the heading "Theoretical Interpretations." They are concerned with speculations and hypotheses. As archaeological studies they are all grounded in the material data, but they move very rapidly away from such data to formulations about the nonmaterial past, the processes of social, po-litical, economic, and ideological development, and attempts to evoke the quality of ancient Maya life. Clearly, such essays are more suscep-tible to and provocative of discussion than those confined to the pri-mary archaeological or ethnohistorical data, and this is reflected in our introductory comments here.

At the same time, the next five essays, those on archaeological "Data Presentations," are not without their implications for questions raised in the theoretical essays. They deal with the specifics of a major site settlement pattern, with Pre-Columbian agricultural production, and with aspects of art, iconography, and crafts which give us some sense of the complexity of the cultural matrix in which both producers and patron operated. The final four essays offer a bridge from the Pre-Co-lumbian Maya into the Colonial European-Maya world. Like all such ethnohistoric-archaeological bridges, this one for the Maya is limited in the weight and kind of interpretive traffic it will bear. It is no open and smooth thoroughfare into an understanding of the past. Nevertheless, these articles tell us a good deal about the way the transition from a native to a European Colonial social order was made; and in so doing they reflect back upon the quality of Maya civilization.

To return to what we have defined as the central theme—the nature of ancient Maya civilization, its structure and functions—Becker has cast his essay in an epistemological and critical frame. According to him, early Maya archaeologists thought of the great Maya sites as true cities. That is, they were considered the nuclei of large populations with all of the attendant functions of government, trade, and manufacturing that the Old World model of the city generally implies. Later, according to Becker, from sometime in the 1920's into the 1940's and later, this model was replaced by J. E. S. Thompson's "ceremonial center" concept. In this, the principal Maya sites were believed to have been only temple-and-palace precincts—essentially "vacant cities"—inhabited only by a priestly aristocracy and their retinues, who were supported by a lowly agrarian peasantry living in scattered farmsteads or hamlets at some distance from these centers of the elite. Now, in more recent years, as we have come to know more about the Maya centers and the overall dispositions of Maya settlement, the earlier, or "true city," model is being revived, particularly in view of the evidence from Tikal (Haviland 1970). The potentially wide implications of these two models are, of course, self-evident. One might say that the "true city" model brings ancient Maya society into the mainstream of cultural evolution, entailing as it does the institutions of state-level governance, an urban-type economy, and the correlates of a complex class system. As opposed to this, the "ceremonial center" model presents the Maya as a somewhat aberrant development, in which all of these above-mentioned institutions are less developed or have proceeded along courses more peculiar to themselves. New data now coming in from various sectors of research do indicate that the "true city" model as a nexus of trade, bureaucracy, and a "rising middle class" has much to recommend it. Becker takes one of us (Willey) to task for not following the basic evidence of settlement patterns all the way to a realization of the full applicability of the "true city" model; but that author would respond that settlement evidence, as he has seen it, does not lead all the way to such a clear conclusion. There are ambiguities in the data, and Thompson's concept, although overly polarized, still has to be kept in mind as we try to find our way through the literal and figurative jungle of Lowland Maya settlement and its demographic, social, political, and economic significances. As an aside, Becker reads much of Thompson's own social, political, and religious background into the "ceremonial center" formulation. True, but our only comment would be that the millennial goal of absolute objectivity in model building is still a long way off and that fashions in thought and circumstances are still operative on the archaeologist today. As a concession to objectivity, as we argue the matter out, we suggest David Webster's (1977) term "organizational center" as preferable to either "ceremonial center" or "city" as these may be applied to the great Lowland Maya sites.

Both Dahlin and Coggins are concerned with the rise of Classic Maya civilization. Dahlin examines this development from the vantage point of the Protoclassic Period and with an emphasis on external influences. Along with some of his colleagues (Sheets 1971), he looks to El Salvador and sees the eruption of the Ilopango volcano, about A.D. 250, as the triggering event. This disaster forced western Salvadoran populations north into the Maya Lowlands. The archaeological evidence for this migration is seen in the Lowland occurrences of the Floral Park or Holmul I ceramic complex, with these occurrences being concentrated mainly along the eastern, or Belize, edge of the Peten. Dahlin then reasons that these immigrants brought with them the skills of cacao production and that as cacao producers they established a successful economic symbiosis with the Lowland Maya heartlands, especially Tikal. Such economic stimulation, in turn, was a major factor in the buildup of the Tikal Classic. This explanation favors the "true city" model, arguing as it does for the rise of major trade nuclei as early as the end of the Late Preclassic. It is a hypothesis to be kept in mind, although whether the appearance of the Floral Park ceramic complex signals migration, as opposed to more casual diffusion of some salient elements into a basically Lowland development, is a matter that is still under debate (Hammond 1976; 1977; Pring 1977).

Coggins's data and arguments are drawn largely from the intricacies of Tikal political history as this is read and extrapolated from the hieroglyphic texts and iconography of the site. She defines a "Middle Classic Period" for Tikal, which corresponds approximately to the Classic Maya "hiatus" (Willey 1974b) and is the two hundred years or so following the reign of Stormy Sky and preceding the "renaissance" of Ruler A's accession to the throne (Jones 1977). This is a time of relatively low cultural profile following a rupture of relations with Teotihuacan. Coggins's treatment of this whole Tikal-Teotihuacan relationship is the most fascinating part of her paper. She sees Curl-Snout, the founder of the Teotihuacanoid Early Classic dynasty at Tikal, as the synthesizer of Mexican ritual and calendrics with those of the resident Maya. Such a synthesis was, in effect, the sanctification of a new mercantilist philosophy which the Central Mexican Highlanders had succeeded in grafting onto the polity of conservative, ancestor-worshiping Lowland Maya society. Such a philosophy and outlook then prevailed throughout the reigns of Curl Snout and his successor, Stormy Sky, or until the beginning of the "Middle Classic Period" at about A.D. 480. During the "Middle Classic Period" (A.D. 480–680) Coggins sees a constant dialectic between the older Lowland Maya values and those which Curl Snout had implanted at Tikal, with no clear winner or ruler emerging to maintain the dominance of one side or the other. Finally, after A.D. 680, the powerful Ruler A emerged to revive the symbols, and presumably the international trading policies, of Curl Snout and Stormy Sky. Such an interpretation takes one back to Becker's "true city" and "ceremonial center" models. It may very well be that the Maya were themselves ambivalent about these two models and at loggerheads with each other over just what kind of political and socioeconomic structure they wanted to design. We are inclined to think that there must have been tension within Lowland Maya society from a quite early time as aristocratic lineages attempted to control, channel, and to a degree restrict trading contacts which otherwise might have been disruptive to an existing social order. This probably began during the Late Preclassic with the first organizational centers, which were, primarily, "ceremonial centers." Trade and contacts from the south, possibly mediated through immigrant colonies from Salvador as Dahlin argues, would have increased Lowland Maya wealth but also would have increased the tensions within a conservative society. A few centuries later the Teotihuacan connections, whatever they may have been in all of their ramifications, were obviously much more difficult to deal with. The dilemma was a real one, for without these external contacts and pressures Lowland Maya Classic greatness seems to have grown dim, as in Coggins's "Middle Classic Period." With the "renaissance" of Ruler A, Teotihuacan contacts, per se, were not revived. By this time it was too late for that. Teotihuacan was no longer a Mesoamerican power; but Late Classic Maya culture did assimilate Central Mexican influences. These are seen in art and iconography, as Coggins points out, and her assumption that this represents ideological change seems well taken. From an even longer historical perspective, going beyond the Late Classic to the "great collapse" of the ninth century, it would appear that the Lowland Maya never did fully resolve the tension between the old local, "ceremonial center–oriented" way of life and the trend toward the "true city" that characterized other parts of Mesoamerica. For whatever reasons—and a search for these constitutes one of the major concerns of Maya archaeology—the Lowland Maya were never able to effect fully the synthesis which Curl Snout had proposed.

According to Cowgill, one of these reasons for Lowland Maya failure may have been a predisposition for endemic warfare. Cowgill's case is a sophisticated and subtle one, drawing on comparisons from Teotihuacan as well as China and ancient Greece. The thrust of his argument is that population increase may be a result of conscious cultural (sociopolitical) choice. Such a decision may have been dictated—as Cowgill believes was true for the Lowland Maya—by a desire for military advantage. This reverses the process whereby warfare is a result of population growth and pressure. Cowgill notes that Teotihuacan achieved its population maximum by about A.D. 200. After that, population remained constant and static until the sudden collapse of the city, probably by military conquest, about A.D. 700. The Lowland Maya population growth profile is quite different. From Preclassic times onward there appear to have been peaks and dips, with the highest peak occurring in the cultural climax of the Late Classic Period. Cowgill rejects the idea that this Late Classic Maya population growth was an "overshoot" that precipitated the "great collapse." Instead, he sees it as the result of deliberate policy on the part of numerous warring "city-states." Such warfare may lead eventually to the domination of all contenders by a single successful "empire-builder," as in the case of ancient China, or it may result in very long periods of exhausting conflict without political integration, as with the Greek city-states.

The Lowland Maya would appear to have followed the latter course. If Cowgill is right, and there are an increasing number of clues to indicate that the old idea of the "peaceful Maya" is an erroneous one, then this militaristic competition is surely another token of the attempt on the part of the Maya to move toward state-type and "true city" organization in, at least, their later centuries.

Puleston's essay, on Maya fatalism and the eventual fate of the "great collapse," is enough to set a good materialist's teeth on edge. It is true, though, from what we have learned from ethnohistoric sources, that the Maya did have a cyclical view of history. In their calendar a katun of the same name came up every 256 years, at which time history was expected to repeat itself. The prophecies of the Chilam Balam state this with reference to the Itza abandonment of Chichen and to the fall of Mayapan possibly some 260 years or so later. Counting backward in time Puleston notes that the beginning of the "great collapse" precedes the Chichen abandonment by about this same span of time (thirteen katuns) and that, still earlier, the "hiatus" low point of Maya achievement began at thirteen katuns prior to the beginning of the "great collapse." We are left with the interesting proposition that ideology–"an epistemological error, a self-validating myth"–can provide a positive feedback for destruction in a cultural system. Is this no more than a series of coincidences, linked to rather vague ideas about "cycles of creation," the kinds of myths that are common to peoples in many parts of the world? Apparently the Maya themselves thought not, as Gordon Brotherston discusses in his essay at some length. The katun cycles had "undeniable historical dimensions," as well as supernatural sanctions, to their priests and scholars. Was their fatalism a subconscious expression of the tensions and instability within their culture and society? Were they somehow aware that the attainment of the urban state would always be just beyond their grasp and that their efforts to achieve it would lead to disaster?

Among the "Data Presentations" the essay by Gordon Willey and Richard Leventhal on Copan Valley settlement is most directly pertinent to Becker's "ceremonial center" or "true city" question. The Copan Valley, or that segment of it which forms the natural basin setting for the big site, is twelve kilometers long and four kilometers wide. The main center takes up less than a square kilometer of this territory, more or less in the center of the valley. Moving out from this center in all directions, on the valley floor as well as the bordering hillsides, are thousands of smaller structures. The pattern is relatively dense. As one moves further away from this segment of the valley such small mounds are fewer in number or are not found at all. In other words, there is a nucleation, or "knotting up," of apparent house or residential structures around the Copan organizational center if one views regional settlement in the large. The pattern, though, is not the urban pattern of Teotihuacan or Tenochtitlan. Spacing of fifty to one hundred meters between residential units is not the equivalent of street-to-street living. Of course we do not know, as yet, just what this Copan settlement distribution means socially and politically, although we have hopes that further surveys and excavations will give us more of a basis for developing ideas about this. This physical dimension of the

Lowland Maya urban problem—the study of settlement patterns and systems—is one of the important starting points for research into the whole question, and much remains to be done.

B. L. Turner's article is really the first to describe Maya agricultural terracing in any detail and as such merits particular commendation. This is done, especially, for the Río Bec region where Turner (1974a; 1974b) has worked, but he also includes a more general survey of Lowland Maya terracing as a whole. Mainly as the result of Turner's investigations we know now what we didn't five years ago, that terracing was extensive and important, at least in Late Classic times, and that the Maya were considerably more advanced as farmers than the simple long-fallow swidden method would imply (Harrison and Turner, eds., 1978). They had addressed themselves seriously to the problem of supporting large populations.

The essays by Jacinto Quirarte, Merle Greene Robertson, and Susanna Ekholm add to our knowledge of Maya sophistication in various realms of endeavor and regions. Quirarte is undoubtedly correct in his interpretation that much of Maya art and iconography pertains to the underworld, the afterlife. Yet in conceding this we do not think that anyone can seriously dispute the proposition that the Maya vision of the world of the dead reflected behavior in the world of the living. Status, rank, and interpersonal relations were an overriding concern in both. Greene Robertson gives us an insight into the high technical competence of one aspect of this art, a competence rooted in centuries of practice. Ekholm opens up another regional aspect of Maya art in her descriptions of the pottery and figurines of the Lagartero site in Chiapas. The styles here are clearly related to, yet significantly different from those of what we have recognized as the "standard" Peten-Usumacinta modes. This is another example of Late Classic regional diversity.

Peter Harrison's discussion of the Lobil Phase of the southern interior of the Yucatan Peninsula gives us a first glimpse of Postclassic culture and settlement pattern in this part of the Maya Lowlands. It would appear that Lobil is Late Postclassic in date, coming up to the time of the Spanish Conquest and beyond. The concentrated town pattern seems to obtain for Lobil—communities of perhaps fifteen thousand people. Tom Lee's Coapa study is set in the Upper Grijalva, out of the Maya Lowlands proper, but its analysis of Maya-Spanish acculturation makes it germane to the ethnohistoric approach. This approach is pursued in the question of religious syncretism by Arthur Miller and Nancy Farriss in their study of the east coast of Yucatan. They argue that Christian beliefs and iconography were not, at least in the Maya way of thinking, completely incompatible with old native beliefs and that the syncretistic results came not from bewilderment or misunderstanding but from an intellectual attempt on the part of the Maya to synthesize the old and the new (cf. J. E. S. Thompson 1970). Gordon Brotherston makes this same point still more dramatically in his analyses of the Chilam Balam. The early Spanish fathers were dealing with neither esoteric obscurantists nor bedazzled heathens. Rather, their Maya opposite numbers were highly sophisticated and somewhat cynical scholars, secure in what they believed the superiority of their ancient intellectual traditions offered them but willing, albeit under some pressure, to attempt accommodation to a new, if nevertheless inferior, theology. They were old hands at treating with foreigners. One was about as bad as another (or so they thought). Toltecs and Itza had come and gone. (And are there ancient memories here of the Teotihuacanos before them?) The Spaniards were yet another set of vulgar invaders, the kind of thing prophesied in the katun cycles, and were to be borne, along with famine and pestilence, as another of many preordained woes. Following Brotherston's interpretation, there can be no doubt that old, native Maya ideology survived the era of "Mexicanization" and was still an intellectual force in the sixteenth century.

To conclude this introduction, it is our opinion that a reading of these essays, disparate as they are in subject matter and approach, leaves one with the idea that while Maya cultural history and cultural processes cannot be understood in terms of the Maya alone, a Maya world, a Maya idea set, a Maya tradition, or whatever one wishes to call it, must always first be taken into account. While there is nothing particularly new in this statement of a basic anthropological tenet of cultural relativism, it is to be borne in mind as we attempt to formulate hypotheses for the explanation of the Maya past.

Theoretical Interpretations

1 Priests, Peasants, and Ceremonial Centers: The Intellectual History of a Model by Marshall Joseph Becker

As I look over the result of archaeological work, this fact forces itself upon me: how hard it is for an investigator, with a pet theory, to avoid moulding the facts to suit his theory rather than to shape his theory to suit the facts – E. H. Thompson 1886:248

Kuhn's (1962:151) observation that paradigms are accepted on faith rather than on the basis of logical argument can be demonstrated to apply quite well to theories about Maya social structure. A review of the history of the major theories concerning Maya society demonstrates how a major thesis came into existence, and continues as the model best known to the public, despite the lack of supporting archaelogical evidence. In keeping with Rogge's (1976) ideas concerning the examination of premises within one's own discipline we should consider the development of various models of Maya social structure and the evidence supporting each.

Although Classic Maya (ca. A.D. 250–900) social class structure has been inferred by numerous scholars during the past century, the evidence in most cases has been meager (see Clarke 1968:14–20). Recent advances in anthropology "have led Maya prehistorians into detailed consideration of demography, class structuring, economic systems, the nature of social integration mechanisms, and other matters previously thought to be beyond detection in the archaeological record" (Adams 1969:13). Various premises about the Maya which had been accepted as "facts" for years were discussed in 1970 at the Maya "Collapse Conference" (see Culbert 1973a). As Webb (1973) noted, the concepts regarding the structure of a society may be used to infer the reasons for changes in that society. For the Maya a sudden "collapse" had been postulated, but not demonstrated. The idea of an antagonistic system consisting of cruel priests and afflicted peasants provided a model for society which would explain a "collapse" due to a revolt of the peasantry. Although entirely undocumented, this was skillfully presented in the popular literature, and few scholars called for the evidence.

Assumptions regarding maize agriculture as the basis for Maya economics also have been called into question. The relationships between the agricultural system, population size, and social systems, as well as other assumptions regarding the ancient Maya, now are being reconsidered. This essay offers a detailed review of the development of the major theories regarding the structure of ancient Maya society. Despite numerous statements about Maya social organization and social integration, including those by Willey (in Willey et al. 1965), Haviland (1966b), and Sabloff (1973), and one excellent review (Kurjack 1974), no detailed study of these theories exists. A presentation of the literature pertaining to the development of the "ceremonial center" concept may clarify some of the basic conceptual problems relating to Maya social stratification and provide a basis for understanding the various models developed over the years (see Table 1-1) regarding the organization of Classic Maya sites. The extensive list of scholars who were concerned with this topic requires that the evidence be presented in historical order to provide the best perspective. Four periods of research, reflecting research methods and trends in thought, will be considered.

THE EARLY PERIOD OF RESEARCH: 1838–1923

Attracted by stories of the Conquistadores and research into Maya epigraphy (e.g., Beltrán 1746), a number of Europeans visited the ruins to gain a firsthand contact with these ancient people. The primary goal of scholars during this period was the recovery of information to formulate a general overview of the people of Mesoamerica. Efforts were directed toward surveys, recording of monuments, and excavating a few large structures at various sites. The first European visitors to Maya sites (Waldeck 1838; Stephens 1843; Maudslay 1886; Maler 1901–1903; 1908a; 1908b; 1911) generally considered that the ancient Maya had lived in large cities which had complex social class structures. The use of the term *city* by these "Great Explorers," including Caddy and Walker in 1830–1840 (Pendergast, ed., 1967), rather than terms such as *village* or *hamlet* indicates that these men believed that these sites once had relatively large and socially differentiated populations. Maudslay, for example, noted "stone roofed houses, probably dwelling houses" on raised foundations and in proximity to the ruins of "temples" on pyramidal foundations at Copan (1886:575) and at the "living city" of Tikal (1886:575,591; see also Church 1900).

The Yucatecan and coastal Maya sites, which had been largely ignored since Stephens's travels, became the focus for the attention of the American explorer E. H. Thompson. Thompson's astute observations at sites such as Sayil and Labna were similar to those made by Maudslay in Peten. Thompson perceived myriad house platforms surrounding the great temples (1886:253) and defined the "principle of abundance." This concept argues that the vast number of such small structures is prima-facie evidence for interpreting them as having been houses. Thompson later (1892) became the first Maya scholar to infer social organization from his field observations.

Cyrus Thomas, however, provided American scholars with a consideration of the Maya area which was a unique interpretation of Maudslay's work and may be the progenitor of J. E. S. Thompson's ceremonial center concept. Thomas called Terrace A at Copan "the heart of the sacred city," which he believed "was probably a religious center" (1899:554–556). Thomas concluded that Palenque and Copan "were evidently sacred centers." The possibility that J. E. S. Thompson may

Table 1-1. *Theories of Maya Social Class Structure*

Periods	Traditional View: Complex Cities and Numerous Classes	Thompson's Popular Model: Ceremonial Center with Priests and Peasants	Thompson Spin-off: Egalitarian Towns with Rotating Office Holders
Early Period 1838–1923 (Sites as inhabited cities)	Waldeck 1838; Stephens 1843; Maudslay 1886; E. H. Thompson 1886; Holmes 1895–1897; Bowditch 1901; Maker 1901; 1908a; 1908b; 1911; Morley 1910; 1915; Tozzer 1911; Spinden 1913; Gann 1918	Thomas 1899	
Middle Period 1924–1945 (Development of the Ceremonial Center concept)	Lothrop 1924; Morley 1924; Gann 1927; Wauchope 1934; Mason 1938; Kirchoff 1943	J. E. S. Thompson 1927; 1931; 1942; Ricketson and Ricketson 1937; Satterthwaite 1937b Ethnographers: Bunzel, Parsons, Redfield, Wagley (see Table 1-2)	
Transitional Period 1946–1954	Morley 1946; Kidder 1950(?); Ekholm 1949; Barrera Vásquez and Morley 1949; Barrera Vásquez 1951; Satterthwaite 1951(?); Brainerd 1954	Kidder 1950(?); J. E. S. Thompson 1954a:86–90; Brainerd 1954	
Late Period 1955–1970 Complex models (and a third model develops)	Morley 1956 (rev. Brainerd); Shook and Proskouriakoff 1956; Borhegyi 1956a; 1956b; W. R. Coe 1957; 1965a; Palerm and Wolf 1957; Olivé and Barbá 1957; Wolf 1959; Willey and Bullard 1965(?); Haviland 1966a; 1968; Adams 1970	Morley 1956 (rev. Brainerd); Willey and Bullard 1956; Willey 1956a; 1956b; W. R. Coe 1959; Bullard 1960; Smith et al. 1963; Willey and Smith 1963; 1969; Willey and Bullard 1965(?); Willey et al. 1965; M. D. Coe 1965(?); J. E. S. Thompson 1966; 1970	Bullard 1964; M. D. Coe 1965(?) (see Vogt 1961 through 1969)

have used this idea makes Thomas's statement a significant part of this review.

Nineteenth-century studies of Mesoamerican sites were summarized by W. H. Holmes (1895–1897), who referred to all sites as "cities." Continuing research reaffirmed the general assumption that all Maya sites were once cities. By the turn of the century greater efforts were being made to explore and record the numerous newly discovered Maya ruins. Bowditch (1901:697–700) and Maler (1901:10; 1908*a* passim; 1908*b*:61; 1911:5, 10) both directed their efforts at dating these "ruined cities." Maler, who already had implied a residential function for certain structures by the use of the term *casa* (1901:52–53), later became concerned with the structure of the city, reaching much the same conclusion as Maudslay and E. H. Thompson. Maler's analysis of the relationship between various aspects of the large "city" of Tikal led him to conclude that the "monumental sections of the city were surrounded by thousands of houses and huts built of perishable material and covered with roofs of palm leaves" (1911:55).

A year before Maler published his great classic, Morley published his study of Uxmal (1910). This work includes the first attempt to present evidence for a structure as having had religious functions. Morley (1910:1, 17) identified one building, variously called a "temple," a "sanctuary," and the "supreme sanctuary," as having been ceremonially important on the basis of its large size, high elevation, and relatively distinct position within its group.

Tozzer's *Preliminary Study of the Prehistoric Ruins of Tikal* and Maler's observations on Tikal were published by the Peabody Museum in 1911 (Tozzer 1911; Maler 1911). Like Maler, Tozzer (1911:93) considered Tikal, Holmul, etc., as cities. Tozzer (1911:120) was the first to recognize that the Central Acropolis at Tikal was "primarily for residence," and agreed with Maler that the North Acropolis was primarily ceremonial in function. Tozzer, who questioned various interpretations in Maya archaeology, noted that a major difficulty in evaluating city size resulted from questionable conclusions concerning what constitutes the "environs" of a site (1911:95). This problem continued to plague scholars for over fifty years (see Puleston and Callender 1967).

Between 1911 and 1920 other scholars reaffirmed the earlier evaluaations of Maya sites as complex cities. Morley (1915:2–4, 15) considered all the great Classic sites as cities and assumed that an extremely complex social and political organization was necessary to maintain them. Morley, like Spinden (1913:3ff.), considered these to be cities such as those described by Landa and others after the Conquest (see also Brunhouse 1975:139). But Morley also supported this conclusion with direct archaeological evidence when he indicated that the vast differences in mortuary customs found within various sites were significant indicators of social class differences (Morley 1915:7). He referred to Landa's observation that when people of high estate were buried they had temples built over them. Morley thus inferred that differences in burial form reflected differences in social class. He later suggested that the vast size of these sites, the evidence for middle class trades and occupations, and the elaborate system of worship which required a numerous and highly organized priesthood supported the concept of these sites having been complex "cities."

Direct archaeological evidence for a complex class structure accumulated rapidly. As Morley (1920:7, 14) continued his hieroglyphic studies of monuments at Copan and other "cities," T. W. F. Gann was reviewing his earlier (1900) statements regarding differentials in mortuary customs and formulating methods by which social differences could be inferred (1918:127). As the Early Period of research drew to a close Gann led the shift from pure data gathering and exploration to the beginnings of analysis. At this time Maya sites generally were seen as cities or large towns organized as parts of a complex society. The development of Thompson's popular model, traced below, offered an interpretation vastly different from that which had existed. Although today the consensus supports a theory of relatively complex social class structure among the Classic Period Maya (see Culbert 1973a), a review of the development of the predominant models may clarify current theoretical positions. Only two of the three schools of throught regarding Classic Maya social structure have been significant in archaeological research. These two may be characterized as dichotomous (priest-peasant hypothesis: J. E. S. Thompson 1954a), and complex (a number of ranked social classes: Borhegyi 1956a).

THE MIDDLE PERIOD OF RESEARCH: 1924–1945

The Middle Period of Maya research was characterized by excavation rather than discovery. Although the concept of Maya sites as "cities" continued, the formulation of the "ceremonial center" concept took place at this time. The Carnegie Institution of Washington was the most active agency during these two decades (see Adams 1969), bringing outstanding field methods to Maya archaeology. However, the Carnegie staff, in the Boasian tradition, developed few theories by which the data could be integrated. Paralleling the archaeological activities of this period were numerous endeavors directed at recovering ethnographic information from the Modern Maya. This research sustained interesting interactions with archaeological interpretation, as noted below.

Publication of Lothrop's material from Tulum (1924) marked the beginning of the Middle Period. Lothrop considered Tulum a city with a dense settlement. This situation differed markedly from that confronted by Morley in Peten. On the basis of calculations made by Love and Ricketson, Morley (1924:272) suggested that ". . . for example, Tikal and Uolantun are so close together, 3.5 miles, that they must be regarded as parts of the same city." This reflects continuing concern with the problem of defining site boundaries.

Gann's (1927:166–175, 223) observations provided useful details supporting the ideas and interpretations of his colleagues. His later statements offered greater detail to his earlier observations (1918) regarding social structure. Gann conceptualized all of the Maya cities under a single political ruler residing at Tikal (1927:233). Gann did not believe that the various Maya cities were independent city-states as found in the Classical world, but he did perceive each as being a complex city operating within a pan-Maya political system. This idea was published in the same year that J. E. S. Thompson published his first popular leaflet for the Field Museum. The ideas in this pamphlet were diametrically opposed to those then current in the scholarly world. Gann and Thompson later coauthored a work in which Thompson stated (1931:199) his popularized idea that the Maya lived in small agricultural settlements while the religious centers were uninhabited, while Gann suggested just the opposite. This divergence from the complex model, however, only appeared in Thompson's popular work.

Wauchope's concern (1934:113) with residential structures and the nature of social structure at Uaxactun marked the inception of an important shift in the goals of Mesoamerican archaeology (see Mason 1938:308). The work of Wauchope, who directed his research toward proving various hypotheses concerning the internal structure of Uaxactun, and others was characterized as anthropological archaeology. Wauchope noted (1934:113) that prior to his work primary attention had been directed toward the "civil and religious center of the sites investigated." Wauchope believed that such concern was justified in Maya cities, but "furnished us with knowledge of the customs of only the highest social stratum, the priests and the chieftains, who always form a very small percentage of any population." Interest in "housemounds" (Wauchope 1934) intensified during the Middle Period as scholars sought to understand the entire cultural situation (see J. E. S. Thompson 1939:1–2).

Subsequent to Wauchope's consideration of problems related to residence and building identification and in the tradition of Morley (1910), Linton Satterthwaite, Jr., attempted to quantify specific techniques by which temples could be recognized at Piedras Negras (1937a:162–174). This work anticipated the trends in research during the Transitional Period. Satterthwaite's detailed inquiry (1937b), based on trait analysis, led to several breakthroughs in the evaluation of building function. Both sweat houses and ball courts (Satterthwaite 1944:38–39) were described by analysis of traits, and other building functions were suggested (Satterthwaite 1954). Satterthwaite (1951:21) also was the first to propose a specific program of excavations to determine "how people of each class lived." Despite these innovations Satterthwaite's views did not develop a strong trend in research. Perhaps his precise and objective writing style together with a tendency to publish in journals with limited circulation precluded the wide dissemination of his ideas. On the other hand, Thompson's popular "syntheses" of field data achieved wide distribution and acceptance of his views, even by scholars in the field.

*Ethnography in the Middle Period (1924–1945):
Influence on Archaeological Interpretations*

While excavating at Uaxactun, O. G. Ricketson suggested that modern "pueblos" in the highlands could serve as models for understanding the ancient site. His belief that the modern towns were used primarily for trade, government affairs, and more important religious festivals (Ricketson and Ricketson 1937:15) indicated a concern with ethnographic analogy. However, his ideas led to numerous interpretive problems. Ricketson assumed that the great ruins to which "we refer as cities" were never urban communities, but more like modern Sololá and Chichicastenango because (1) he discerned no housing around groups of temples; and (2) he could find no limits to the housemounds, which would indicate the end of a city. Once again the problem of defining site limits had created an interpretive problem.

Ricketson did not realize that all modern Highland villages were not like Chichicastenango (see Borhegyi 1956a:6), nor did he have the skill to recognize the archaeological remains of small residential structures, as later developed at Tikal (Carr and Hazard 1961) and Dzibilchaltun (Stuart et al. 1965; see also Puleston and Callender 1967). What is more important is that Ricketson's ideas regarding modern village organization derived in part from ethnographic concepts which in turn had been partly based on Thompson's false archaeological conclusions.

A brief summary of ethnographic research in the Maya area provides insights into the archaeologists' evaluations of cultural behavior among the Classic Period Maya. Although much of this research was not published until long after the completion of field work, reports, papers, and informal communication disseminated the basic information among the small group of Mesoamericanists (see Table 1-2).

One of the more important studies of the period was that conducted by Bunzel. Although unpublished for some twenty years, her information relative to highland Guatemalan settlement pattern and social organization was available in manuscript form (see Wagley 1941:bibliography).

Table 1-2. *Ethnographic Field Work*

Scholar	Dates of Field Work	Date(s) of Publication	Area
Bunzel	1930–1932	1952	Chichicastenango
F. W. McBryde	1931	1934	Sololá
E. C. Parsons	Early 1930's	1936	Southern Mexico
Redfield and Villa Rojas	1920's	1934	Chan Kom
M. Steggerda	1931	1941	Yucatan
S. Tax	1925 to 1941	1937; 1953	Panajachel (Highland Guatemala)
C. Wagley	1937	1941	Santiago Chimaltenango
C. Wisdom	Ca. 1931	1940	Chorti Indians

Evidence for the relationship between ethnographers and archaeologists may be found in Wisdom's earlier position as assistant to J. E. S. Thompson in the excavations at San José. Redfield subsequently was employed by the Carnegie Institution to provide ethnographic information to complement their archaeological interpretations.

Bunzel, Parsons, and Redfield all suggested that modern Mesoamerican villagers maintain what has been described as a dispersed settlement pattern. Similarly, Wagley assumed that most villages were only political, economic and ritual centers. While contending that Santiago Chimaltenango was unusual since the majority of its population lived in the pueblo, Wagley made a most significant undocumented comparison. "The majority of Guatemalan Indians, however, live near their fields, as did their ancient ancestors; the Spanish pueblo with its church and market center has supplanted the aboriginal ceremonial centers" (1941:8–9). The importance of this comparison was the absence of *published* archaeological data regarding these "ceremonial centers." One must conclude that Wagley based his ethnographic evaluation on Thompson's ceremonial center hypothesis. Apparently this concept or the use of the term *ceremonial center* was sufficiently well established when Wagley first wrote this paper in 1938, or by the time of its revision in 1940, that he could make this statement without quoting a source. Prior to 1938 only J. E. S. Thompson (1931:334) offered a model of a vacant ceremonial center with population residing in dispersed hamlets. Wagley applied that specious archaeological model to an ethnographic situation, despite the fact that it contradicted the evidence from Santiago Chimaltenango. Such uses of Thompson's data created biases among ethnographers which in turn generated ethnographies which were used to interpret archaeological "evidence."

One also might note that Wagley, like Sol Tax, considered Indians and Ladinos in the highlands to be part of a cohesive cultural unit. Perhaps only Stuart Chase (1931), a nonanthropologist, recognized the gulf which still exists between Indians and Ladinos in Mesoamerica.

The belief that the ancient Maya were sustained by a milpa economy with minimal potential for supporting complex technology (see Linton 1940) supported archaeological inferences concerning a dispersed settlement pattern. Variations on this theme appeared for many years (Hester 1952; 1953; 1954). This also established a circular argument concerning maize economics and residence patterns. Miles (1957; 1958) tried to alter the concept of vacant "towns," and Willey (1956c: 780) suggested using Redfield's (1941; 1956) useful data on peasants and their relations with city people. Chang (1958) only recently demonstrated that very *few* societies of swidden farmers actually live in dispersed settlements. However, nearly fifteen years were to pass before Kubler (1972b) provided a perceptive statement on the fallacious use of ethnography in reconstructing Maya social integration. Price's (1974) consideration of ethnographic models and archaeological inferences offers further insight into this important relationship.

The Middle Period of research, however, was characterized more by theory construction than by theory testing. Mason's summary (1938: 300) of the problems which plagued the archaeology of this area was of great intellectual utility, but was unnoticed by the scholars of the day. Mason pointed out that the "size and architectural wealth of Maya cities" was of general concern to archaeologists. His review statement concerning the decline of Maya cities offered a modification of Thompson's peasant revolt hypothesis (1931:230), but without interpretation of political or social organization. Although Mason noted ideas of Satterthwaite with which he agreed, Mason was not a supporter of the "priest-peasant" hypothesis as Webb (1964:745n.166) suggested. During the Middle Period of Maya research only J. E. S. Thompson specifically stated that Maya social organization was different from the complex model described by Landa at the Conquest.

Thompson the Popularizer: The Ceremonial Center Concept

The vast quantity of data generated during the Middle Period of Maya research supported the concept of Classic Maya sites as urban in character. Thompson's scholarly works did nothing to challenge this position, but his popular works developed a completely different thesis which had a significant influence on the course of Mesoamerican studies. The wide influence, prose style, and oratorical abilities of Eric Thompson were matched only by his enthusiasm and generosity with his colleagues. One must be fully aware of his dynamic personality in order to comprehend the significance of his contribution to and influence upon the course of Maya studies.

Thompson's first published statements regarding Maya sites and Maya social organization appeared in 1927 with the first edition of *The Civilization of the Mayas*. His statements regarding a dichotomized class organization appeared quite early, leading one to speculate on their origin. Neither historic sources nor excavation records supported this position, and one might consider what biases led to this conclusion, which evolved through four editions of this popular work.

Thompson began with a conclusion, which may be called the "priest-peasant hypothesis," and then interpreted his excavation data to support the correlated "ceremonial center" theory. The development of these two interrelated theories in the popular literature (with one exception) may be summarized as follows:

1927:12–23   Priest-peasant hypothesis first noted.

1931:334   First use of the term *ceremonial center*, without definition (in a scholarly report on four "sites" chosen because they were supposedly associated with residences).

1931:230   Introductory statement that occupation of these four sites resulted from open revolt of peasants against the "priest class."

1942:12–13   "Cities" really vacant "religious centers" (cf. Ricketson and Ricketson 1937:15).

1954*a*   The developed popular theory.

A detailed review of the development of this idea and counter arguments (Becker 1971) enables the reader to trace the history quite closely (see also Willey 1976). However, a brief summary of this development serves to show how Kuhn's (1962) thesis applies to theory in Mesoamerican archaeology. After years of excavating and studying Maya archaeology, Thompson's scholarly works remained noncommittal regarding interpretations of social structure. On the other hand, his popular works became more and more fanciful. Thompson never offered evidence, documentation, or tests of these concepts. The basis for these popularized ideas derived more from English social structure and Bolshevik history than from archaeological evidence. A number of factors which may have given rise to these ideas ought to be explored for their influence on the development of the "priest-peasant hypothesis" and to explain why it rapidly gained wide public acceptance.

Thompson grew up in English society, where well-defined and sharply separated social classes existed. European scholars of that time also believed that the medieval period, which was characterized by an extreme concern for the sacred reflected in cathedral construction, had a sharply divided order of social classes. Only recently have we learned that the medieval cathedrals were not the work of inspired and toiling peasant volunteers directed by their priests, but the coordinated efforts of corps of middle-class artisans. The idea of divinely directed peasants building these "temples" was accepted in 1927, and may have been transferred by Thompson to the New World.

In addition to this intellectual attitude, in the explosive first decade of the twentieth century the idea of the lost city of Atlantis was in great vogue. The more rapidly the scientific revolution changed the world, the greater the clamor for simplistic explanations and phantasmagorical theories of culture history. The Maya cities could be explained as being the products of inhabitants of the lost Atlantis, who seemed to be forever doomed to be lost again. The lost-city theme also may have been a projection of what many in the landed classes felt to be a growing horror: "urbanization." The growth of cities throughout the world created a climate in which many wished to escape back to nature. The antiurbanists of 1910 found the idea of cataclysm to be an attractive and fitting end of the unbearable urban lifestyle.

Other problems of twentieth-century urbanization generated more realistic fears among the aristocracy. Trade unions in England and America turned meek workers into violent strikers. The suffragists added to the stress by turning docile housewives into rebellious seekers after the vote. Socialism, in theory and in practice, had gained great strength between 1900 and 1910 and threatened "capitalism." The Great War, in which Thompson served as an underage youth, ended in the Russian Revolution and the establishment of a Marxist state. Almost immediately after the war, Thompson left for the family estancia in Argentina. His four years as an administrator on lands which had been held by his family for one hundred years (Graham 1976) involved him in a situation where harsh masters actually were terrorizing the peasant masses. Bloody revolts were frequent in Argentina. When combined with a growing fear of Communism in Europe this situation easily could have generated the "peasant revolt" theory of Maya decline. Thompson's subsequent studies at Fitzwilliam House, Cambridge, continued his exposure to Bolshevik ideas, and conservative fears. When this young student of Maya hieroglyphics arrived in Yucatan in 1924, a Bolshevik party had been in political control for six years (Brunhouse 1975). The beginnings of Thompson's popular peasant revolt theory could have been the historical events taking place in modern, not ancient, Mexico. A latent fear of Communist uprisings may have led Thompson to his priest-peasant hypothesis, and would also explain why Thompson *never* accepted the principle of Maya writing's being composed of syllabic elements (Graham 1976:319). This discovery was announced, amid much Communist bombast, by Yuri Knorosov in 1950. Years were to pass before Knorosov's work was demonstrated to have substance, and Thompson always refused to recognize its successes.

In retrospect one must consider that the prodigious output of J. E. S. Thompson, the persuasiveness of his style, the persistence of his theme, and his great production of popular works were all factors in disseminating this theory. A sharp distinction exists between Thompson's scholarly publications (1939; 1941; 1943; 1945; 1948; 1954*b*; J. E. S. Thompson in E. H. Thompson 1938), to which must be added his coauthored work on Cobá (J. E. S. Thompson et al. 1932), and his popular works (1927; 1942; 1954*a*; 1966; 1970). In Thompson's scholarly articles (except 1931 as noted above), priest and peasants do not appear, and sites are *not* designated as "ceremonial centers." Not only was Thompson neutral in his scholarly depictions of Maya sites, but he also indicated quite clearly that he recognized the complexity of these sites (e.g., 1948:47–49). His (1945:23) scholarly description of the process by which the "cities" came to be abandoned includes no reference to a peasant revolt theory.

On the basis of earlier observations (see Becker 1971) and conversations with Thompson after 1970, I was *not* surprised, as was Ian Graham (1976:319), that *Maya History and Religion* was issued as a trade book. Thompson's scholarly publications omit references co priests and peasants, while his popular works are based on these ideas. Perhaps he enjoyed playing the devil's advocate, and found it amusing that pap for the masses became grist for academic mills. In 1970, after noting this dichotomy in Thompson's work, I mentioned the observation to him. Thompson was completely at ease when he acknowledged the lack of a data base for his popular speculations on the nature of Maya society, ending this portion of our conversation with the statement that he had "never held a university appointment." The full meaning of this comment became clear only with Professor Glyn Daniel's opening address to the Second Cambridge Symposium on Recent Research in Mesoamerican Archaeology. Daniel noted that there had never been an English university position in American archaeology prior to 1966; Thompson, like Alfred Maudslay, G. H. S. Bushnell, and Louis Clark, could never aspire to a position which could support scholarship, and had to support his research by other means.

To better understand why J. E. S. Thompson's popular thesis took the form that became so widely accepted, one also should consider the intellectual relationship between the two Thompsons, the early interpretations of the evidence by Cyrus Thomas (1899), the impact of Satterthwaite's interpretation of the broken thrones at Piedras Negras (1937b:20), and the growing fear among many people during the Great Depression of a Communist revolution by the "peasant masses" bringing the destruction of traditional society (see Terkel 1970:passim). Few of these factors appear in the archaeological literature, but they are of importance in understanding how certain conclusions could be reached without the support of direct evidence. A further difficulty lay with two problems which continue to plague Mesoamericanists in their attempts to understand the structure of Maya society.

Tozzer (1911:95) first noted one of these problems when he observed that one difficulty in Maya archaeology was the definition of the *environs* of a city. Thompson's popular works shifted the terminology away from the use of *city* toward *ceremonial center*, producing a conceptual reorientation which inhibited generalized research programs such as the Tikal project. The second problem, the analysis of the social and political relationships which existed between the inhabitants of a site, had also been considered by Tozzer. In a review article Tozzer (1937) criticized archaeology for concentrating on excavation techniques and description without developing a body of theory which would lead to an understanding of how the inhabitants of a site lived, a difficulty not reconciled throughout the remainder of the Middle Period of research (see Kirchoff 1943). As Kluckhohn (1940) noted, "The industry of workers in this field is most impressive as is, for the most part, their technical proficiency, but one is not carried away by the luxuriance of their ideas."

Not until the application of anthropological models and the development of new approaches in archaeology, already under way at Uaxactun in the 1930's, was Maya research to produce significant information regarding the "culture" of the Classic Period. By the end of the Middle Period the theoretical structure of two strongly divergent models of Maya social structure had been developed. The following period of research found anthropological data considered more closely, and means were considered by which these dichotomous theories could be tested. Although the ceremonial center model was commonly employed, considerations were given to the nature of Maya sites of great size. A reconciliation of these two views was at hand.

THE TRANSITIONAL PERIOD OF RESEARCH: 1946–1954

During this brief period there was a decline in the activity of the Carnegie Institution of Washington and an increase in university-based research (see Adams 1969:20–23). This shift brought more anthropological theory to bear on archaeological problems by replacing scholars trained in the classical tradition with researchers broadly schooled in culture and its analysis. The use of anthropological theory, with its concern for developing models of behavior, was the most important factor characterizing this period. The evaluation of the existing evidence and creation of specific field projects led to new solutions of long-standing problems in Maya research, and toward a reconciliation of the two principal and opposing theories regarding Classic Maya social organization. Thompson's popular summarization (1954a) appeared at the close of this period. This was diametrically opposite Morley's (1946) position, which was later considered by Kidder (1947; 1950) and restated by Brainerd (1954). These authors had firm backgrounds in anthropology, and were able to bring specific data to bear on archaeological interpretation. The statements of these scholars suggested that ancient Maya social organization included a relatively complex series of closely spaced social classes. Thompson's research at Mayapan (1954b) and his other scholarly works did not dispute this problem, but his popular publications established a point of view which continues to be held by the public and even a few Mesoamericanists.

The Transitional Period produced a reformulation and, to a limited extent, a clarification of the positions regarding the analysis of Classic Maya social organization. New excavation data and other relevant publications, such as *The Maya Chronicles* (Barrera Vásquez and Morley 1949), added to the fundamental knowledge of the area (see also Barrera Vásquez 1951). Ekholm (1949) even went so far as to interpret Shook's data from Kaminaljuyu as indicating that an "advanced" social organization and economy existed as early as the Preclassic Period. This concept was supported by Brainerd (1954:20) and elaborated upon by Culbert (1974:xiii). Despite such farsighted observations, the lack of a sound theoretical basis for research among Mesoamericanists continued to plague the field. These problems had drawn criticism from several scholars (Tozzer 1937; Kluckhohn 1940; Taylor 1948). In general, the Transitional Period may be characterized best as a time of formulation of basic concepts as well as the continued publication of field reports and translations of historic documents.

Just as Thompson's *Rise and Fall of Maya Civilization* (1954a) links the Transitional Period with the preceding epoch, Brainerd's *The Maya Civilization* (1954) introduces the next period. Almost every aspect of Brainerd's work indicates that he was resynthesizing earlier concepts of Maya social organization by reflecting on Willey's studies (1953) in the Virú Valley, Peru. The positive aspects of Brainerd's work include its impressive brevity, the clear distinction made between "settlement pattern" and social organization, and following from this a clear indication that a complex social class system existed among the Maya as early as 100 B.C. Brainerd was the first scholar concerned with Mesoamerica to distinguish between settlement pattern data and the inferences which could be made therefrom regarding social classes. His separation of field data from conclusions and his logical order of making inferences were the most important legacy which Brainerd left to scholars of the Late Period.

Recent research in settlement pattern has formalized, restated, and to some extent confused the issue relative to Classic Maya social class systems. The two primary models and their variations were formulated during earlier periods. Proponents of both theories found support in new field data. Despite the long history of science applied to this area, most authors failed to consider means by which these theories could be tested (see Clarke 1968:34–40), and every variety of theory came to be proposed.

The year 1956 was most notable for publications regarding the subject of Classic Maya settlement patterns. Perhaps the best statement concerning the problem came from Shook and Proskouriakoff, who summarized the subject in the following fashion (1956:93): "These settlements were towns with nuclei of civic and religious buildings, which typically included pyramidal substructures of temples. Until recently, archaeological work was concentrated on these nuclei or 'ceremonial centers,' and data on the extent of sites and on the arrangement of dwelling units within them are very scant. The widely held opinion that ceremonial centers, particularly in the Maya area, served scattered rural populations and had few permanent inhabitants has recently been challenged . . ." Borhegyi (1956a; 1956b) and others were among the challengers who focused more clearly on the complex nature of Maya society.

Willey (1956b), ignoring his own dicta regarding settlement studies (1953), supported the ceremonial center model and, as might be expected, was joined by his own students (Willey and Bullard 1956; Bullard 1960). These supporters of a simple social class model also produced a minor intellectual aberration on this theme. Bullard (1964) suggested the "egalitarian" model of Classic Maya social organization, derived from comparisons with Vogt's ethnographic data. This homogenizing approach, which assumed rotating offices, came from Vogt's work (1961 through 1969), much of which was based on the ethnographies of McBryde, Tax, and Wagley, who in turn had used Thompson's archaeological "conclusions" in organizing their theories, as noted earlier. The "egalitarian model" held that the peasants were also part-time priests holding administrative offices for limited periods, a relationship which Vogt believed continued unchanged from the Classic to the present (see Table 1-1; also Haviland and Coe 1965:38). This theory was supported almost exclusively by scholars from Harvard.

Thompson's ceremonial center concept, however, continued to hold considerable attention and create confusion. Even Brainerd's revision of Morley's classic (1956) adopted a great deal from Thompson. Details of the complex positions held by various scholars are found elsewhere (Becker 1971).

During this recent period of research two main concepts continued to be used in the evaluation of Maya class systems. Thompson's simple model for Classic Maya social organization, which assumed dichotomous priest and peasant categories, was correlated with the idea of vacant ceremonial centers. Supporters of the second major position (complex class structures) found the simple model incapable of explaining many of the problems developed through the accumulation of vast amounts of field data.

Over the past few years most Mesoamericanists have been drawn to interpretations of Maya society as being more complex. This trend has become so general that few have considered the intellectual history of the ceremonial center concept or why it was ever invented.

SUMMARY OF "COMPLEX SOCIETY" MODELS

The model Kidder (in Shook and Smith 1950) provided for Classic Maya social organization was the first significant attempt to describe complex social class relationships as important to human interactions within Lowland Maya sites. Whereas Morley (1946) assumed these sites to be complex, Kidder attempted to understand their internal organization through an examination of the evidence. Borhegyi was among the first to state clearly that numerous social classes may have existed among the Classic Maya (1956a:348) and to provide the basic data needed to substantiate this hypothesis. Palerm and Wolf (1957) clearly pointed out the problems inherent in the ceremonial center hypothesis, although they utilized only indirect evidence to support an alternate model similar to that presented by Borhegyi. In reviewing the ceremonial center hypothesis and the attendent concept of a small and dispersed population Palerm and Wolf (1957:27) pointed out two "obvious weaknesses." The first weakness, repeatedly indicated above, was the *assumption* "that the non-urban character of Maya civilization is a demonstrated fact." Palerm and Wolf (1957:27) also found that this hypothesis "postulates the existence of a kind of social and political organization (based on the dichotomy between ceremonial center and rural population) which—it would seem—could hardly develop under the conditions of slash-and-burn agriculture." Palerm and Wolf then pointed out how the development of the ceremonial center concept violated any logical order of inference (see also Brainerd 1954:20; Olivé and Barbá 1957). The ceremonial center concept was a conclusion regarding social relationships drawn from an undocumented assumption regarding the structure of a Maya site, and never tested.

Prior to 1970 little direct evidence had been collected to demonstrate the social stratification at large Maya sites, but the idea had been gaining momentum (see W. R. Coe 1965a). As late as 1971, Willey and Shimkin could state that the evidence for the development of a class society was not yet clear from the archaeological record. The various indicators of cultural complexity were just being considered, and over the next few years the evidence for technological and concomitant social complexity were to be presented. Six indicators of cultural complexity are as follows (see Becker 1971: Ch. 2):

1. "Urbanism" and large population size (see Adams 1974; Haviland 1970; Millon 1973).
2. Evidence for occupational specialization, which suggests hierarchical social groupings ranked by expended time, energy, and

associated skill (Adams 1970; see also Houston and Wainer 1971; Andrews and Rovner 1973; Becker 1973*a*; Krotser and Krotser 1973).

3. Indications of differential access to goods and services:
   A. Dynastic lines (Proskouriakoff 1960; Kelley 1962*a*).
   B. Ceramic manufacture (Gifford, in Willey et al. 1965:35).
   C. Others (Adams 1970; Andrews IV and Rovner 1973; Becker 1973*b*).
4. Evidence of stratification from depictive sources (e.g., the Bonampak and other murals).
5. Implications from linguistic reconstruction (see Ehret 1976).
6. Gradations and distinct categories of structures at a site; presence of large structures (Becker 1971; Andrews IV and Rovner 1973; Sharer 1974).

The contemporary view of large Classic sites as cities also depends upon an understanding of the complex economic base which supported large populations. The old concept of slash-and-burn milpa agriculture, with all its productivity limitations, has been altered with ideas of tree crops, root crops, use of marine resources and ridged fields, and combinations of all these in a complex intercropping system. Despite this trend, the term *ceremonial center* often appears in varied contexts. Hammond's (1972; 1974) use of the term *ceremonial center* derives from Sjoberg (1955; 1960), in the sense of a "pre-industrial city in function and in most aspects of form except population density" (Hammond 1974:329). Having equated the term with the concept of city, Hammond says that "a ceremonial centre is after all a service centre for a population in much the same way as a modern shopping/civic centre/church complex is." Perhaps W. R. Coe's term *epicenter* might be used in these and similar situations. Dahlin (1976), following Coe, distinguishes between "epicentral Tikal" (ceremonial nucleus of the site) and "central Tikal" (the epicenter as well as the surrounding residential zone). Perhaps the "epicenter" is what Marcus (1973) intends when she uses the term *ceremonial-civic centers*. Terminological confusion has long plagued research in this area and should be eliminated. A further difficulty stems from analyzing a site with the ceremonial center in mind prior to excavation. This model may preclude a search for the vast number of small platforms upon which were built most of the structures of a Classic Period site, as at Altar de Sacrificios (Willey and Smith 1969). At this site Bullard's map indicates only 41 housemounds, all at least one meter high. Fourfifths of the 2,500 structures at Tikal are platforms less than one meter high (Carr and Hazard 1961), suggesting that the mapping at Altar de Sacrificios was incomplete. Willey and Smith (1969:23) concluded that the occupants of 41 structures represent a population which could "not be sufficient to have built or maintained a ceremonial center of the size of the one at Altar de Sacrificios." The original hypothesis (sites as vacant "ceremonial centers") influenced the research design and the final interpretation, leading Willey to ignore his own warning (Willey et al. 1955:20) against defining a community without being able to recognize house sites.

The implications set forth by this review include a need both to re-evaluate our theoretical models and to examine the evidence from a neutral point of view. Similar re-evaluations might also be in order for sites such as Chan Chan in Peru and the "palaces" on Crete. The basic archaeological problems in all areas of the world may be much the same. The evolution of ideas does not occur as an automatic process as new data is produced, but may occur for reasons entirely distinct from scholarly research.

CONCLUDING SUMMARY

The Early Period of Maya research can be characterized largely as a period of data gathering. During the Middle Period, which marks the beginning of extensive excavations such as those of the Carnegie Institution of Washington, little was done in the way of developing theoretical models, except in the popular writings of J. E. S. Thompson. His ceremonial center concept, with its attendant priest-peasant dichotomy, placed the population into two sharply distinguished and antagonistic social classes. This model, which is conspicuously absent in Thompson's scholarly works, dominated the thinking and research methodology of most Mesoamerican scholars between 1935 and 1960 and continues to pattern the thought of numerous people today.

The Transitional Period was characterized by the confusion generated by attempts to fit new information into an as yet undemonstrated model of social organization. However, during this period anthropological concepts were being applied with greater frequency to various archaeological situations. The recent period of research is marked by the development of new models based on anthropological theory and the archaeological evidence. More direct archaeological efforts to test and verify the various hypotheses developed also characterize this period. Use of the traditional ceremonial center concept as a rubric, while ignoring fundamental evidence concerning how the Classic Maya really lived, no longer characterizes research in Mesoamerica (see Parsons 1972). As M. D. Coe noted (1976:69), archaeological knowledge does not proceed by popular consensus. The slow but sure development of settlement pattern archaeology has generally eliminated the priest-peasant theory and the ceremonial center concept.

Culbert's (1974:19–22) useful discussion of the various theories of Classic Maya society assumes a complex social structure, with extensive trade and social stratification. However, E. Wyllys Andrews V (1976) offers what may be the most succinct sentence regarding the matter: "Many Classic Maya sites, until recently viewed as concentrations of ceremonial and civic buildings surrounded by small and dispersed populations, were in fact the seats of tremendous and obviously stratified populations." Contemporary scholars are concerned with the problem of defining the *variations* to be found within Classic Maya sites and analysing what these mean. From such evaluations of new data and re-evaluations of accumulated knowledge will come greater comprehension of how Classic Maya sites were organized, how the inhabitants of these sites interacted, and how the Classic Period adaptive strategy changed, resulting in the decline of the great cities, but not of the Maya people.

ACKNOWLEDGMENTS

Sincere thanks are due to D. Bryce, Robert H. Dyson, Jr., Ward Goodenough, W. A. Haviland, N. A. Hammond, Ruben E. Reina, and Norman B. Schwartz for reading earlier versions of this manuscript and offering valuable suggestions. Special thanks are owed the late J. Eric S. Thompson, whose kind words and scholarly advice continue to guide me in my work. Norman Hammond is responsible for enforcing a drastic shortening of this paper, and for its similarly shortened title.

Responsibility for the ideas and interpretations set forth in this paper as well as any errors which may appear are entirely my own.

2 Cropping Cash in the Protoclassic: A Cultural Impact Statement by Bruce H. Dahlin

Things fall apart; the centre cannot hold;
Mere anarchy is loosed upon the world.
—W. B. Yeats, "The Second Coming"

INTRODUCTION

In this paper I would like to review the evidence for the existence, nature, and sociological implications of a single geological event which can be dated to the Protoclassic Period in the Maya Lowlands. I will, for convenience, use the absolute date of A.D. 250 for the event itself (see below), and a date of A.D. 250 to 300 for the Protoclassic Period. It was at this time that a truly catastrophic eruption of Volcán Ilopango caused an unknown number of Late Preclassic Period peoples to flee from western El Salvador. They had previously been heavily involved in the production of finely decorated ceramics, cacao, cotton, and chipped stone (obsidian) (among other valuable commodities), and they are believed to have migrated into particular regions of the Guatemalan, Belizean, and Mexican Lowlands to the north where their activities could be continued at approximately the same scale. Their success in their new home was due to the fact that they could, and did, settle in areas along major river systems where conditions were propitious for conducting their former economic pursuits.

THE PROTOCLASSIC PERIOD

The chronological and cultural unit now known as the Protoclassic Period was first defined in the Maya Lowlands in 1932 with Merwin's and Vaillant's publication of Merwin's 1910–1911 excavations at the site of Holmul in northeastern Peten, Guatemala. It was defined then, and is normally defined today, on the basis of a complex of stylistic and formal ceramic traits that cohere in time, and it was formerly thought to cohere in space throughout the Maya areas as a whole. The complex of ceramic traits derived from the "Q Complex" which was first enunciated in 1927 by S. K. Lothrop and Vaillant and includes mammiform tetrapods, stucco painting, Usulutan-type decoration, spouted jars, potstands, and ring-based bowls. Basal flanges and Z-angles on bowls, and polychrome painting are listed sometimes also (cf. Willey et al. 1967:297). The first of Vaillant's phases, Holmul I, contains many of these traits.

These ceramic traits are not uniformly distributed in the Lowlands, however. Moreover, other nonceramic diagnostics can be used to identify archaeological contexts of the period as well. These include barkbeaters, spindle whorls, and spindle rests (Willey et al. 1965) and points-on-blades (Rovner 1975). I will have occasion to discuss some natural phenomena which help serve to date the period as well. For the meantime it is clear that the Protoclassic Period spans the juncture between the Late Preclassic (Chicanel Horizon) and the Early Classic (Tzakol Horizon) (Willey and Gifford 1961:152–153).

It would seem that indigenously and independently developed pottery traditions are found side by side with the full-blown Floral Park Horizon pottery at Barton Ramie (Willey and Gifford 1961:152–153; Willey et al. 1967), at Holmul, at Altar de Sacrificios (Adams 1971), and possibly at Nohmul (Pring 1975; 1977). In each case, the Floral Park Horizon does not appear to have derived from local ceramic traditions, although there may be some attribute sharing. Nor does the Floral Park appear to be a pottery complex that was reserved for special occasions by Maya elites such as one would expect with a mortuary complex, although such may have been the case in the Late Preclassic, when some decorated wares appear to have been imported from the southeastern highlands. This is no more clear than at Barton Ramie. Willey and Gifford explain that the new ceramic complex at Ramie

> differs radically in a stylistic sense from contemporary and earlier indigenous pottery, 2) is abundant in the frequence of its occurrence, and 3) occurs in many deposits throughout the site which can only be considered of domestic origin. . . . It is our belief that the Floral Park ceramic complex was made and used at Barton Ramie (paste and temper do not differ profoundly from types of local manufacture) by an intrusive population element that would have brought with it the stylistic attributes (broadly speaking the Holmul I style) so out of place in the pottery of the region prior to this time. This intrusive element, however, did not eclipse previous developmental trends. (1961:167)

By the middle of the following Hermitage Phase at Barton Ramie we appear to be seeing a settling in and assimilation of the incoming population.

Sharer (1968; 1969; 1974) and Sharer and Gifford (1970) have shown that the southeastern highlands can be viewed as the original home of at least the Barton Ramie intruders. They base their findings on specific ceramic similarities in both "ceremonial" and "utilitarian" wares. In the case of one very common ceramic group, Aguacate Orange, Sharer and Gifford (1970:454–455) found local varieties at both Chalchuapa, El Salvador, and Barton Ramie to be "virtually indistinguishable." Chalchuapa shows the earlier appearance and a dated development sequence in the relevant ceramic types and modes (ibid.: 456), whereas these same types and modes burst on the scene fully developed at Barton Ramie. In fact Sharer and Gifford (1970:454) state that the Aguacate Orange pottery at Barton Ramie "is far more diverse and developed there than at Chalchuapa. This elaboration could be an indication that the Aguacate ceramic group is later at Barton Ramie than at Chalchuapa."

Duncan Pring is not in full agreement, although I am not convinced by his arguments in his latest summary article (1975). He admits strong links between Barton Ramie and Chalchuapa, but he also postulates a "possible precursor" to the Aguacate Orange group in a Mount Hope Phase variety at Barton Ramie—San Antonio Golden-Brown: Variety Unspecified (1975:199). Sharer, on the other hand, has documented a long developmental sequence of the Aguacate Orange group at Chalchuapa. It is also one of the most popular wares here in the Late Preclassic. Moreover, Sharer and Gifford (1970) found some Aguacate Orange varieties at Barton Ramie to be "virtually indistinguishable" from those at Chalchuapa. If, then, there is any link between San Antonio Golden-Brown and Aguacate Orange at Barton Ramie, it seems highly improbable that San Antonio Golden-Brown is the sole parent of the Barton Ramie Aguacate Orange. Given the fact that Chalchuapa traded out some of its more popular, and probably more prestigious, wares in the Late Preclassic—among them Aguacate Orange —it seems plausible that San Antonio Golden-Brown was originally influenced by Chalchuapa Aguacate Orange trade items, and/or San Antonio Golden-Brown lent some specific attributes to the Barton Ramie Aguacate Orange group after it was brought in by the migrants.

Pring also finds an antecedent of the Guacamayo Red-on-Orange in Escobal Red-on-Buff: Variety Unspecified, yet he is stuck, on the basis of slip texture (and presumably other features) with the similarity between the Nohmul specimens and those from Chalchuapa. He argues that these ceramics arrived at Nohmul by trade from Chalchuapa rather than by migration; yet he admits that the influx of people at Barton Ramie from Chalchuapa is plausible. Although he reserves doubts about the latter assertion and is perhaps playing the role of devil's advocate, I find that the simpler explanation is that both the Barton Ramie and Nohmul ceramics arrived on the scene by a single agency—the mass migration of people from the southeastern highlands (see below).

It should be noted that variability in both time and space among Floral Park Horizon ceramics is to be expected. Such variability must be accounted for, but presumably such differences should be confined to the varietal level (in Type-Variety-Systematics). First the newcomers probably migrated in from several disparate localities in the southeastern highlands (not just from Chalchuapa) to new and equally disparate localities in northern and central Belize and elsewhere. In this light, the chance recovery of identical and nearly identical varieties at two sites so widely spaced is a remarkable and fortunate accident of site sampling. We might have missed all hope of seeing such connections if Willey and company had decided to survey and excavate in some other area than the upper and middle courses of the Belize River valley, or if Sharer had decided to excavate some other site than Chalchuapa. Where particular groups of migrants actually decided to settle may have been dependent on variables which we find exceedingly difficult to control, such as pre-existing kin and/or trading alliances that were established in the Late Preclassic. It would seem extremely problematic to find very many more similarities on the varietal level than we already have. But let us hope we can.

Second, varietal differences might also be expected as the ceramic styles would tend to differentiate through time between themselves, as well as from the original stock of Preclassic southeastern highland styles, after the users became established in different river valleys in northern Belize and elsewhere. In this type of situation, one might expect to find only a very small amount of pottery showing exact similarities with that from particular sites in the southeastern highlands. Probably a large number of sociological variables conditioned this differential varietal distribution. For example, daughter populations may have budded off from the original Belize valley settlements into northern Belize, thus accounting for some of the spatial (and temporal) varietal differences. This, emphatically, does not obviate the migration hypothesis, although it will blur the effectiveness of distribution maps. Bearing these complicating factors in mind, I think it is advisable to weight the remarkable ceramic identities between Chalchuapa and Barton Ramie more than we ordinarily would, and seek corroborating evidence in other artifact categories and relevant natural phenomena.

Ceramics do not tell the whole story in any case. In addition to the intrusion of a new ceramic complex, there is a set of utilitarian, i.e., household, items. Barkbeaters made of stone appear for the first time (Willey et al. 1965). Rovner (1975) has identified a characteristic point-on-blade. And significantly, spindle whorls and spindle rests make their appearance (Willey et al. 1965); these are among the most conspicuous artifacts found in the stratified deposits at Chalchuapa and point to a well-developed cotton processing technology (see below). These items (barkbeaters, points-on-blades, and spindle whorls and rests) would all appear to relate to everyday economic activities; certainly they should not be confused with artifacts found in ritual contexts such as the fine ceramic vessels in burials and caches.

No less significant than the ceramic and utilitarian artifact linkages is the fact that Barton Ramie experienced a doubling of housemounds and burials, in what Willey et al. (1965:342) have called "a high point in population density" at this time (also see Pring 1975: 200). Whether this population increase and "site unit intrusion" is general throughout northern Belize and eastern Guatemala is not yet certain.

Lacking detailed and quantitative settlement studies at a large sample of sites, we can only say that the frequency of Protoclassic occurrence appears to grow as more sites are investigated. For example, three of the five large to moderately sized sites presently under excavation in northern Belize (Nohmul, Santa Rita, and San Estevan, versus Cerros and El Pozito; see Pring 1975:199) have quite substantial Protoclassic components. Again, this is hardly evidence for a population increase, since we do not know the relative sizes of the Preclassic components, but neither is it evidence against it. I am afraid that useful information concerning Protoclassic population dynamics will not be forthcoming until quantitative measures are applied to both Pre-classic and Protoclassic materials at these and other sites. Any statement about a population increase outside of the Belize valley would be premature at this time, therefore, although I feel that the Belize valley data tip the balance in favor of one.

In and of itself, the present inability to demonstrate a demographic increase in an area where massive in-migration is hypothesized is a serious fault, and it would be ludicrous to maintain this position if there were not other supporting evidence. But perhaps the greatest difficulty in seriously advocating the in-migration of droves of as yet invisible people into northern Belize is an explanation of why western Salvadoreños would want to migrate hundreds of kilometers north in the first place. Those of us who worked on the Chalchuapa Project (Sharer, ed., 1977) believe we have that explanation, and that is that almost the entire population of areas tested by us (and subsequently by Payson Sheets, personal communication) was forced to leave because of volcanic activity (see Sheets 1971).

El Salvador is dominated by a chain of twenty volcanoes, one of which, Volcán Izalco, is still intermittently active. Sheets (1976) summarizes all the previous work done on the subject and offers the hypothesis that a gigantic eruption of one of these volcanoes, Volcán Ilopango, located on the southern outskirts of the modern city of San Salvador, devastated large portions of the otherwise fertile valleys and Pacific coastal plains in the central and western parts of the country. He lists several known sites or site zones in El Salvador with an ash layer; in most cases the ash is known to cap Preclassic deposits, while in other cases the reportage on some of the earlier stratigraphic excavations leaves some doubts. The depth of the ash deposits overlying well-known Preclassic deposits range from twelve meters at Cerro Zapote, seventeen kilometers west of Volcán Ilopango, to sixty centimeters at Chalchuapa and Tazumal, which are located seventy kilometers west-northwest of Ilopango. These measurements do not take adequate account of the obvious wind and water erosion that would have reduced their thicknesses before they were colonized by plants and held fast.

Over this apparently ubiquitous ash seal, and where stratigraphic and dating controls are good, an exceedingly sparse Early Classic occupation is found following a probable occupational hiatus (cf. Sheets 1976). That the entire area had to be abandoned for at least a generation and perhaps as long as two hundred years (except perhaps in hillslope areas where the ash might wash away more rapidly) is clear. First, the effects of the ash would have been devastating to local vegetation. The ash is toward the acidic end of the scale and consists of potash, feldspar, and quartz, "which weather slowly to relatively infertile soils" (Sheets 1976:13). Without plant roots to hold the soil, sheet erosion must have been massive. Within the one-meter isopach, or approximately within a radius of up to one hundred kilometers from the source, all plant life would have suffered, perhaps fatally, by structural overloading, chemical attack, or wind abrasion. Second, the faunal biomass, both aquatic and terrestrial, would have suffered both from ingestion of the chemical-laden ash and from lung and gill damage. One would expect that such devastation would have lessened with increasing distance from Ilopango, and Sheets is still in the process of measuring the thickness of deposits and their environmental effects. But it already is becoming reasonable to argue, for example, that the abandonment of such areas as Ocos, which was heavily dependent on aquatic protein, much of it fresh-water, was due to tephra damage to fish and shellfish (see M. D. Coe and Flannery 1967; Sheets 1976:17). In fact, human populations living on the Pacific littoral and southern slopes of the southeastern highlands as far away as Chiapa de Corzo (Sharer 1974) may have felt the indirect effects of this massive eruption and its consequences. Shook and Proskouriakoff (1956) in their survey of settlement patterns in the southeastern highlands note a virtual abandonment of much of this area until the Late Classic Period, or perhaps somewhat before. L. A. Parsons (1969, vol. 1:27) notes a probable population decline, but not abandonment at Bilbao.

Sharer (1968; 1969) and Sheets (1976) have some suggestive evidence that the abandonment of at least Chalchuapa was immediate and directly related to the eruption. First, Sharer (1969:36–37) reports deliberately mutilated monuments (stelae, etc.) immediately under the ash layer and suggests that the mutilations were responses to the first stages of the eruption. Second, Sheets reports a partially finished plaster surface on a pyramid with ash deposits directly on top of it; this deposit was subsequently sealed over by later construction, thereby preserving it. According to Sheets, "The Preclassic inhabitants were actually in the process of surfacing ('plastering' with a clay-pumice mixture) the pyramid when the eruption struck" (1976:9).

The issue of the dates for the Protoclassic Period is a confusing one, mainly, I think, because the period has been defined by ceramic developments at a number of disparate sites (some of which have been dated by C[14]) rather than by a single datable event which encompasses the area as a whole. As a result, various beginning and end dates for the period have been estimated based on the vagaries of excavation, site sampling, interpretations of standard deviations on C[14] dates, and ceramic sequencing by various ceramicists. Moreover, many of the ceramic elements conventionally assigned to the Floral Park Horizon were widely traded from the southeast highlands in Late Preclassic times, thus confusing the issue further (see below).

According to the reconstruction given here, the end date of the Protoclassic Period should vary in accordance with the rate of assimilation of the highland refugees at each site. The Ilopango eruption and hasty abandonment of most of western El Salvador and the Pacific littoral of Guatemala, on the other hand, must be taken as the initial date for the Protoclassic Period in the lowlands and the highlands. The most plausible absolute date for that eruption is that given by Sheets (1976:9), who cites a German geological mission's investigations of Volcán Ilopango; the mission produced a C[14] date of A.D. 260±85.

The violence and nature of the Ilopango eruption suggest a means by which a close correlation between the abandonment of western El Salvador and the intrusion of migrants on the Caribbean side of the continental divide may be traced, insofar as there appear to have been sone long-distance atmospheric effects. Sheets has described the eruption in the following terms:

> What evidently happened is that such tremendous pressures built up on a very hot and gas-laden acidic magma inside Ilopango volcano that, when the pressure was suddenly released, the magma exploded high into the air. The explosion was sufficiently violent to take a major portion of the volcanic cone with it, depositing this material as a layer of ash and pumice over the country-side. Then, the hot magma left at the base of the volcano subsided, leaving a depression which subsequently cooled and now holds Lake Ilopango. . . . The prevailing surface wind direction does not seem to have had much effect in pushing the ejecta to the down-wind side of the volcano. A relatively uniform distribution of materials is common with violent eruptions, evidently because the ash is blown upwards through many layers of the atmosphere to as high as fifteen kilometers. (1971:28)

In a more recent article, based on fresh field data, Sheets states, "As far as we presently know, this eruption occured in three stages, two ashflows (nuée ardente or glowing avalanche) and an airfall ash. The ashflows, consisting of incandescent clouds of pumice, ash and gases, rolled downhill and buried villages and forests in their paths as far as 45 km from their source. Shortly thereafter, perhaps hours to weeks, the airfall ash was deposited in a more uniform blanket over the countryside" (1976:33). As with the August 27, 1883, eruption of Krakatoa, we can probably measure the volume of volcanic ejecta from Ilopango in terms of several cubic miles. Such violent eruptions as those of Krakatoa and Ilopango send vast amounts of tiny ash particles into the upper atmosphere, where they are carried extraordinarily long distances by stratospheric winds. Wexler (1952:74) remarks, for example, that "the sun's radiation . . . dropped suddenly from 30 per cent above normal to 20 per cent below normal" at the Montpellier Observatory in France just three months after the explosion of Krakatoa halfway around the world. Subnormal solar radiation persisted for three years as the dust pall hung in the air. Similar observances have been made repeatedly since. The reasons seem simple enough. Dust in the air scatters, reflects, and absorbs solar radiation in the upper atmosphere, thus reducing the amount of sunlight and thereby cooling the ground below it. Moreover, "A pall of volcanic ash might increase cloudiness in the atmosphere, which would add to the effect of the dust itself in reducing our sunshine" (Wexler 1952:79).

But what goes up must come down, and it is not likely that nucleated ice crystals ultimately descended in the form of rain or hail. But some regions and latitudes would be affected more than others, thus leaving open the question of whether northern Guatemala and Belize would have been greatly affected by volcanic events to the south in El Salvador. Ash clouds from the relatively tiny 1974 eruption of Volcán Fuego outside Guatemala City were carried across the continental divide to the north and west and into the extreme northern latitudes. More dramatic was the abundant ash fall at Tikal from the larger 1962 Fuego eruption (Hattula Moholy-Nagy, personal communication). The ash was so thick that it could be scraped off the zinc rooftops of the Tikal Project Camp. The small-scale Fuego eruptions demonstrate that ash-laden winds can cross the continental divide despite the prevailing surface winds, which would be contrary to this movement. Neither eruption would even approach the scale of a Krakatoa or Ilopango.

What I am proposing here, then, is that the heavily burdened winds carrying Ilopango ash and ash-nucleated ice crystals cooled and descended on the northern slopes and lowlands to the north, causing torrential rains and subsequent flooding.

There is some evidence for something of this sort having happened. Capping the black, organically stained soil stratum which contains exclusively Preclassic occupation in the Belize River valley is a sterile brown clay layer. Upon this sterile clay layer is the fully developed Protoclassic ceramic horizon (Willey et al. 1965:565). Thus the "site unit intrusion" is on top of, and apparently never under, this clay layer. The layer itself has been plausibly interpreted by Willey et al. as the result of extensive flooding of the Belize River. This flooding even covered the upper terraces, minimally seven meters above the dry season level where the Preclassic and Protoclassic housemounds were located. Probably not coincidentally, fresh-water shellfish virtually disappear from the archaeological record at Barton Ramie at the same time (Sheets 1976:17), and possibly the same thing happens at Copan (Longyear 1952), again implicating respiratory and/or digestive damage. At Altar de Sacrificios, Willey and Smith (1969:46) note the reduction in the practice of using the common river mussel, *Amblema nickliniana*, as an element of concretions used for building materials after the Preclassic Period. Does this decreased usage reflect a decrease in the population of this ubiquitous mussel?

The only quantified information on shellfish population dynamics comes from Rice (1976). He notes a decline in the number of mollusks recovered in housemound excavations throughout the sequence in the Lake Yaxha/Sacnab region and ascribes it to overexploitation due to population increase in the area. While population doubles between each two periods (i.e., between the Middle Preclassic and the Late Preclassic, the Late Preclassic and the Early Classic, and so on) the mollusk population is roughly halved—except for one period transition, the transition between the Late Preclassic and the Early Classic periods, when the number of mollusks exploited is reduced by two-thirds, not by half as between the other periods. This would suggest that some other factor was at work, and again I would propose that this disproportionate reduction in the number of mollusks was due to respiratory or digestive damage caused by unusually high quantities of volcanic ash in the lake sediments. Continued pressure on mollusk exploitation was probably linked to population growth throughout the sequence as Rice suggests, and this, combined with the short-term (or relatively short-term) reduction in the Early Classic mollusk population caused by volcanic ash, may not have allowed the mollusk population to recover its former high level.

Recent inquiries to colleagues have provided some tantalizing suggestions that short-term and reasonably well-dated flooding of river regimes and other water sources might have been common throughout the Maya Lowlands during the terminal Preclassic. Payson Sheets has directed my attention to another sterile clay layer capping the Late Preclassic deposits along the Ulua River flood plain at Playa de los Muertos in Honduras (also see Stone 1972:62). Other possible alluvial layers are turning up in northern Belize. For example, Mary Neivens (personal communication, 1975) has informed me of a sterile brown layer capping Preclassic occupation at the site of El Posito, which is located about midway between the New and Hondo rivers near their middle courses. Going north from there, excavations in raised fields (see Siemens and Puleston 1972) near San Antonio on Albion Island in the Hondo River have revealed a number of layers of *sascab* (soft mud), which may indicate a concern for elevating these planting platforms above their previous mean water levels. We do not know if, in fact, these *sascab* layers represent successive construction phases for this purpose, nor if they date to the Protoclassic, but again there is the possibility of it. Finally, David Freidel (personal communication, 1974), working at Los Cerros on Chetumal Bay, has uncovered what may be ash layers over what appears to be a terminal Late Preclassic burial.

The evidence, except for the Belize Valley flood, is admittedly weak, but it leads to the formulation of the testable hypothesis that the alluvial clay is the result of a single atmospheric event rather than a longer-term climatic shift, that it contains traces of ash, and that it represents the long-distance climatic effects of the Ilopango eruption. Payson Sheets, Robert J. Sharer, and I are currently testing this hypothesis. We are attempting to collect likely deposits for analysis. If the deluge posited here was the result of ash-laden winds from El Salvador, as we suspect, then one might expect to recover traces of ash in the sterile clay layer. By trace element analysis, this ash could be compared to the ash which is confidently attributed to Ilopango. Sheets has already initiated investigations of the Salvadorean ash (1976), and several samples of alluvium from lowland riverine sites have already been submitted for analysis. Also, the Ilopango eruptions probably were of sufficient magnitude to have produced the same sort of observable atmospheric disturbances as the Krakatoa eruption produced throughout the Northern Hemisphere. Krakatoa produced a dusty haze that made "the sun and moon look blue, purple or green, and produced gorgeously-hued sunsets and rose-colored twilights that lasted more than an hour after sunset" (Wexler 1952:74). A search for pertinent dated atmospheric observations will be made among the historic documents of Europe and Asia between ca. A.D. 100 and 300. While this last evidence would not be conclusive evidence for obvious reasons, it would be supportive. Finally, Lonnie Thompson of the Institute of Polar Studies has agreed to search the Greenland Ice Cores for possible traces of the Ilopango ash. If he should recover any of it, we shall have some very good oxygen isotope dates. He, too, already has some samples in his possession.

The Chalchuapa site zone was densely populated and contained some of the largest pyramids in Mesoamerica during its pre-eruption phase. Mound groups are found in broad, fertile alluvial valley bottoms or coastal plains. Ceramic evidence, including that from well-dated Preclassic deposits in the lowlands to the north, indicates far-flung exchange networks, as does the presence of a rock sculpture done in Olmec style. My own analysis of the Chalchuapa figurines (1977) confirms the hypothesis that western El Salvador was intimately involved in a vast and voluminous exchange network which extended throughout southern Mesoamerica and into eastern Costa Rica, and even as far as the Tumaco region of coastal Colombia, where, incidentally, some Protoclassic migrants may have established themselves. Because of the diversity and richness of the artifacts found in both excavations and local private collections, Chalchuapa and nearby sites (e.g., Ahuachapan, Atiquizia) appear to have been trade centers par excellence during the Middle and Late Preclassic (see Sharer 1974). For example, the zone was located along the "trade route" by which the Olmec were supplied blue jade from Costa Rica (see Stirling 1961 and Easby 1968). Moreover, much of Preclassic El Salvador was a major production and distribution center for a brisk trade in fine ceramics, cacao, cotton, and obsidian. And, as we shall see, these products were in great demand in the Northern Lowlands where many of the migrants finally settled.

Sharer (1974) and Sharer and Gifford (1970) have discussed the Preclassic ceramic exchange, which will not be dealt with here. The sparse but broad distribution of such fine wares as Usulutan suggest that ceramic ware was a costly sumptuary item.

Cacao's importance in the economic life of Postclassic Mesoamerica can hardly be overemphasized, since cacao beans served as a "consumable currency" in both long-distance exchange and local market transactions (see Blom 1932; J. E. S. Thompson 1948; 1956; Millon 1955; Chapman 1957; L. A. Parsons 1969; L. A. Parsons and Price 1971; Feldman 1971; and Sharer 1974). Cacao served a variety of medicinal and ritual functions, perhaps as a mild hallucinogen and certainly as a prestige beverage (J. E. S. Thompson 1956). That it was of equal importance in the Early and Middle Classic periods in the southeastern highlands is evident from its iconographic attention in the sculptural art of the Cotzumalhuapan region to the west of Chalchuapa, as discussed by L. A. Parsons (1969).

There are several references to cacao production in El Salvador immediately after the Conquest, and one gets the distinct impression that cacao was a major economic product of the area. Girolamo Benzoni (1857) noted cacao in his travels in El Salvador sometime between 1541 and 1556. By the 1570's, "it is clear that the Izalco region had developed into one of the most important cacao producing areas in Mesoamerica" (Millon 1955:72). In yet another passage, Ciudad Real (1872) mentions the cultivation of cacao by means of irrigation in what seems to have been an arroyo near Santa Ana. The present town of Santa Ana is located about fourteen kilometers from Chalchuapa.

Large-scale cacao production in western El Salvador during the Postclassic period was highly probable. Cacao was definitely grown to the west in Xoconusco in Middle Classic times according to sculptural representations recovered by J. E. S. Thompson (1948) and L. A. Parsons (1969). Recently Sanders and Price (1968) and Parsons and Price (1971) have postulated its cultivation along the south coast and piedmont region of Guatemala and Chiapas generally, in the Late Preclassic, if not earlier. And, significantly, such highly suitable areas for cacao cultivation as Sonsonate, Chalchuapa, Atiquizia, and Ahuachapan also have some of the largest standing architecture at this time in the southeastern highlands; they are perhaps the richest sites in terms of trade goods as well.

Evidence for Preclassic Period cotton cultivation along the Pacific littoral can hardly be doubted and requires little in the way of comment. What may be spindle rests (sherd discs with incompletely drilled holes) have been reported for the Ocos Phase (1300–1100 B.C.) and the Conchas Phase (800–300 B.C.) at the site of La Victoria (M. D. Coe 1961:104). A modeled Crucero Phase (300 B.C.–A.D. 100) spindle whorl comes from the same site (ibid.:109). Scores of incompletely and completely perforated sherd discs were excavated in Preclassic contexts at Chalchuapa, indicating their use as spindle rests and spindle whorls respectively. Because this area and the neighboring Pacific coastal lowlands to the south are ideally suited to cotton cultivation (it is a major commercial crop here today), it is easy to imagine that cotton spinning (and probably weaving and decorating) was a major industry in Preclassic times.

Obsidian is a well-known, major production item in western El Salvador. Control of the Ixtepeque obsidian source and the production of prismatic blades must have been an important industry from the very beginning of occupation by settled agriculturalists there. Ixtepeque obsidian has been recognized among the Tikal obsidian artifacts, and although reliable figures are still lacking (Jane Wheeler Pires-Ferreira, personal communication, 1976), Ixtepeque obsidian was probably more common there in the Preclassic period than at any later time.

In sum, it is not unlikely that, at the time of the Ilopango eruption, western El Salvador was a long-established and highly successful center for long-distance trade and for production of cacao, cotton, and obsidian. It seems reasonable, therefore, to suspect that areas colonized by the posteruption migrants would be located in areas where (1) cacao and cotton could be grown and marketed in quantity, (2) good quality chipping stone was concentrated, and (3) goods could be easily shipped to consumer centers.

CASH CROPPING IN STRIP DEVELOPMENTS

As has been previously mentioned, the major concentration of Protoclassic materials appears to be in northern Belize, including Santa Rita near Chetumal Bay and Nohmul on the Hondo River (Anderson and Cook 1944; Gann 1918; Gann and Gann 1939). Norman Hammond's Corozal Project has confirmed a sizable Protoclassic ceramic component at Nohmul and recently recovered a cache of jade figurines which look very much like southeastern highland ceramic figurines (cf. Dahlin 1977) but in another medium. The site of San Estevan produced some Protoclassic vessels as well (Bullard 1965:50–51).

Further to the south, of course, is the "site unit intrusion" of the Floral Park ceramic complex in the Belize River valley. Smaller amounts of Protoclassic materials have also been recognized at the nearby sites of Mountain Cow (Mountain Cow II, J. E. S. Thompson 1931) and San José (J. E. S. Thompson 1939). To the south of these central Belizean sites, along the western flanks of the Maya Mountains in the southern Peten, a Protoclassic presence is seen at Poptún (Shook and Smith 1950). Finally, there is the Salinas complex at Altar de Sacrificios on the Pasión/Usumacinta river confluence (Adams 1971).

Protoclassic models, though not the full complex, diffused widely in southern Mesoamerica (see Willey et al. 1967); Pring (1975) has recognized about two dozen sites with some Protoclassic wares. Of concern to us here, however, are only those areas which experienced a heavy influx of what would appear to be migrants; and except for the Salinas complex the greatest contribution of Protoclassic pottery seems to be in Belize, north of and including the Belize River valley. All sites having Protoclassic components are located on major river systems or within easy access distance to them (e.g., Poptún). These rivers have their headwaters in the Peten and are navigable for considerable distances. How long a portage it would take from the terminus of navigability on the New, Hondo, and Belize river tributaries to Tikal is not yet clear, but two or three days appears to be more than ample. A couple more days' portage to the west of Tikal would bring trading parties to the uppermost navigable portion of the San Pedro Martir near what is presently the village of Paso Caballos. It is a fairly easy canoe trip from there, via the lower Usumacinta River, to the Gulf of Mexico.

Tikal, apparently the largest and most complex of the Early Classic lowland sites, would have stood astride this portage then and mediated the east-west water-borne trade in what is becoming known as the "Trans-Peten Trade Route." Moreover, central Peten society was much more nucleated and more highly stratified than the more dispersed and more egalitarian settlements on its peripheries (see, for example, Dahlin 1974). Therefore, in addition to becoming a "depot city" (Jacobs 1969; Dahlin 1976) which facilitated the trans-Peten trade, Tikal, in particular, would have been the greatest consumer, style-setter, and distributor of exotic raw materials, subsistence commodities, and finished status goods for the central Peten. In this case the economic growth of Tikal would have stimulated economic production both along the riverine routes to the east and west and along the overland trails to the north and south.

The productivity of the riverine routes was obviously greater than that of areas adjacent to the overland trails, however. For example, aboriginal cacao production was an important trade commodity in the provinces of Uaymil and Chetumal at the beginning of the Conquest Period. Ciudad Real reports that cacao was grown in moist soils near lagoons close to the town of Bacalar (cited in Millon 1955:83). Roys (1943; 1957) discusses a debarkation point for the shipment of cacao (to the Xiu towns to the north of the town of Ucum). Ucum is located on the Hondo River a few kilometers north of Nohmul. While it is possible that the cacao mentioned by Roys was produced in Honduras and then shipped from Ucum overland, I concur with Millon that "at least part of what was carried overland would have been grown in the Chetumal area" (1955:83).

Finally, cacao was grown until very recently along the Belize River in the neighborhood of Barton Ramie; in fact, one cacao orchard can still be seen there.

There can be little doubt of the antiquity and importance of cacao in Classic and Preclassic times in the Maya Lowlands. In fact, it is all but inconceivable that cacao was not used in the Classic Maya Lowlands when all of Mesoamerica outside of the Lowland Maya area was trading with it, fighting over it, and venerating it in art work (J. E. S. Thompson 1966; L. A. Parsons 1969; L. A. Parsons and Price 1971). It would be strange indeed if the Maya wealth in exotic trade goods was not also achieved through the use of cacao as a medium of exchange passed through the hands of both Maya and foreign merchants.

Cacao, however, does not grow well in the interior Peten, where river banks are scarce but where Classic Maya society achieved its most spectacular florescence. Nor does it grow well in northern Yucatan, the scene of Postclassic Maya growth and development. In the north, it is too dry and the soils are too thin; in the Peten, the dry season is too long and there are no rivers amenable to irrigation. Cacao must have been imported into these florescent areas if it was to be consumed in any great quantity. Looking at the distribution of former cacao-producing regions, we can see that the nearest major production centers for cacao were probably along the major drainage systems of the extreme eastern Peten and in northern Belize. The most important drainage systems would be the Hondo River, New River, and Belize River. This is precisely where we have the greatest and the most secure evidence for Protoclassic intrusions. It also seems clear that the cacao produced here was grown on raised fields on the river flood plains and active low-lying swampy *bajo* systems, since the climatic and edaphic conditions of the upland portions are not too unlike those of the Peten and Yucatan, where, as I have said, cacao does not grow well.

In fact, the Hondo and New river flood plains appear to be ideal environments for cacao production, particularly in the Hondo and Pucte clay zones, where the vast majority of the raised fields actually appear to occur. In addition to the appropriate drainage conditions on the raised fields, the soil waters of both these zones are alkaline and rich in calcium and magnesium (Wright et al. 1959: 61, 101). Urquhart (1961:42) emphasizes that adequate amounts of these nutrients are essential for cacao production. Moreover, where magnesium and calcium are not abundant in the wet alluvial bottom lands, that is, in

8 015

FERNALD LIBRARY
COLBY-SAWYER COLLEGE
NEW LONDON, N.H. 03257

the more acidic Sibal peaty sandy clays, raised fields appear to be much less frequent. Moreover, cultivation of cacao by means of irrigation was a fairly widespread phenomenon in the tropical New World in historic times. Van Hall (1914) reported on recent drained-field cacao plantations in Nicaragua, Colombia, Venezuela, the island of Guadeloupe, and Surinam.

Cacao cultivation does not require large amounts of labor. Nor does it require a large capital investment, except, of course, in constructing the fields to plant on. Today most cacao throughout the world is small family-owned orchards, although some is grown in rather large plantations also. We have no pollen evidence for the cultivation of cacao in Belize, but it seems reasonable to assume that it was grown as a cash crop on raised fields that were located at some distance from habitation centers, while more labor-demanding crops (such as maize and cotton; see below) were grown closer to the settlements.

I think that a fairly good case can be made for the cash cropping of cotton on the raised fields along the New and Hondo rivers also. Large (1975:13), citing Landa, states that two types of cotton were raised by the northern Maya in the sixteenth century: *Gossypium hirsutum*, a small annual, and *G. hirsutum*, var. *punctatum*, a larger perennial which lasts from five to six years. An unidentified species of cotton was recovered in the only two cores to be thus far published from the Río Hondo Project's core samplings of raised fields (Bradbury 1974).

The northern lowlands generally are climatologically well suited to cotton cultivation (Large 1975). Large does not specify the edaphic requirements of *punctatum*, but those conditions listed by her for *G. hirsutum* suggest that raised-field edaphic conditions would probably have been ideal: loose, fine-textured soils with a continuous water supply and yet continuous aeration, "so the soil must be capable of holding and transporting water but not become waterlogged" (ibid.:15). Calcium, nitrogen, phosphorus, and potassium must also be in abundance. Because cotton "suffers heavily from overhead shade or heavy competition" (ibid.:15), it was probably grown in open fields closer to the residential sites than crops requiring less protection from weed competition for light and soil nutrients.

In addition to the cotton pollen, spindle whorls have been recovered in central Belize at Barton Ramie. They are of the perforated sherd disc type which is so common at Chalchuapa during the Preclassic Period; these sherd discs enter the archaeological record at Barton Ramie with the Protoclassic intruders. A few spindle whorls of the same kind have been found at Uaxactun and Copan in the Preclassic, so it cannot be said that the Protoclassic peoples actually introduced cotton into the entire northern lowlands. In fact, spindle whorls have not been reported in northern Belize, where the Protoclassic population appears to have been heaviest. This is probably due to the fact that few excavations have been published from there as yet. Then lack of spindle whorls might also mean that only raw cotton was exported; it may have been shipped in bulk via canoe to cloth-production centers. Based on the distribution of spindle whorls, these may include Piedras Negras, Altar de Sacrificios, Tikal, Uaxactun, Mayapan, and Chichen Itza, and, in fact, most of the large excavated sites (see Large 1975).

In addition to cacao and cotton, the strip developments along the major riverine routes may have produced other valuable cash crops. In his discussion of the raised field complexes that Siemens and Puleston (1972) examined along the Candelaria River in Campeche, J. E. S. Thompson (1974) has suggested that the primary focus of economic activity was not the fields themselves but rather the canals between them; in short, Thompson believes that the canals were fish farms. Schorr (1973), with a more detailed knowledge of raised field complexes in South America, has found supporting evidence for this hypothesis, and it is pertinent that the British land use survey of Belize (Wright et al. 1959:102) has suggested that fish farming be introduced in at least one of the broad alluvial soil zones where Pre-Columbian raised fields are most common.

Pring and Hammond's excavations into a riverside platform on the Hondo River, 3.7 kilometers west-northwest of Nohmul, are interesting in this regard, as they produced a large quantity of "netsinkers." They deduce from this that "fishing, and therefore perhaps also fish-drying, was an activity associated with the platform" (1975:117). Even if the fish farming was not actively practiced here, fishing potentials of the raised field complex canals and nearby rivers may have been quite high; this is particularly true if the problems associated with oxygenation and removal of toxic gases in the canal waters were solved (see Hickling 1961 and below).

It is interesting to note that cacao orchards would have had a beneficial effect on fish harvests from the canals. Cacao trees are pollinated by small insects of the midge family. Therefore, where large stands of cacao trees are found, there is usually a large midge population feeding from them (Urquhart 1961:11). Midge larvae require an aquatic environment and often occur "by the thousands per square metre" (Hickling 1968:55). What is of particular interest is that midge larvae are a major source of fish food in temperate and tropical hatcheries around the world (Hickling 1961; 1968). Therefore, the planting of cacao in wet lands, in this case raised field platforms, would attract large numbers of bottom-feeding, carnivorous fish. Moreover, canoe traffic and periodic fertilization of the raised fields by scooping out the rich organic sediments from the canal bottoms might have restored much of the oxygen that the fish need in the canal water; this oxygen would otherwise be consumed by the millions of pelagic and bottom-dwelling microorganisms which may have served to reduce the number of fish which could otherwise have been sustained. This relatively easy, but ecologically complex, system would have required very little labor (after the raised fields were initially built) in exchange for an abundance of fresh protein and cacao. Both cacao and dried fish could have formed valuable and easily transportable exports that were needed and wanted in the Maya core zone as well as in the Mexican and Guatemalan highlands.

Rovner (1975) has isolated another resource which he believes was traded widely from northern Belize, and that is the fine local cherts. Either chert nodules or finished products arrived at some Peten and Yucatecan sites along with a diagnostic point-on-blade which appears "most frequently in the Belize region and most frequently made of

Belize fine chert" (ibid.:5). Barkbeaters arrived in the region at about the same time (ibid.:6). Both the point-on-blade and the barkbeaters appear to be primarily of Protoclassic date. It should be noted that some of Rovner's analyses cannot be taken to be conclusive, since the identification of some of the source materials was done on the basis of color and not petrographic analyses. The finding of a specialized lithic workshop at Colha (Hammond 1975) has lent some support for Rovner's hypothesis, however.

David Pendergast's excavations at Altun Ha have demonstrated the wealth that even moderate-sized sites controlling marine resources might achieve (for example, see his 1969). The nearby Caribbean coast furnished a large quantity of sea salt, shells, sting ray spines, sharks' teeth, and so on to the interior Maya, and probably also to the Central Mexicans when they took an interest in the Maya Lowlands. Northern and central Belize would have been favored as far as these products were concerned, not because they were not available elsewhere–they were–but because they could be funneled along with the volume of goods which were unique to this area alone.

This sort of thinking led Norman Hammond (1975:9) to search for a possible port installation on the Hondo River near the apical northern Belizean site of Nohmul. He reports a possible port (previously mentioned in regard to possible fish-drying activities) in the form of a broad, flat platform (ca. one meter above the dry-season water level of the river) which contains a single low substructure. Pring and Hammond (1975:117) date the construction to the Early Classic Period, but they also found a sizable Protoclassic midden dumped in the earliest levels of one of their excavational units. They report other "riverside mounds" near Nohmul, yet one wonders if some of them are actually raised fields, since the Río Hondo Project's 1973 mapping efforts produced a large number of very well defined raised fields in this general vicinity.

As it stands now, no positive evidence for a port function has been found on the excavated platform. No exotic materials were in fact found in excavations, something one might expect if the platform was used for loading and unloading canoes. Probably a better place to look for such materials is not on the platform itself, but in the bottom sediments where the canoes would have been loaded. Yet the location (Nohmul), its form, and the date of the platform do conform to what one would expect of a port facility.

CONCLUSIONS

The information that is currently available on the distribution of substantial Protoclassic migrants is in accord with the hypothesis previously stated; that they were concentrated primarily along the river systems in nothern Belize (and probably on the Pasión River at Altar de Sacrificios) where high levels of economic production of the goods formerly produced in El Salvador could be had. Such goods, including cacao, cotton, chipped stone, and possibly dried fish, to say nothing of staple crops such as maize, were in increasing demand as the populations and economies of the central Peten developed.

A final word should be said about ceramics. As previously mentioned, the Floral Park Horizon includes both fine wares and utilitarian wares, and this has been taken as evidence of migrations into northern Belize and at Altar de Sacrificios. At least the fine wares were exchanged over long distances in the Preclassic, so there is some reason to suspect that their possession conferred a certain degree of status. It is even likely that some attributes were borrowed in local ceramic traditions before the Protoclassic migrants arrived on the scene. Pring (1975) argues for an independent invention of some of these attributes in northern and central Belize. While he is probably correct concerning one or two specific attributes (e.g., polychrome painting), the long developmental sequence of the complex as a whole at Chalchuapa presents a stronger case for a limited amount of attribute borrowing in the Preclassic Period. One would expect this sort of thing if, as appears to be the case, the fine wares were considered as sumptuary items.

During the Protoclassic Period, on the other hand, fine Floral Park Horizon wares are scarce or perhaps even absent in high-status burials and ritual deposits in the central Peten. Both the Matzanel ceramic complex at Uaxactun (Smith 1955:22) and the Cimi ceramic complex at Tikal were postulated prior to detailed ceramic analyses in anticipation of their being found in substantial numbers and as dating controls. This anticipation was not borne out, as very few Floral Park Horizon vessels or sherds were actually found there; the few that were found could as easily date to the Preclassic, or they might be Late Preclassic heirlooms showing up in Matzanel or Cimi graves. Even if some few vessels did enter Uaxactun and Tikal during the Protoclassic Period, their infrequency suggests that they had lost much, if not most, of their value as trade and status items. After all, if the migration hypothesis is correct, then we are dealing with an initial influx of desperate "squatters," literally in the inhabitants' own backyard, as opposed to a wealthy and powerful elite who formerly controlled access to sumptuary items from some far distant land.

Such was apparently not the case closer to the locus of migrant settlements in central and northern Belize. Floral Park Horizon ceramics were not popular for very long there, either (except perhaps at Altar de Sacrificios), as the horizon gradually blended in with the local ceramic traditions to form local varieties of the Tzakol Horizon. How long this took is anyone's guess, but I would estimate that the entire Protoclassic Period—from the volcanic eruption and initial migrations to the completion of the assimilative process—took probably less than three generations, or perhaps about fifty or sixty years; the assimilative process may have taken longer at Altar, if Adams's terminal date for the Salinas complex has any validity at all.

3 A New Order and the Role of the Calendar: Some Characteristics of the Middle Classic Period at Tikal by Clemency Coggins

A Middle Classic Period may be defined at Tikal in a number of different ways. Most clearly and dramatically it may be defined as the two centuries that separated the reigns of Tikal's two most illustrious rulers: Stormy Sky and Ruler A, both of whom represented a fusion of indigenous Maya culture with intrusive Mexican traits. This Middle Classic period may also be described as a time in which there was little major construction, in which very few rich burials were known to have been made, and during which there was a continuous stylistic development in the local polychrome ceramic industry. Politically this appears to have been a period of instability with strife between factions of two different types of government: one-man dynastic versus divided rule. There is little justification, at Tikal, for emphasis on the traditionally accepted break between the Early and Late Classic period, placed at A.D. 550 (Coggins 1976a). The two hundred years between 9.2.10.0.0 and 9.12.10.0.0 (ca. 480–680) are, in sum, understood as a Middle Classic Period characterized throughout by political unrest and, in terms of cultural remains, by the *absence* of elite goods imported from the Mexican Highlands.

In the century preceding this Middle Classic Period, about A.D. 380–480, there is evidence for the presence of an intrusive elite of markedly Highland Mexican character at Tikal (Coggins 1976b). The historical events of this period are detailed in a long inscription on the back of Stela 31, which depicts a Maya Lord, provisionally named Stormy Sky, who is flanked by two men dressed in the manner of Highland Mexicans (Fig. 3-1). The ruler who preceded Stormy Sky acceded to the rule of Tikal on 8.17.2.16.7, or A.D. 378. This date is recorded on Stela 4 with a Calendar Round date, a notation which indicated a calendric position in the pan-Mesoamerican 260-day ritual calendar, rather than a specific position in the Maya Long Count. This man, whose identifying glyph (Fig. 3-1, J3, N2) has suggested the name Curl Snout, is represented frontally on Stela 4 seated Mexican fashion (with legs hanging down) and wearing regalia of a type common at Teotihuacan but previously unknown at Tikal. Stela 18 is the second stela known to have been erected to Curl Snout. Here he is again represented seated frontally Mexican fashion and wearing foreign regalia, but this stela commemorates the completion of the katun, or twenty-year period, that ended at 8.18.0.0.0. This is the first example of a katun-celebrating monument at Tikal. (The only two earlier Tikal-associated dates known—Stela 29 and the Leyden Plate—record specific historic dates, in the Maya Long Count.)

Further evidence of the relationship between Curl Snout and Teotihuacan is found in his tomb (Bu. 10), which included imported pot-

FIGURE 3–1. Tikal Stela 31, front and sides. Stormy Sky. Drawing by W. R. Coe. Courtesy Tikal Project, University Museum, University of Pennsylvania.

tcry and personal regalia and evidence of exotic ritual. The contents of this tomb also resemble tomb furnishings of Teotihuacanoid character with some Veracruz traits found in the tombs of Mound A at Kaminaljuyu in the Guatemalan Highlands. The Kaminaljuyu tombs have long been noted for their Mexican traits, and it has been suggested that there was a colonial relationship between Teotihuacan and Kaminaljuyu (Kidder et al. 1946).

Curl Snout's accession at Tikal is described on Stela 31 with a vulture glyph (E10) which Proskouriakoff (n.d.) believes stands for a military role; and the glyph which apparently refers to the followers of, or nationality of, Curl Snout (ibid.) is composed of a four-cornered Cauac shield surmounted by a hand holding a spearthrower (Fig. 3-1, L4, N3). The Cauac glyph is Maya for 'rainy or stormy sky', and it may be understood as a translation into Maya of the foreigners' description of themselves as followers of Tlaloc, who was their national god of rain and storm, and who was depicted on the shields which they carried along with spearthrowers. If the archaeological distribution of projectile points is reliable evidence (Moholy-Nagy 1975), spearthrowers were a type of weapon previously foreign to the Maya, and they doubtless served the dual purpose of identifying the military role of these people and referring to their association with Tlaloc the Lightning-Hurler. Another example of the translation of these foreign concepts into Maya is found on Stela 4, where in the position of the traditional Maya figure in the sky thought to be an ancestor, Curl Snout has a long-nosed deity head. This is one of the earliest known examples of the Maya rain deity much later known as Chac. In this case, the form is a transformation of the Teotihuacan Tlaloc with its lightning bolts into a Mayoid figure with a smoking axe, connoting lightning, hafted in its forehead. This particular long-nosed deity, which first appears at Tikal as the translated Tlaloc ancestor of Curl Snout, later became the emblem of this Mexicanized Maya dynasty and eventually was transformed into the Manikin Sceptre, which is an analog of the spearthrower itself (Fig. 3-2).

Unlike Curl Snout, who by Maya standards had no proper ancestor, his successor, Stormy Sky, had Curl Snout himself to put in the sky as his ancestor figure on Stela 31, and he proclaimed the affiliation of this young dynasty with the lightning-rain deity by the form of his own name Stormy Sky. This name, visible in his headdress on Stela 31 (Fig. 3-1), consists of a cleft sky glyph from which emerges the long-nosed deity figure with the smoking axe in its forehead. Stormy Sky became ruler of Tikal at about 8.19.10.0.0, and he erected Stela 31 to himself at the end of his first katun of rule. The synthesizing character of his reign is evident on the stela itself, where he wears the elaborate insignia of a traditional Maya ruler and also displays Mexican emblems such as the skull on his helmet, the quail on his wrist, and a Teotihuacan owl and weapon badge in the headdress of the mask above his upraised hand. He is, furthermore, flanked by and apparently identified with two figures whose simple Mexican dress is in marked contrast to his own.

Sometime during the reigns of Curl Snout and Stormy Sky at least three ritual deposits were made at Tikal which may have been the

FIGURE 3–2. Tlaloc/Manikin Sceptre. After Proskouriakoff 1950: Fig. 35, Copan Miscellaneous Sculpture.

cremation burials of Mexicans. These deposits (Problematical Deposits 22, 50, 74) include charred bones, ceramics, and other objects imported from some Mexican region and suggest the practice of burial rites appropriate to a member of a Mexican elite. The tomb of Stormy Sky (Bu. 48) followed more traditional Maya patterns however and included relatively few objects of foreign origin or inspiration. By the time of his death, at approximately A.D. 455, the Mexican influence at Tikal was waning, and as far as luxury imports were concerned it disappeared within the next katun or two.

The Middle Classic Period at Tikal begins as foreign luxury trade stops. In my work on the period of Teotihuacan influence at Tikal (Coggins 1975; 1976b) the Tikal tombs of Curl Snout and Stormy Sky, which can be dated quite accurately in the Maya Long Count, were linked to the series of tombs in Mounds A and B at Kaminaljuyu excavated by Kidder et al. (1946). This analysis suggested that Curl Snout's tomb (Bu. 10) at about A.D. 425 corresponded roughly to the relatively early Tomb A-III at Kaminaljuyu and that Stormy Sky's tomb (Bu. 48, A.D. 455) corresponded best to the somewhat later tombs A-V and B-I at Kaminaljuyu. These comparative relationships still hold, but recent analysis by Charles Cheek of the contents of the Kaminaljuyu tombs suggest that they may have been made a generation later in the highlands than they were at Tikal (n.d.); or that Tomb A-III, which apparently corresponds to Curl Snout's tomb at Tikal, was really not made until about the time of Stormy Sky's tomb. If the obsidian dating upon which Cheek relies can be accepted, the relationship between Tikal and Kaminaljuyu could be re-explained by reversing their relationship. I had originally assumed that Kaminaljuyu was the donor site partly because of Tikal's ancient and continuing dependence upon obsidian from the southern highlands, and partly because the Maya elite of Late Preclassic Tikal had apparently come from the far south.

These hypotheses may still be tenable, but it might alternately be postulated that Curl Snout came from the north or northeast to Tikal, perhaps even from Mirador, which may have served as a redistribution center for Kaminaljuyu throughout Late Preclassic times (Coggins 1975:59–62). A documented historic event that may also support a northern origin for Curl Snout and for intrusive Mexicans is found at Uaxactun, directly north of Tikal on the principal access route from that direction. Stela 5 at Uaxactun depicts a simply dressed, clearly foreign figure who carries a club and a spearthrower. This person is associated with the date 8.17.1.4.12 11 Eb (A.D. 377). This same date is found on Stela 22 (Proskouriakoff n.d.). The arrival of these people, or this person, was clearly of particular importance both at Uaxactun and at Tikal, where it was associated with the end of the old dynasty and with the accession of the foreigner Curl Snout a year and a half later.

If this new interpretation of the relationship between Teotihuacan, Tikal, and Kaminaljuyu, suggested in part by Cheek's data, is correct, then the absence of Mexican cultural remains at Tikal, and at Uaxactun, in the Middle Classic Period may suggest a withdrawal of an early Mexican base of power and its removal to the southern highlands and coast, where evidence for a diversified Mexican presence is manifest throughout the Middle Classic Period.

At Tikal after the death of Stormy Sky and the withdrawal of a foreign elite, the local polychrome ceramic industry resumed its primacy in elite ritual as the Mexican-associated rectilinear monochrome vessels declined in importance. During the two centuries of political instability that followed Stormy Sky's reign, foreign ritual paraphernalia was apparently no longer desirable, but these two centuries are nevertheless characterized by powerful Mexican influences of a more ideological nature.

Two (perhaps three) stelae were erected to Stormy Sky after his death (nos. 1, 2, 28?). These suggest the extraordinary power and fame that had accrued to him as the most illustrious ruler of Tikal before the reign of his descendant (Ruler A) who adopted a variant of Stormy Sky's name and acceded to power thirteen katuns later. These posthumous stelae also suggest a period in which no ruler had emerged, or been powerful enough to succeed, and in the subsequent centuries the struggle for power was between those who claimed descent from Stormy Sky and other factions of less clear association.

The first resolution of the succession problem was apparently a divided reign. Between 9.2.13.0.0 and 9.4.0.0.0, a period of only twenty-seven years, at least ten stelae were erected. These depict profile individuals who hold staffs of varying complexity and wear relatively simple costumes. They stand upon the bare ground without the basal panels below and sky motifs above that had characterized the traditional Maya portrait from Late Preclassic times. Most of the inscriptions on these stelae are short, and half note the completion of a katun. None of the Sky or Manikin titles used by earlier and later rulers are associated with the names on these stelae; neither are any birth or accession dates identifiable; a final unusual aspect of these inscriptions is that a woman's name is mentioned for the first time at Tikal.

Four of these stelae probably commemorate the completion of the katun 9.3.0.0.0 2 Ahau (nos. 7, 9, 15, 27). These four stelae apparently depict only two rulers: Kan Boar and Claw Skull. Kan Boar's stelae note the katun ending with a Calendar Round alone. Claw Skull's stelae, however, note the katun ending with complete Initial Series, using the Maya Long Count. In my interpretation the name Claw Skull is a variation on the Tikal Jaguar Paw family name that belonged to the ruler who preceded Curl Snout (Coggins 1976a). Thus the four stelae erected at the completion of the katun 9.3.0.0.0 belong to two men who may have been joint rulers of Tikal and possibly represented two different factions. Claw Skull was a descendant of the ancient ruling dynasty and was associated with the use of the date recorded in the Long Count. Kan Boar, however, may represent a new merchant elite that derived its power from the trade instituted in the previous period of Mexican contact and from the families involved in its administration. It is in association with the name Kan Boar that a woman's name first appears on a stela (13). This may refer to his mother or his wife. It is likely that the new significance of a woman at traditional Tikal may be explained as validation of the legitimacy of the co-ruler Kan Boar through a Tikal woman of appropriate birth. In the Books of Chilam Balam the newcomers (the Itza) were repeatedly described as having no fathers and mothers (Roys 1933:178). We have seen that this was also considered to be the case with Curl Snout, as he is represented in Stela 4 without a proper ancestor figure in the sky. It might, in fact, be considered true of any foreign intrusive group which had no significant kinship ties with those they invaded. By Middle Classic times at Tikal the Mexicanized Maya who had come to power modified the local form of stela erection so that sky ancestor figures were no longer depicted. As a representative of this relatively new element of society, Kan Boar's legitimacy as co-ruler nevertheless may have depended upon a woman of ancient local lineage. Furthermore, his stelae commemorate the katun ending with a Calendar Round alone, or with the universal dating system used by the Mexicans when they first came to the Maya regions—not with the privileged Initial Series.

The four stelae erected at 9.3.0.0.0 may represent a joint rule that divided administrative responsibility between internal and external affairs in a moiety system of the kind Becker has recently suggested existed at Teotihuacan, as at later Tenochtitlan (Becker 1975). Claw Skull as a member of an ancient lineage may have been concerned with internal affairs while Kan Boar managed the external affairs of trade and warfare.

The most significant long-term effects the Mexicans had upon the Maya of Tikal probably derived from the introduction of trade-generated wealth and the transfer of power to foreigners who were outside the entrenched dynastic system. Ancient Maya imagery, and presumably related practice, at Tikal derived from an aristocratic ancestor veneration that had dictated forms since Preclassic times. The relationship of man to the cosmos was conceived of as primarily vertical, with the earth depicted below and the ancestor in the sky above. Time was conceived cyclically, but it reached into the remotest past and thus fixed rulers in a single historic continuum. Proskouriakoff believes that Maya social organization was originally based upon three ruling lineages for which there is evidence in the three structures that underlay Structure A-V at Uaxactun, and in the three temples at Palenque; to these examples may be added the North Acropolis at Tikal, which had three principal shrines throughout most of its centuries of development.

With the arrival of Curl Snout at Tikal there began a modification of these primarily historic, tripartite, vertical conceptions of the Maya universe. During the following two centuries of Middle Classic times there was a period of accommodation with a Mexican ideology that was based more on the Tlaloc cult and an expanding economy than on ancestor veneration. The Classic Period Mexican conception of the cosmos was horizontal and probably quadripartite. The Maya may have believed there were four quarters of the world as well, but their ancient emphasis was on East and West. For postclassic Mexicans, quadripartition was a basic principle which governed their perception of the world and time, the organization of their principal cities, and the form of their government.

At Teotihuacan, quadripartition appears to have determined the final layout of the city and may have been celebrated in the great square compound known as the Ciudadela which encloses the Temple of Quetzalcoatl. This pyramidal structure with its projecting heads was probably involved in the celebration of both the solar year and the ritual calendar (Drucker 1974); thus in the Ciudadela as in many of the surviving ritual manuscripts we have a four-sided figure surrounding a cult image to represent the calendric count (Codices Borbonicus, Borgia, Vaticanus B, Fejervary-Mayer, etc.). A four-sided, or four-lobed, diagram was associated with the completion of a calendric count for many Postclassic Middle American peoples. Xochitl or 'flower' was the last, completing day of the twenty-day month for thirteen of the thirty-one counts listed by Caso (1967; cuadro IX). A similar four-petaled floral form is also one of the commonest iconographic motifs at Classic Period Teotihuacan (Kubler 1967: Figs. 23, 29, 33, 42, 44), and it is likely that it signifies the completion of a calendric count as does the similarly formed Classic Maya glyph (T173) for the completion of a time period.

The introduction of Tlaloc, the Mexican national rain and storm deity, was among the most important innovations of Curl Snout at Tikal, where the concept was rapidly Mayanized. At Teotihuacan, agricultural aspects of the omnipresent Tlaloc cult probably involved calendric ritual deriving from the seasonal availability of rain; thus, if calendrically conceived, the Temple of Quetzalcoatl at Teotihuacan and its vast surrounding plaza, located opposite the market place, may have functioned as a source of prognostication for the thousands of farmers, merchants, pilgrims, and tourists who flocked to the great city from all over Mesoamerica (Millon 1966:151). At Tikal, Curl Snout may have introduced a similar emphasis on the short-term cycles of the ritual calendar along with the Tlaloc cult. Before his arrival at Tikal those shorter cycles would probably have been considered the concern of the commoners, who knew little of the millennial records of the Maya Long Count, which were the esoteric province of the aristocracy. If Curl Snout did not actually try to impose a Mexican type of celebration of the ritual calendar at Tikal, it is likely that it was he who introduced a brilliant compromise between the two calendar systems that would eventually become Tikal's principal public cult. This compromise was the celebration of the completion of katuns, or twenty-year periods. Katuns were firmly anchored calendrically within the Maya Long Count but for most purposes they were identified only by their ending day, and they were conceived of as part of a closed and repeating series of thirteen katuns of which each katun had a predictable character and an augury for mankind. This cycle of thirteen 20-year katuns was thus a Long Count approximation of the thirteen 20-day months that composed the basic Mesoamerican calendar: the latter cycle composed of 260 days, the former of 260 years.

Evidence for the introduction of katun celebration by Curl Snout is found on his Stela 18, which commemorates 8.18.0.0.0, the first katun completed after his accession to power. This is the first katun-celebrating monument at Tikal, and except for two stelae that celebrate the completion of 8.16.0.0.0 at Uaxactun it is the earliest known. The presence of these two monuments at Uaxactun may indicate, as previously suggested, that the Mexican influences came to Tikal by way of Uaxactun, as may the presence of Stela 5 at Uaxactun portraying a weapon-bearing foreigner.

After 8.18.0.0.0 there are no more katun-celebrating monuments at Tikal until the four stelae already discussed that were erected after the death of Stormy Sky at 9.3.0.0.0. In the intervening century there is evidence that the old lineages of Tikal were struggling to regain power and that the reign of Stormy Sky represented an accommodation between the old order and the new. The struggles following his death were apparently resolved, temporarily, by a joint rule that acknowledged both factions. These four stelae have no identifiable foreign symbolism, yet they suggest the survival of a foreign ideology and political order. These are evident in the presence of four monuments, in the absence of the old Maya earth/man/sky composition, in the simple costumes of the rulers, in the absence of traditional Maya titles in the inscriptions, in the importance of katun celebration, and in the selective use of Calendar Round dates in place of historic dates written out in the Long Count.

Throughout much of the rest of the Middle Classic Period at Tikal, power appears to have changed hands a number of times but to have belonged to the weakened and impoverished Jaguar Paw dynasty most consistently. Claw Skull may have been sole ruler in 9.4.0.0.0 (Stela 6), and a posthumous stela was apparently erected to him at about 9.5.0.0.0 (Stela 26). During this period there was little major ceremonial construction, and most of the carved monuments that were erected were eventually damaged and moved. The population of Tikal was, however, increasing steadily, and it seems likely that the administration of the extended city continued below the level of the monument-erecting ruling elite, run by a less aristocratic class which administered trade as well as local government.

Toward the end of the Middle Classic Period there may have been a second period of divided rule, perhaps as early as 9.9.0.0.0 (Stelae 10, 12; A.D. 613). These rulers may have come to power at Tikal through dynastic connections with a southeastern Peten site near Pusilha in modern Belize (Coggins 1976a). During this period there appears to have been a revival of the emphasis on katun celebration and the further development of the cult into the completely Maya katun ritual. This was institutionalized at Tikal with the construction of twin pyramid complexes. These were apparently first made at Tikal at about 9.9.0.0.0, A.D. 613 (Jones 1969:85–87). In their developed form, twin pyramid complexes consisted of two four-stairwayed pyramids located one on the east and one on the west side of a plaza (Fig. 3-3). On the south side of the plaza there was a nine-doorwayed range-type structure and on the north a walled enclosure with a stela and altar which commemorated the completion of the katun and depicted the current ruler making a scattering gesture. The altars frequently have four-part designs around the periphery with Pop, or mat, signs framing the divisions. Jones has discussed the katun-celebrating nature of these complexes and emphasized their great size and probable function in large public ceremonies (1969:128–137). Such ceremonies would have been concerned particularly with the prophecies for the current katun and with auguries for crops and personal health. These popular rituals may have been analogous to those held at the "Temple of Quetzalcoatl" at Teotihuacan with its vast surrounding plaza, and markedly different from the ancestral ritual of Tikal, which was concentrated among the tombs of the ancestors at the ancient center of the site.

The twin pyramid complexes at Tikal with their monuments that depict rulers casting seed in divination involved the ruler in public ceremony and thus tended to expand the traditional role of the aristocracy of Tikal. The twin pyramid complexes also popularized the form of the central Great Plaza itself. There the tombs of the ancestors and their stelae are located on the north side, and a nine-doorwayed range structure is on the south. As Guillemin has pointed out (1968) this same grouping of buildings was copied in the (later) twin pyramid complexes. Guillemin further points out that the twin pyramids with their stepped profiles provide a diagram for the Mesoamerican conception of the path of the sun as it rises and declines and passes below the earth to traverse the underworld (Fig. 3-3). This trajectory of the sun was also viewed by the Maya as analogous to the life of a ruler, who was identified with the sun when he ruled, and after his death similarly passed through the underworld then rose into the sky to join his ancestors. Thus the twin pyramid complexes provided a popular religion which combined the veneration of a semi-divine ruler and prophet with the issuance of practical prognostication for everyman.

Twin pyramid complexes evolved as a ritual form during the last part of the Middle Classic Period at Tikal. It is likely that the institution of the ball game developed concurrently, having been intro-

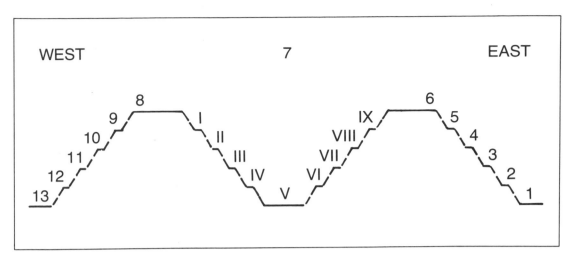

FIGURE 3–3. The Twin Pyramid Complex as a cosmic diagram. After Guillemin 1968:24.

FIGURE 3–4. Tikal, Twin Pyramid Complex, Group 4E–4. Reconstruction by Norman Johnson. Courtesy Tikal Project, University Museum, University of Pennsylvania.

duced in the years of strong Mexican influence. Prosperity returned to Tikal at about 9.11.0.0.0 (A.D. 650), or at least rich burials became common again. At this time twin pyramid complexes had been in use for two katuns at least, and there were probably joint rulers of Tikal. Two noblemen were ultimately buried sequentially on the axis of the North Acropolis, and katun celebration plates were included in the tomb furnishings. The next ruler of Tikal, Ruler A, arranged his accession on the thirteen-katun anniversary of the accession of Stormy Sky, who was his ancestor. Thus his arrival at Tikal symbolized the end of the preceding 260-year cycle of history and he proclaimed himself the inaugurator of the new cycle.

We know about the Maya cyclic view of history and about the celebration of the completion of katuns from the Maya Chronicles, or the Books of Chilam Balam (Barrera Vásquez and Morley 1949; Roys 1933; 1954). These are compilations of ancient Maya prophecy and history that were still recorded in manuscripts and part of the oral tradition in colonial Yucatan. It has generally been considered unlikely that the history in these accounts could have any long-term accuracy. Recently, however, analysis of the excavations at Tikal has suggested that the thirteen-katun cycle was operative in the Classic Period conception of history at Tikal (Coggins 1975).

Events described in the Maya Chronicles, since they occur in association with repeating cycles of thirteen katuns, are identified only by the Ahau day upon which each katun was completed; it has thus been thought likely that the described events of each katun may represent the arbitrary reorganization of the past by subsequent recordkeepers "who were more interested in the magic of numbers [than in] pinpointing historical events" (J. E. S. Thompson 1970:25). Nevertheless, if we take the most conservative (or currently radical) point of view and assume that these chronicles do extend into the Classic Period as they purport to, then we find some extraordinary parallels with our expanding knowledge of the history of the southern Maya Lowlands. (See also Puleston, Ch. 5 of this volume.)

Most compelling is the historical evidence now available in the Peten for the Katun 8 Ahau that was completed in 9.13.0.0.0. This is the katun in which the Itza are said to have abandoned Chichen Itza for the first time and started for Chakanputun, a place which it apparently took them decades to reach and settle (Barrera Vásquez and Morley 1949:30, 32). It has recently been suggested by Joseph Ball that Chakanputun was the site we call Seibal on the Pasión River, a tributary of the Usumacinta (1974a), and he postulates that the Itza went to Chakanputun about 10.0.0.0.0 (A.D. 830). A broad association of Seibal with Chakanputun seems possible, as does the general identification of these southward-migrating Itza with a Chontal Putun people, as Thompson (1970:1) and Ball both assert. Evidence at Tikal, however, suggests that an Itza-related group settled Seibal and other nearby Pasión River sites earlier, close to 9.13.0.0.0, after the region had been depopulated for a century or more (Sabloff 1975: 41). These Itza-related people apparently supported the return to Tikal of Ruler A, who was the legitimate descendant of Stormy Sky, and who may have gone to Tikal from the Pasión River site of Dos Pilas, which had originally been founded from Tikal. Contemporaneously, in this same Katun 8 Ahau, Shield Jaguar became ruler at the Usumacinta River site of Yaxchilan, which was probably also founded from Tikal (Proskouriakoff n.d.), having brought with him a variant dating system which was in use in the Puuc region well to the north. It is possible that Chakanputun was the general name for the sites along the Usumacinta River and its tributaries that were settled by interrelated Mexicanizing Maya peoples in late Middle Classic times.

While there is no question that we are dealing with different Maya groups which developed variant rituals and monument-erecting practices in Late Classic times, many of these ritual forms probably derived originally from Early Classic Period Tikal, where they had been practiced by the earliest people to whom the colonial Maya Chronicles refer. Most prominent among these practices are katun celebration with a seed- or water-scattering divination ritual and the display of the Manikin Sceptre as a national emblem. This group of Maya peoples first established their identity and began their history at the completion of Baktun 9, or 9.0.0.0.0 8 Ahau. The most important Maya site known to have been in existence at this fateful date is Tikal, which was ruled at that time by Mexicanized Maya who had apparently introduced katun celebration and the Manikin Sceptre concept to the Peten.

During the Katun 8 Ahau, which completed Baktun 9 and completed the thirteen-katun cycle before the beginning of Itza history, the foreign people who had accompanied Curl Snout to Tikal wore the costume and carried the weapons of Mexicans, and I have specifically suggested that katun celebration and the Manikin Sceptre were Mayanized Mexican concepts introduced to Tikal by Curl Snout. Perhaps Curl Snout also introduced a Mexican language along with these other basic cultural concepts. It is said of the later katun-celebrating Itza that they spoke the language of Zuyua, at least for ritual purposes (Roys 1933:88–89). Zuyua was apparently Nahuatl, and according to Brinton the word derives from the mythical location of the Seven Caves from which most Highland Mexican peoples are said to have derived (Barrera Vásquez and Morley 1949:26, 27). Heyden has recently suggested that the lobed cave found beneath the Pyramid of the Sun at Teotihuacan was associated with the one in this origins myth (1975); thus it is possible that the language of Zuyua was the language of Teotihuacan, and that it was also the language in esoteric ritual use by the Mexicanized Maya of Tikal at the beginning of the history of the Itza, as well as the archaic language still used by the Itza of Yucatan over a millennium later.

During Middle Classic times, between A.D. 480 and 680, Teotihuacan was at its height and probably controlled most Mesoamerican trade networks. The presence of Teotihuacan as a foreign, perhaps even as a colonizing, culture abroad was most clearly evident at this time in southern Guatemala. Elsewhere in the Maya regions a prosperity derived from this trade, and vigorous new cultures, born of the combination of Maya and Mexican border peoples, flourished along the rivers and around the peripheries of the Peten. At Tikal, during this Middle Classic time the aristocracy declined, population grew, and Mexican ideology implanted in the previous century spread throughout the society until it had revitalized ancient Maya culture as exemplified by the region of Ruler A.

ACKNOWLEDGMENTS

This essay was presented as a paper at a symposium entitled "Pattern and Process in the Maya Middle Classic Period" at the American Anthropological Association meetings in Washington, D.C., November 21, 1976, and derives from the original paper read at Cambridge in August 1976.

The historical conclusions found herein are based on my work on the elite ritual contexts (especially tombs) of Tikal (1975), as are the hypotheses offered. I am particularly grateful to Christopher Jones, George Cowgill, and George Kubler for criticism of this essay, but I must bear complete responsibility for the final version.

4 Teotihuacan, Internal Militaristic Competition, and the Fall of the Classic Maya
by George L. Cowgill

In very broad terms, the Teotihuacan civilization, centered in the Mexican Highlands, and the Classic civilization of the Southern Maya Lowlands exhibit a similar developmental trajectory. That is, both enjoyed a period of development, flourished for a time, and then collapsed. But as soon as one looks beyond these gross generalities, the evidence from each region shows striking differences in the pace and timing of events. These differences are of interest in their own right, and one of my objectives is to call attention to them. In addition, however, they help to direct our attention to some of the distinctive features of the Maya trajectory which are relevant for understanding the functioning of Late Classic Maya society and for explaining its collapse. My main concern is to point out difficulties in some recently proposed explanations, to draw on evidence from China and Greece to make some points about causes and dynamics of serious militaristic competition, and to suggest that escalating internal warfare may have been more a cause than a consequence of serious trouble for the Maya. I do not suggest warfare as a monocausal explanation for the Maya collapse, but I do think it may have been an important contributing factor, and old evidence should be re-examined and new evidence sought with this possibility in mind.

Emphasis on Maya warfare is part of a widespread recognition that the Maya were not the gentle pacifists that some archaeologists would have them be. But there is a difference between sporadic raiding, with occasional enslavement or sacrifice or captives, and what David Webster (1977:363–364) calls *militarism*: institutionalized warfare intended for territorial aggrandizement and acquisition of other capital resources, with military decisions part of the conscious political policy of a small elite, semiprofessional warriors, and lethal combat on a large scale. Webster and I both argue that the Late Classic Maya may have become militaristic in this sense, but we differ about the probable dynamics and consequences of Maya militarism.

Although it is clear that there were important contacts between the Highlands and the Southern Maya Lowlands, I should stress that I am *not* arguing that either Teotihuacan intervention or the withdrawal of Teotihuacan contacts played a decisive role in the Maya collapse. Direct or indirect contacts with Teotihuacan are important and extremely interesting (e.g., Coggins 1975; Ball 1974b; W. R. Coe 1972; Pendergast 1971), but I doubt if they explain much about either the rise or the fall of the Lowland Maya. In any case, my use of the Teotihuacan data here is purely as a contrastive example.

It is often assumed that Teotihuacan developed rather steadily up to a distinct peak somewhere around A.D. 500 to 600, after which it soon began a fairly rapid decline (e.g., Sanders 1965: Fig. 14). Within the last few years, largely through the data obtained by the comprehensive surface survey and limited test excavations completed by the Teotihuacan Mapping Project, under the direction of René Millon, evidence for a very different pattern has emerged. Much of this evidence has been published, fully or in part (e.g., Bernal 1966; Millon 1973; 1974; 1976; Cowgill 1974; J. R. Parsons 1974), but it has not been emphasized and the implications have not been discussed. I believe that most Mesoamericanists do not yet appreciate how different the Teotihuacan pattern is from the Maya pattern. Furthermore, recent results from computer analyses of Teotihuacan Mapping Project data suggest that the contrasts may be even more striking than has been indicated in previous publications.

Briefly, it appears that the city of Teotihuacan enjoyed an early surge of extremely rapid growth, followed by a four-to-five-century "plateau" during which growth was very much slower or may even have ceased altogether. Then, probably not before the eighth century A.D., the city collapsed, apparently rather rapidly. This pattern is most clearly suggested by the dates of major monumental construction in the city (Millon 1973), but it is also suggested by the demographic implications of quantities and areal spreads of ceramics of various periods, both in the city itself and in all parts of the Basin of Mexico which have been systematically surveyed (Sanders 1965; J. R. Parsons 1968; 1971; 1974; Blanton 1972a; 1972b). Further support comes from data on Teotihuacan obsidian industry (Spence 1975).

In contrast, the Maya site of Tikal was settled at least as early as Teotihuacan but developed more irregularly to a modest Late Preclassic climax, followed apparently by something of a pause. There seems to have been a second peak in Early Classic times, and then a distinct recession for a century or so (Willey 1974b; 1977). Then there was a relatively brief burst of glory in the seventh and eighth centuries, immediately followed by rapid decline and very drastic population loss (Culbert, ed. 1973; 1974; Coggins 1975). Tikal population may have been relatively stable from about A.D. 550 until after A.D. 800 (this view is argued by William Haviland, 1970 and in personal communication), or it may have shot up rapidly during the 600's to a short-lived maximum in the 700's (Culbert 1974:113–117). In either case, however, it seems clear that the Late Classic population of Tikal was larger than that at any previous time. Other major sites in the Southern Maya Lowlands had rather different trajectories, but they also generally peaked during the Late Classic and collapsed during the ninth or tenth centuries.

There are also striking contrasts in spatial patterns. The early growth of Teotihuacan is concomitant with rapid and marked decline in the number and size of other settlements in the Basin of Mexico. Teotihuacan quickly achieved, and for several centuries maintained, a size probably twenty or more times larger than any other known Basin of Mexico settlement. Even Cholula, in the Valley of Puebla some ninety kilometers away, does not seem to have covered more than a sixth of the area of Teotihuacan (Muller 1973: Fig. 3), and other settlements in the Tlaxcala–Northern Puebla area were much smaller (Snow 1969; Dumond 1972; García Cook 1974). In the Southern Maya Lowlands there were other major centers comparable in size to Tikal, and below these there was a hierarchy of other sites ranging from fairly large secondary centers to small hamlets and individual households. (Hammond 1974 and Marcus 1973 and 1976 give recent reviews of this evidence. In contrast to Marcus, Hammond [1974:318] argues that present evidence is insufficient for assigning specific sites to specific hierarchical levels, although hierarchies probably existed. The very fact of the controversy points up the contrast with Teotihuacan, where there is no dispute at all about its primacy in the settlement hierarchy.) There is no suggestion that Tikal or other major centers ever drew people away from other sites or monopolized power to anywhere near the extent that Teotihuacan did in central Mexico.

THE TEOTIHUACAN EVIDENCE

During the Cuanalan Phase, corresponding to Ticoman elsewhere in the Basin of Mexico, around 500 to 150 B.C., Teotihuacan did not yet exist. The several small villages in what was to become the urban zone did not cover more than a few hectares and could hardly have totaled more than one to three thousand people. During the Patlachique Phase, about 150 to 1 B.C., Teotihuacan grew far more rapidly than at any other time, and it came to cover some six to eight square kilometers—about a third of its eventual size. During the Tzacualli Phase, about A.D. 1 to 150, nearly the entire area of the later city was occupied, as well as some parts not occupied later. By the end of this phase, most of the enormous Pyramid of the Sun had been completed and more than twenty "three-temple" complexes had been built (Millon 1973:52). Millon (1973:42) stresses the "audacity" of early building in Teotihuacan. The Ciudadela was close to its present bulk before the end of the Miccaotli Phase (ca. A.D. 150–200). The Temple of Quetzalcoatl may also have been completed this early, and is surely not later than the Tlamimilolpa Phase (ca. A.D. 200–450) (Millon 1973:55).

The latest major building phase of the Pyramid of the Moon dates to Tlamimilolpa, but it was probably already very large in the Miccaotli Phase, if not earlier. In contrast, monumental building during the Xolalpan (ca. A.D. 450–650) and Metepec (ca. A.D. 650–750) phases was very substantial in total amount, but it consists primarily of renovations and additions to existing structures. There seems nothing at Teotihuacan after about A.D. 300 or 400 at the latest that is comparable to the Late Classic outburst of monumental building in the Southern Maya Lowlands, when numerous structures were built that far surpassed Early Classic Maya achievements.

In fact, the most important new architectural idea in post-Miccaotli

Teotihuacan pertained to residential rather than monumental building. This was the apartment compound, a relatively large room complex surrounded by a massive outer wall. There was great variety, rather than standardization, in the internal arrangements of these compounds, but usually there were several apartments, each focused around its own inner patio. They did *not* generally have a single large inner courtyard, as Willey (1974a:136) suggests. These apartment compounds were doubtless basically an adaptation to somewhat crowded urban living, but their differences from residential architecture in Tenochtitlan or other preindustrial cities are as notable as their resemblances (Millon 1973:40, 56).

After this, throughout the Xolalpan and Metepec phases, there was constant rebuilding, renovation, and alteration of apartment compounds, and continued variety in the details of each. Construction quality remained good. But in residential architecture, as in monumental architecture, after Tlamimilolpa there seem to have been no really new ideas, nor anything further that can be called "audacious."

A second line of evidence about the tempo of Teotihuacan's development is provided by the obsidian industry. Michael Spence (1967; 1975) finds that obsidian working was probably well under way in Patlachique times, and was certainly an important craft by the Tzacualli Phase. More than four hundred workshops are recognized for the Tlamimilolpa Phase, and it appears that there was little if any subsequent increase in the number of obsidian workshops (Millon 1973:57). Computer studies suggest that, if anything, there may have been a slight decrease. At least for obsidian, the major Teotihuacan industry whose chronology we now know the most about, it appears that, as with architecture, there was early development followed by a long plateau.

Absolute population estimates for the Xolalpan Phase have been derived by Millon (1970:1079–1080; 1973:45) by making estimates of the number of occupants of apartment compounds of various sizes and then counting the numbers of compounds in each size class. Although sizable uncertainties remain even with this procedure, it has the great advantage that the surface evidence about the number and approximate sizes of Xolalpan apartment compounds is reasonably clear. For earlier periods my population estimates have to rely on (1) the spatial extent of substantial sherd cover, and (2) relative sherd frequencies, adjusted for the differing durations of the phases. I have discussed elsewhere problems in such inferences from surface surveys (Cowgill 1974). It is some comfort that, because we have counts of sherds collected systematically in the course of complete coverage of the city, we are better off than most persons who have attempted to estimate prehistoric population trends. Usually such attempts rest on general impressions of area and density of sherd cover. Nevertheless, all we can say is that we have fairly good figures on "sherds per century," but we cannot be sure that these figures give a correct impression of "people per century."

With this caveat firmly in mind, it is still worth looking at the main outlines of the sherd frequency trends. Adjusted for duration, there are more than a third as many Patlachique as Xolalpan. Miccaotli, Tlamimilolpa, and Metepec sherds per century are about the same as Xolalpan. In other words, if one *were* to take these sherd counts as a good index of population trends, it would seem that Teotihuacan population grew very rapidly during the Patlachique Phase. Any reasonable smooth curve fitted to the sherds-per-century histogram suggests a Patlachique growth rate probably over twelve per thousand per year. During the Tzacualli Phase the implied rate is still high, but slowing rapidly. By very late in the Tzacualli Phase, the curves already come close to the total reached in subsequent phases. During the Miccaotli through Metepec phases, from ca. A.D. 150 until nearly A.D. 750, although there may have been short-term fluctuations, there appears to have been practically no long-term change.

Thus, the sherd-count trend does not show a steady increase as one approaches the Xolalpan Phase; it shows instead very rapid early growth and then a long plateau. The sherd data by themselves do not compel us to believe that this was the actual trend for people as well as pots. It is entirely conceivable that people in the earlier phases used and/or broke significantly more pots per person per year than did people of the later phases. It is also conceivable that redeposition makes very early material much better represented on the surface than is less early material. The question of demographic trends at Teotihuacan cannot be resolved until we have a substantial amount of data on residential structures throughout the city for each period. Nevertheless, it seems significant that the sherds-per-century pattern is consistent with other evidence: the early expansion and then relative stability of the city's borders, the very early dates of much of the most impressive architecture, and the good evidence for early development in the Teotihuacan obsidian industry.

If one projects Millon's (1970:1079–1080) "middle range" estimate of 125,000 people in Xolalpan Teotihuacan back into the past, an average Patlachique population of possibly 30,000 to 40,000 and an average Tzacualli population something like 60,000 to 80,000 are suggested by the ceramic abundances for these phases. These estimates are notably higher than previous estimates. Because of the highly ambiguous implications of the sherd counts, one cannot say that the evidence for such a large early population is strong. Nevertheless, I do think that the possibility that Patlachique and Tzacualli urban populations were this large has to be taken seriously. And estimates on the order of 10,000 for Patlachique or 30,000 to 50,000 for Tzacualli Teotihuacan now seem definitely conservative. Of course, using Millon's minimum or maximum estimates for the Xolalpan Phase will scale all other estimates down or up accordingly.

IMPLICATIONS OF THE TEOTIHUACAN EVIDENCE

Several implications of the Teotihuacan pattern suggest themselves. The long duration of Teotihuacan seems unreasonable unless economic and political power were quite strong and quite effectively centralized in the city, and much other evidence also suggest this. In contrast, both the more or less concomitant development of many

Lowland Maya centers and the dynastic evidence so far gleaned from inscriptions indicate that no single Southern Lowland Maya center ever gained long-term firm political or economic control of any very large region, although there is plenty of evidence for brief domination of one center by another, and of political alliances often bolstered by dynastic marriages (Marcus 1976; Molloy and Rathje 1974).

The obvious next step is to suggest that Teotihuacan was long-lived and highly centralized because it was a "hydraulic" state, based on intensive irrigation agriculture in a semiarid environment, while the Southern Maya Lowlands was politically less centralized and enjoyed a much briefer climax because of critical deficiencies in its tropical forest environment. I do not think that environmental considerations are unimportant, but I do feel that there are extremely serious difficulties with these explanations.

Discussions of Teotihuacan irrigation usually do not deal adequately with its *scale*. Evidence for pre-Toltec irrigation in the Teotihuacan Valley remains circumstantial rather than direct, but it seems quite likely that canal irrigation there does date back to Patlachique or Cuanalan times. But the maximum area available for permanent canal irrigation is less than four thousand hectares (Millon, Hall, and Diaz 1962; Sanders 1965; Drewitt 1967; Lorenzo, ed. 1968; Sanders et al. 1970). This is not a very large area, nor does it call for large or complex canals, dikes, or flood-control facilities. Assuming a peak population of 125,000, there would have been about one irrigated hectare for 30 people. It is clear that the city grew well beyond any population limits set by irrigation agriculture, and a substantial fraction of its subsistence must have come from other sources, including riskier and much less productive alternative forms of agriculture, and collecting and hunting wild plants and animals. Faunal analyses (Starbuck 1975) and paleoethnobotanical studies (Ford and Elias 1972; McClung de Tapia 1976) provide evidence that Teotihuacanos ate a wide variety of wild as well as domesticated plants and wild animals.

It seems unlikely that there were any environmental or purely technical factors which would have made it impossible for the Teotihuacanos to have practiced intensive chinampa agriculture in the southern part of the Basin of Mexico. Chinampas were an important subsistence source for the Aztec population, which was much larger than the Teotihuacan population. Yet there is no evidence for extensive use of chinampas in Teotihuacan times (Armillas 1971). It is tempting to speculate that technical difficulties in assembling food for more people in one place may be at least part of the reason that Teotihuacan grew so little after Tzacualli times (a point also made by J. R. Parsons 1974:105). If indeed there were environmental reasons, such as a change in lake levels, which prevented extensive chinampa exploitation in Teotihuacan times, then Teotihuacan is an instance of a population which expanded until it approached a perceived subsistence limit and then stabilized, rather than disastrously exceed that limit. If, as seems more likely, there was no environmental reason why the Teotihuacanos could not have fed more people by simply moving part of the population down to the chinampa area and investing in chinampa developments, their apparent failure to do so must have been for social or political reasons. If so, Teotihuacan population growth in the Basin of Mexico halted at a level well below the number of people it would have been technically possible to feed.

Teotihuacan's behavior has particular significance for the Maya because Culbert (1974) suggests that the Maya collapsed because they were unable to control runaway expansion which caused them to "overshoot" disastrously the productive limits of their environment.

Whether or not I am right in suspecting that Teotihuacan population growth leveled off before environmental limits were approached, it is logically inescapable that it was biologically possible for Teotihuacan population to have continued to expand until it "overshot" all technically feasible subsistence possibilities. If it were simply the case that rapid development tends to acquire a sort of momentum which carries it beyond environmental limits and into disaster before it can be stopped, then the ability of the Teotihuacanos to slow down and stop short of disaster would be puzzling.

An extended discussion of Teotihuacan's eventual collapse is not possible here, but I should add that I do not know of any convincing evidence that even the end of Teotihuacan was primarily due to climatic deterioration or other environmentally generated subsistence difficulties. Growing competition from other Highland centers was probably important (cf. Litvak King 1970), and I suspect that Teotihuacan may have collapsed for political, economic, and military reasons, rather than purely ecological reasons.

Proponents of either "population pressure" or "hydraulic" explanations for early states may perhaps argue that Teotihuacan "plateaued" instead of overshooting because the power of the state was very much stronger and more centralized than in the Maya cities, so that when the disastrous consequences of further expansion of the city became evident, the state had the power to intervene effectively and halt further population growth. Possibly this may be part of the explanation, but I do not think this explanation is required. The main reason may have been that there was simply no advantage in further expansion that would have offset attendant inconveniences. There is much evidence that population growth rates are very responsive to shifts in other variables (Cowgill 1975a; 1975b). Assuming the Southern Lowland Maya did indeed "overshoot" their environment, even in the face of growing subsistence difficulties, it is the Maya behavior which is puzzling—far more puzzling than Culbert assumes—and it is the Maya "overshoot" rather than the Teotihuacan "plateau" which is most in need of explanation.

Culbert's (1974:113–117) "overshoot" explanation of the Maya collapse is one of the least unsatisfactory suggestions made so far. Culbert himself (1974:111–112) cogently disposes of most previous explanations. And archaeological evidence for the Southern Maya Lowlands in the eighth century does suggest a population so large that, in spite of evidence for terraces, ridged fields, and tree and root crops in addition to swidden (Turner 1974a), a subsistence crisis seems a real possibility. Nevertheless, there are serious problems with Culbert's explanation. He speaks of many causal factors, but inspection shows that excessive population growth plays a central role in his model. And, in his 1974 book, he offers no particular explanation for the population growth itself. More recently (Culbert 1977) he has attributed population growth to economic development. But the question remains: what would have driven the Maya to expand population and/or environmental exploitation to the point where a subsistence crisis was produced? And if, instead, there was little population growth after about A.D. 550, as Haviland (1970 and personal communication) argues, then the postponement of collapse for some 250 years seems even more puzzling.

A different explanation for the Maya collapse suggests that the eighth-century Maya "florescence" was not, in fact, a time of Maya prosperity at all, but instead an attempt to cope with already serious troubles (Rathje 1973). This theory, if I understand it correctly, suggests that ability to obtain foreign goods by trade was critical for elite Maya prestige, for the power that derived from that prestige, and as a means of providing incentives for local production. Exclusion of central Peten elites from developing Mesoamerican trade networks supposedly precipitated a crisis for these elites, in which they attempted to offset their sagging prestige by even more ambitious monumental construction projects. But clearly nothing indispensable for subsistence was lacking, and prestige games can be played with whatever one defines as status markers, as Sanders (1973) points out. Goods need not be obtained by long-distance trade in order to be scarce and valuable. Furthermore my guess is that the decline of Teotihuacan, if anything, expanded the possibilities for profitable trade by Southern Lowland Maya elites. Webb's (1973:391–403) postulated development of new Mesoamerican trading networks following the decline of Teotihuacan seems, in very broad outline, a reasonable possibility. But I am much less persuaded than either Webb or Rathje (1973) that, at least at first, the Southern Lowland Maya were unable to participate in these new developments. The scale and substance of Late Classic Maya material civilization argues that they *were* able to profit from the situation, at least for a time. To be sure, there is some evidence for poor nutritional status for some Lowland Maya (Saul 1973), but the same was probably true for much of the English and Western European population at the height of rapid economic growth in the early decades of the Industrial Revolution. It may well be that Late Classic Maya wealth was very unevenly distributed, and it also may be that the Late Classic Maya of the Southern Lowlands were increasingly "living off ecological capital," but this does not mean that the elites were already badly off, or were doing what they did in order to cope with resource pressures or an unfavorable balance of trade. The argument that the Late Classic Maya were already in serious trouble in the seventh or eighth centuries is unconvincing. Exclusion from trade networks does seem a good explanation for nonrecovery after the collapse, but not for the collapse itself.

SOME POINTS FROM CHINA AND GREECE

It is instructive to consider some episodes in the history of China and Greece. Clearly Maya culture, technology, and environment differed drastically from those of both China and Greece, and I do not want to suggest that any two of the three belong in any useful sense to a similar "culture type" or that one can prove an argument about the Maya by referring to Greek or Chinese data. Instead, my use of the Chinese and Greek material has two objectives. First, knowing what happened in these cases enables us to ask whether something slightly similar *might* have occurred in the Southern Maya Lowlands. It broadens the range of possibilities we can seriously imagine. Second, knowing what seemingly *did not* happen—especially in China—awakens or intensifies doubts about some comfortable assumptions about processes in the Maya area.

In China, the Chou Dynasty came to power around the eleventh century B.C. and for a while exercised fairly centralized control over most of northern China (Creel 1970). But effective control soon passed into the hands of the leaders of a large number of localized, more or less feudal states (Bodde 1956). In the seventh and sixth centuries warfare between states was fairly frequent but was limited in scale and duration, and a "chivalrous" code of rules was honored. In the fifth through third centuries economic, political, technological, and intellectual development was rapid. As some states were annexed by others, the remaining states grew fewer, larger, and more competitive, and the scale and intensity of warfare escalated. Brief raids and combat between chariot-riding aristocratic heroes were replaced by long campaigns, great troops of conscripted infantry, and the bloody slaughters of the "Warring States" period (Hsu 1965). Feudal governmental institutions tended to be replaced by bureaucratic institutions (Creel 1964), at least partly because of a felt need to make governments more centralized, more efficient, and more ruthless in order to survive in an increasingly competitive arena. The eventual outcome, however, was not catastrophe, but the triumph of one state, Ch'in. It defeated all the others, and the ruler of the Ch'in became the first emperor of a unified and highly centralized Chinese empire. His particular dynasty was short-lived, but it was quickly followed by the Han Dynasty, which held effective control for most of the next four centuries.

In any holistic comparative sense, the differences between "Warring States" China and the Southern Maya Lowlands are extremely great. The Warring States had an iron-age technology, metallic currency, and at least the beginnings of bureaucratic institutions and intensive large-scale irrigation agriculture. Many individual states had more people and sometimes more territory than the entire Southern Maya Lowlands. What can Warring States China suggest about the Maya?

China gives an example of escalating competition for a prize—the empire—which was resolved when one state eventually gained the prize. It seems quite clear that conflict *did not* escalate because of growing population pressure or subsistence problems. On the contrary, rulers of states often felt that their states were *under*populated. They needed people as conscripts for the huge armies, and they also needed people to intensify agricultural production in order to feed the huge armies during their long campaigns. Some rulers adopted policies explicitly intended to encourage population growth, and rulers also attempted to induce peasants to flee from other states and settle on underdeveloped lands in their own states (Bodde 1956:67; Eberhard 1969:53–45).

This is worth emphasis because the direction of causality is exactly opposite to the direction suggested by Steward (1955:202–203) and assumed by Carneiro (1970) and many others. It is wonderfully reasonable to assume that as long as there is plenty of land, conflict will be minimal, and that conflict will increase in severity as population, owing to natural fecundity, increases, "filling up" the landscape and engendering competition for resources which are becoming increasingly scarce. But the Chinese evidence shows the opposite. States which still had plenty of land were fighting so that their rulers could gain the wealth and power attendant on control over other states, and to defend themselves against being deprived of wealth, power, and even life, by the rulers of the other states. They encouraged population growth *because of* escalating warfare, as well as for economic reasons, rather than escalating warfare because of population growth.

The Peloponnesian War of Greece provides further food for thought (Bowra 1971). It seems clear that it would not have involved virtually the whole Greek world or had the serious consequences that it had, if Athens had not looked as if it might really succeed in gaining control over most of Greece. Greece had been divided into city-states for a long time, and by the fifth century B.C. there was a long history of shifting quarrels, alliances, wars, and peaces, with no one state dominating all the others. But by the mid fifth century, after having turned back the Persian threat, Athens was far more than a city-state. Between vassals and states which were nominally "allies" but in fact dominated by Athens, it already controlled an empire of respectable size and great wealth. It was quite realistic of Sparta and its allies to fear that unless Athens were stopped, it would gain control of the whole Greek world, as indeed Alexander did a few generations later. The severity of the Peloponnesian War was surely due to the fact that the stakes were so high. Conceivably it could have ended as in Warring States China, with some one faction gaining a decisive advantage and establishing a Greek Empire. Instead, the contending states only succeeded in debilitating themselves, without any one gaining a true victory.

Although there were serious plagues and the population of Attica itself declined (Gomme 1933), it seems as if the most that can be said for Greece as a whole is that the period of rapid growth preceding the war was brought to a halt. Only later does it seem that Greek population actually declined markedly (Angel 1972:100). Certainly Greek civilization did not "collapse" as a consequence of the Peloponnesian War. Indeed, such men as Plato and Aristotle flourished in the generations following it. Nevertheless, the competition and warfare between Athens and Sparta was very damaging, and the results that the Athenians hoped for were not achieved.

A SUGGESTION ABOUT THE MAYA

61
Teotihuacan,
Militaristic
Competition, &
Fall of the
Classic Maya

It seems likely that in Late Classic times there was general economic development in a number of regional centers in the Southern Maya Lowlands, perhaps at least in part because of the weakening of Highland states such as Teotihuacan and Monte Alban. More speculatively, the elites of the individual centers may have increasingly seen it as both feasible and desirable to extend strong control over a relatively large surrounding area—a control based more on conquest and annexation than on political alliance and elite intermarriage. Population growth may well have been a concomitant of this economic and political development. My argument here and previously (Cowgill 1975a; 1975b) is not that population growth rarely occurs, nor that population growth does not have important reciprocal effects on other variables. My objections, instead, are to the idea that population can be counted on to increase for no reason except human procreative proclivities, and to the idea that competition and militaristic warfare would intensify mainly as a response to subsistence shortages. Instead, I suggest that if population was increasing, it was because it was useful either to elites, to peasant households, or to both. And I suggest that intensified militaristic competition is a normal extension of intensified economic competition.

Mayanists are accustomed to assuming that the political institutions of the Classic Maya Lowlands were marginally statelike. I suggest that we should seriously consider the possibility that by the seventh and eighth centuries the combination of economic development, population growth, and social changes was leading to the emergence of more highly developed and more centralized governmental structures—the kinds of structures which would make the incorporation of many small states into a single reasonably stable empire seem a realistic possibility. I would not venture to make further conjectures about the specific forms of these new political and economic developments. However, archaeological and epigraphical evidence promises not only to test the general proposition, but also to shed a great deal of further light on the precise forms of Maya political and economic organization.

What I suggest, then, is that eventually the major Maya centers may have begun to compete for effective political mastery of the whole Southern Lowlands. This postulated "heating up" of military conflict, for which there is some support in Late Classic art and inscriptions (Graham 1973:209; Marcus 1974), may have played a major role in the Maya collapse. If, indeed, population growth and/or utilization of the environment expanded beyond prudent limits, the spur may have been provided by militaristic competition. And even if population and production did not expand beyond feasible steady-state values (under peaceful conditions), intensified warfare may have precipitated disaster through destruction of crops and agricultural facilities and through disruption of agricultural labor cycles. Clearly, internal warfare is not "the" single cause of the Maya collapse, but I believe it deserves renewed consideration as a contributing factor.

Webster (1977) also places new stress on the role of warfare in Maya history, but our views and emphases differ in several important ways. First, he is mainly concerned with Preclassic and Early Classic warfare as one of the causes of the *rise* of Maya civilization. This is a topic I have not discussed here. My feeling is that Webster makes some good points—there is certainly clear evidence for some Maya warfare quite early—but he probably overestimates the explanatory importance of early warfare. Second, Webster tends to see warfare largely as a response to shortages in land or other subsistence resources. I believe that this underestimates other incentives for warfare, especially for large-scale militaristic warfare. Third, Webster places much less stress than I do on Late Classic economic development, and he differs sharply on the matter of political integration. He feels that even the largest autonomous political units were never more than forty to sixty thousand people and that incorporation of further large increments of population, especially at considerable distances, proved unworkable. Presumably, although Webster does not explicitly discuss the matter, he would assume that serious attempts to incorporate many more people and more land and other resources within single states did not play a significant role in Maya history. He does feel that warfare may have contributed to the Maya collapse, but he explains intensified warfare mainly as a consequence of the manipulation of militarism by the Maya elite for bolstering their control of their own subject populations, rather than for any extensive conquests of other states. He says that conflicts may also have intensified over strategic resources, especially capital improvements for intensified agriculture, in the intermediate zones between major centers, but he does not suggest that there may have been major attempts to expand beyond the intermediate zones to gain control of the other centers as well. He does not suggest, as I do, that an important contributory element in the Maya collapse may have been a struggle—violent, protracted, and unsuccessful—to bring into being something like the kind of polity Teotihuacan had succeeded in creating several centuries earlier.

ACKNOWLEDGMENTS

Valuable comments on earlier versions of this paper were made by René and Clara Millon, Robert Hunt, William Haviland, David Webster, Clemency Coggins, Gordon Willey, Cynthia Cowgill, Donald Lathrap, Arthur Miller, David Drucker, and B. Turner. The computer work has been supported by NSF grants GS-36960 and SOC73-09075 AO1 to Brandeis University and by an ACLS grant-in-aid.

5 An Epistemological Pathology and the Collapse, or Why the Maya Kept the Short Count by Dennis E. Puleston

The cyclical view of time held by the Pre-Conquest Maya had a profound effect on their cosmology. It has also been recognized that it had significant impact on their history: "A katun of the same name recurred after approximately 256 years, consequently, at the end of that time history was expected to repeat itself. The events recounted in the Maya chronicles . . . offer excellent grounds for believing that this belief was so strong at times as to actually influence the course of history. A surprising proportion of the important upheavals in Maya history appear to have occurred in some katun named either 4 Ahau or 8 Ahau" (Roys 1967:184).

The hypothesis to be presented here is that whatever other factors may have been involved, the collapse (Culbert, ed. 1973) was an event fully anticipated by ancient Maya scholars and priests, who by means of consultations with their books and prophecies were well aware of their impending fall. In order to appreciate this proposition it will be necessary to review certain aspects of the Maya calendar and its relationship to the katun prophecies of Chilam Balam.

The basic unit for the 256-year cycle was the *katun*. A survival of the Classic Period Long Count, the katun was a 7,200-day unit composed of twenty 360-day *tuns*. Running beside the count of tuns and katuns was the repeating 260-day Sacred Round, dates of which were determined by the intermeshing of the 20 named days and a sequence of 13 numbered day coefficients. Each katun was labeled with the Sacred Round date coinciding with the completion of an old katun and the beginning of a new one. Because both calendars have a common denominator of twenty, this day at the fold of the katun was always an Ahau, the last of the 20 named days. Its coefficient, which could be any number between 1 and 13, followed an orderly progression yielding a sequence of 13 distinctly named katuns, as shown in Figure 5-1, which started with 11 Ahau and continued through 9 Ahau, 7 Ahau, 5 Ahau, 3 Ahau, 1 Ahau, 12 Ahau, 10 Ahau, 8 Ahau, 6 Ahau, 4 Ahau, 2 Ahau, and 13 Ahau in that order. This cycle of 13 katuns, or 260 tuns (roughly 256 years of the Christian calendar), formed the repeating historical cycle, called the Short Count, which Roys refers to in the above quotation.

It is clear that the Maya conception of historical repetition did not entail an exact replication of past events but rather a conformance of history to certain underlying, predictable patterns as revealed in the katun prophecies. The prophecies, in turn, seem to have been largely based on an accumulation of recorded history and were even

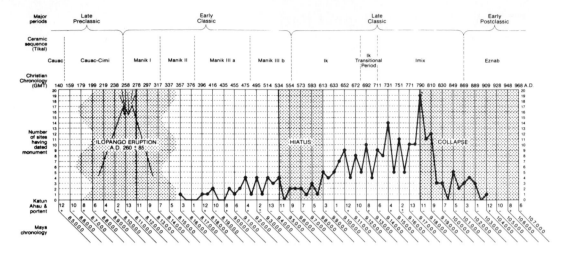

FIGURE 5–1. A relationship between the collapse and hiatus on the one hand and the thirteen-katun time cycle on the other is suggested by this frequency distribution of sites with katun-ending monuments (adapted from Morley 1956: Fig. 2; prepared by Phyllis E. Mauch Messenger).

referred to as the *u kahlay katunob* or 'record of the katuns' (Roys 1967:185). Particular prophecies, such as that for Katun 8 Ahau, refer directly to events of the past because of their relevance to the demonstration of underlying patterns: "Katun 8 Ahau is the ninth katun. The katun is established at Izamal. There is Kinich Kakmo. The shield shall descend, the arrow shall descend [upon Chakanputun] together with the rulers of the land. The heads of the foreigners to the land were cemented [into the wall] at Chakanputun. There is an end of greed; there is an end to causing vexation in the world. It is the word of God the Father. Much fighting shall be done by the Natives of the land" (Roys 1967:160).

It is the reference to Chakanputun that is of especial interest here because of its reference to the expulsion of the Itza from Chakanputun as recorded in the First Chronicle of the Book of Chilam Balam of Chumayel. Here, in a record of successive katun histories, we find that on each Katun 8 Ahau the Itza were being driven from a currently occupied home. How exactly this history corresponds to reality is not of primary concern: the point is that this is how it was viewed.

The First Chronicle begins with Katun 6 Ahau, which supposedly dates the discovery of Chichen Itza. We might imagine the immediately preceding Katun 8 Ahau was witness to the founders' departure from some unrecorded homeland. Using the Goodman-Martínez-Thompson correlation, this probably imaginary event would have occurred in the mid-fifth century A.D. Upon the arrival of the succeeding Katun 8 Ahau, thirteen katuns or 256 years later (the end of the seventh century A.D.), the chronicles intone the abandonment of Chichen Itza: "8 Ahau was when Chichen Itza was abandoned. There were thirteen folds of katuns when they established their houses at Chakanputun" (Roys 1967:136). Chakanputun, commonly identified as Champoton (Roys 1967:136; but see J. E. S. Thompson 1970:15), thus becomes home for the Itza for another thirteen katuns, at the end of which time they are driven out, once again leaving an established home: "8 Ahau was when Chakanputun was abandoned by the Itza men. Then they came to seek homes again. For thirteen folds of katuns they had dwelt on their houses at Chakanputun. This was always the katun when the Itza went beneath the trees, beneath the bushes, beneath the vines, to their misfortune" (Roys 1967:136). The reference to going beneath trees, bushes, and vines refers to defeat, for among the Maya wars typically were terminated by driving the vanquished into the forest (Roys 1967:157).

Following their departure from Chakanputun, according to the First Chronicle, the Itza returned to Chichen Itza. There they reputedly resided for another thirteen katuns until the treachery of Hunac Ceel in the twelfth century A.D. resulted in their second expulsion from that site.

The chronicles intone once more: "8 Ahau was when the Itza men again abandoned their homes because of the treachery of Hunac Ceel, because of the banquet with the people of Izamal. For thirteen folds of katuns they had dwelt there, when they were driven out by Hunac Ceel because of the giving of the questionnaire of the Itza" (Roys 1967: 137).

From Chichen the Itza seem to have divided up, one group heading south into the Peten to settle at Tayasal in Lake Peten. Another group, according to the chronicles, seems to have remained in Yucatan and after forty years regained power by taking Mayapan. Here they reigned under conditions of relative stability, but with the completion of another cycle of thirteen katuns and the arrival of the fateful Katun 8 Ahau the inevitable repetition of history occurred once more. Of the two ruling families at that time, the Cocoms and the Xiu, the Xiu were the lesser, and it was through a conspiracy planned by them that the chiefs subject to Mayapan rose up and killed most of the Cocom family. Mayapan was destroyed and abandoned: "8 Ahau was when there was fighting with stones at Ich-paa Mayapan because of the seizure of the fortress. They broke down the city wall because of the joint government in the city of Mayapan" (Roys 1967:137).

Before a fifth cycle could be completed the Spanish Conquest occurred. The fall of Mayapan marks the end in so far as the chronicles of the Books of Chilam Balam are concerned.

But this was not quite the end. Far to the south, in the fastnesses of the Southern Lowland forest, the Itza of Tayasal continued on virtually undisturbed by the Conquest which was brutally dismantling traditional Maya culture to the north and west in Yucatan, Campeche, and Chiapas and to the south in the Guatemalan Highlands.

In 1618 the Padres Fuensalida and Orbita penetrated this preserve and attempted to persuade the ruling cacique, Canek, to bring his people into the fold of Christianity. Our interest in this event is that in apparent reference to katun prophecies Canek, in the words of the padres, replied that "the time has not yet arrived in which their ancient priests had prophesied to them they were to relinquish the worship of their Gods; because the period in which they then were was

Oxahau, which means Third Period . . . and so they asked the padres to make no further attempts in that direction at that time, but to return to the Village of Tipu and then, on another occasion, to come again to see them" (Means 1917:72). Oxahau, of course, refers to Katun 3 Ahau, for which the prophecies predict "fighting" and "rains of little profit" but make no reference to an overturn of government or a change in religion. *Entradas*, or expeditions, made by other padres were similarly unsuccessful, though Avendaño (who had done his homework, spoke Maya fluently, was well-versed in the nature of katun prophecies and even in hieroglyphic writing) convinced the ruling Canek in 1696 that their time to become Christians was at hand. Avendaño, who seems to have had access to prophecies like those of Chilam Balam, very probably argued his case on the basis of a version of the Katun 10 Ahau prophecy found in the Chumayel version of this prophet's works:

> Katun 10 Ahau, the katun is established at Chablé. The ladder
> is set up over the rulers of the land. The hoof shall burn; the
> sand by the seashore shall burn. The rocks shall crack [with the
> heat]; drought is the change of the katun. It is the word of our
> Lord God the Father and of the Mistress of Heaven, the portent
> of the katun. No one shall arrest the word of our Lord God, God
> the Son, the Lord of Heaven and his power, come to pass all over
> the world. Holy Christianity shall come bringing with it the time
> when the stupid ones who speak our language badly shall turn
> from their evil ways. No one shall prevent it; this then is the
> drought. Sufficient is the word for the Maya priests, the word
> of God. (Roys 1967:159–160)

Though the ruling Canek and many of his followers appear to have been convinced of Avendaño's interpretation both of their history and of their future, other groups were not, and the good father was forced into an exodus that took him beneath the trees, bushes, and vines, all but killing him in the process.

The conquest of Tayasal was finally accomplished in the following year by Sargento Mayor Martín de Ursua y Arizmendi. On March 13, 1697, after a brief display of resistance the Maya fled. The town was abandoned; the people plunged into the lake and swam to the mainland. The idols were cleaned out and a church was founded in the principal temple. Though this event occurred within a Katun 10 Ahau, there lacked but 136 days to achieve the customary 8 Ahau (Tozzer 1957:64) for Itza displacement.

While the existence of a repetitious cyclical history and katun prophecies can be demonstrated for Postclassic and historic times, how sure can we be that such a system also existed during Classic times when the much grander Long Count was still intact and in its heyday? The First Chronicles of the Book of Chilam Balam of Chumayel suggest it with a history that supposedly goes back to the fifth century A.D., but as valid historical records the chronicles are suspect, since events which are likely to have been contemporaneous are placed in separate thirteen-katun cycles. As Roys (1967:185) suggests,

they very possibly were drawn up from historic allusions in hieroglyphic texts and other sources and then manipulated to fit a precon-
ceived model after the fact. Perhaps this whole Short Count was new,
replacing a more sophisticated, less mechanical, longer-term system
that went out with the collapse of Classic civilization. Accepting this
possibility for the sake of argument, it might be claimed that a thirteen-katun cycle of repeating history was a Postclassic invention without relevance for Classic Period conceptions of time. However, recent
work by Clemency Chase Coggins on the iconographic and textual
material from the Classic Period site of Tikal utterly vitiates any
such argument (Ch. 3, this volume).

Coggins's study of Tikal iconography has revealed the striking similarity in the reigns of Stormy Sky (fifth century A.D.) and Ruler A
(seventh century A.D.), whose accessions both fell within a Katun 8
Ahau and were within a few days of being exactly thirteen katuns
apart. As she points out, "The arrival of Ruler A at Tikal at the completion of 13 katuns was probably the most extraordinary combination
and transposition of calendric and historic events in the history of
Tikal" (Coggins 1975:444).

Stormy Sky was certainly one of the greatest rulers Tikal ever had.
Probably twelve years of age at the time of his accession at 8.9.10.0.0
(426 A.D.), he is suggested to have been the son of a Mayanized Mexican from Kaminaljuyu (Coggins 1975:141). "Curl Nose," the Mayanized Mexican father (or possibly grandfather) of Stormy Sky, though
deposing the traditional Jaguar Paw dynasty at Tikal, seems to have
married into local Jaguar Paw nobility, thereby obtaining a certain
degree of legitimacy. Although the accession of Stormy Sky clearly
represents a return to the previous Maya dynasty, it is significant that
he did not repudiate his predecessor, whose important role is historically commemorated in the two Mexican figures on the sides of Stormy
Sky's Stela 31 (Coggins 1975:186). "It is precisely in his role as the
objective synthesis of [Mexican and Mayan culture] that Stormy Sky's
rule became the most venerated at Tikal; and perhaps why his reign
was restored at the completion of thirteen katuns by another Mexicanized Maya who was his descendant—Ruler A" (Coggins 1975:186).

The progeny of Stormy Sky seemingly moved away from Tikal during the difficult times that marked the transition between the Early
and Late Classic Periods. The folding of the new Katun 8 Ahau, however, brought Ruler A back from the west as his lineal descendant.
Ruler A assumed, or was given, the entire Manikin Sky title which
restated Stormy Sky's name (Coggins 1975:444), and he may even have
been conceived of as a reincarnation of Stormy Sky (Coggins 1975:
449). Be that as it may, with him came a return to wealth and power
for Tikal and a renaissance in architecture dramatized by the construction of the great temples—a theme which once started was carried to even greater heights by his son, Ruler B.

With this new understanding of Classic Period history, it seems
undeniable that a thirteen-katun historical cycle was recognized and
was of great significance during the Classic Period. Even the katun
prophecies which survived in the Post-Conquest period may reflect
something of these events which must have already had a rhythm of

their own which, like waves on an ocean of time, had a momentum that carried the fortunes of civilization with them.

The Postclassic Katun 8 Ahau prophecy quoted above is a very positive one despite its reference to battle. "The shield shall descend, the arrow shall descend. . . . There is an end to greed; there is an end to causing vexation in the world. . . . Much fighting . . ." (Roys 1967:160).

Much fighting and the descent of arrows and shields seem to refer to the overthrow of a Mexican regime which has outlived its time: in Postclassic times the phrase was in reference to the displacement of the Itza. It would not be surprising to discover, at some future date, that the accessions of Stormy Sky and Ruler A in Tikal were not entirely peaceful.

Now we may at last turn to consideration of the collapse. The collapse has been characterized in many ways, and obviously many aspects of Maya culture were ultimately involved, including population, demographic patterns, subsistence, economics, and political structure. In the archaeological record we seem to be viewing the remnant evidence of a relatively rapid sequence of interrelated events, which can perhaps best be viewed as a breakdown driven by positive feedback linkages that worked like a chain reaction. What clues do we have as to the kind of mechanism which might have touched off such a sequence of events?

The first indication of the impending decline that we are aware of is a marked drop-off in monument and stela dedications which begins after the all-time high achieved at the katun ending of 9.18.0.0.0 (see Fig. 5-1). This fold of the katun marks the beginning of a Katun 11 Ahau. This in itself is significant, for the Katun 11 Ahau was viewed as the first katun of the thirteen-katun cycle—it marked the beginning of a new era in that cycle. Further, with regard to the general portent of the katun prophecies extant in Post-Conquest times, it is second in a long series of decidedly negative prophecies, as the following summaries (J. E. S. Thompson 1960:181) indicate.

13 Ahau: "There is no lucky day for us."
11 Ahau: "Niggard is the katun, scanty are its rains . . . misery."
 9 Ahau: "Bread is mourned, then water is mourned . . . excessive adultery."
 7 Ahau: "Carnal sin, roguish rulers."
 5 Ahau: "Harsh his face, harsh his tiding."
 3 Ahau: "Rains of little profit, locusts, fighting."
 1 Ahau: "The evil katun."

Finally, and most importantly, it follows by exactly thirteen katuns the beginning of the hiatus that falls between the highpoints of the dynastic reigns of Stormy Sky and Ruler A. The dimensions of this hiatus, which starts during a Katun 11 Ahau and runs from 9.5.0.0.0 to 9.9.0.0.0, have been most recently brought into focus by Willey (1974b).

First recognized by Morley (1937–1938, Vol. 4:333) as an area-wide slump in monument dedications which occurs at this time, the hiatus has since been discussed in terms of monument reports for specific sites, including Tikal (Satterthwaite 1958:122) and Altar de

Sacrificios (J. A. Graham 1972:116). More comprehensive studies carried out at Tikal now reveal that it was also a period of comparatively poor burials (Coggins 1975:258), "muted artistic expression" (Coggins 1975:252), and economic isolation possibly contemporary with the construction of the great earthworks system around that site. Willey (1974b) draws long overdue attention to the dimensions of this hiatus and refers to it as a "rehearsal for the collapse." He remarks that it has been considered remarkable that the Maya were even able to recover from the difficulties of these times. Evidently within the downward positive feedback cycle, which must have existed even at that time, stability was achieved before complete collapse occurred. We may well wonder how and why.

Viewed from the perspective of the thirteen-katun cycle, then, the hiatus was not so much a rehearsal for the collapse as the collapse was a full-bore re-enactment of the hiatus without recovery. Assuming that these events were related, because of their comparable positions in the thirteen-katun cycle, we might wonder if something similar might have occurred during an even earlier Katun 11 Ahau. Looking at Figure 5-1 we can observe that, counting backward, the next so designated katun would fall at the beginning of the final quarter of the third century. As there are no hieroglyphically dated monuments or tombs at Tikal, or for that matter anywhere else in the Maya Lowlands, for this time, we must turn to other data. Doing so, we find evidence of another general slump overlapping the indicated period of time. This is just after the end of the time period when late Late Preclassic, or Protoclassic, Cauac-Cimi ceramics were in use (A.D. 150–250). There is also evidence to suggest this slump extended into the beginning of the Early Classic, at least for the duration of Manik I (A.D. 250–320). The Protoclassic's beginning is signaled by an abrupt termination of Tikal's Preclassic relationship with Kaminaljuyu and the initiation of a period of seemingly dispirited isolation (Coggins 1975:86–93). Very briefly, in contrast to the rich burials which occur both before and after this time, there is only one tomb that has been found in the North Acropolis which dates to this time period. This one tomb is unusual for the fact that it contains no more than a single large male skeleton unaccompanied by any form of burial furniture. Though stucco architectural decoration is less obviously degenerated, the almost graffitilike wall paintings on Structure 5D-Sub.3-1st are in strong contrast to the beautiful and sophisticated painting styles which were already in evidence in the Late Preclassic (W. R. Coe 1965b:13).

Explanation for this regression, which occurs during the transition from Late Preclassic to Early Classic, has been sought in disruptions ultimately caused by the incursions of populations from the region of El Salvador and Honduras, an event suggested by the sudden appearance of nonlocal ceramic types in sites along the southern and eastern edges of the Southern Lowlands. Payson Sheets (1971) has recently implicated the Salvadorian volcano, Ilopango, in these upheavals by proposing that a single devastating eruption (dated by a German Geological Mission [Sheets 1976:9] to A.D. 260 ± 85) produced a tephra-fall that precluded agriculture over an area of three thousand square kilometers. Unable to cope with these conditions, the affected populations or some portion of them supposedly moved up into the Southern Maya Lowlands. The suggestion here, of course, is that something related to these events occurred during the Katun 11 Ahau that comes up at this time; perhaps something to do with the human incursions, perhaps the eruption of Ilopango itself. Until more specific data are generated for this time period and dating is better controlled, it is difficult to do more than refer to such a possibility in the most general way.

By way of conclusion then, I wish to suggest that the collapse of Classic Maya civilization was triggered by an internal mechanism. I am not denying that the system in which the Maya participated was under various forms of stress, but the timing of this ultimate event seems to have been linked to very specific and deeply rooted assumptions that the Maya had about the nature of time. Apart from providing an "initial kick" (Flannery 1968) for the collapse, these assumptions may also have supplied a good deal of the drive which kept the reaction going once it had been catalyzed. The notion that the course of natural and human events was predictable and cyclical and, more specifically, could be pegged to the thirteen-katun cycle of 256 years appears to have been, in Bateson's (1972:480) terms, an epistemological error which became a self-validating myth, and ultimately a positive feedback mechanism of awesome compass.

Thus it is extremely likely that the Classic Maya fully anticipated at least the initial stages of what eventually came to pass. Something of the vigor that characterized the final burst of temple building during the reigns of Rulers A and B as recently chronicled by Jones (1977) may have been derived from this knowledge.

It would seem that the first to respond to the arrival of the fateful katun were the elite, who apparently began to pull out of energy- and time-consuming ritual projects. I would suggest that at this point behavioral and attitudinal changes spread outward in the system and, presumably in a classic demonstration of the principle of hypercoherence (Flannery 1972), began to affect the social, political, and economic structure. What were at first minor disruptions in the system gained momentum; changes that had a negative effect on the stability of the system as a whole could only be taken as evidence for the truth of the central assumption; and in a very real sense the prophecies of the katun were self-fulfilling. In this case, however, unlike that of the previous cycle, there was essentially no recovery. The survival of the system and of the population that sustained it was too dependent on established patterns to maintain itself without them. The disruption of social mechanisms that maintained control affected production and the maintenance of vital services, including perhaps the reservoir system, the distribution of food, even the tasks and behavior directly linked to the maintenance of public health. It is not difficult to imagine how a combination of factors might have resulted in increased mortality in a system that was already under stress. Essential to the argument here is that every step, in this vortex of positive feedback relationships, confirmed the predictions of prophecy and the general sense of fatalism. In the social and economic holocaust that followed, the fundamental epistemological error was the only thing left of the old system of order that could be believed in. Stability was not achieved, as in a great forest fire, until virtually everything was consumed.

Data Presentations

6 Prehistoric Settlement at Copan by Gordon R. Willey and Richard M. Leventhal

INTRODUCTION

This is a preliminary, interim, and essentially descriptive account of a settlement pattern study in the Copan Valley of Honduras by a Peabody Museum, Harvard University, expedition in 1976. The idea of the study was conceived in the spring of 1975 when the senior author, as a guest of the Honduran government, spent a week looking over the valley. Further preliminary preparations were made in the summer of that year when the junior author made a two-month on-the-ground survey of the valley. A two-year program of research was then drawn up with a February 1976 starting date. Through the good offices of J. Adán Cueva, director of the Instituto Hondureño de Antropología e Historia, and of Vito Véliz, Chief of the Technical Section of that body, a contract arrangement was made between Harvard and the Honduran government. The National Science Foundation of the United States provided a generous grant of funds for the research so that work was able to commence as planned. The investigations were under the senior author's direct field supervision during February and March 1976, with the junior author taking over for the April–August period.

Since this account of the 1976 field work was prepared, the Harvard group has conducted a second and continuing season of investigations in the Copan Valley. Although the results of this second season are still in the preliminary stages of preparation, we can say that the additional mapping and excavation of the 1977 season (February through July) generally confirmed our results and impressions of the first season. Mapping in the second season was largely confined to the hillslopes of the northern side of the valley. A medium-large Type 3 site was excavated in some detail in the valley bottom area, not far from the location of site CV-20 reported upon here. This 1977 excavation was in the CV-43 unit, apparently an elite residential group that had been built and occupied over essentially the same time span as CV-20.

It should be added that this Copan settlement study, carried out by the Harvard group over the 1976 and 1977 seasons, will form an integral part of a much larger Copan regional archaeological project to be carried out by the Honduran government under the immediate field supervision of Claude F. Baudez. This larger program, which will incorporate field excavations and restorations in the main Copan center, as well as additional mapping and digging in the valley at large, is envisaged as a five-to-seven-year undertaking.

As with most of the great Maya ruins, interest in Copan, to date, has been largely with the imposing structures and monuments of the main ceremonial center. Little attention has been given to outlying or surrounding smaller constructions. In the last two decades, however, settlement pattern and settlement system studies have become an increasingly important part of many Maya archaeological investigations, and such investigation at Copan seemed long overdue. It would involve the disposition, number, size, form, dating, and functions of the numerous minor or small ruins that surround the main Copan center; and it is anticipated that the information developed in this kind of an investigation will be crucial in determining such things as ancient demography, sociopolitical structure, and economic activities.

At this juncture let us say that we are well aware that a proper Maya settlement pattern study is an undertaking demanding considerable archaeological sophistication. To begin with, there must be a substantial data base control. This means, among other things, a real working knowledge of the local regional ceramics and their chronology. It also means an appreciation of the *in situ* remains–including architectural detail of structures and, more generally, what might best be referred to as the local "digging conditions." As of now, we do not have a mastery of these things although, thanks to some previous research at Copan, we do have some partial knowledge. We will have to acquire more as we proceed with our study; but this means that we are not yet ready to define all of our specific research aims. Broadly, we obviously want to define a settlement-sustaining area for the Copan center; but this is a complex matter, for the sustaining area concept can be projected in various ways. Basic economic subsistence is only one of these. How might the institution of trade define another? What were the political or religious allegiances related to Copan? And how might all such projections overlap, cross-cut, or incorporate with each other? A great many hypotheses and questions can be framed and asked that will bear upon these and other matters. To take a simple example, we might advance the hypothesis that the larger and more complex of the outlying Copan structures were the former residences of the elite who governed at the center and that the smaller mounds found around and among these larger ones mark the houses of lesser persons, perhaps retainers or servants to the ruling aristocracy. Tests for such a hypothesis would be in the differentials in structure unit contexts and contents, as in exotic trade goods versus ordinary manufactures, or elaborate tomb constructions as opposed to simpler graves. But while keeping these things in mind, and being committed to their pursuit as research progresses, we must also move very directly to basic data gathering. This includes adequate mapping of the structures, both in their overall distributions and in their individual structure unit details. We must also excavate some of them for purposes of dating and to determine the uses to which they were put. Were they all, indeed, residences, and how do they differ one from another? In saying this we are not arguing that the research strategy for Copan settlement problems should be a rigidly defined two-stage enterprise, with a long period of problem-blind data collecting preceding a more edifying interpretive phase. The objectives of information accumulation and interpretation should go along together. Still, in taking the first steps in a venture as important and, eventually, as comprehensive as this is bound to become, it would be premature and absurd to claim that we have formulated all pertinent and interesting hypotheses and research designs.

COPAN ARCHAEOLOGICAL DATA BACKGROUND

On the face of it, the great ruin of Copan "needs no introduction" to informed archaeological circles, but this is also a very superficial appraisal. There are some salient facts that we start with that should be kept in mind.

Copan is the largest ceremonial or organizational center in what has been called the Southeastern Zone (Culbert 1973: Fig 1) of the Maya Lowlands. This southeastern position means that almost immediately to the east and south of Copan Classic Maya civilization, at least in those well-known hierarchic aspects of vaulted architecture, hieroglyphic inscriptions, and monumental art, thins and disappears. Conversely, it also means that Copan and the Southeastern Zone show linkages in ceramics and other minor artifacts with the Ulua-Yojoa region of Honduras and with western Salvador, so that our better-known Peten typologies do not altogether apply here. A perusal of J. M. Longyear's sound study on Copan ceramics (Longyear 1952) indicates some of the problems. He has made a good beginning, but we still have a way to go on pottery systematics for this part of the Maya area.

Maya Initial Series dates at Copan span a period beginning with 9.1.10.0.0 (A.D. 465) and ending with 9.18.10.0.0 (A.D. 800), according to Morley's (1920) readings. Ceramics which Longyear and others have found in or near the main center, in so far as these can be related to the Uaxactun-Tikal sequences, accord with this Early and Late Classic dating. In addition, earlier pottery, aligning chronologically to the Late Preclassic Period, has been found at Copan, and some Middle or Early-to-Middle Preclassic vessels have been found in caves on the outlying edges of the Copan Valley. Whether or not Copan was an important ceremonial center, or even a center of any consequence, in Preclassic times is as yet unknown; but, to us, this seems likely. Obviously, more and very deep digging in the main ruins will be necessary to determine this point. This does not fall within the scope of our immediate project, but if we do identify substantial outlying residential settlement of Preclassic date, this would certainly suggest very strongly that Copan was a major center at that time. Just when the first Early Classic, or Tzakol sphere, pottery was introduced to the Copan Valley is uncertain. It may not have arrived until the first appearances of Classic Maya hierarchic culture, that is, along with the stelae cult and hieroglyphic writing, in the mid-fifth century A.D. Longyear (1952) was inclined toward this view, and he may be right; but, if so, the Copan appearance of Peten-type Early Classic pottery was considerably later here in the Southeastern Zone than in the Northeast Peten "Core" Zone. Related to these questions are those concerning the processes by which Classic "Mayanization" developed at Copan. Was it a matter of "colonization" from the "Core" Zone, as Longyear thought, or were the contacts less direct than this? After A.D. 800 Copan declined as a place of importance. There have been some finds that indicate a desultory occupation in the Postclassic, but it is likely that the great center was abandoned for long periods of time. At the time of the Spanish *entradas* in the sixteenth century, the center was not functioning, although there were some populations in the valley.

THE COPAN VALLEY

The Copan River is a smallish stream in southwestern Honduras which flows in a westerly direction, crossing the border into Guatemala and joining with the northward-flowing Motagua. The Copan Valley lies in hilly terrain and is divided into a number of natural wide sections or "pockets" which are separated from each other by narrower passages where the bordering hills close in upon the river. The Copan pocket proper, where the ruins are located, is the largest such wide section or pocket in the valley. It measures about 12.5 kilometers long (east-west) and from 2 to 4 kilometers wide (north-south). To the east it is separated from the smaller Santa Rita pocket by about a kilometer where the river flows through a narrow gorge. To the west, the valley bottom narrows to gorgelike conformations throughout the rest of its course in Honduras.

It is in the Copan pocket that all of our activities to date have taken place. The pocket is semidivided into a longer western section, 7 kilometers in length, in which the main ruin is situated, and a shorter eastern section, 5.5 kilometers long. This division or semidivision is created by a place where the bordering hills jut out into the valley, although they do not entirely eliminate the valley bottoms at this point. These jutting hills are relatively low, especially on the north side of the valley, where they form a kind of small tableland; and it is on this tableland that the modern town of Copan, or Copan Pueblo, is situated. In generalized cross section the Copan pocket consists of a flood plain, of varying width, immediately adjacent to the stream channel; directly above this flood plain, on both sides of the river, are somewhat higher flat bottomlands which we will refer to as the "second terrace"; back of this second terrace, on both sides of the valley, low foothills gradually rise up to the high hills or small mountains which compose the outer borders of the valley catchment basin. The only exception to this rather regular transect is in the western section of the Copan pocket, where a short range of east-west hills rises out of the valley floor to create a little division in the bottomlands on the north bank of the river.

The Copan Valley floor is approximately two thousand feet above sea level; and, as has often been remarked, this makes the ruin of Copan somewhat atypical in that it is a truly Maya Classic manifestation that is not in typical tropical rain forest country (below one thousand feet). Today, while there are junglelike patches and parklike stands of trees (as in the preserve around the main ruin), the general impression is that of an almost semiarid region, especially during the dry season (January–May). Much, indeed most, of the valley is under cultivation. The largest tracts of arable land, especially the first and second terraces of the river, are in tobacco. Farther back from the stream, in the low hills, maize and other crops are grown; and in the hills, as well as in some patches of bottomlands, there is pasturage for cattle. Because of this farming activity, as well as the somewhat higher and drier conditions than those of the Peten, the small mound remains of the Copan Valley are much more readily visible than those in the rain forest surroundings of a site such as Tikal or Seibal; and one comes back from a walking tour of the valley, such as those we made in 1975, impressed with the great number and density of these minor, outlying structures.

MAPPING STRATEGY AND TECHNIQUES

Prior to our 1976 efforts the only extensive mapping in the Copan Valley was that done by Robert Burgh of the Carnegie Institution in connection with their archaeological work of the 1930's and early 1940's. This map, published in Longyear's ceramic report (1952: Map 1), takes in most of the Copan pocket. It is useful in that it gives an initial idea of the numbers and general dispositions of the valley's smaller structures; however, it was done at too small a scale to reveal details of individual structure unit arrangements. Also, our own surveys indicate that it is not an altogether complete record of the valley's many mounds, especially those in the upper or hilly terrain. We decided that there were at least two ways to improve upon the Burgh survey. One of these was to map individual site or structure units in much greater detail and at a larger scale; the other was to achieve greater thoroughness in valley-wide coverage. In the two years, or two field seasons, we have set for our initial Copan settlement study it will be impossible to attain these objectives fully; however, we shall make a beginning, and in making this beginning it has been our strategy to proceed slowly and in great detail in a relatively small sector of the Copan pocket. That is, we have opted for the first of our objectives as the way to begin.

For this we selected a sector comprising approximately 1.25 square kilometers lying immediately to the east of the main Copan ceremonial center ruins. This is on the north side of the river and is comprised almost entirely of second terrace elevation bottomland. The selection of this particular sector was not entirely arbitrary. A preliminary survey of the valley—as well as an inspection of the Burgh map of Copan shows that medium- and small-size ruin density here is very great, there being a more or less continuous distribution of at least five hundred mounds grouped into what we have called structure units. Mapping here was by transit and rod, and we mapped a total of eighty-three structure units (Fig. 6-1). This was done by ourselves, aided by one or two workmen, so that each stadia rod point on a mound or other feature was selected by an archaeologist rather than by the workman holding the rod. In the mapping we faced many prob-

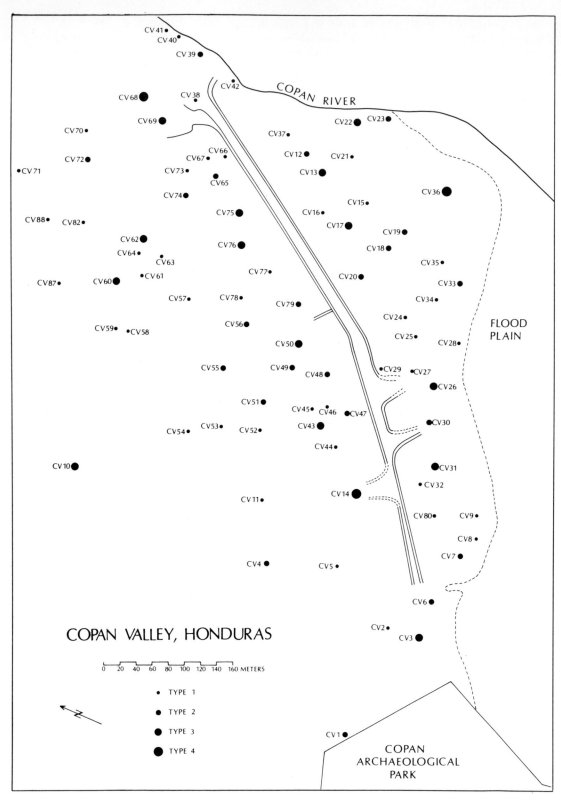

FIGURE 6–1. Eighty-three sites (of different types) in Zone 2, east of main Copan center.

lems. Mound and structure preservation in the valley is reasonably good; but, still, ancient looting and erosion have taken their toll, and structure corners were not always readily evident on surface examination. As a rule, stadia shots were taken from all basal and summit platform corners so that our mapping of sites is based upon a rough field rectification of mounds–a methodology common to Maya archaeology. Final results indicate the shape, size, height, and orientation of mounds, as well as the rough organization and composition of a plaza grouping or structure unit. These results have also benefited, or suffered, from some further rectification in drafting. Short of excavation, however, there is no sure way of insuring greater accuracy. One particular problem or difficulty is that many mounds have raised, but rather amorphous, appendages extending out from them, or such raised areas between them, which may or may not have been true terrace or other constructional features. Our decisions to map or not to map these were made on an ad hoc and somewhat subjective basis. We can only close here by saying that our thorough excavation of one site, structure unit CV-20, revealed that our surface mapping of seven mounds and two plazas which composed the site was reasonably accurate. Some minor terracings of the larger mounds had gone undetected, as had a very narrow division or passage through one mound; but general sizes, shapes, and orientations had been properly recorded.

But to return to our 1.25 square kilometers of carefully mapped structures, we can say, first, that there is no observable and obvious overall pattern in the arrangement of the eighty-three structure unit groups. Most of them appear to have been placed with regard to minor terrain fluctuations that would have favored drainage for the buildings in question, although even this was not always the case. The overall pattern for the eighty-three must be described, essentially, as a random one. The individual structure units were, on the other hand, almost always definitely patterned, and this pattern is the general Maya–or perhaps Mesoamerican–one of a plaza or plazuela arrangement of mound platforms. Two to four or more mounds were placed around a central rectangular court. There is, though, considerable variation in the sizes of these structure unit groups. They range all the way from units of no more than two mounds to those of forty to fifty mounds. The designation and numbering of these sites or structure units, in a series running from CV-1 through CV-83, was, inevitably, somewhat arbitrary. While most of the structure units or mound groups could be set apart from each other spatially, there were instances where units were very close together or where small, semi-isolated mounds were found between unit groups. In such cases we had to make judgments as to unit groupings that were, to a degree, subjective.

A preliminary site or structure unit typology was developed. This was to serve as a trial classification, based entirely upon observable surface forms, that might be checked later, through excavation sampling, in an attempt to arrive at possible functional differentiations between the various types of units. The criteria of individual mound size and of the complexity of the mound groupings within a site unit determined the type classes. These two criteria co-varied: smaller

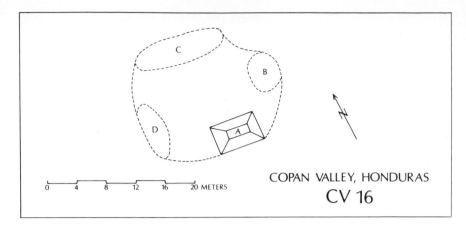

FIGURE 6–2. A Type I site in the Copan Valley.

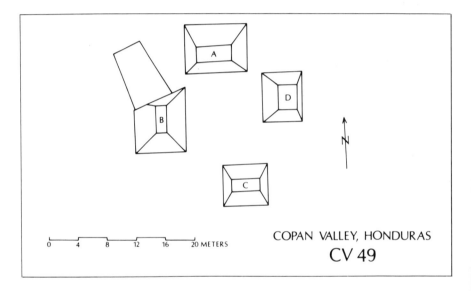

FIGURE 6–3. A Type 2 site in the Copan Valley.

mounds were found in simpler plaza arrangements, larger mounds in more complex arrangements.

Type 1 units are at the small end of the size and complexity scale (Fig. 6-2). These number, as a rule, from three to five mounds around quite small plazas or courts. Such mounds are from .25 to 1.25 meters in height. Their general constructional makeup is earth fill and small- to medium-sized, undressed stone rubble.

Type 2 units may have one or two plazas, and surrounding mounds number up to six or eight (Figs. 6-3, 6-4). Maximum height of such mounds is 2.50 to 3.00 meters. There is more surface stone on these sites than is the case with Type 1; most of it is undressed, but there are some instances of dressed blocks. The one site we have excavated, CV-20, belongs to this Type 2 class, and excavations revealed both uncut and cut stone.

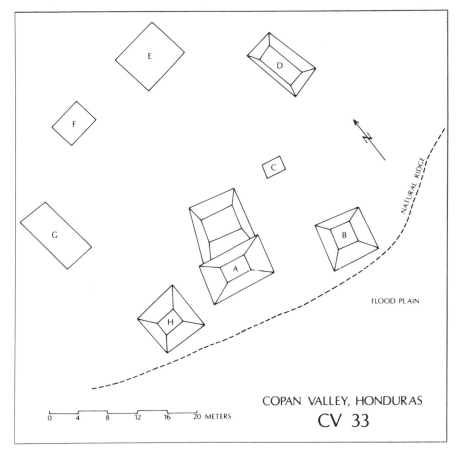

FIGURE 6–4. A Type 2 site in the Copan Valley.

Type 3 units have mounds as high as 4.75 meters (Fig. 6-5). Dressed stone is much more in evidence on their surfaces than in Type 2 units. Plaza arrangements and numbers of mounds are not, however, much different than in those of Type 2.

Type 4 units are by far the largest ones in the entire 1.25-square-kilometer mapped sector (Fig. 6-6). Mound heights may be as much as 10 meters. There are only three sites of this type, CV-14, CV-36, and CV-68, and all are very complex groupings with multiple plazas. CV-36, the largest of all and probably the largest ruin in the Copan pocket, except for the main ceremonial center, has five major plazas and over forty mounds. These Type 4 sites are covered with large stones, both rough and dressed, and among the latter are probable vault stones.

The entire 1.25-square-kilometer sector was mapped at a scale of 1:1,000. Then each individual mound group or unit structure was drawn up, from our transit and stadia figures, at a scale of 1:200. Final publication size of these maps remains to be decided, but the survey engineering data are available for very large scale, detailed presentations.

In our mapping during the 1976 season we did have recourse to

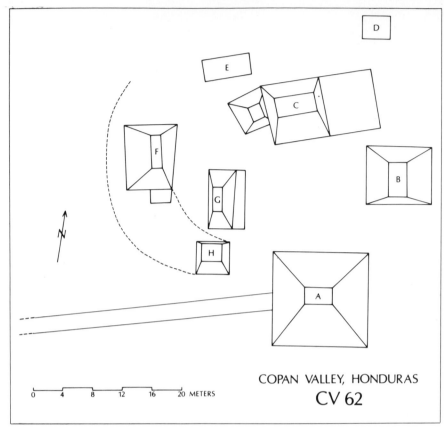

COPAN VALLEY, HONDURAS
CV 62

FIGURE 6–5. A Type 3 site in the Copan Valley.

air photographs. These were from a survey flown at a scale of 1:5,000, and the prints are available at the Honduran national Servicio Geográfico in Tegucigalpa. Because of the relative scantiness of vegetation, it is easy to spot or locate many of the larger of the mounds, those of the Type 3 and 4 classes, in our intensively surveyed area to the east of the main center; however, smaller structures, of the Type 1 and 2 classes, are very difficult or impossible to see by megascopic inspection of the photo quads. We are informed, however, that with sophisticated air photo interpretation techniques and appropriate viewing instruments even quite small structures can be detected. Such would greatly facilitate mapping, particularly more extensive mapping of other areas of the Copan pocket and the valley as a whole.

Some of this more extensive mapping was begun by our party in the summer of 1976. Using air photos simply as aids for map orientations and the location of whatever sites on them could be detected megascopically, Lori Wrotenberry of Wellesley College explored a sector of the valley lying in the foothills or valley slopes immediately to the north of the 1.25-square-kilometer sector of our intensive transit-stadia mapping. Ground exploration here revealed other, smaller sites, not seen on the air photographs, and site unit locations were also checked with Brunton compass triangulations. Eleanor King, of

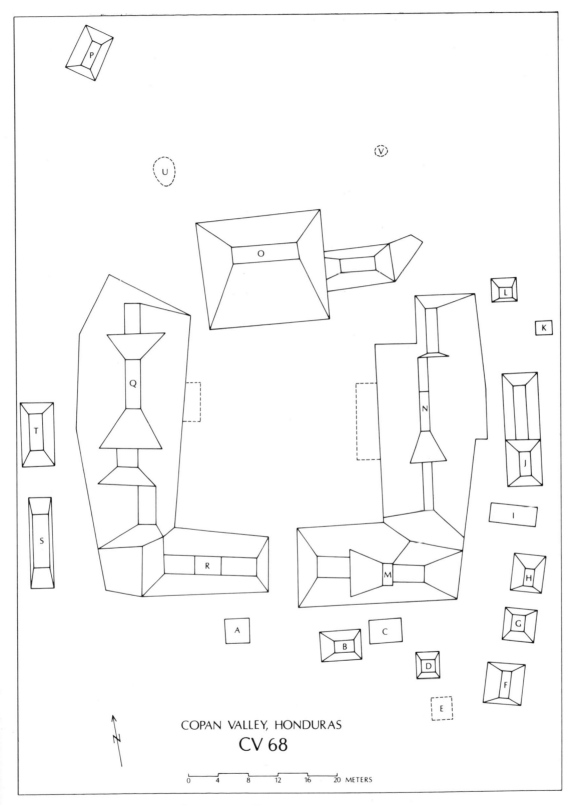

COPAN VALLEY, HONDURAS
CV 68

N

0 4 8 12 16 20 METERS

FIGURE 6–6. A Type 4 site in the Copan Valley.

Radcliffe College, conducted a similar exploration in the relatively narrow flatlands and in the bordering hills on the south side of the river and to the east of the main ruins. In both of these sectors it is anticipated that transit-and-stadia rod maps will be made of at least a sampling of the structure units in the forthcoming season.

THE COPAN VALLEY OVERALL SETTLEMENT

A preliminary description of the overall settlement of the Copan Valley pocket is, at this stage of the research, most easily presented under the headings of five zones. These zones are defined by a combination of topographic features and archaeological remains (Fig. 6-7).

Zone 1 corresponds to the flood plain or first terrace of the river. This topographic zone is found for the length of the pocket, with its largest segments in the western end and also along the northern river bank in the eastern end. So far, no archaeological sites have been located within Zone 1; however, it is possible that mounds once were on this lower terrace but have since been either scoured away or covered with alluvium by river action. Clearly, further investigation is required here—both more intensive surface inspection and random test pit sampling.

Zone 2 is essentially the second terrace of the valley bottomlands, in the eastern section of the valley and on the northern bank of the river. As such, this zone includes the main Copan ceremonial center, an area some five hundred by three hundred meters, and the outlying eighty-three site unit groups mapped during the 1976 field season. The zone is delimited by the modern Copan Pueblo on the west and by the disappearance of the second terrace flatlands some 2.5 to 3.0 kilometers to the east of Copan Pueblo. Our map (Fig. 6-1), as drawn to date, is not a complete archaeological map of Zone 2, as there are more sites, at both its western and eastern ends, which have not yet been entered.

We have already discussed the different site unit types found in Zone 2. An interesting aspect in the arrangements of some of them is that small, Type 1 mounds and mound group units are often found in close proximity, or literally around the edges of, larger Type 3 and Type 4 units. A hypothesis to be advanced in the interpretation of such an arrangement is the one previously mentioned, that the smaller units represent the quarters of servants and retainers to those persons dwelling in the larger units.

A notable archaeological feature of Zone 2 is the *sacbe*. This artificial raised road began somewhere in the vicinity of the east side of the main Copan ruins. Perhaps it was once attached to the main center, although, if so, this is no longer evident. It runs for approximately one-third kilometer due east and then angles sharply to the northeast for perhaps two-thirds kilometer. The roadway is well defined for most of its course, being 10 to 12 meters in width and from .25 to .75 meter in height, depending upon the terrain over which it passes. It is indicated on the Burgh map, although little has ever been said about it in any archaeological reports dealing with Copan. A test

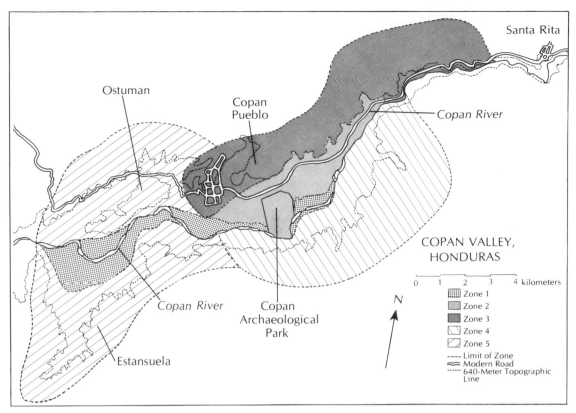

FIGURE 6–7. Archaeological-topographical zones in the Copan Valley.

excavation in the sacbe revealed a cobble-paved surface, earth and rough rock rubble fill, and a basal level of more compact rock rubble. Whether this basal rubble stratum marks an earlier sacbe construction or whether it is simply a prepared base for subsequent construction was not determined in our limited excavations. Perhaps the most interesting features of the sacbe are its branches or appendices. At three places along its course it widens to the side to form plaza areas that lead into site units of the Type 3 and 4 classes; and at its terminus it bifurcates into two plaza areas, each relating to a separate site unit. There is also one quite narrow branch or extension which leaves the sacbe at right angles and runs into the plaza of site unit CV-79. The sacbe, with these branching features, does, indeed, suggest that the Zone 2 area was one of important residences, an aristocratic preserve for the rulers of Copan.

Zone 3 is the foothill region located directly above the Zone 2 second terrace. It extends all along the north side of the valley, from the modern Copan Pueblo on the west to a distance of some 6 to 7 kilometers to the east. In general settlement or mound distribution there is no real break or hiatus between Zones 2 and 3, the separation between the two being one of topographic difference. This topography, however, may have influenced site size and complexity in Zone 3. Most of the sites here seem to have been constructed to take advantage of the many natural or hillside terrace or spur tops. Out of approximately 250 site units in Zone 3, the great majority are of Types 1 and 2; there are a few Type 3 sites scattered among these; but we located only one Type 4 unit. This latter site lies about 2.5 kilometers to the northeast of the main Copan ceremonial center. It must also be noted that among the smaller sites in Zone 3 there are some which do not adhere to any kind of plaza arrangement but could best be described as small, haphazard clusterings of mounds or, in some instances, isolated mounds. To date, in our preliminary recording these have been counted in with either our Type 1 or Type 2 sites; but their presence indicates that a revised site form typology will have to be expanded. Finally, with reference to Zone 3, it should be mentioned that site density is greater at lower hillslope elevations and that sites are not found all the way to the crests of the bordering hills. At these elevations the hillsides are steeper, natural terrace locations for structures few or absent.

Zone 4 is the entire southeastern section of the Copan pocket, both bottomlands and hillslopes. These bottomlands are less extensive than those on the north side of the valley, with their bordering hills rising more abruptly than the northern hills. Sites are much less numerous here than in either Zone 2 or 3. Most of them are of the smaller, Type 1 and 2, classes. Only two Type 3 sites have been located within the zone and no Type 4 sites. Nor is the effect of a continuum of sites, as seen in Zones 2 and 3, present in Zone 4. Instead, sites tend to be grouped in small clusters with large empty areas between. Of the six such clusters in the zone, four are situated in the extreme southeast corner of the pocket, at a considerable distance from the valley center and the main ceremonial group. The reasons for the relative scarcity of sites in Zone 4 and their somewhat different distribution than those on the north side of the valley are not obvious, at least from any natural environmental standpoint. Current agricultural practices would indicate that land in Zone 4 is as good as that on the north side of the river.

Zone 5 is the entire western end of the Copan pocket, both north and south sides of the river. We have made no systematic survey of sites there, as yet, but it was walked over in the 1975 surveys. The zone divides naturally into two parts, separated by a ridge of hills rising out of the valley floor. Each of these two parts is dominated by a large Type 4 site: Ostuman on the north and Estansuela on the south. There are three Type 3 sites in the Ostuman subzone, as well as a scattering of other, smaller sites; around Estansuela, however, there are only small sites.

EXCAVATIONS

During the 1976 field season, our excavations within the Copan Valley consisted mainly of intensive architectural clearing and cross-sectioning of a single site unit, CV-20. Such excavations were designed to give us some formal understanding of a representative site unit lying outside of the main ceremonial center, to throw light on its functions, and to begin a study of the chronological correlations of the valley settlement units. We devoted a three-month period to this operation,

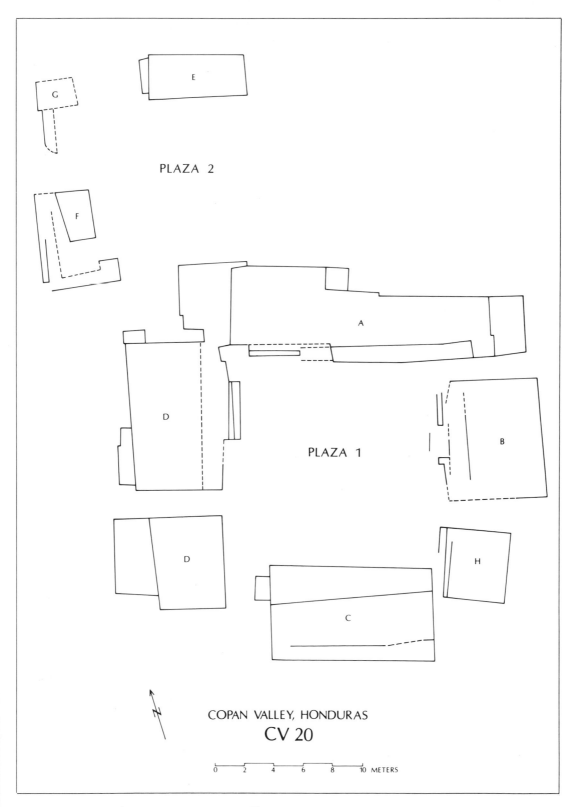

FIGURE 6–8. Map of site CV–20, Copan Valley.

from mid-March to mid-June, working with a digging crew of twelve to fifteen men, supervised by ourselves and with the assistance of Oscar Cruz Melgar and César Alvarez of the local staff of the Instituto.

The site unit selected for these excavations was CV-20, located in the midst of the mound groups which we mapped in Zone 2. CV-20 is a Type 2 site, consisting of a main plaza surrounded by five mounds (A, B, C, D, H) and a minor, subsidiary plaza formed by three smaller mounds (E, F, G) arranged adjacent to the main plaza (Fig. 6-8). As is consistent with our typology, the largest mounds of CV-20 are no higher than 2.50 meters; the total site diameter is within approximately 25 meters; and the surface of the ruin was strewn with construction stone, mostly rough but with some dressed blocks. Surface alignments of stones on the mounds gave some indications of basal and summit terraces and other features.

Our excavations in CV-20 can be conveniently separated into two sequent operations. The first of these was the clearing of the two plaza areas and all of the mound structures. This clearing revealed the final occupational and constructional phase at the site. From ceramic evidence, this phase can be placed in the Late Classic Period and probably, from the presence of the type Copador Polychrome, in the latter part of that period, or at least after A.D. 700. Tentatively, in these discussions, we will refer to this as the Copador Phase.

Following this complete clearing and mapping of surface, or Copador Phase, architecture, the second stage of our excavations consisted of trenches carried down into all of the CV-20 structures. These deeper excavations disclosed an earlier building and occupation phase, to which we will refer as simply the Early Phase. The ceramics of this Early Phase do not include Copador ware, although other polychromes of a definite Maya genre are present. Some of these also feature both positive and Usulutan technique painting on the same vessels. There is some question about the proper dating of this CV-20 Early Phase pottery. Longyear (1952:55) states that Usulutan technique continues on as late as his Full Classic (Late Classic) Period at Copan; and some of the vessels which he illustrates (ibid: e.g., Fig. 102g) are quite similar to those from CV-20. On the other hand, two archaeologists who had seen the CV-20 specimens, or photographs of them, are of the opinion that they pertain either to the latter part of the Early Classic Period or to a time range that would include this and the very beginning of the Late Classic (ca. A.D. 450–650) (C. F. Baudez and R. J. Sharer: personal communications, 1976). But, however dated on the Early Classic–Late Classic scale, the internal stratigraphy within site CV-20 shows that our Early Phase is clearly antecedent to our Copador Phase. Bearing these two occupational-constructional phases in mind, let us briefly review some of the excavations.

Structure B, located on the east side of the main plaza, was the highest mound in CV-20, although not the largest in extent. Its surface contours suggested a compact, slightly oblong, flat-topped little pyramid, and our excavations bore this out. Clearing revealed a well-built platform retaining wall and the foundations of a platform summit room of nicely dressed stone blocks (Fig. 6-9). The floor of this single room was the only well-smoothed or polished plaster floor encount-

FIGURE 6–9. CV–20, Structure B, from the plaza. Interior of dressed masonry wall of summit room seen at back.

ered in any of the CV-20 excavations. Our subsequent deep-trenching into structure B disclosed no earlier, interior structure; indeed, this was the only one of the four main mounds at the site that did not have such an earlier building. Instead, within the body of the mound fill of Structure B, was our richest grave of the site, Burial 9. This badly disintegrated skeleton of an adult had been covered with uncut boulders and pottery vessels. Six pottery vessels and three small jade beads were associated; and it is these vessels that compose our best sample of the Early Phase pottery of the site (Figs. 6-10–6-13), including those pieces displaying the Usulutan technique. As no later major alterations or rebuilding was evident in Structure B, this grave would appear to relate to the construction of the building; or, in a word, Structure B was constructed during the Early Phase of the site's history and never covered with a later, Copador Phase building. The relative height, form, and good-quality masonry and plaster construction of Structure B and its surmounting building all suggest that it may have been a small temple or shrine; and this surmise may be further re-

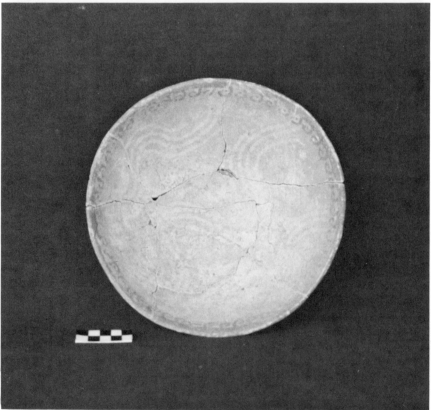

FIGURE 6–10. Side and interior views of bowl with interior Uusulutan decoration, from Burial 9.

FIGURE 6–11. Small red-on-orange bowl, Burial 9.

FIGURE 6–12. Red-on-orange olla or jar, Burial 9.

FIGURE 6–13. Side and interior views of large polychrome plate found over Burial 9.

inforced by its position on the east side of the plaza, a circumstance noted elsewhere in Maya elite domestic site units (Willey et al. 1975: 37).

Structure D, on the west side of the main plaza, was originally mapped, from surface observations, as one long, low platform; but excavation revealed that it was actually two such platforms cut by a narrow passage leading from outside the compound into the plaza. The southern section of Structure D consisted of a rather nebulous series of three or four small terraces. The surface of the northern (and larger) section was divided up into smaller roomlike subsections by basal structure walls. Perhaps these do represent the walls of domestic room divisions. A subfloor cache in one of these rooms consisted of two small Copador bowls (Fig. 6-14), dating the upper levels of Structure D to our Copador Phase. The trench through the building then revealed an earlier construction; and a cache within this earlier platform, of three unslipped vessels, two manos, a barkbeater, and a polished black (diorite?) rock, can probably be assigned to the site's Early Phase. The "domestic" nature of this cache lends additional weight to the interpretation of Structure D, probably for both of its phases, as a dwelling subunit of the CV-20 complex.

Structure A, on the north side of the main plaza, also had what looked like the foundations of room walls, similar to those of Structure D. These walls, together with bench features in the rooms, would seem to indicate a range of dwelling units. There are also several constructional additions attached to and extending to the east of Structure A. Until ceramic analyses from the fill materials of these walls and small platforms is completed it is impossible to say to which of the site phases these extensions may date; however, it is most probable that they and the rooms on the main platform are of our Copador Phase. Earlier construction, dating to our Early Phase, was found within Structure A, though. Our cross-sectioning trench located a platform retaining wall and a crude plaster floor. Two caches were directly associated with this early construction. One cache consisted of two pottery vessels: a small monochrome vase and a lidded incensario decorated with animal head adornos (Fig. 6-15). The other cache, resting directly on the plaster floor, was made up of eight polished and slightly worked diorite stones and a miniature stone "table." Within this early platform, below the floor, we found a tightly flexed burial of an adult. This individual had a large jade inlay in one of the upper incisors. Associated was a carved blackware vase covered with a thin layer of green stucco. Such vessels have been placed by Longyear in the latter part of the Early Classic (Longyear 1952:97: Figs. 64, 65), a dating which would confirm our estimates of the CV-20 Early Phase.

Structure C, the lowest of the four main mounds around Plaza 1, situated on its south side, was also cleared and trenched. There had been more than one building level here, also; however, the dating of the inner and outer platforms must await sherd refuse analysis. It is to be noted that Structure C is on what is generally the "downwind" side of CV-20. This, and the fact that it is a relatively simple low platform, might imply that it was a "kitchen" or cooking area; but no ash concentrations or other indications of cooking or kitchen

FIGURE 6–14. Two Copador Polychrome bowls, from cache in Structure D.

FIGURE 6–15. Incensario from cache in Structure A.

functions were found here. Some metate and mano fragments were recovered in the Structure C area, but they were also as plentiful, or more so, on other main structures, especially A and D.

Structure H, a small separate platform near Structures B and C, not seen in our surface mapping, and Structures E, F, and G of Plaza 2 were all cleared of surface debris. It is quite difficult to delineate the exact forms of the Plaza 2 mounds, owing to their small size and extremely crude construction. No concentrations of metates, manos, or other culinary or food-preparing implements, or possible cooking fires, were found associated with the Plaza 2 structures or in the plaza itself. This does not preclude the possibility that this plaza and its structures may have been the location of quarters for servants or retainers, although it does nothing to support this conjecture.

In connection with our excavations of the Plaza 1 structures, substantial portions of a rubble and cobble plaza floor were uncovered. This floor clearly related to the Copador Phase construction levels. Excavation below the floor did not reveal an earlier one. Subfloor refuse was a mixture of both Copador Phase and Early Phase debris, with the former concentrated in the top 30–50 centimeters of the deposit and the earlier materials found on the original ground surface. Copador Phase burials were found under the floor. One of these was the extended burial of a young child in a stone cist grave, and the other was a secondary burial, probably of an adult. Caches of pottery (Copador Polychrome), fine flint blades, and long obsidian bladelets were found near these burials.

In general, potsherd material was abundant throughout the CV-20 excavations. This included a fair number of polychrome and bichrome pieces, although these were in the minority. As indicated, such decorated material included both the later Copador and the earlier Usulutan types. Perhaps half of the pottery recovered was unslipped; and sherds from striated, handled jars were extremely common in the collection. This striated ware was included by Longyear (1952:89–90) in his Coarse Ware category. We also found a great many red-slipped sherds, including those which may have had an overall slip and others on which red paint had been applied to the outer and inner surfaces of rim collars.

In addition to the pottery vessels already described, and the ubiquitous sherd material, a class of incensarios deserves special mention (Fig. 6-16). These all appear to date to the later Copador Phase, and they differ, in form and decoration, from the single Early Phase incensario found in Structure A. All of them, eight in number and found either whole or in large sherds, are sizable cylinders, decorated with appliqué spikes and fillets and some crude incisions. Five of them were found along the back basal terraces of the main platform of Structure A, two on the platform top of Structure A, and one on the back basal terrace of Structure D. At least six of these vessels (and probably all eight) had been buried in their platform or terrace locations intentionally. That is, they were set in earth fill up to the rim of the vessel. The earth around the rim was, in each case, burned, blackened, and hardened some 5 to 15 centimeters in outward extent and to a similar depth. Two of these incensarios from Structure A and the one from

FIGURE 6–16. Large cylindrical incensarios, dating to the Copador Phase.

Structure D had been placed within roughly constructed semicircles of stones. On excavation and cleaning it was noted that the interior basal areas of the vessels showed no evidences of fire or blackening, although the upper interior and upper exterior walls did have such blackening. These burning patterns, as well as the placement and contexts of the vessels, are somewhat peculiar, and it is difficult to specify just how the incensarios had been used. Their "built-in" architectural settings, especially in the two structures of CV-20 that would appear to have been residential quarters, is quite different from what

FIGURE 6–16 *continued*.

R. E. W. Adams (1971:139) found at Altar de Sacrificios. There incensarios were found almost entirely in temple contexts. At CV-20 our apparent temple structure, Structure B, did not have the incensarios in association.

We have mentioned cache finds of artifacts other than pottery in CV-20—manos, polished pebbles, finely chipped flint blades, and obsidian bladelets. Nonceramic artifact refuse also came from the general digging. Broken manos and metates were found on the surface, as well as the subsurface. The metates were of the legged form (probably three

FIGURE 6–16 *continued.*

legs). Flint refuse, either as broken artifacts or as wastage, was extremely rare. Obsidian, on the other hand, was quite common. This included thousands of bladelets, a substantial number of cores, usually exhausted, and a plenitude of chips and scrap, some of which showed cortex surfaces. All of this would indicate that obsidian knapping had been carried out at the site or residence. As yet, this obsidian material has not been examined for source identification. A cursory inspection seems to indicate that it is all black or grey in color.

After a season's work in the Copan Valley we have only begun a proper settlement pattern study, so that our results, to date, can be summarized rather simply and rapidly. The Copan pocket of the greater Copan Valley is a territory about 12.5 kilometers long and 2 to 4 kilometers in width. Evidences of "small structure settlement" ("small" as opposed to the great structures of the main Copan ceremonial center) are found throughout this territory. The densest distributions of this settlement are found in the valley bottoms, on the second terrace above the present course of the river. Notably, there is such an aggregation of structures or mounds in the kilometer or so immediately to the east of the main Copan ceremonial center, on the north side of the river. There are others on similar terrain toward the western end of the Copan pocket. Mounds are also found on the hillslopes bordering the valley flats, on both sides of the valley. Generally speaking, there are more large and elaborately arranged site structure units on the flat lands than on the hillslopes. A hierarchy of site structure unit types, ascending from small, simple units to large, complex ones, has been devised as a tentative scheme of classification; and this classification has been applied, particularly, to the carefully mapped strip immediately to the east of the main center. Quite probably, this was an area of elite residences, pertaining to the aristocratic class of old Copan. It was served by a sacbe, or raised road, leading from the center through this dense zone of settlement.

The spatial organization of Copan Valley settlement still remains to be fully mapped and understood. The size-complexity differential in outlying small structures appears to apply to all portions of the Copan pocket, both valley bottom and hillslopes, although it is to be noted that in some regions, particularly those farther out from the main Copan ceremonial center, the larger and more complex plaza-mound arrangement units are few in number or absent.

As a very tentative estimate, on the basis of the archaeological settlement evidence seen superficially and the land areas involved, we would say that the Copan pocket could have sustained ten thousand persons. As such, it may have been the basic subsistence "sustaining area" for the Copan center. Admittedly, all this is very much a guess, at this stage of the survey; but it is a guess guided by experience in other Lowland Maya settlement studies. We would further surmise that the Copan center also drew upon and served peoples from a wider area, quite probably those from the full range of the Copan Valley with its other agricultural pockets. Beyond this, Copan undoubtedly had prestige, and certainly power of a kind (obviously not fully understood), over a much wider sphere, probably the whole Southeastern Zone of the Maya Lowlands.

We have excavated, quite thoroughly, a modest-sized site structure unit (Type 2 in our classification) in the dense settlement aggregate immediately to the east of the main ceremonial center. This unit (CV-20), consisting of two small plazas and eight structure platforms, appears to have had primarily residential functions, although one building within it (Structure B) seems, in its architectural form, to be a temple-type building, perhaps a household shrine. The unit was first constructed, at least in its major plaza arrangement, in an Early Phase, corresponding in time to the latter part of the Early Classic Period and the beginnings of the Late Classic Period (total span of A.D. 450–650). It was built over, and probably enlarged, in a later Copador Phase (A.D. 650–700 to ca. 800). During both phases, burials, accompanied by polychrome pottery and some other luxury artifacts, were made within the buildings or plaza of the site. These burials suggest that CV-20 was a reasonably prosperous household, probably not at the top of the elite class but pertaining to it. Hypothetically, higher echelons of this class are represented by site units of Types 3 and 4; lower social orders pertain to Type 1 (quite small) site units. This, however, remains to be demonstrated by further excavations.

7 Prehispanic Terracing in the Central Maya Lowlands: Problems of Agricultural Intensification by B. L. Turner II

Population growth in the Lowland Maya Classic civilization was associated with a growth in the areal extensiveness and the intensification of agriculture.[1] Although the growth of population and agriculture fluctuated temporally and spatially throughout the Maya region, it probably peaked during the latter stages of the Classic Period (ca. A.D. 550–1000) in the Central Lowlands.[2] During this period the number of occupied civic-temple centers reached its zenith (Hammond 1974), and numerous areas within the Central Lowlands were densely settled (Puleston 1974; Turner 1976).[3] Also during this period, large-scale terrace and raised-field cultivation was pursued by the lowlanders, as was a form of cultivation associated with stone demarcated fields.

The implementation of terracing, raised fields, and field demarcation was emblematic of increasing pressures to produce agricultural goods during the Classic Period. The use of terraces and raised fields was employed both to expand the amount of land under cultivation and to permit an increase in the frequency of cultivation. The expansion and intensification of agriculture, however, presented several ecological problems with which the Maya had to cope. Failure to adequately solve these ecological problems would have resulted in a diminishing food supply that could have been a contributing factor influencing the collapse of the Classic civilization (Willey and Shimkin 1973).

This essay focuses on terracing as a technique utilized by the Classic Maya to expand intensive cultivation throughout the upland zones of the Central Lowlands. Special emphasis is placed on Prehispanic terracing in the Río Bec region of Campeche and Quintana Roo, Mexico (Fig. 7-1). The physiography of the upland zone is described, and the principal ecological problems confronting intensive terrace cultivation in these zones are discussed. A description of relic terraces and their reported distribution in the uplands is presented. Finally, specific attention is given to the probable functions of the terraces and the manner in which these functions may have facilitated intensive cultivation.

UPLANDS

Constituting one of the more dominant features of the landscape, the undulating uplands of the Central Maya Lowlands may be divided into at least three zones: the northern ridge lands, the southern ridge lands, and the flank lands (Fig. 7-1). The northern ridge lands comprise the backbone of the base of the Yucatan Peninsula. Situated in the center of the peninsula, the northern ridge lands extend along the border of Campeche and Quintana Roo, Mexico, into central Peten, where they diminish north of Lago Peten Itza. The southern ridge lands are geologically distinct from their counterpart to the north, being part of the east-west anticlinal ridges that push into Peten from Chiapas, Mexico (Wadell 1938). The flank lands are the limestone foothills that surround the Maya Mountains of central and southern Belize and the adjacent sectors of Peten.

The uplands share numerous physical characteristics, particularly sloping terrain, well-drained soils, and seasonal tropical forests, but differ in elevation, ruggedness, and degree of karstic relief. The Río Bec region of southern Campeche and Quintana Roo typifies most of the northern ridge lands. Local relief is dominated by elongated limestone ridges that rarely exceed an elevation of 330 meters above sea level. Elevation differences between the crowns of the various ridges and the surrounding terrain are often 50 meters or more with slopes ranging up to 45°. In Peten elevations may reach 500 meters above sea level. This increased elevation is generally accompanied by an increase in the prevalence of steep slopes, especially in the flank land zone. In the southern ridge lands, numerous conical hills or cones, characteristic of karstic relief, share the landscape with ridges. Interspersed throughout the ridge lands are small areas of level terrain and depressions, including savannas and *bajos*.

Drainage is largely subterranean in the northern ridge lands, and the water table often exceeds a depth of 100 meters. During the rainy season intermittent streams develop and depressions often retain water. The southern ridge lands are dissected by several river systems, although poorly drained terrain is common.

The uplands are composed largely of well drained to moderately well drained fertile loams, mostly Lithic Troporendolls or Rendoll-like soils (Mollisols) in the Río Bec region. These soils are shallow silt and clay loams with an A horizon ranging in depth from 5 to 45 centimeters to bedrock. Slope soils tend to be alkaline, with a pH range of 7.4 to 8.0, and are consistently low in organic matter (particularly if cultivated), 2.2 to 10.0 percent by weight, and phosphorus, 3.4 to 14.5 kilograms per hectare. Colluvial in origin, the Mollisols are fertile for agriculture, particularly if adequate phosphorus and nitrogen levels are maintained and erosion is controlled (see Simmons et al. 1958; Olson 1969). The variety of upland soils may be greater in Belize and Peten than in the Río Bec region, but various Mollisols are prevalent. The calcareous loams of the southern uplands maintain similar characteristics to those described for the Troporendolls of the northern ridge land zone, but may be more subject to erosion due to the ruggedness of the terrain and the increased rainfall of the region.

Annual precipitation in the Río Bec area averages about 1,200 millimeters, with variations up to 100 millimeters. Southward annual

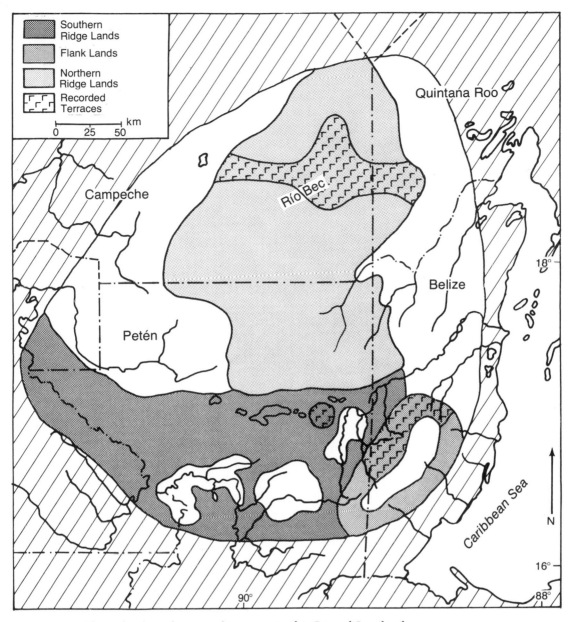

FIGURE 7–1. The uplands and reported terraces in the Central Lowlands.
Prepared by Mary Goodman.

precipitation in the ridge lands of Peten and portions of the flank lands
may approach 2,000 millimeters. Precipitation is distinctly seasonal,
with about 80 percent of the annual rainfall in the Río Bec region
occurring between May and November. This precipitation regime is
characteristic of other sectors of the Central Lowlands, although the
rainy season tends to lengthen in the southern ridge lands.

It is not surprising that the Classic Maya civilization flourished in the Central Lowlands of the Yucatan peninsular region, despite notions to the contrary. The Central Lowlands are dominated by good agricultural soils, especially the fertile Rendolls and other Mollisols that cover much of the uplands. Furthermore, the Haplaquolls (Mollisols) of the *bajo* zones, and the Entisols and Inceptisols of the river valley zones are fertile for cultivation if properly treated (Turner 1974*b*:93–97). These soil types, especially the Mollisols of the ridge and flank lands, constitute some of the best agricultural land in the tropics and typify the type of tropical land that historically has been associated with high population densities (Sanchez and Buol 1975: 600–601). That the Classic Maya recognized the fertility of the soils in the Central Lowlands is evidenced by their use of the uplands, as well as river valleys and *bajos,* for large-scale intensive cultivation.[4]

Despite the high native fertility of the upland Mollisols, several problems had to be overcome in order to pursue intensive agriculture. First, the well-drained but shallow slope soils were subject to erosion when cultivated, particularly when the cleared and dried soils were exposed to the onslaught of the rainy season.[5] Second, intensive cropping necessitated the maintenance of soil fertility, particularly in regard to the nitrogen and phosphorus content of the soils. Third, to ensure adequate crop yields during periods of excessive rain or drought, or in order to double crop, the moisture content of the soils had to be manipulated.[6] The Maya of the Central Lowlands used terracing and associated techniques to confront some of these problems.

TERRACING

Relics of Maya terraces have been recorded over several extensive areas in the uplands of the Central Lowlands (Fig. 7-1). These features are especially prevalent in the Río Bec region, where hundreds of thousands of terraces and related stone works are spread across an approximate contiguous area of ten thousand square kilometers.[7] Terraces have also been observed south of the Río Bec region near the Peten-Campeche border and in Peten about thirty-five to forty kilometers southeast of Tikal (Turner 1974*a*:124).[8]

Relic terraces have long been recorded in the flank lands of Belize and the adjacent portions of Peten (Ower 1927:384).[9] Indeed, a four-hundred-square-kilometer segment of the flank lands has been identified as containing extensive relic terracing. This area is demarcated by Benque Viejo on the north, Mountain Cow (Tzimin Kax) on the south, the Río Macal on the east, and the Río Chiquibul of Peten on the west (Lundell 1940:9; J. E. S. Thompson 1931:228–229). Flank-land terracing actually extends east of this zone to the Río Sibun of Belize (Ower 1927:384; Rice 1974:129–130). The number of terraces in the flank lands are not known, and data of the type necessary to estimate the number are not available. Nevertheless, the number must be large as indicated by the observations of Ower (1927:384) and Thompson (1931:228–229). Indeed, fifty-one terraces have been reported as occurring on only one hillside (Lundell 1940:9).

Two varieties of relic terraces have been identified in the central lowlands: the linear sloping, dry-field terrace and the channel bottom weir-terrace (Turner 1974a).[10] The dry-field terrace is the more common type, particularly in the Río Bec region. This type of terrace breaks the slope with a series of embankments, often poorly contoured, creating small, level or near level planting surfaces immediately behind the embankment and a gradual increase in slope up to the next embankment (Fig. 7-2). In the Río Bec region the level surfaces range from one to five meters in width and maintain soil depths ranging from twenty-five to forty-five centimeters. The sloping section of the terrace field may maintain a width of twenty meters or more, with soil depths rarely exceeding ten to fifteen centimeters.

The weir terraces, also referred to as check dams (Ruppert and Denison 1943:13, 50) or *terraplenes agrícolas* (Blom 1946:5), are composed of embankments constructed laterally across small drainage channels, creating level silt-laden planting surfaces (Fig. 7-3).[11] The soil depth of the weir terraces often exceeds fifty centimeters. Planting surfaces range in width from three to eight meters.

Two types of embankments have been identified in conjunction with the two varieties of terraces. A broad-base embankment is most prevalent among the weir and dry-field terraces (Hopkins 1968:41; Willey et al. 1965:574–575). This form of embankment is composed of a fronting wall of dry-laid limestone, and a rearward and lower rock-rubble fill (Fig. 7-4). The fronting walls are commonly 100 centimeters in height but range from 80 centimeters to 140 centimeters. The fill is composed of small rocks extending about 40 to 260 centimeters rearward and 20 to 40 centimeters below the front wall, depending on the size of the terrace.

In the western segment of the Río Bec region a second type of embankment—stone slabs—is prevalent in the gently sloping ridge lands. The stone-slab embankments are composed of small rows of upright rock (Fig. 7-5). These slabs are sunk about twenty centimeters into the ground and create an embankment of about forty centimeters in height, with basal widths ranging from sixty to eighty centimeters. This form of embankment is often difficult to distinguish from various forms of field demarcation but may be identified by the more or less contouring nature of the walls.

Other than embankments, several stone works are associated with terraced fields in the Río Bec region. Large stone ridges or barriers often dissect terraces, running perpendicular to the contour of the slope. These ridges are composed of two parallel walls separated by a rubble fill, and vary in height from 80 to 130 centimeters and in basal width from 200 to 400 centimeters. The ridges may have functioned as walkways that would have facilitated movement through the fields, especially in the rainy season. Other functions may have included field demarcation, although the ridges are rather large for this singular function, and serving as windbreaks to protect crops from the high winds associated with hurricanes which frequently cross the peninsular area.[12] Small stone walls also occur in conjunction with terraced fields, though they are less common than the larger ridges.

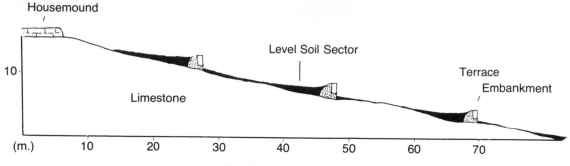

FIGURE 7–2. Profile of a linear sloping, dry-field terrace.

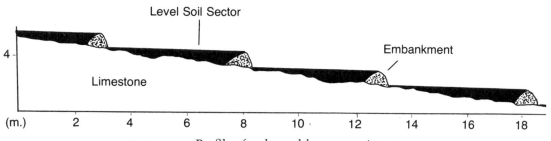

FIGURE 7–3. Profile of a channel-bottom weir terrace.

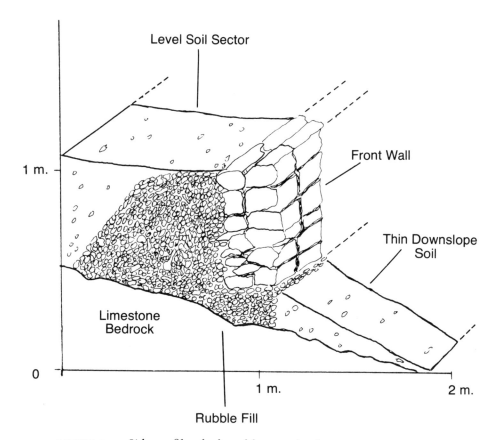

FIGURE 7–4. Side profile of a broad-base embankment.

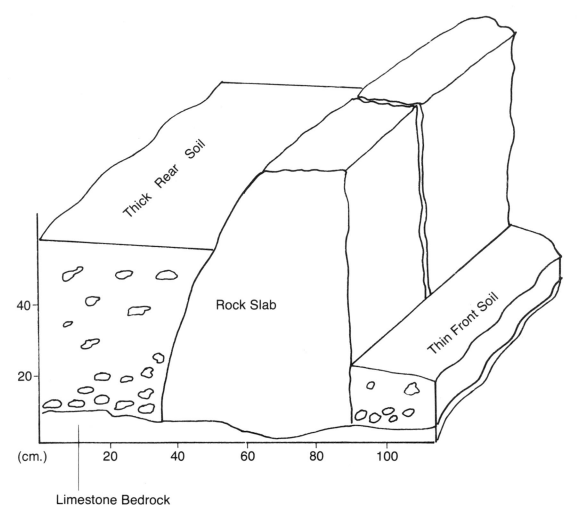

FIGURE 7–5. Side profile of a rock-slab terrace.

These features consist of small stone slabs of limestone that tend to be oriented diagonally across terraced slopes. With the addition of large ridges and small stone walls to the terraced fields, as well as house sites, the composition of a terraced slope may be quite complex (Fig. 7-6).

Terracing in the Central Maya Lowlands was probably initiated as a means to impede the erosion of the fertile but shallow Mollisols, preserving soils on slopes and providing a superior and enlarged cultivatable medium. Both the dry-field and the weir terraces acted as barriers to impede soil erosion and created deeper and more level segments of land immediately behind the embankments. These level segments may have been developed by the accumulation of eroding soils, or soil may have been transported and deposited behind the embankments of the dry-field terraces. Indeed, evidence of aquatic snail shells taken from terrace fill in the flank lands near Mountain Cow, Belize,

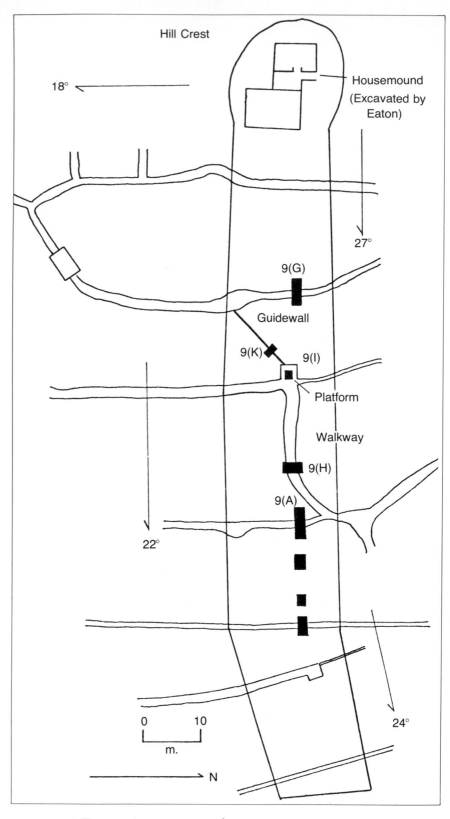

FIGURE 7–6. Terrace site 3—excavated.

suggests that the soil may have originated from inundated zones not native to the terraced slopes (Hopkins 1968:41). Among the weir terraces, the level soil sections were created by the capture of silt carried down drainage channels.

The implementation of terracing and the impedimentation of erosion may have had several negative effects on soil fertility. Most of the Mollisols in the region are colluvial in origin and maintain their fertility by the frequent exchange of soil materials created by the continuous circulation of mineral fragments (Wright 1962:97). This exchange of minerals occurs between the limestone bedrock and the shallow top soils, and by the continual movement of soils downslope. The use of terracing may have impeded soil movement sufficiently to have led to excessive leaching and loss of fertility.

The Maya of the Central Lowlands may have utilized at least two methods to offset the negative effects of the impedimentation of soil movement. As noted previously, soils may have been transported up the slopes and used as terrace fill. This practice would have provided a source of fresh, fertile soils for cultivation, but would have been time and labor consuming. Nevertheless, the pressure to produce agricultural goods may have reached a level that necessitated such measures. The design of the terraces may have been utilized to confront the impedimentation problem also. The sloping section of each terrace may have facilitated soil movement from the base of the upslope embankment to the level section of trapped soils behind the downslope embankment. The use of slope sections in this manner over lengthy periods of time may have depleted the slope soils in each section. Soil depletion may have been countered by carrying fresh soils or the soils collected behind the terrace embankments back to the slope section. The manipulation of soils in this manner would have required considerable time and energy.

Leaching and alteration of soil textures are further problems that may have developed with the implementation of terracing in the ridge and flank lands. The accumulation of runoff water on the thicker sections of soil immediately behind the embankments would have led to excessive leaching and to the transformation of soil textures from loams to clays. These leached clays would have provided a cropping medium that was poor in plant nutrients, poorly aerated, and, perhaps, waterlogged. Such conditions would have reduced crop production and may have placed sufficient pressure on the terrace embankments to cause structural damage.

The Maya may have attacked these problems with the use of several drainage techniques. The rubble fill behind and below each terrace wall may have allowed some seepage of excess water downslope. This suggested drainage technique (Turner 1974a:120) would not have worked, however, if clays developed and clogged the base of the terrace embankments around the fill. The small stone walls that cross terraced fields at various angles may have functioned as drainage devices to divert runoff water to collection points before it could accumulate behind the embankment. Furthermore, the slightly noncontouring construction of the embankment may have allowed runoff that reached the wall to flow to collection points. Whether or not the proposed collection points existed and the manner in which the collected water may have been utilized are uncertain.[13]

Tillage was another technique that may have been used to control soil accumulation and packing behind the embankments. Tilling loosened the soils and improved conditions for drainage and aeration. The Maya probably tilled the deeper terrace soils, although proof of this activity is lacking. The Prehispanic cultivation technique of mounding (the construction of hillocks for planting crops) was a form of tillage. The Classic Maya constructed such mounds with the use of dibble sticks and, perhaps, mattocks or hand hoes. The style of the Maya dibble stick—curved handle and blunt or chisel-shaped point —suggests a tillage usage (Donkin 1970:509). Evidence of the mattock comes from bifaced "celts" uncovered in the Río Bec region, often in conjunction with house sites near or within terraced zones.[14] These celts may have been hafted and used as hand hoes to till the soils.

The Mollisols of the ridge lands were fertile, but repeated cultivation diminished soil nutrients that are essential to crop growth, particularly phosphorus and nitrogen content.[15] The construction of terraces did not directly confront this problem, and the manner in which the Maya may have coped with the maintenance of soil fertility is based largely on speculation. Intercropping (the cultivation of several crops in the same field), which is characteristic of contemporary slash-and-burn cultivation in the Maya Lowlands, and crop rotation may have been employed in order to maintain adequate levels of nitrogen in the soil. The obvious crops to be used for this purpose would have been several varieties of beans (*Phaseolus* spp.) and various other legumes. Composting and manuring were probably employed to maintain adequate levels of nutrients in the soil, especially nitrogen, phosphorus, and iron. The large populations of the civic-temple centers would have provided an excellent source of human excrement. Animal manures may have been collected from several semidomesticated or tame animals and used as well (Turner 1974b:166–169). Wood ash would have been an effective fertilizer to replenish potassium in the soils. Terracing probably enhanced the effectiveness of fertilizers by retaining the materials on the slopes.

The back filling of terraces with fresh soils is another method with which the Maya may have maintained adequate levels of soil fertility. Finally, the terraced fields may have been fallowed occasionally, but probably not for lengthy periods of time. The growth of woody species on the terraces would have created considerable damage to the embankments and would have been difficult to clear among the various stoneworks on the slopes. Furthermore, the construction and maintenance of the terraces would have been economically unfeasible if the land were not cultivated fairly continuously (Wilken 1971:434).

Soil moisture balance constituted yet another consideration with which the Maya cultivator had to cope. The inundation of soils behind the terrace embankments would have retarded crop growth and inhibited crop production. This problem may have been circumvented with the use of the several drainage techniques described. Terracing may have facilitated double cropping on the level sections behind the embankments of the dry-field and weir terraces. The depth of the soils in these level sectors may have permitted sufficient moisture retention to allow the cultivation of a dry-season crop other than beans.[16] Finally, pot irrigation may have been utilized to improve crop production during periods of drought or during the dry season, although direct evidence of the use of irrigation techniques on the terraces is lacking.[7]

SUMMARY

Research dealing with Prehispanic intensive agriculture in the Central Maya Lowlands is in its infancy. As a result, our knowledge of the mechanics of various agricultural techniques employed by the Maya is limited and based largely on speculation. Furthermore, two assumptions are implicit in such research: that contemporary environmental conditions in the Central Lowlands are similar to those during Prehispanic times, and that technological comparisons between relic agricultural features and operative agricultural systems are valid. The evidence suggests that both assumptions probably are correct (Cowgill and Hutchinson 1963; Tsukada and Deevey 1967).

Despite the obvious inadequacies of our knowledge, a coherent picture of Maya agriculture is emerging. The Classic Maya possessed the technology to pursue intensive cultivation throughout a variety of physical zones in the Central Lowlands. The fertile Mollisols of the uplands were intensively cultivated throughout the Central Lowlands, and the major problem of soil erosion was confronted with the use of terraces. Apparently, other problems connected with intensive cultivation in the ridge and flank lands, such as the maintenance of soil fertility and drainage control, were countered sufficiently to sustain intensive agriculture. Maya farming, then, was of a quality comparable with any Prehispanic indigenous cultivation in the Western Hemisphere.

ACKNOWLEDGMENTS

Funding for graphics was provided by the Faculty Research Council, University of Oklahoma. The map (Fig. 7-1) was prepared by Mary Goodman.

NOTES

1. Incipient agriculture in the Maya Lowlands need not have been an extensive, swidden type of cultivation. Intensive agricultural practices may have been introduced or developed very early in the area, as is suggested by the dating of a canal associated with raised fields in Belize at 1110 ± 230 B.C. (Puleston 1977).
2. The chronology used here was developed by Ball (1977) to include the Río Bec region of southern Campeche and Quintana Roo, Mexico.

3. Increasing evidence indicates that the so-called Maya civic temple centers were densely settled relative to "rural" areas in the Lowlands and served diverse functions (Kurjack 1974). The density of occupation and pattern of settlement within the Lowland sites, however, differed from those in Highland cities such as Teotihuacan. The future nomenclature for Lowland sites will probably shift to that applied to most forms of settlement: hamlet, village, and so forth.

4. The distribution of soil types is critical to understanding Maya settlement patterns and land use. Relics of intensive land settlement and use in the Río Bec regions are strongly associated with Mollisols (Rendzina). A similar relationship between prime agricultural soils and the location of Maya sites has been found in other sectors of the Lowlands, particularly in southern Peten (Voorhies 1972) and northern Belize (Green 1973). Whether this relationship will be substantiated by spatial examinations of intersite settlement patterns remains to be seen.

5. The susceptibility of tropical slope soils to erosion when they are cleared and cultivated is discussed by Ochse et al. (1961:239–247).

6. Double cropping refers to the cultivation of the same plot twice within the same year.

7. Río Bec terraces were first reported by Ruppert and Denison (1943: 13, 50) and reidentified by various members of the National Geographic Society–Middle American Research Institute, Tulane University, Becan Project, including Eaton (1972:54).

8. Stone walls similar to terraces have been observed south of the Río Bec region by Jack D. Eaton (personal communication). Blom (1946:5) refers to terraces in Peten, but fails to specify a more precise location.

9. Joyce (1926:226–227) made an earlier reference to terraces in the Lowlands near Lubaantun, Belize, but failed to distinguish them as agricultural or monumental.

10. These terms follow the classification of terraces developed by Spencer and Hale (1961).

11. Blom (1946:5) neither described the features he called *terraplenes agrícolas* nor specified their location. I have assumed that Blom was referring to the terraces of the foothills of the Maya Mountains that occur in eastern Peten. I did not consider the possibility that these features may have been raised fields for several reasons. Blom was familiar with various forms of raised fields that occur in the Highlands, and he did not choose to refer to the Lowland features by the Highland nomenclature, either *tablón* or *chinampa*. Also, it is doubtful that relic raised fields could be discovered in the Lowlands by ground observation. Barrera et al. (1977:55), however, have referred to raised fields in Campeche as *terraplenes agrícolas*. This reference raises questions concerning the meaning intended by Blom.

12. The possible function was first suggested to me by Martin A. Nettleship. For a discussion of the use of windbreaks in tropical agriculture, see Wilken (1972:557–559).

13. At least one identifiable drainage spout was found on a terraced hillside in the Río Bec region by Jack D. Eaton. The constructional context of the spout, however, could not be determined.

14. The celts were uncovered by the author and other members of the 1973 National Geographic Society–University of Texas at San Antonio–University of Wisconsin-Madison Río Bec Project. Of the forty-one bifaced celts uncovered, twenty-two were taken from "rural" house sites and two from terrace fill. The celts were examined by Stoltman (n.d.) and Irwin Rovner.

15. As field clearance and weeding is increased and as the crop-fallow cycle is shortened, the loss of nitrogen and phosphorus in the soil becomes an exceedingly acute problem because of increased leaching and oxidation (Ochse et al. 1961:201–209).

16. A dry-season crop is rarely attempted in the Río Bec region. In the more humid southern portions of the Central Lowlands, however, a dry-season crop of beans is often planted.

17. The relic raised fields found in the Central Lowlands may have some bearing on the ancient use of terraces. Raised fields were located in river valley and *bajo* zones, where sufficient water may have been available during the dry season to directly or indirectly irrigate. Double cropping was more feasible on the raised fields than on terraces.

8 The Representation of Underworld
Processions in Maya Vase Painting:
An Iconographic Study
by Jacinto Quirarte

A number of Maya polychromed vases, related to death and
the underworld, have been appearing in private and public collections
in Mexico, Guatemala, and the United States in recent years. Among
these are vases which show processions of two, three, and sometimes
four figures moving from right to left within the narrative register.
The vases clearly depict deities, supernaturals, and/or their impersonators in the underworld. There are death figures accompanied by jaguars, monkeys, deer, and composites of some or all of these. Signs
of death are often included in these vases. Some of the figures wear
death spots, death eyes, and the sign for death—division or percentage
sign—on parts of the body or on banners. The death eyes are also attached to a death collar worn by these figures and the death god in
the codices (J. E. S. Thompson 1960: Figs. 13-11 and 19). Nicholas
Hellmuth refers to the scenes painted on these vases as decapitation
and/or death dances (personal communication).[1]

Although several vases showing processions have been known for
over fifty years, no one as far as I know has thoroughly analyzed this
particular theme. Enough pieces are now available to make a preliminary analysis possible.

In this essay I discuss the procession scenes depicted on ten of the
more than seventeen vases with similar representations presently
available.[2] The discussion concentrates on the protagonists in the processions and their identification as deities, supernaturals, and/or impersonators, as well as their placement within the processions, in order
to determine the significance and meaning of the themes portrayed.
The glyphic columns associated with the procession figures are studied with those ends in mind. The glyph bands directly below the rims
of the vessels are not discussed.

LITERATURE

References to the vases with processions of deities, supernaturals, and
their impersonations have appeared in the literature for many years.
The earliest of these vases was found in Yalloch before 1918 by
Thomas Gann (1918: Pl. 24). It is presently held in the collection of
the Museum of the American Indian (Catalog No. 9/6544) in New
York. Two pot-bellied figures wearing scarves are shown moving from
right to left in procession style. The figures are black; they have monkey tails and oversized saurian heads. They wear voluminous scarves

around their necks. Although no references to death are apparent, the posture as well as the articulation of the figures, along with details such as the scarves, relate these to the others to be discussed below.

A related vase was found fifty years ago in the Guatemala Highlands at Chama and reported by Dieseldorff (1926, Vol. 1: Pl. 22). The vase shows a procession of four figures: a jaguar with water lily and *ahau* unit on its head leading two armadillos and a rodentlike animal playing gourds, a drum, and a turtle carapace with a deer antler, respectively. The jaguar wears a death collar. Nicholas Hellmuth has recently photographed three almost identical vases (correspondence). These are still unpublished.

Some of the figures involved in these processions have been known in isolated contexts for over sixty years. Spinden (1913:77, 135, Figs. 101, 185) discusses two representations of water-lily jaguars with scarves, one on the famous Peto carved jar presently part of the Peabody Museum collection at Cambridge and the other on a polychrome vase fragment from Copan.

Michael Coe (1973:100–101) discusses a three-figure procession scene painted on a vase which he designates as a "codex style vase." The procession is led by a death figure wearing death eyes and a death collar. A severed head is placed over a container directly in front of the first figure. A second figure also wearing death eyes and death collar assumes a similar posture. The third figure wears jaguar paws on hand and feet and a jaguar head and tail. These slightly paunchy figures are related to the figures represented on the vases to be discussed below.

PROVENIENCE

Most of the vases included in this study have been obtained through uncontrolled excavations (see Coggins 1976c for a discussion of this problem). Not only is it difficult if not impossible to determine where each was found; it is also difficult to date the vases with any certainty. Most of the vases considered here are reportedly from the southern Campeche, northern Peten, western Belize region. This corresponds to the Southern Lowlands of the Maya area or the Peten-Belize area of the Central Region. The temporal horizon for these vases corresponds to the Late Classic period (A.D. 600–900), indicated by their stylistic affinities with properly excavated materials.

THE VASES SELECTED FOR THIS STUDY

The protagonists in the procession scenes usually do not do anything other than walk from right to left or face to the observer's left if sitting or crouching. There is no specific position occupied by the participants in the single-file processions.[3] Positions occupied by death figures, jaguars, and others vary from procession to procession.

Those vases which show a representative range of figural presentations and a variety of positions occupied by protagonists in the processions have been selected for this study. Other factors considered include differences in background color, the number of procession figures, and their interpretation as deities, supernaturals, and/or their impersonators. Such distinctions have been used as a basis for the grouping of the vases to be discussed below.

In addition, the vessels selected for this study have been assigned numbers, letters, and Roman numerals for identification purposes based on the type of procession—single file (1) or tiered (2); background colors (A, B, or C); glyph bands (I) or lack of them (II); and the number of the vessel within each grouping, as follows:

1AI: Single-file procession on a red-orange ground with glyph band on a tan or buff ground. (See Fig. 8-1.)

1AII: The same as 1AI but with the glyph band.

1BI: Single-file procession on a tan or buff or white ground with glyph band framed by single or multiple black lines. Red-orange bands almost always cap the lip and the base of the vessel. Occasionally the same color is used to frame the glyph band.

1BII: The same as 1BI but without the glyph band.

2BI: The same as 1BI but with complicated (tiered) processions. (See Fig. 8-10).

1CII: Single-file procession on a tan or buff ground with chevron bands framing the narrative scene. No glyph band.

The descriptive titles used incorporate references to the protagonists in each procession.

DEITY AND SUPERNATURAL IMPERSONATORS

1AI-1. "Dancing Jaguar; Dancing Deer; Dancing Death Figure" Vase. This vase from Peten (Fig. 8-1) is presently held in the collection of the Logan Museum, Beloit, Wisconsin. It has a ratio of 1:1.79 of height to diameter.[4] It shows a procession of three figures moving from right to left. All three figures are pot-bellied. Columns of glyphs are associated with each figure (Fig. 8-11a). The glyph band near the rim of the vessel and its treatment as well as the red-orange background color of the vase relate it to the Initial Series vase found in Uaxactun in 1931 (Smith 1934: Pls. 4, 5; Fig. 19). The procession is led by a human figure with death spots on its body, jaguar paws, and bearded, feline head (Quirarte 1976: Pl. 1).[5] It wears a death collar from which a banner with death signs (T-509) is draped over the extended right arm. The second figure in the procession, a deer impersonator with long, flowing tail, assumes exactly the same posture, with upraised right leg, which gives the impression of arrested movement, as in a dance. It wears the same signs of death around the collar and on the banner. A double flower emerges from the mouth of the deer head, while another flower is attached to the figure's tail. The procession is com-

FIGURE 8–1. A death impersonator with death collar and a banner with death sign. This is the third figure in a procession of three figures (1AI–1). The first figure is a jaguar impersonator with death spots. The second, a deer impersonator with long, flowing tail, wears the same signs of death as the first. Photograph by Nicholas M. Hellmuth, courtesy of the Foundation for Latin American Anthropological Research, St. Louis, Missouri. The vase is from the collections of the New Orleans Museum of Art, Purchased through the Ella West Freeman Foundation Matching Fund. Used by permission of the Museum.

pleted by the third figure wearing the death costume (Fig. 8-1). The figure also wears the death collar as well as the banner with death signs. It is bearded and extends its arm like the leader of the group. It wears a death eye on the forehead.

1AI-2. "Dancing Death; Dancing Jaguar; Dancing Composite Figure" Vase. This vase, found in the collection of the New Orleans Museum of Art (Catalog No. 70-18), is almost identical to vase 1AI-1 and must come from the same region. Its ratio of 1:1.94 is similar to that of the other vases reviewed here (see Table 8-1). The glyph band below the rim of the vessel, as on vase 1AI-1, is painted on a light tan ground with additions of the overall red-orange background color and then outlined in black. Columns of glyphs separate the figures in the procession (Fig. 8-11b). The first dancing figure represents death. It hold a container in its right hand. The second dancing figure wears a scarf, mittens (?), a long, flowing tail, and a feline head (Quirarte 1976: Pl. 2). The feline head, like countless others represented on painted vases from the Maya Lowlands and Highlands, has an attachment behind the ear comprised of the day sign *ahau* topped by a double scroll. One scroll curls inward; the other extends outward as if released from its taut configuration. This is a typical combination of the contained and released aspects of the scroll motif found in Maya art. The third figure, a composite with saurian (?) head, a deer's ear, and a jaguar's tail, wears a death collar and the front and back paws (mittens) of the jaguar.

1AI-3. "Seated Jaguar; Crouching Deer" Vase. This vase, like vases 1AI-1 and 1AI-2, has a red-orange background, but it is slightly different in terms of the configurations, as well as the postures of the seated jaguar followed by a crouching deer (Fig. 8-2). The figures are perhaps getting ready for the procession or have momentarily stopped. The spotted jaguar wears a voluminous scarf, a water lily sprouting from its head, and the *ahau* unit with the double scrolls directly behind it. The crouching deer with antlers also wears an equally large scarf tied around its neck. The glyph column immediately behind the deer is associated with the jaguar.

1BI-1. "Jaguar; Saurian Death; Monkey/Deer" Vase. This vase from the Peten has a ratio of 1:1.50. The three figures moving from right to left extend their arms and bend from the waist down (Fig. 8-3). The procession, represented on a tan or buff background, is led by a heavily scarfed, spotted feline. An abbreviated version of the *ahau* attachment extends horizontally behind the jaguar's ear. A column of three glyphs is shown in front of this figure. Another column of three glyphs separates the jaguar from the second figure, which wears a skeletal, saurian head with a deer's ear flowing behind it. It wears a death collar and spotted jaguar paws on its hand and feet. References to a skeletal figure are made by the elbows and knees as well as the rib cage, spinal column, and scapula. The procession is completed by a crouching monkey whose tail flows upward. It wears a voluminous scarf like the jaguar and has deer accents in the form of antlers and

Table 8-1. *Procession Vases*

Inventory				Format		
Vase No.; Designation; Source and/or Illustration	Site and Provenience	Present Location	Participants in the Procession	Dimensions (Cm.)		
				Ht.	Dia.	Ratio

Type 1AI: Single-file procession; red-orange background; glyph band

[a]1. "Dancing Jaguar; Dancing Deer; Dancing Death Figure"; Quirarte 1976: Pl. 1; Figure 8-1	Peten	Beloit College, Logan Museum, Beloit, Wisc.	Three impersonators	20.4	11.4	1.79
[a]2. "Dancing Death; Dancing Jaguar; Dancing Composite Figure"; Quirarte 1976: Pl. 2	Unknown	New Orleans Museum of Art, #70-18	Three impersonators	21.6	11.1	1.95
[a]3. "Seated Jaguar; Crouching Deer"; unpublished; Figure 8-2	Peten	Private Collection	Two impersonators?			[b]
[a]4. "Serpent–Saurian Death; Jaguar/Flame"; *Tesoros Mayas de Guatemala*, 1974 Japanese Exhibition Catalogue: Fig. 1; Figure 8-4	Peten-Belize Area	Carlos Nottebohn Collection, Guatemala City	Two deities?	20.0	11.5	1.74
[a]5. "Wailing Seated Jaguar; Seated Deer with Monkey's Head"; unpublished; Figures 8-5 and 8-6	Unknown	Museo Popol Vuh, Guatemala City	Two deities?			1.68[c]
[a]6. "Three Death Figures"; unpublished; Figure 8-7	Peten	Private Collection	Three deities			1.60[c]
7. "Death; Deer/Monkey; Rodent?"; unpublished	Peten	Jorge Castillo Collection	Three impersonators			1.65[c]
[a]8. "Death; Jaguar/Flame; Death; Jaguar"; unpublished; Figure 8-8	Peten	Private Collection, Europe	Four deities			[b]
9. "Two (?) Jaguars"; unpublished	Unknown	National Museum of Anthropology, Mexico City, Dec. Kam. 1971	Three (?) deities?	23.0	11.7	1.97

[a]Vases discussed in the text.

[b]Only the rollout drawings for these were available. These show the narrative register and sometimes the rim glyph band but not the size of the vessel. Since the format or ratio is based on the actual size of the vessel, it is not possible to make such determinations.

[c]Dimensions for these vases were not available; the ratios of vessel height to diameter were taken from photographs and slides.

Table 8-1 *continued.*

Vase No.; Designation; Source and/or Illustration	Site and Provenience	Present Location	Participants in the Procession	Dimensions (Cm.) Ht.	Dia.	Ratio
Inventory				Format		

Type 1AII: Single-file procession; red-orange background; no glyph band

1. "Spotted Jaguar; Monkey/Deer; Jaguar"; unpublished	Unknown	Witte Museum, San Antonio	Three impersonators	15.3	10.0	1.53

Type 1BI: Single-file procession; tan, buff, or white background; no glyph band

[a]1. "Jaguar; Saurian Death; Monkey/Deer"; unpublished; Figure 8-3	Peten	Private Collection	Three impersonators?			1.54[c]
[a]2. "Dancing Monkey; Composite Avian God"; unpublished; Figure 8-9	Peten	Private Collection	Two deities			1.63[c]
3. "Codex Style Vase"; M. D. Coe 1973:100–101	Southern Campeche or Northern Peten	Private Collection, New York	Three impersonators	21.5		2.00
4. "Yalloch Vase"; Gann 1918: Pl. 24	Yalloch, Chultun Burial, before 1918	Museum of the American Indian, New York, #9/6544	Two supernaturals? or impersonators?	27.6	15.2	1.82

Type 1BII: Single-file procession: tan, buff, or white background; no glyph band

1. "Monkey; Deer; Composite"; unpublished	Peten	Private Collection, United States	Three supernaturals?	20.5	11.3	1.81

Type 2BI: Complicated (tiered) procession and decapitation scenes; glyph band

[a]1. "Decapitation Scene"; *Archaeology*, January 1976:4; Figure 8-10	Peten	Private Collection	Three deities; four humans?			1.81[c]

Type 1CII: Single-file procession on a tan or buff ground with chevron bands framing the narrative scene; no glyph band

1. "Jaguar; Armadillo Gourd Player; Armadillo Drummer; Rodent Playing a Turtle Carapace"; Dieseldorff 1926: Pl. 22	Chama	Unknown	Four impersonators			1.41[c]

[a]Vases discussed in the text.

[b]Only the rollout drawings for these were available. These show the narrative register and sometimes the rim glyph band but not the size of the vessel. Since the format or ratio is based on the actual size of the vessel, it is not possible to make such determinations.

[c]Dimensions for these vases were not available; the ratios of vessel height to diameter were taken from photographs and slides.

ear. Two columns of two glyphs each are found directly in front of its head and above its extended right arm and directly below its tail. The jaguar points to these glyphs.

DEITIES AND SUPERNATURALS

1AI-4. "Serpent–Saurian Death; Jaguar/Flame" Vase. This vase has the same red-orange background as the other 1AI type vases. It also has a similar ratio of 1:1.74 and is reported to be from the Peten-Belize area (see Table 8-1). Like vase 1AI-3, it has a two-figure procession (Fig. 8-4). The lead figure has a skeletal, long-lipped saurian head with a flower attached to its forehead and a column of four glyphs in front of it. It is pot-bellied and moves from right to left. A long, flowing spotted tail extends below and behind its legs and is topped off by an attachment with the usual double scroll typical of Maya art. This figure wears a long death collar.[6] Second position is occupied by a frontally presented dancing jaguar wearing a voluminous scarf around its neck. The feline looks to its right toward the skeletal figure. It is backed up by what appear to be flames. It has obviously lost its tail. A column of five glyphs is associated with it.

1AI-5. "Wailing Seated Jaguar; Seated Deer with Monkey's Head" Vase. This two-figure vase, like vases 1AI-1, 2, 3, and 4, has a red-orange background and a glyph band painted on a tan ground. Its ratio of 1:1.68 is similar to the others of this type. Glyph columns separate the two seated figures—a wailing jaguar wearing a red scarf and a deer with a monkey's head, deer's antler and ear (Figs. 8-5, 8-6). The former has four glyphs associated with it, the latter five (Fig. 8-11c). The deer/monkey holds a cacao pod in its right paw. It also wears a scarf.

1AI-6. "Three Death Figures" Vase. This vase from the Peten has a ratio of 1:1.60 and a red-orange background. It has three death figures moving from right to left separated by columns of four glyphs each and a glyph band near the rim of the vessel (Figs. 8-7, 8-11d). The first two figures have the same type of object attached to the front end of each death collar. All three have a death eye on the forehead. The second figure has a greatly distended abdomen area (Fig. 8-7). The third figure appears to be hopping and holds its hand up to its mouth. A larger banner with death eyes depicted on a black ground appears to be appended to the death eyes on the capes of a number of dancing bat figures found in the Chama area in the Guatemala Highlands.

1AI-8. "Death; Jaguar/Flame; Death; Jaguar" Vase. This vase has a four-figure procession composed of alternating death and jaguar figures moving from right to left (Fig. 8-8). Like other 1AI type vases, this vase has a red-orange background. Glyph bands on a tan ground below the rim and near the base of the vessel frame the narrative register. A glyph column is associated with each figure. Leading the procession is a smoking death figure who wears a death collar, has a death eye on the forehead, and carries a container in the left hand. The second

FIGURE 8–2. A preprocession (?) scene comprised of a seated jaguar as Lord of the Underworld and a crouching deer (1 AI–3). Drawing by Barbara Van Heusen, Foundation for Latin American Anthropological Research; illustration provided courtesy of the director, Nicholas M. Hellmuth.

FIGURE 8–3. A procession comprised of: the jaguar as Lord of the Underworld; a saurian death figure with a deer's ear and jaguar mittens; and a monkey with deer traits (1BI–1). Drawing by Persis Clarkson and Barbara Van Heusen, Foundation for Latin American Anthropological Research; illustration provided courtesy of the director, Nicholas M. Hellmuth.

figure in the procession is a water-lily jaguar enveloped by flames. A second death figure with greatly distended abdomen occupies the third position in the procession. It wears a death collar and a death eye over the forehead. The fourth figure is another water-lily jaguar shown holding a cup in its left paw and a staff (?) with its right.

1BI-2. "Dancing Monkey; Composite Avian God" Vase. This white-ground vase from the Peten has a ratio of 1:1.63. Two figures are represented moving from right to left (Fig. 8-9). The glyph band is directly below the rim of the vessel. The procession is led by a monkey whose legs are flexed in such a way that its weight, resting on the balls of

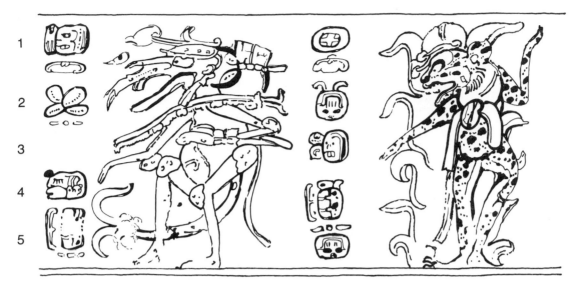

FIGURE 8–4. A procession comprised of a saurian death figure with a jaguar's tail and a dancing jaguar amid a wall of flames (1AI–4). Rollout drawing made from slides. Used by permission of Karl-Heinz Nottebohm, Guatemala City.

its feet, is about to be shifted, thus giving it the appearance of a dancer. It carries a long staff with curvilinear attachments in front under its left arm. This could be the long-stemmed flower of the water lily (see Spinden 1913: Fig. 186 and M. D. Coe 1973:119). It wears a double (?) scarf. The headdress, difficult to make out, extends in cantilever fashion behind the monkey's head and has downward flowing feathers. This is echoed at ground level by a curving tail made doubly thick by the inclusion of a red sash running the length of it on the outside. Death eyes are attached to the outer contours or sash. Death eyes are also placed over the scarf. The monkey balances a long object in its upraised right hand which may be a death collar. The upper part of its headdress could conceivably be a reference to the antlers of a deer.

The second figure appears to have an avian head. It wears a serpent tied around its neck instead of the usual scarf worn by all figures reviewed above. It has long-lipped head references on either side of the decorated *ahau* attachment (see M. D. Coe 1975a: Pl. 11).

Great rhythmic patterns are created by the manner in which these figures and their accessories are represented and arranged.

2BI-1. "Decapitation Scene" Vase. This vase from the Peten has a ratio of 1:1.81 and a light tan background. It has seven figures, in contrast to the other vases reviewed above. The usual protagonists in the procession scenes are represented in this vase along with a number of human figures (Fig. 8-10). The human and supernatural figures are placed above and below on the narrative register similar

FIGURE 8–5. A seated wailing jaguar with scarf and long-lipped head attached to its tail (1AI–5). Its companion is illustrated in Figure 8–6. Photograph by Nicholas M. Hellmuth, courtesy of the Foundation for Latin American Anthropological Research, St. Louis, Missouri, and Museo Popol Vuh, Universidad Francisco Marroquín, Guatemala.

FIGURE 8–6. A seated deer with monkey's head. It wears a scarf and holds a cacao pod in its right hand (?) (1AI–5). It follows the jaguar shown in Figure 8–5. Photograph by Nicholas M. Hellmuth, courtesy of the Foundation for Latin American Anthropological Research, St. Louis, Missouri, and Museo Popol Vuh, Universidad Francisco Marroquín, Guatemala.

FIGURE 8–7. A death figure as Lord of the Underworld. This is the second figure in a procession of three death figures (1 AI–6). Photograph by Nicholas M. Hellmuth, courtesy of the Foundation for Latin American Anthropological Research, St. Louis, Missouri.

FIGURE 8–8. A procession of: a hopping death figure (smoking); a jaguar in flames; a death figure with distended abdomen; and a jaguar (1 AI–8). Drawing by Barbara Van Heusen, Foundation for Latin American Anthropological Research; illustration provided courtesy of the director, Nicholas M. Hellmuth.

to the arrangement in the Altar de Sacrificios vase (Adams 1971: Fig. 92). The leader is a skeletal death god which holds a decapitated human head in its extended right hand. It is twice as big as any of the others and occupies the entire height of the narrative register. A double scroll—a combination of a curving and an undulating form—emanates from its abdominal cavity and extends vertically the entire height of the figure. The undulating portion of the scroll terminating behind the severed head has markings on the inner side similar to those of a serpent's body. The double scroll actually emanates from a container held by the death god at waist level.[7] Death eyes are attached to various parts of the death figure.

The death figure is followed by two figures (2 and 3). One is seated and placed within a cartouche (a similar motif is found in the Bonampak murals of Structure 1, Room 2). Death eyes may be part of the image. Directly below is a spotted jaguar with a water lily on its head and the *ahau* (?) unit behind its ear. This jaguar wears an actual serpent around its neck instead of a scarf.

The next two figures (4 and 5) are a composite serpent with deer and monkey traits above and a human figure enveloped by flames below. A human head emerges from the open jaws of the serpent. This is reminiscent of the several Yaxchilan lintels with similar motifs (Lintels 15 and 25). The human figure rests its upturned body on its shoulders and head and is smoking. This is followed by two more human figures arranged in similar fashion (6 and 7). The upper figure clicks its heels and has a two-headed fleshless serpent draped over its shoulders. The serpent heads face in opposite directions at the level of the figure's thighs. Death eyes are attached to the serpent's body. The figure wears spotted (jaguar?) anklets, belt, and breech clout, and the jaguar's ear over its own ear. The fanged serpent attached to its headdress is similar to the serpent heads already described. The final figure is seated and holds another severed human head. It is confronted by two seemingly floating saurian heads attached to an arching serpentlike body. The lower head appears to be fleshless. There are glyph columns and bands associated with each of the seven figures. Figures

FIGURE 8–9. A procession comprised of a dancing monkey with death eyes and a composite avian creature with serpent scarf (1BI–2). Drawing by Persis Clarkson and Barbara Van Heusen, Foundation for Latin American Anthropological Research; illustration provided courtesy of the director, Nicholas M. Hellmuth.

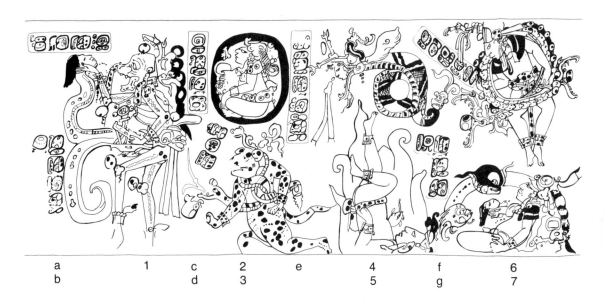

a   1   c   2   e   4   f   6
b   d   3   5   g   7

FIGURE 8–10. A decapitation scene comprised of: (1) a death god holding a severed human head; (3) a jaguar as Lord of the Underworld with a serpent scarf; (4) a composite serpent with deer and monkey traits; (6) a heel-clicking figure with a skeletal two-headed serpent; (2), (5), and (7) appear to be human figures (2BI–1). Only figures (1), (3), and (4) are considered procession figures; position designations in text refer only to them. Figure (1) is in position 1, (3) is in position 2, and (4) is in position 3. Drawing by Persis Clarkson, Foundation for Latin American Anthropological Research; illustration provided courtesy of the director, Nicholas M. Hellmuth.

1, 2, 3, 4, and 6 have glyphs located immediately in front of each figure, to the viewer's left. Figures 5 and 7 have glyphs behind or to the right of each one.

JAGUARS, WATER LILIES, AND DECORATED AHAU UNITS

Jaguars or references to jaguars are included in thirteen of the sixteen procession vases found in the Southern Lowlands and in one Highland Maya vase (see Table 8-2). Some are bearded; others are enveloped by flames; some are seated; most wear a water lily on the head; some also wear an *ahau* attachment on the head. One has death spots. At least four wear death collars. Six wear a voluminous scarf around the neck. The jaguar occupies the lead position in seven vases. In five it is second, and in four others it is third.

The water lily and the decorated *ahau* unit are not exclusively attached to jaguars, nor do they always appear on the head. The *ahau* unit is sometimes attached to the tail of a jaguar or composite creature with jaguar traits. The tail attachment is seen on a carved vase discussed by Michael Coe (1973:127). This is the same water-lily jaguar depicted on the Peto vase (Spinden 1913: Fig. 185). The *ahau* unit also appears attached to the head of the earth monster. It is evident that the *ahau* unit simply refers to the wearer as Lord, in this case, the Lord of the Earth.

The water lily is also worn by a procession figure representing a serpent–saurian death creature who retains the jaguar's tail (Fig. 8-4). Other wearers of the water lily are deities of the underworld as well. One of these is God L, who has a number of jaguar traits (J. E. S. Thompson 1970:292–294 and Fig. 1b), including the water lily and jaguar paw attached to the head and ear, respectively. It also has the cruller element placed on the bridge of the nose and the usual deity eye. It wears a jaguar skin.

The ubiquitous procession jaguar with water lily and decorated *ahau* attachment on its head is the personification of the night sun as it goes into the interior of the earth or underworld. The *ahau* signals this creature as a Lord of the Underworld. J. E. S. Thompson (1960: 12, 72) discusses this Maya deity, which he considers to be the same as the Central Mexican deity Tepeyollotl, or 'Heart of the Mountain'. Under this guise, then, the jaguar wears a water lily and the title of Lord on its head—the main sign T-533 or *ahau* topped by the typical scroll found in Maya art.

There are no readily apparent references to rulers in the vases under discussion. The deities and their impersonators involved in the processions do not appear to represent or refer to specifically named rulers. More pointed references to rulers are made in several Guatemala Highland vases in which the bodiless jaguar head with water lily and death collar is attached to the bundle (cushion) of rulership placed as a seat or backing on a throne (see L. A. Parsons 1974: Pl. 189 and M. D. Coe 1973:40–41). On another Highland vase (Dieseldorff 1926, Vol 1: Pl. 22) the same water-lily jaguar god with death collar leads

Table 8-2. *Jaguars, Water Lilies, and Decorated Ahau Units*

Vase No.; Source; Posture	Jaguar Spots	Jaguar Traits	Procession Figures No.	Procession Figures Position	Water Lily	Ahau	Scarf	Death Collar	Other
Type 1AI									
1. Quirarte 1976: Pl. 1 Walking			3	1				X	Impersonator with death spots
2. Quirarte 1976: Pl. 2									
(a) Dancing		Head	3	3			X		Impersonator with deer's hooves and tail?
(b) Dancing		Mittens	3	2				X	Impersonator; composite with jaguar tail
3. Figure 8-2 Seated	X		2	1	X	X	X		Deity or impersonator?
4. Figure 8-4 Dancing	X		2	2	X		X		Deity; flames
5. Figure 8-5 Seated	X		2	1	X (Attached to scarf)		X		Deity?
8. Figure 8-8									
(a) Walking	X		4	2	X				Deity; flames
(b) Walking	X		4	4	X				Deity; flames
9. Unpublished									
(a) Squatting?	X		?	?	?				Deity?
(b) Squatting?	X		?	?	?				Deity?
Type 1AII									
1. Unpublished									
(a) Walking	X	Head and paws	3	1	X				
(b) Walking			3	3	X?			X	Impersonator?
Type 1BI									
1. Figure 8-3 Walking	X		3	1	X?	X	X		Impersonator?
3. M. D. Coe 1973: 100–101 Standing		Head and paws	3	3					Impersonator? smoking jaguar?

Table 8-2 *continued.*

Vase No.; Source; Posture	Jaguar		Procession Figures		Attachments				Other
	Spots	Traits	No.	Position	Water Lily	Ahau	Scarf	Death Collar	
Type 1BII									
1. Unpublished Walking		Head? and paws	3	3	X (Head and tail)		X		Supernatural; black body
Type 2BI									
1. Figure 8-10 Walking	X		3 (7 total)	2	X	X			Deity; serpent scarf
Type 1CII									
1. Dieseldorff 1926: Pl. 22 Walking	X		4	1	X	X		X	Impersonator?

a procession of musicians (Table 8-2). The jaguar figure is an impersonator of this deity.

The jaguar may perhaps announce the actual death of a specific ruler whose kinship to some feline-related lineage is reported in the texts. The glyphic texts associated with the procession figures may provide some answers.

Adams (1977) suggests that references are made to a Lord Jaguar lineage by the glyph T-539 in the Altar de Sacrificios vase. This glyph usually accompanies references to specific rulers on the Altar vase. The same glyph is found repeatedly in most of the vases included in this study. It may refer to the deceased who is announced or personified by the supernatural or impersonator painted on the vases.

GLYPHIC COLUMNS ASSOCIATED WITH JAGUARS

Glyphic columns associated with jaguars in six vases are reviewed and discussed below. The numbers assigned to affixes and main signs are based on the Thompson catalog (1962).

Vase 1AI-1, Position 1: Jaguar Impersonator with Death Spots (Fig. 8-11a, Column A)

A1	122:?	
A2	?:563a?	Fire
A4	128.609:125	Rulership[8]
A5	168:561:?	Ben Ich–Sky
A6	?.?	

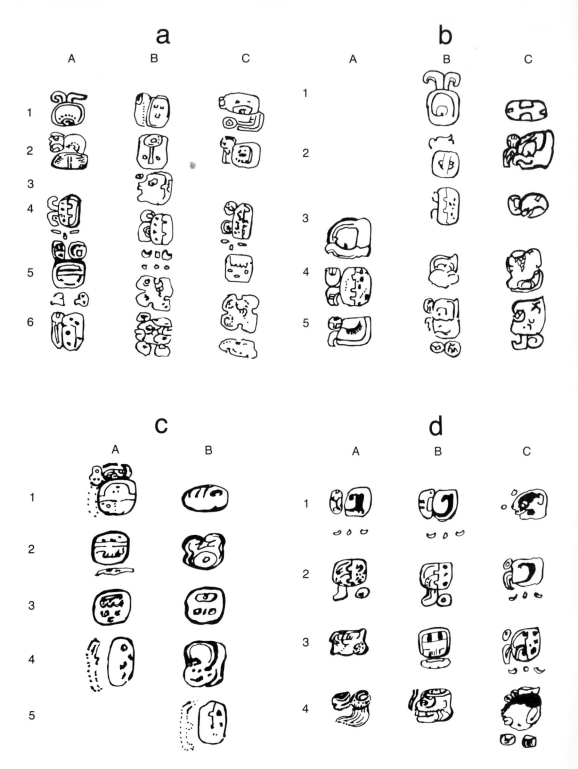

FIGURE 8–11. Columns of glyphs associated with each of the following procession figures: (a) three impersonator figures from vase 1AI–1 (Fig 8–1); (b) three impersonator (?) figures from vase 1AI–2; (c) two seated figures—a jaguar and a deer with monkey traits—from vase 1AI–5 (Figs. 8–5 and 8–6); (d) three death figures from vase 1AI–6 (Fig. 8–7).

Vase 1AI-2, Position 2: Dancing Composite Jaguar Impersonator
with a Scarf
(Fig. 8-11b, Column B)

B1	129?:578	Spiral
B2	78?:518c	Muluc Variant
B3	1?.609	Rulership
B4	?	
B5	Portrait:168	Portrait–Ben Ich

Vase 1AI-4, Position 2: Jaguar/Flame
(Fig. 8-4, Column b)

B1	281:23	Kan Cross
B2	129:524	Ix (Jaguar)
B3	130?.?	
B4	1.130:609:125	Rulership
B5	524	Ix (Jaguar)

Vase 1AI-5, Position 1: Seated Jaguar
(Fig. 8-11c, Column A)

A1	40.168:?	Emblem Glyph
A2	561:23	Sky
A3	524	Ix (Jaguar)
A4	1.539 or 609	Lord/Jaguar Lineage? or Rulership

Vase 1AI-8, Positions 2 and 4: Jaguar/Flame
(Fig. 8-8, Columns B and D)

B1	129:563	Fire
B2	524	Ix (Jaguar)
B3	3?.539:125:126	Lord/Jaguar Lineage?
D1	?.?	Portrait?
D2	524	Ix (Jaguar)
D3	3?.539:125	Lord/Jaguar Lineage?
D4	?	

Vase 2BI-1, Position 2: Jaguar with Serpent Scarf
(Fig. 8-10, Caption d)

F1	?.?	
F2	524	Ix (Jaguar)
F3	1.539	Lord/Jaguar Lineage?
F5	?.?	

The glyph columns associated with the water-lily jaguar have references to Ix (T-524) in four vases (1AI-4, 5, and 8; 2BI-1). This glyph precedes all references to the Lord/Jaguar Lineage? or Rulership glyph (T-539 or T-609) with various affixes in these four vases. In vase 1AI-4 (Fig. 8-4) Ix follows a reference to T-609 as well. It is interesting to note that there is no reference to Ix in vases 1AI-1 and 1AI-2 in which *impersonators* of a jaguar and a composite with jaguar head are depicted—one with death spots, the other with a scarf (Quirarte 1976: Pls. 1 and 2).

According to J. E. S. Thompson (1960:82), Ix represents the jaguar god and is also the fourteenth day in the Maya calendar. This corresponds to *ocelotl* 'jaguar' of the Mexican plateau.

There is a jaguar figure in vase 1BI-1 (Fig. 8-3) not included in the review of glyph columns. The three glyphs in front of the jaguar are drawn in a very cursory manner and are presently not clear enough to warrant a reading. It is possible that T-539 may have been intended in column A3, although it is unlikely that T-524 (Ix) was included, since this too may be an impersonator of the jaguar god.

The presence of T-524 (Ix) in the texts verifies that the figure represented is the jaguar god of the underworld. Its absence indicates that we are dealing with an impersonator.

Glyphs T-539 and T-609, a possible variant of it, are usually found in the glyphic columns associated with the procession figures. The main sign of T-539 is a combination of *ahau* 'lord' and a jaguar pelt bundle. The reference to *ahau* is not found in T-609. This glyph is associated with the jaguars (shown on vases 1AI-4 and 5) who do not wear the *ahau* on the head (see Table 8-2). In vase 1AI-4 the jaguar enveloped by flames has been divested of its tail by the serpent–saurian death figure in front of it (Fig. 8-4). It wears the tail and points to glyph a4, which precedes another reference to T-609. On vase 1AI-5 the seated jaguar is shown with its jaws open (Fig. 8-5). The small commalike elements emanating from its jaws make it look as if it is howling or lamenting. The jaguar in flames on vase 1AI-8 (Fig. 8-8, position 2) still has its tail, but, unlike the 1AI-4 jaguar, it has T-539 associated with it. In addition, it has T-563, the fire glyph, associated with it.

Kelley (1962*b*: Pl. XVII) reads T-539 as a reference to the equinox. R. E. W. Adams (1977) interprets this glyph as a reference to a broad Jaguar/Lord Lineage/Ruler system operating in the Southern Maya Lowlands during the Late Classic period.

Thompson (1960:74, 212) places T-609 in the Lunar Series as Glyph F. A variant of this is the knot motif, an affix (T-60) which, when used as a main sign, stands for Glyph F. This is an interesting combination, since the water-lily jaguar of the underworld often wears an elaborately tied scarf around the neck. This may in turn stand for the serpent (see Fig. 8-10).

As so often happens in Mesoamerican art, what is represented is a specific state of being rather than a figure's unchanging identity and position in space and time. Thus motifs as well as glyphs demonstrate and signal a constantly changing state and location for deities and supernaturals which is difficult to pin down.[9]

In any case, the jaguar pelt bundle (T-609) undoubtedly refers to rulership. These bundles are often shown as actual cushions used by a ruler on a throne for sitting or as a backing. Thrones are shown in Maya art with jaguar skins over them or carved in the form of a jaguar.

Thus, T-609 refers to the mat or throne, the symbol of authority in the Maya area. According to Thompson (1960:107) the mat, or Pop, "has a secondary meaning of chief in some Maya languages or dialects."

The similarity of contexts in which T-539 and T-609 appear indicates that these two glyphs may have very similar meanings. They may, in fact, be variations of the same glyph. For the moment we can say that T-609 refers to rulership and T-539 to a possible Lord-Ruler system similar to that suggested by Adams, a "Lord/Jaguar Lineage."

DEATH FIGURES AND DEATH COLLARS

The death figures demonstrate all of the usual representations and signs of death in Maya art. These include skeletal figures, death eyes on various parts of the body, death collars, and the division or percentage sign. In no case do the death figures wear a scarf around the neck. Eleven death figures wear death collars in at least eight vases (they appear two and three times in some of the vases) (see Table 8-3). They occupy the first position in seven vases, the second position in three, and the third in three.

The death god appears often in these processions as a human skeleton. On occasion the skeletal figure has saurian characteristics. Sometimes the death figure is characterized by an excessively distended abdomen. This appears in at least two vases in which the more "normal" pot belly of the death figure is also shown (Fig. 8-8, positions 1 and 3; Fig. 8-7). The serpent–saurian death figure mentioned above also has a distended stomach, a water lily on its head, and a jaguar's tail, and wears a death collar (Fig. 8-5). Jaguar impersonators also wear death collars. In another example, the saurian death figure wears the deer's ear and jaguar paws on its hand and feet (Fig. 8-3).

Like the columns associated with jaguars, those next to death figures have references to T-539 and T-609 and in one case to T-524 (Ix). A review of the glyphic columns associated with death figures follows.

GLYPHIC COLUMNS ASSOCIATED WITH DEATH FIGURES

Nine death figures with glyphs depicted on six vases are discussed below.

Vase 1AI-1, Position 3: Dancing Death Impersonator
(Fig. 8-11a, Column C; Fig. 8-1)

C1	523:93	Uinal Semblant
C2	360 or 228.?	
C4	168.609:125	Ben Ich; Rulership
C5	524	Ix (Jaguar)
C6	530:130	Cauac Variant

Table 8-3. *Death Figures and Death Collars*

Vase No.; Source; Posture	Death		Other Traits	Procession Figures		Attachments			Other
	Skeletal	Saurian		No.	Position	Water Lily	Death Collar	Death Eyes	
Type 1AI									
1. Figure 8-1 Walking	X			3	3		X	X	Impersonator
2. Unpublished Dancing			Death head	3	1				Impersonator
4. Figure 8-4 Walking		X	Decorated jaguar's tail	2	1	X	X	X	Deity
6. Figure 8-7									
(a) Walking	X			3	1			X	Deity
(b) Walking	X			3	2		X	X	Deity; distended stomach
(c) Hopping	X			3	3		X	X	Deity; death banner
7. Unpublished Seated	X			3	1		X	X	Impersonator
8. Figure 8-8									
(a) Hopping	X			4	1		X		Deity; smoking
(b) Walking	X			4	3		X		Deity; distended stomach
Type 1BI									
1. Figure 8-3 Walking		X	Deer's ear; jaguar's paw	3	2		X		Impersonator
3. M. D. Coe 1973: 100–101									
(a) Standing	X			3	1		X	X	Impersonator
(b) Standing (Dancing?)	X			3	2		X		Impersonator
Type 2BI									
1. Figure 8-10 Walking	X			3 (7 total)	1		X	X	Deity

Vase 1AI-2, Position 1: Dancing Death Impersonator
(Fig. 8-11b, Column A)

A3	578	
A4	130.609	Rulership
A5	15.736	Cimi (Death)

Vase 1AI-4, Position 1: Saurian Death with Water Lily and Jaguar's Tail
(Fig. 8-4, Caption a)

A1	70.?:23	
A2	727?:125	
A4	1052	Portrait Death
A5	1.609:125	Rulership

Vase 1AI-6, Positions 1, 2, and 3: Death Figures
(Fig. 8-11d, Columns A, B, and C)

A1	112.577:125	Flint Knife Spiral
A2	539:130	Lord/Jaguar Lineage?
A3	528	Cauac
A4	556?.501?:116	Imix Title? (R. E. W. Adams)
B1	16.577:125	Spiral
B2	539:130	Lord/Jaguar Lineage?
B3	561:?	Sky
B4	1041?	Death?
C1	?.?	Portrait; personal name? (R. E. W. Adams)
C2	130.577:125	Spiral
C3	130.539:125	Lord/Jaguar Lineage?
C4	1000?:168	Portrait?–Ben Ich

Vase 1AI-8, Positions 1 and 3: Death Figures
(Fig. 8-8, Columns A and C)

A1	125.?	Portrait
A2	?.577:125	Spiral
A3	3?.539:125:126	Lord/Jaguar Lineage?
C1	16.?:?	
C2	?.577:125	Spiral
C3	561:23	Sky
C4	758?	

Vase 2BI-1, Position 1: Death God
(Fig. 8-10, Caption a)

A1	?.5?:?	Ben? = main sign (R. E. W. Adams)
B1	?.528?	
C1	1 or 11.539	Lord/Jaguar Lineage?
D1	142.548:141	Tun

There are clearly several death gods represented in the processions. The hopping death god with a "normal" pot belly is shown on Vase 1AI-6 in the third position, and in first position on vase 1AI-8 (Fig. 8-8). In each case, it is accompanied by another death god with unusually distended abdomen (Fig. 8-7 and Fig. 8-8, Position 3). The "normal" death god has basically the same first three glyphs associated with it on vases 1AI-6 (Fig. 8-11d, Column C) and 1AI-8 (Fig. 8-8, Column A). In the former, there is a fourth glyph, a possible reference to an individual.

The companion "obese" death gods have references to sky in both vases (Fig. 8-11d, Column B, and Fig. 8-8, Column C) in third positions, followed by T-1041, a death (?) glyph, on vase 1AI-6 and T-758 (?) on vase 1AI-8.

The first glyph in each column differs in almost every case. The one recurring glyph is T-539 in almost all columns associated with straight rather than composite death gods. The references to T-609 in vases 1AI-1, 1AI-2, and 1AI-4 coincide with a similar one found in relation to jaguars. Whenever *impersonators* (vase 1AI-2) or composite death figures (vase 1AI-4) are shown, the glyph is T-609. The Lords of the Underworld as holders of the mat are the actual deities and supernaturals depicted on the vases. Impersonators refer to the mat itself. *Ahau* is not included in their attire nor in the glyphs associated with them.

Glyphs T-539 and T-609 may refer to the rite of passage through the underworld by the deceased. T-609, associated with impersonators, may signal the ruler's death before his passage through that nether world. And once the ritual is initiated, all references to *ahau* or deities of the underworld may indicate that such passage is in progress or completed.

DEER, MONKEYS, COMPOSITE CREATURES, AND VOLUMINOUS SCARVES

Monkeys and deer sometimes appear as straight representations. At other times they comprise the parts of a composite figure. Often the monkey will have the deer's antlers and ear; on other occasions the deer will have a monkey's head and tail. Both figures or composites of them often wear scarves. They appear in ten of the sixteen Lowland Maya vases (see Table 8-4). In four of these they wear scarves around the neck. Of three vases with processions of two figures, they occupy the first position in one, the second position in two. Of five vases with processions of three figures, they occupy first position in one, second position in three, and third position in one. A deer wears a death collar. This is of course an impersonator, which may account for the exception. Monkeys or composites of these do not wear death collars.

It is unclear what role monkeys and deer play in these scenes. Even more perplexing is their appearance as composite figures with attributes of one or the other. The key may be found by studying the use of the scarf, which is probably worn by impersonators of these

Table 8-4. *Deers, Monkeys, and Composite Figures*

Vase No.; Source; Posture	Deer				Monkey			Procession Figures		Attachments			Other
	Body	Head	Ear	Antler	Body	Head	Tail	No.	Position	Scarf	Death Eyes	Death Collar	
Type 1AI													
1. Unpublished Walking	X	X	X	X				3	2			X	Bearded impersonator; flowers in mouth and attached to tail
3. Figure 8-2 Crouching	X	X	X	X				2	2	X			Impersonator
5. Figure 8-6 Seated	X		X	X				2	2	X			Deity; holds cacao pod in right hand; water lily on end of scarf
7. Unpublished Standing	X	X	X	X			X	3	2				Impersonator
Type 1AII													
1. Unpublished Walking		X	X		X		X	3	2				Impersonator
Type 1BI													
1. Figure 8-3 Walking			X	X	X	X	X	3	3	X			Impersonator?
2. Figure 8-9 Dancing				X?	X	X	X	2	1	X	X	X?	Deity
Type 1BII													
1. Unpublished													
(a) Playing drum	X	X	X					3	2				Supernatural; water lily on tail
(b) Dancing					X	X	X	3	1				Supernatural
Type 1BI													
2. Figure 8-9 Avian				X?				2	2		X		Deity; serpent scarf
4. Gann 1918													
(a) Walking							X	2	1	X			Impersonator? (saurian)
(b) Walking							X	2	2	X			Impersonator? (saurian)
Type 2BI													
1. Figure 8-10			X	X	X (as tail)			3 (7 total)	3				Deity (has serpent body)

creatures in lieu of a serpent wrapped around the neck. Serpents with associated death eyes appear in various scenes worn by the jaguar as the night sun or announcer of the deceased (Fig. 8-10, Position 2), and by another procession figure with avian traits (Fig. 8-9, Position 2). In both cases the creatures wearing the serpents in this fashion also have the *ahau* unit attached to the back of the head. The *ahau*, as already noted, refers to the wearer as a lord of that abode.

The voluminous scarf worn by jaguars, deer, and monkeys stands for the serpent (Figs. 8-2, 8-3, and 8-4). This is clearly seen in the depictions of a jaguar wearing a serpent in one vase (Fig. 8-10, Position 2) and a scarf in several others (e.g., Fig. 8-2, Position 1, and Fig. 8-3, Position 1). In the first example (Fig. 8-10, Position 2), the water-lily jaguar wears an actual serpent around its neck with head and tail extending in opposite directions and under the jaguar's arms. In one

FIGURE 8–12. Composite figures with serpent, deer, and monkey traits taken from vases illustrated above: (a) from 2BI–1 (Fig. 8–10), (b) and (c) from 1BI–1 (Fig. 8–3). Drawings by Persis Clarkson and Barbara Van Heusen, Foundation of Latin American Anthropological Research; illustration provided courtesy of the director, Nicholas M. Hellmuth.

of the others (Fig. 8-3, Position 1), the fringe of the scarf could conceivably be a reference to the underside of the serpent's body.

The scarf may identify the wearer as an impersonator traveling through an imagined underworld. This is true for the water-lily jaguars, deer, monkeys, and composites of the latter two.

In another confusing context the serpent itself becomes the central motif to which the attributes of the deer and monkey are added. A human head emerges from the open jaws of the serpent (Fig. 8-10, Position 3). Is this a shorthand reference to the normal procession in which the jaguar, serpent, deer, and monkey play a part?

Obviously the deer can be evoked by the inclusion of the antlers and ear. M. D. Coe (1973:126) suggests that the deer's antlers are selected for their bonelike appearance. But what about the ear? The inner markings on the deer's ears worn by three composite creatures on vases 1BI-1 and 2BI-1 differ in each case (Fig. 8-12a, b, and c). The serpent with deer antlers and monkey head tail (Fig. 8-12a) has a single query sign. This sign also appears on the ears of a deer playing an upright drum on Vase 1BII-1 (see Table 8-4). The saurian death figure with jaguar paws (Fig. 8-12b), has a leaflike ear. The monkey with deer's antlers (Fig. 8-12c) has an ear with a series of dots running the length of it. Both the query sign and the dots are probably elements of Caban (Earth).

Reference to the monkey on the serpent composite figure is made by including the head and tail. All the information we have on the monkey as artisan and its licentiousness does not seem to apply here.

GLYPHIC COLUMNS ASSOCIATED WITH DEER,
MONKEYS, AND COMPOSITES

Three figures with glyphs depicted on three vases are discussed below.

Vase 1AI-1, Position 2: Deer Impersonator
(Fig. 8-11a, Column B)

B1	325.537 or 538	Xipe
B2	534	Inverted Ahau
B3	755	Monkey
B4	128.609.125	Rulership
B5	529	Cauac Variant
B6	1078:?	Portrait?

Vase 1AI-5, Position 2: Deer with Monkey Head
(Fig. 8-11c, Column B)

B1	666	
B2	671	Manik (Deer)
B3	534	Inverted Ahau
B4	755	Monkey?
B5	1.539 or 609	Lord/Jaguar Lineage? or Rulership

Vase 2BI-1, Position 3: Serpent with Deer and Monkey Traits
(Fig. 8-10, Caption e)

G1	?	
G2	168.?:23	Portrait
G3	1.539	Lord/Jaguar Lineage?
G4	62.?	
G5	168:741?:130	Xul Emblem Glyph?
		(R. E. W. Adams)

T-609 rather than T-539 is associated with the deer impersonator
in vase 1AI-1 (Fig. 8-11a, B4), as in all previous examples of impersonators reviewed above. T-539 may be intended in vase 1AI-5 (Fig.
8-11c, B5) since T-524 (Fig. 8-11c, A3) indicates that the seated jaguar
is a deity. T-539 is clearly intended in vase 2BI-1 (Fig. 8-10, Caption e),
where an actual deity or supernatural is represented.

It is interesting to note that T-534 (inverted *ahau*) is included in
the columns associated with two deer composite figures bearing monkey traits on vases 1AI-1 and 1AI-5. The glyph following in each case
is T-755 (monkey).

SUMMARY

Impersonators as well as deities and supernaturals participate in the
processions through an imagined underworld or the interior of the
earth itself. Although there is no indication of place in the paintings,
the death figures and other signs of death demonstrate that the underworld or an evocation of it is intended.

All participants move from right to left, as is appropriate for such
a journey in the paintings. The direction of the procession reflects
the manner in which the Maya visualized the journey through the
underworld. The Maya saw the procession in terms of their position
facing south, with the east to the left, west on the right, and north
behind them. Consequently, at night the sun journeyed through the
underworld as the night sun by moving from right to left to emerge
anew in the morning as the sun in the east.

Evidently, the number of participants has no significance as far as
figures involved are concerned. No two or three participants are ever
the same. A jaguar does not always follow death, and so forth. The
impersonators and deities must be determined by the particular journey depicted. There were obviously several different types of processions in which deities and supernaturals were involved.

The water-lily jaguar as a god of the underworld plays an important
role in these processions. It is one of the lords of that region. It leads
the procession in a number of cases. In two instances the jaguar is
enveloped by flame.[10] At no time do these jaguars wear actual signs
of death.

Jaguar impersonators can wear the *ahau* unit and the water lily,
assuming that the absence of T-524 (Ix) in the glyphic columns associated with them designates them as such. As impersonators, these

figures can also wear death collars. The actual water-lily jaguar as a Lord of the Underworld—as the night sun—does not wear a death collar. It wears a serpent tied around its neck and possibly the voluminous scarf. It is not entirely clear whether the scarf is simply a substitute for the serpent or whether it stands by itself. In any event it identifies the wearers (jaguars, deer, monkeys, and composites of these) as travelers through the underworld.

Death figures abound. Actual death gods lead processions in three cases. When there is only one death figure in a procession, it is relegated to the third position in only one case. It may be that as an impersonator this figure naturally occupies this position in the procession.

There are two saurian death figures. Both wear other attributes. One (Fig. 8-4, Position 1), leading a jaguar in flames, has a water lily and the jaguar's tail. The other (Fig. 8-3, Position 2) follows a regular jaguar but wears jaguar paws on hands and feet and a deer's ear.

Only the death god always moves through the underworld without a scarf. It wears a death collar but is not one of the Lords of the Underworld. Nonetheless, like all the gods of that region it has T-539 (Lord/Jaguar Lineage?) associated with it. T-609, as has been noted, is associated with impersonators.

Deer, monkeys, and composites of the two usually follow the jaguar or death gods when these are included in the procession. A notable exception is the procession headed by a monkey balancing on the balls of its feet and wearing deer antlers (?) (Fig. 8-9, Position 1). It in turn is followed by a composite creature with avian beak topped by a decorated *ahau* unit. It wears a serpent tied around its neck.

Deer and monkeys generally do not wear death collars. They usually wear scarves.

Those specifically designated as Lords of the Underworld by the *ahau* unit are the water-lily jaguar, a composite avian creature, and the earth monster. Death figures are simply designated by their configuration and the paraphernalia of death. The deer, monkeys, and composites are supernaturals rather than deities.[11]

The glyphic columns refer to some of the procession deities (T-736, *cimi* 'death', and T-524, *ix* 'jaguar'); supernaturals (T671, *manik* 'deer', and T-755, 'monkey'); to rulership (T-609), and a possible Lord/Jaguar Lineage Ruler (T-539).[12]

A study of the other vases with underworld processions will allow a more precise picture of the participants and the many variations each can take as it "borrows" attributes from the others. For instance, it is still unclear whether the death figures with jaguar mittens (and a tail in one case) are simply death figures or whether they are, in fact, "dead" jaguars after immolation (the two jaguar/flame vases). In other words, should each figure be identified as a unique full-fledged participant in the processions with no relation to the others, or is it possible that some of the figures are presented more than once in a single image but in a changed state—before and after, so to speak?

Another question has to do with the identification of specific participants such as the jaguars and death figures. How many and which ones are to be considered discrete entities? Also, why are some figures presented as leaders in some of the processions and as followers in others? Why are some immolated? These are a few of the questions that remain unanswered.

A thorough analysis of the other vases will undoubtedly help answer these and other questions regarding the participants and the nature and meaning of the processions.

ACKNOWLEDGMENTS

I am indebted to Nicholas Hellmuth and his associates Persis Clarkson and Barbara Van Heusen, staff artists for F.L.A.A.R., for supplying me with photographs, slides, and copies of the rollout drawings. N. Hellmuth, P. Clarkson, R. E. W. Adams, Clemency Coggins, and David Kelley reviewed the first draft of this paper. Their many comments concerning the text and the reading of the glyphic materials in particular are greatly appreciated.

A portion of this paper dealing with the water-lily jaguar in the underworld processions was published in *New Mexico Studies in the Fine Arts* (Quirarte 1976a).

APPENDIX 1

Vase 2BI-1: Decapitation Scene (Fig. 8-10)

Captions a, d, and e, associated with the death god, water-lily jaguar god, and composite god have already been discussed in the text. Only captions c, f, g, and b are included here.

Caption c (associated with figure 2)

E1	511?:102	Muluc?
E2	?.521:102	Uinal
E3	1.539?:?	Lord/Jaguar Lineage?
E4	529	Cauac Variant

Caption f (associated with figure 6)

H1	58.501:?	
H2	542a.181?	Ahau Semblant
H3	111?.586a:102	Hatched Dot
H4	1.539:?	Lord/Jaguar Lineage?
H5	111:?	

Caption g (associated with figure 5)

I1	2.586:	Hatched Dot
J1	?.539:	Lord/Jaguar Lineage?
J2	2.?:?	
J3	758.528	

Caption b (associated with figure 7)

A1	501:	Imix
B1	23?.521:102	Uinal
B2	1.539	Lord/Jaguar Lineage?
B3	?.579	
B4	?	Portrait

NOTES

An excerpt from this essay has been previously published in *New Mexico Studies in the Fine Arts*, copyright The Regents of the University of New Mexico. Reprinted by permission.

1. Nicholas Hellmuth reproduces a vase with an Underworld scene discussed in this paper in *Archaeology* 29, no.1 (January 1976): 4.

2. Nicholas Hellmuth (correspondence) adds fourteen other vases with death and/or sacrifice by decapitation scenes to the fifteen included in this study. While many of these vases have representations of deities and supernaturals involved in underworld scenes of sacrifice by decapitation, they do not all fit into one single thematic classification. An attempt is made here to deal with only those figures involved in the single-file procession scenes. Some procession scenes have references to decapitation. Others do not.

3. Exceptions are the Chama style vases exemplified by the Dieseldorff vase (1926, vol. 1: Pl. 22). The same participants with assigned positions appear in all three known vases. Highland Maya vases are not included in this study.

4. Kidder (1946:159) used the ratio of vessel height to diameter to classify the vessels found in Kaminaljuyu according to size as tall, medium, and squat. I have used the same procedure (Quirarte 1973) to discuss the difference between the visual surfaces used by Teotihuacan and Maya painters. The format thus obtained, whether vertical (Maya) or horizontal (Teotihuacan), affected the manner in which the painters dealt with the task of creating images.

5. The position of each figure within the procession is determined by the occurrence of the initial sign found in the rim glyph bands discussed by Michael Coe (1973). His interpretation of the initial glyph as the determinant of the figural sequence is followed here. The meaning or decipherment of the glyph bands is not included in this study. Only the glyph columns associated with each figure are discussed.

6. The vase is reproduced in color in a Japanese catalogue of a Maya Art Exhibition (*Tesoros de Guatemala*, 1974: Pl. CN3).

7. R. E. W. Adams (personal communication) calls my attention to the St. Andrews cross—a sky element—inside the vessel.

8. Persis Clarkson (correspondence) prefers to identify this main sign as T-609 due to the indication of "upholstery tabs." She adds

further that "The reference to Balam is clear and important regardless of identification."

9. In Maya art each figure, whether human or supernatural, retains its spatial and configurational integrity. It never loses its essential identifying features. Whenever part of a figure is attached to another, it is done in patchwork fashion. One unit does not fuse into the other. It retains its identity no matter how minuscule its role may be in its new context. Attributes are thus added figuratively. The spatial envelope surrounding each figure is equally inviolable. There is always enough negative space between the positives represented by the figures themselves to allow easy identification. The Maya artist found it essential to allow each of the narrative units the necessary negative space to function in a visual and thematic fashion. Each carries part of the narrative and is to be considered in relation to the entire scene. While it stands alone as an image, it still must function with other equally semiautonomous images.

10. Nicholas Hellmuth (correspondence) has brought my attention to another unpublished vase in which a jaguar is enveloped by flames.

11. Although the deer, monkeys, and composites of these are undoubtedly related to the gods of the underworld, their identities as gods are not readily apparent. They are certainly not given the status of Lords of the Underworld. I have therefore preferred to designate those not so identified with the decorated *ahau* unit as supernaturals.

12. David Kelley (personal communication) reads T-609 as an accession clause such as "so and so was seated on the throne," and T-539 and T-609 superimposed on *ahau*.

9

A Sequence for Palenque Painting Techniques
by Merle Greene Robertson

There was a time[1] in Palenque's illustrious history when the city was ablaze with brilliant color—palaces and temples all painted a deep dark red, roofs and roofcombs spectacularly adorned with rulers seated on thrones intermingling with gods and serpents—all in reds, blues, and yellows (Plates 9-1 and 9-2). Stucco sculptured piers framing doorways in almost all buildings were likewise dramatic in their shades of red, blue, and yellow.[2]

In the terminal stage of Palenque's building boom, however (just before the collapse), this dazzling display of color was painted over with red in almost every instance. As we shall see, Palenque in Late Classic times was a victim of fads and preferences as to size, detail, and color, as well as artistic subject matter and the manner of treating it. Methods of construction changed also.[3] Whether these changes were due to preferences of kings or rather to a pan-Maya view will not be known until a study has been made of color and painting techniques at other sites over a wide area. It will be shown however, that, at least at Palenque during the Late Classic, color became part of the iconographic language.

Painting practices at Palenque followed a definite sequence: (1) plain painted walls; (2) isolated motif painting on white walls; (3) mural painted walls; (4) stucco sculptured "murals," which I shall refer to in this essay as Narrative Sculpture; (5) painted stucco sculpture on weight-bearing rectangular exterior columns, which changed considerably from Otolum-Murcielagos times to Balunte, that is from the early seventh century until the collapse, somewhere between A.D. 615 and 830 (Rands 1974:35), a period of a little over two hundred years.

Background painting in early Otolum, during the reign of Pacal,[4] was a deep dark red, as evidenced by the remaining paint on the Olvidado, Houses B, C, and E of the Palace, and on the walls of the North Group buildings. Lighter red-pink became more popular during the reign of the following two rulers (A.D. 683–719 [Mathews and Schele 1974]), as can be seen on the piers of the Inscriptions Temple and Houses A and D of the Palace. Finally, at the end of Palenque's period of powerful ruling dynasties, every building, including roof and roofcombs and almost all of the stucco sculpture, was painted over in red, this time a return to the early deep dark red.

ISOLATED MOTIF WALL PAINTING

On the western face of House E there are glyphic motifs which at one time covered most of the exterior of this building. Colors on these include blue, blue-green, yellow, orange, black, and white. Palenque wall painting apparently followed the trend of Teotihuacan, of having outlines divide areas of color, as Miller (1973:174) brings out. Although Teotihuacan outlines are "usually red and, rarely, black" (Miller 1973: 174), Palenque outlines have been more evenly distributed between red and black. The inclusion of white and black in the palette of Palenque wall painting is another Teotihuacan trait, as evidenced by the Mythological Animals Mural of Zone 4, Platform 1 (Miller 1973: 71–72). Palenque House E exterior wall painting motifs do however recall more characteristically the Tetitla Mural 1 fragment shown in Miller's *Mural Painting of Teotihuacan* (1973: Fig. 243). On the House E exterior motifs, the background white stucco wall is used as the ground for the painting, a practice which is not typical of Teotihuacan painting, as Miller (1972:4) points out in referring to the Tetitla Room 7 painting, where the bare stucco is used as the white of the bivalve shells. He feels that this is not typical of Teotihuacan but more in keeping with Maya characteristics. It is quite possible that the use of a white background wall and isolated motif painting was a characteristic of Palenque or some other lowland area which spread to the Mexican Highlands (Teotihuacan and elsewhere) rather than one which originated in the Mexican Highlands and was carried to Palenque. A typical method of painting these glyphic motifs would be as in Figure 9-1. Here, against a white wall background, a quatrefoil cartouche is outlined in black. The second cartouche has two outlines, both in black. Originally these two outlines were blue, as can be seen in many places where the underline still shows. As is noted on the figure, the colors consisted of pink, deep red-orange, light red, and Maya blue.

On the Bonampak Murals (Ruppert et al. 1955) white is used as a color in many areas, such as headdresses, fringe, neck pieces, cloaks, dresses, and parts of the printed or woven design of cloth. The Bonampak painting techniques also followed the Teotihuacan practice, as did Palenque, of using an outline around figures and motifs.

In the Tower at Palenque, all that remains of painting is the large Venus sign on the southern side of the inner stairs. The walls were all painted red at one time, and there are remnants of this red paint on every wall.

MURAL PAINTED WALLS

Remaining evidence of mural painted walls is not abundant at Palenque, although at one time certainly many early buildings (especially those of the Palace) were decorated in this manner. Probably the most brilliant use of transparent paints on mural painted walls is on the northern end of the western corridor of House E (Plate 9-3). Here, cursively outlined in very dark red, one can see the remains of a huge painting depicting a splendid parrot. This painting extends from floor to ceiling on the western wall and extends around the corner onto the northern wall, where the doorway steps up to the eastern court. Colors include reds, blues, greens, yellows, and, by overlaying of pigments, purple and orange. Although not a true fresco, this wall paint-

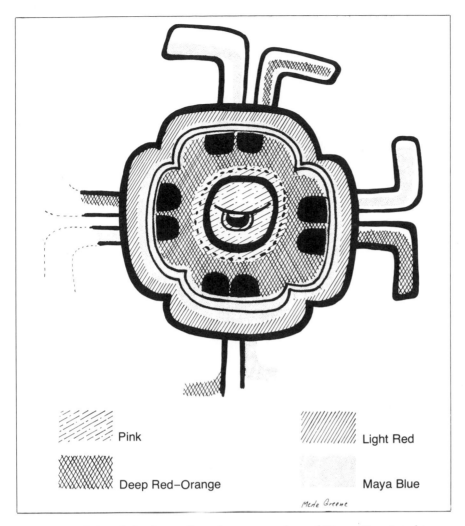

Pink

Light Red

Deep Red–Orange

Maya Blue

Mede Greene

FIGURE 9–1. Painted glyph motif on the western face of House E, painted in Teotihuacan style.

ing must surely have been painted on dampened plaster for the paint to still be so firmly adhered to the wall and for the color to have remained so pure even though the coats of paint were extremely thin. The thin, watered-down pigment made possible the transparent purples and oranges in numerous shades and intensities. The brush marks are clearly visible today, making it evident that the paint was freely applied with clear sweeping strokes of a brush which was probably either of turkey or bird feathers. One area (145 centimeters from the floor on the west wall) indicates that the first paint was a vivid light blue, and on top of this are clear brush strokes of red, creating purple. To the left of this blue area is a large sweep of feathers or circular element in which yellow ochre was the background color. On top of the yellow, circular lines were painted in red. The same procedure was followed in the upper portion of the painting. Outer areas are outlined in thick brush strokes one-half centimeter in width in deep red. This painting has been either retouched or painted over many times.

In one area on the northeastern wall corner, the sequence of painting follows thus: first the white wall, then yellow–red–yellow–blue–yellow–blue–red, with a coat of white having been applied before each new color coat. In another area on the western wall, the painting sequence proceeded from white to red–blue–yellow, again with white having been applied before each color coat. This practice of applying a coat of fresh white paint on top of every existing color before a different color was applied or before repainting in the same color was to be the painting practice throughout Palenque's history and was to be practiced on stucco sculpture as well. All of the pigment in wall painting however, is much thinner and more transparent than that on painted stucco sculpture.

The uppermost remains of another magnificent mural are on the northeastern wall of this same room (Plate 9-4). The profile face of a Maya lord faces south. He wears an intricate headdress containing a gaping-mouth god and a fantastic fish outlined in scrolls. Hieroglyphic inscriptions continue across the top of this wall just below the vault spring. These glyphs are all in cursive black lines. The background of this mural is a bright red-orange. Much vivid blue remains on the headdress elements, the god, and the little fish. All elements of the painting are outlined in black, including the figure's face.

Another notable mural wall painting is in the southwestern corridor of House C. Considerable paint can be seen today on this Hand Extending Bowl Painting, although coatings of lime obscured most all of the mural. A figure's delicately drawn hand with long fingernails (done in the manner of the Tancah wall paintings) is holding out an offering in a beautifully shaped shallow bowl of vivid transparent Maya blue. Other colors in this painting include (besides numerous shades of blue) transparent reds, yellows, and outlines of black, as well as vacant areas of white. Remaining elements of this early wall painting can be seen at floor level, although most of this section is covered over with a sculptured skybank of a Narrative Sculpture. Black glyphic inscriptions are at the upper portion of this wall painting.

In the southwestern room of House B there is some evidence of a mural having been painted on the wall at one time, but for only small areas of painted surface; all that remains on the wall now is a portion of the large Narrative Sculpture.

Perhaps, at the termination of Teotihuacan influence at Palenque, wall painting was no longer in vogue. Gifted Palenqueño artists turned their talents to stucco sculptured scenes which were laid directly on top of existing mural painted walls. The beauty of these sculptured scenes, although evidenced by only scant remains, attests to the expertise of Palenqueño artists, to a skill which later enabled them to create the finest stucco sculpture in all Pre-Columbian America. Painting of all stucco sculpture at Palenque was somewhat different than the painting of wall murals. Whereas the palette for Palenque mural painting included red, red-pink, blues, greens, yellow, orange, purple, and black and white, stucco sculpture was limited to red, red-pink, blues and yellow in all instances. There is no place where any other color was used at Palenque.

NARRATIVE SCULPTURE

The Narrative Sculpture which overlays the previously mentioned Hand Extending Bowl Painting (on the southwestern corridor of House C) portrays a life-size figure on the northern end of the wall. Remnants of an immense headdress of vivid Maya blue feathers extend across the uppermost section. Below the row of feathers which sweep across the top is a row of horizontally laid feathers which end abruptly as they meet with a large 45° backframe. Although it is the only example of a backframe in a headdress at Palenque, headdress backframes are known to have existed in other areas and are portrayed on stone monuments covered with headdress paraphernalia. A notable one is portrayed on Yaxha Stela 31, which supports what is probably a light-weight three-dimensional scene intended to portray a myth, a sacred story being enacted on the towering headdress (Greene et al. 1972:344).

Enormous headdresses which would have required light-weight wooden or wicker frames were the style throughout much of the Lowlands. Some however, appear to have necessitated right-angle frames extending to the rear of the headdress proper in order to bear the weight of the rear superstructure. These were often balanced by a frame held taut by the chin strap. In this category might be listed Yaxha Stela 6, Seibal Stelae 8, 9, 11, and 14, Dos Pilas Stelae 1 and 17, and Bonampak Stela 2 (Greene et al. 1972: Pls. 162, 107, 108, 110, 112, 90, 93, and 69). Also we might include Machaquila Stelae 2, 3, 5, 7, and 8 (I. Graham 1967: Figs. 44, 49, 53, 57, and 59) and Naranjo Stelae 6, 7, 8, 13, and 14 (I. Graham 1975).

In the House C stucco Narrative Sculpture it is difficult to tell just what the vertical portion of the backframe was intended to represent. However, there are six depressed oval areas running up the vertical piece. Each of these ovals was first painted red and then painted over in yellow. This could have been meant to represent a serpent. The serpent bars worn as chin straps on the Inscriptions Tomb stucco figures (Fig. 9-2) look very much like the bottom bar of the House C backframe. The unique feature about the House C Narrative Sculpture is the portrayal of a human figure standing within the headdress backframe.

This is the only known example of a realistic standing figure which is taking part in some kind of action within a headdress. This small (forty centimeters tall) figure is standing in profile position on the angle backframe (Fig. 9-3). The personage is wearing a knee-length gown, large headdress, and a three-knotted element on the upper arm. He holds an umbrella, with ribbons attached to the top, in front of him. A diagonal object supported by a kneeling dwarf can be seen just below the umbrella handle. Gods and animals are well known as being parts of headdresses, but small figures are very rare. They

FIGURE 9–2. The Inscriptions Tomb, Stucco 7, figure wears a chin strap similar to that worn by the small figure on the House C Narrative Sculpture.

FIGURE 9–3. Small figures are rare in Maya sculpture. This one is standing in a headdress back-frame, holding an umbrella in front of him.

appear on the Bonampak Stela 2 in the form of a bird-mask manikin figure (Greene et al. 1972: Pl. 69), as a little gaping-mouth god and a baby jaguar on the Dos Pilas Stela 17 (Greene et al. 1972: Pl. 93), and on the Yaxha Stela 31 in the form of a nonhuman jester and cavorting little jaguar who intermingle with birds, flowers, serpents, and flamboyant scrolls atop a skyband in the headdress superstructure (Greene et al. 1972:164).

Although there is no remaining paint on the small figure in the House C headdress, there is considerable bright blue in the life-size principal figure's headdress which sweeps above the miniature personage standing in the backframe. On the horizontally laid feathers, which end abruptly at the backframe, there are remnants of red paint, but no blue remains.

The stucco sculptured skyband border which overlays the wall painting and is a part of the Narrative Sculpture extends along the base of the wall for its entire length. This skyband is nineteen centimeters in height, including borders. The background, as with all skybands, is a deep red with blue vertical separators between the sky segments. The twenty-three-centimeter sector of the skyband which Tozzer (1910: Pl. 13) refers to as a crocodile was originally blue, but in the many repaintings it is predominantly red that remains. The floor in this room dips down to the eastern side, as, in the many replastering jobs given the floor, each time the workers must have been instructed not to run into the sculptured skyband surface, or perhaps not to cover the painted mural which was on the wall earlier.

Another Narrative Sculpture was on the south-facing wall of the southwest room of House B. Here one can see the remains of a full-size sculptured figure which covers a previous mural painted wall (Fig. 9-4). All that remains of the wall painting are small patches of paint in blue and red, and there is no evidence as to the subject matter. This mural was covered over with a coat of white lime plaster, and the new Narrative Sculpture was then scratched into the still damp plaster. The entire outline of the figure, plus facial features such as eyes, lip, nose and nostrils, fingernails, earlobes, details of feathers (even the center lines), folds in cloth, knots and folds of cloth in the headpiece, were scratched in with a fine instrument, conceivably a pointed bone. On top of the scratched cartoon, the sculptor formed the narrative scene in stucco. Portions of the vivid Maya blue feathers which sweep to the rear of the figure's head attest to the precision of the sculptors in adhering to the outline. I suggest that the artist had a cartoon (probably on bark paper) and, in sketching the scene on the wall, could look at the paper and back to the detailed wall sketch to see if the proportions and effect were going to be as desired. Otherwise there would have been no need to include all of the details in the damp plaster. The free-flowing lines of the cartoon indicate that the design was drawn quickly and in an unlabored way, and that the artist was skilled in knowledge of anatomy and in the ability to draw accurately.

Bright blue feathers of the headdress are all that remains of the stucco sculpture on the western side of the wall space. Scant remains

FIGURE 9–4. A cartoon which included face, eyes, headdress, and feathers was scratched in plaster before the sculpture was started.

of color and stucco and a few scratched-in lines outlining a figure are all that is left on the eastern side to indicate that a figure did exist at one time there also. Considerable amounts of deep stucco sculpture remain however on the mask at the lower center portion of the wall. Abundant blue and red paint are still on the surface of this high (almost three-dimensional) relief of a mask, as well as in the deeply incised lines of the eyes and scrolls.

I would not classify the "fret" motif in the eastern room on this same building (House B [Maudslay IV Plate 18]) (which adjoins, but is not connected with the western room) with the Narrative Sculpture. This room is completely taken over by a powerful symbol of religious significance which we do not understand. The main geometric fret is a deep red, outlined in yellow. The curving ribbons of crossed bands and circular elements are blue with deep red background. The positive space of the Ik sign on the west is blue outlined in red, while the negative Ik on the east is only outlined in red. Positive and negative spaces such as this are seen in a number of instances at Palenque, as for example in the adjoining building, House E, the eastern room. Here positive and negative elements of the same shape and size are seen in the water flowing from the western (front) head of the saurian head of the Bicephalic Dragon (Fig. 9-5). Although there are many portions of the stucco missing in the House B southeastern room, remaining colors are vivid and include excellent examples of early red, blue, and yellow. Unfortunately the sculpture is in a much greater state of disrepair than in Maudslay's time.

PAINTED STUCCO SCULPTURE

Phase four of Palenque's painting procedure is that of painting stucco sculptured figures and gods in isolated instances on weight-bearing rectangular columns which act as pictorial displays intercepting open spaces on the exteriors of buildings. An extension of this phase would be the painting of sculptured heads of rulers, gods, and other divine motifs on substructures to buildings, roofs and roofcombs, and roofs to sanctuaries within temples. There is significant paint on all of these sculptures, especially the substructure tiers of the Palace. Although little paint remains on the western roof of the Temple of the Cross (Fig. 9-6), the blue and red paint are most important indicators that the stucco sculpture on this roof was indeed painted.

Painting of stucco sculpture, as noted, was limited in all instances to a palette of red, blue, and yellow. Although the techniques of painting stucco sculpture were different from those of wall painting, they evolved from wall painting techniques. Wall painting consisted of filling in spaces limited by outlines laid on the surface to be painted. At Teotihuacan, outlines in light red were first laid on, setting the limits for the color to be filled in, and then, after the painting was finished, full dark red border outlines were added (Miller 1973:31). On Palenque stucco sculpture painting, the joining edge of the figure or motif, where it met the flat background surface, became the outline. Stucco sculptured surfaces all rise either perpendicularly or at a decided angle from the flat background surface. This abrupt change of surface in stucco sculpture constitutes the outline. In no instance

PLATE 9–1. Reconstruction painting of the Palace from the North Group, by Merle Greene Robertson, for the Florida State Museum.

PLATE 9–2. Reconstruction painting of the Temple of the Sun, by Merle Greene Robertson, for the Florida State Museum.

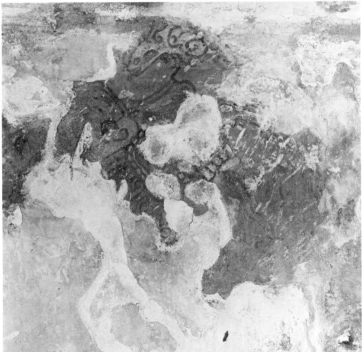

PLATE 9–3. Wall painting in House E, the Palace, western wall of the western corridor.

PLATE 9–4. Wall painting in House E, the Palace, eastern wall of the western corridor.

PLATE 9–5. The Corn God in the Eastern Subterraneo was at one time painted all in blue.

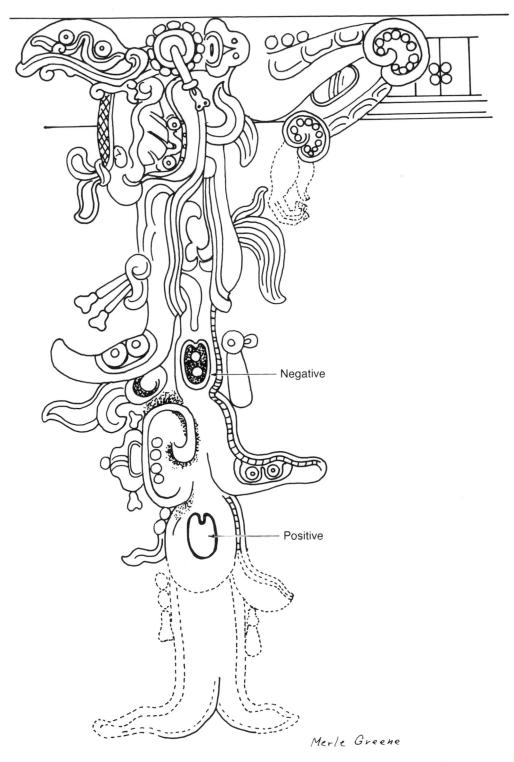

Negative

Positive

Merle Greene

FIGURE 9–5. The western head of the Bicephalic Dragon contains positive and negative motifs, one raised and the other sunken. This is the "play of opposites" in Maya art.

FIGURE 9–6. There are remnants of red and blue paint on these huge symbolic fish on the western roof of the Temple of the Cross. 1,000-mm. lens courtesy of Gillett G. Griffin, Princeton University.

is one color painted next to another color on the same surface. There is always an abrupt change of relief when color changes, although there is not necessarily a change in color when relief surfaces change.

There was no blending of colors or overlapping of colors in stucco sculpture painting as there was in mural wall painting. Paint on stucco sculpture also had a tendency to be thicker. The only time washes were used in stucco sculpture was in a thin wash coat of red or pink, brushed on a damp stucco surface to act as an adherent for the next succeeding coat of paint, or applied before final elements, such as beads, were added.

The sequence of painting color at Palenque can be seen very clearly on the recently turned pier g of the Palace House A-D.[5] All reds were painted first, followed by blue, and then yellow.

The sculptured piers at Palenque were painted over many times, and as I have gone into considerable detail concerning the techniques of construction and painting of them in a previous paper (Greene Robertson 1977), I shall only briefly touch upon them here. The background of the piers was always red or red-pink, and at the end returned to a dark red more like that of earlier times.

Human bodies, as well as hair and clothing, were also red and red-pink, but of a darker and more intense color than the background. Certain elements always remained the same color—for instance, feathers were always blue—whereas other elements, such as gods' heads and serpents, changed color with the times.

A particularly interesting procedure for both sculpting and painting came to my attention while making the reconstruction sculptures of the Palace piers.[6] The detail I am referring to concerns pier d, House D, the Tlaloc section of the loincloth of the principal figure (Fig. 9-7). The procedure for assembling and painting this motif was as follows:

1. The naked figure was formed in stucco on the pier first (greatly depressed at the groin area under discussion).

2. The unclothed figure was given a wash coat of red (Munsell 7.5R 7/4).

3. A one-millimeter layer of lime plaster was laid over this area.

4. Lines were scratched into this plaster to indicate the placement of skirt folds.

5. A six-millimeter layer of more plaster was put over the area next to the loincloth in order to fill it in. Lines were scratched into this.

6. A wash coat of thin watery pink (Munsell 10R 6/6) was applied.

7. The round beads (two centimeters in diameter) and the long beads were placed on the skirt area in the places designated for them. These beads continued directly over the area that was to be covered by the loincloth.

8. A thin coat of red (Munsell 7.5R 7/4) was painted on all of the beaded area.

9. A flat slab of stucco was placed on top of this skirt area *which already had beads on it*.

10. The loincloth was placed on top of everything.

11. The loincloth was painted with a wash coat, some quite bright (Munsell 7.5R 6/8).

12. The loincloth area was incised and modeled to include the Tlaloc motif, etc.

13. The finished loincloth was all painted blue (Munsell 7.5BG 5/4).

The structural as well as the painting procedure on all of the piers was the same and just as detailed and carefully done. It is just as though the sculptor was actually dressing the figure while modeling it. Painting sequence at Palenque seems to follow that of Teotihuacan in sculpture as well as wall painting—first red, then blue. The difference in the painting techniques is that there is no outline on Palenque sculpture, and only red, blue, and yellow were used. At Palenque, as at Teotihuacan, the wash coat is the most strongly bonded, followed by the coat immediately following it. These first coats were almost pure lime.

FRAMING DEVICES

Painted framing devices or lack of them at Palenque progressed as follows: (1) wall painting with no borders; (2) wall painting with painted outline borders; (3) stucco Narrative Sculpture either with no border, as in House B (southwest room), or with painted sculptured border, as in House C (southwest wall); (4) painted sculptured piers with no borders, as on the Olvidado and the House C piers; (5) plain red

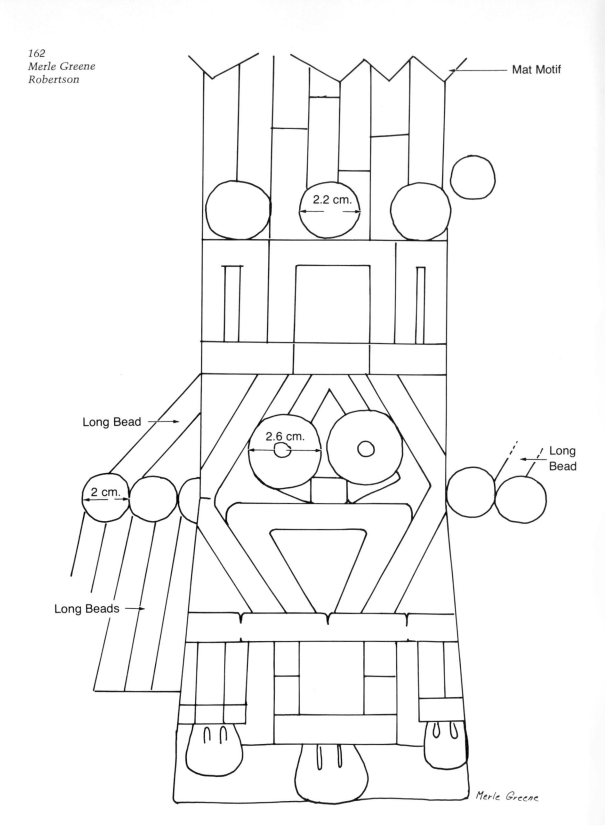

FIGURE 9–7. A Teotihuacan Tlaloc appears on the loincloth of the principal figure on pier d, House D.

borders, as on the North Group buildings; (6) isolated figures, as in the Inscriptions Tomb; (7) painted iguana-house skyband borders with the Earth Monster head acting as a pedestal upon which a central figure stands (Quirarte [1974:133] refers to these latter frames as Terrestrial and Celestial Narrative Polymorphs [as on the Inscriptions piers]); (8) painted skyband borders without pedestal heads, such as the House A piers; (9) painted repeated-motif borders, as on House D piers; and finally, (10) painted sculpture composed of iconographic elements with no line determinants, as in the case of the north Palace substructure tiers.

Skyband borders always had their sunken background painted deep red. The outline borders and the raised dividers between the sky elements seem always to have been blue until the very last stage, when they were painted over in red. The inner borders' color changed over time however, and on both piers a and c of House A, the first painting evidence is deep yellow, then blue, and third red, with a final red. On pier b the only remaining evidence of paint is red over blue. All of the balls within the skyband or at the edge were painted over in blue many times.

COMPOSITION OF STUCCO SCULPTURE

Composition of painted stucco at Palenque progressed as follows: (1) the transference of flat wall painting to Narrative Sculpture on flat walls; (2) the sculpturing of single *small* isolated figures repeated on each pier, as on the House C piers, where seated figures on thrones are all alike except for the iconographic content of their headdresses; (3) single, standing figures, centrally composed and held within defined space, as was done on the Inscriptions piers; (5) balanced triangular compositions of a standing figure flanked on both sides by a seated figure, as on House A; (6) two-figure asymmetrical compositions, such as House D piers; (7) the enlargement of iconographic components and the deletion of the full figure, as on the Palace north substructure and south substructure.

ICONOGRAPHIC CONTENT OF STUCCO SCULPTURE

The iconographic content of Palenque's painted stucco sculpture, like that of its mural painting, developed chronologically by first portraying gods and humans separately, then portraying gods and humans together, and finally portraying humans *as* gods. The development of Palenque's iconographic use of paint and the part it played in stucco sculptural compositions attests clearly to Kubler's (1969:48) statement that "iconography concerns intended meanings and their changes through time and space."

Palenque's first painted sculpture portrayed portraits of humans and divine themes separately, as in the Olvidado and Houses B, C, and E of the Palace. In the Olvidado, from the scant remaining stucco sculpture, it appears that humans were portrayed alone. All that remains on the left pier is the legs and feet of what was a frontal standing figure with widespread legs. On the right pier, all that remains is a double cartouche with one part above the other, joined as two interlocking circles. These are made much in the same manner and size as Medallion 11 of House A with a deep red painted area in the center also. I would expect that there would have been portrait heads in these also, as there were in the House A medallions.

All that remains of North Group painted stucco sculpture is the single frontal standing figure on pier a and minute remnants of stucco feathers on pier c. The background was a deep dark red, while the figure was a lighter shade of the same color.

In House B of the Palace in the two southern rooms, figures and divine elements are portrayed separately. On the Narrative Sculpture in the southwest room there is no evidence that the standing figure wore any apparel that would place it with godly beings. The immense mask in the center of the wall even accentuates the difference between gods and humans. The two figures flanking the wide entrance to this room apparently play no part with the gods either. The eastern room of this building has a symbolic emphasis, undoubtedly of divine nature. No humans are portrayed.

In House C there are gods' masks all along the entire wall in the eastern corridor, while in the western corridor there is the Narrative Sculpture, of whose total contents we know little, except concerning the full standing figure on the left. The House C piers are all sculptured with seated human figures on thrones, and although the figures all wear gods in their headdresses, the interaction of humans and gods is not as involved as it was to become.

House E likewise portrays gods and humans separately. While House E contains the accession plaque of Pacal, the subterranean chambers portray solely gods and divine themes. In the West Subterranean Vault 2, portraying the Corn God's entrance to the underworld, there are remnants of blue paint over the entire stucco sculptured vault (Plate 9-5). The sculptured Eastern Subterranean Vault, entering from House E, likewise has considerable blue paint on the iguana monster, the deer, and the Sun God over the second vault (Fig. 9-8).

In the second phase, when humans and gods were portrayed together, humans had godly attributes. The Inscriptions Tomb stucco figures all carry God K staffs and have rulership gods in their headdresses. The Inscriptions piers portray a distinct involvement between gods and humans. The human standing figures all hold divine babies in their arms, infants who are part human and part divine serpent (Greene Robertson, Scandizzo, and Scandizzo 1976:83). There is no record of any of the infants with heads intact, but I would expect that they would not have had human heads, but rather heads of God K. Even the color used on the infants is that of the serpent—blue for their bodies and red for the serpent scales on their legs.

Although the Cross Group stucco piers have little remaining sculptured stucco, the stone tablets within, the sanctuary roofs, and the roofs to the temples all attest to the intermingling of the lives of gods and humans. The ruler seated on the throne on the east roof of the

FIGURE 9–8. The Eastern Subterranean Vaults were once mainly blue.

Temple of the Sun has a serpent emerging from his body and terminating in the large head of the God of Number 7 (Fig. 9-9) on the right side. Issuing from the serpent to the left of the figure would have been another god. Linda Schele suggested to me when I was making the reconstruction drawing that it might be the God of Number 9. This is a distinct possibility, as the lock of front hair that would be an identifying feature of the god is indeed still there (Fig. 9-10).

On all of the piers of Houses A and D, humans are involved with gods. On House A, the principal figures all carry the staff of God K, the Palenque "lineage god" (Schele 1976:26), and the medallions all contained human heads encircled by divine serpent cartouches. On House D, there is even more action between gods and men. Headdresses, staffs, twisting serpents, and thrones of god heads all bear witness to the divinity of kings.

Third, by the time the north Palace substructure was built, the iconography was proclaiming that kings *were* gods. Meter-high heads of rulers were centered on each of four tiers on each side of the wide central stairway of the north substructure. From each portrait head, a serpent emerges from behind the headdress, and in the serpents' wide-open mouths rest the largest known portrayals of God K in the Maya area. One can imagine the dazzling display of color on the whole north side of the Palace in Late Classic times, when not only were there thirteen brilliantly painted piers extended for the length of the entire Palace, but enormous heads of god-kings, ablaze in red, blue, and yellow, were proclaiming for all to see that the king was a god (Plate 9-1).

ICONOGRAPHY OF COLOR

As stucco sculpture replaced flat wall painting, color took on significant iconographic meaning. Blue, a sacred color, became the color for all things divine, sacred, precious—gods, beads, serpents' bodies, feathers, thrones, god's staffs, mirror cartouches, axes of God K, mat motifs, the *le* motif pertaining to accession, as well as divine infants (as on the Inscriptions piers), and superhuman persons such as the dwarf on the south side of pier c, House C. Glyph blocks were always blue. Major portions of loincloths were blue.

Red was the color used for humans, for background sculptured walls, for serpent scales, fangs, and teeth, and for all clothing and paraphernalia worn or carried by humans which was not considered of divine nature, except in cases where it was allocated yellow. Red was also the color of buildings, inside and out.

Yellow was the color designated for jaguar tails and spots, holes in supraorbital plates of serpents, crosshatched areas in headdresses and medallions, certain glyphs used as parts of compositions (but not inscriptional texts), inner serpent borders of skyband frames, and glyphic sculptured borders, as on the House D piers. Yellow was more than likely used in many more instances than has been possible to record. Because of its very fragile nature, much yellow paint undoubtedly no longer remains.

Some colors changed over time, either by preference of rulers or as determined by iconographic meaning as it changed. The palette of stucco sculpture at Palenque remained the same throughout the city's occupation, and although there was a time in its illustrious past when this metropolis was ablaze in brilliant color, in the terminal stages of Palenque's building boom the complicated system of iconographic portrayals of gods and kings was all painted over in a deep red. Virtually the entire city was red. There were few, if any, elements or portions of sculpture left unpainted in the final days before the collapse. The reason for this "city of red" is an enigma. We might pos-

FIGURE 9–9. The God of Number 7 is still intact on the east roof of the
Temple of the Sun. 1,000-mm. lens courtesy of Gillett Griffin.

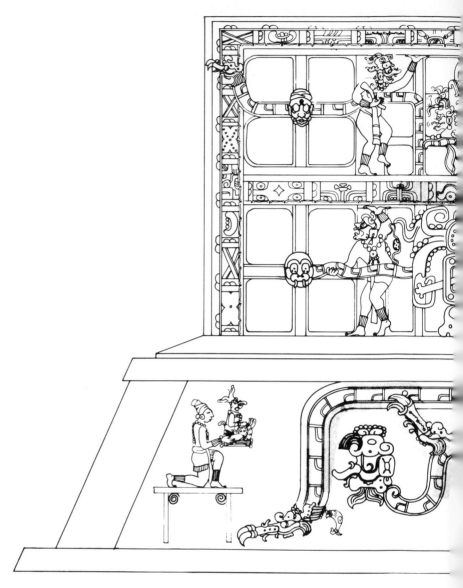

FIGURE 9–10. The eastern roof of the Temple of the Sun portrays a ruler flanked on both sides by gods. Besides the structural part of the temple which is intact, the *dotted* areas are still there.

sibly look to other civilizations when looking for meaning for a "city of red." Homer's use of color in the *Iliad* (Greene 1962) suggests one reason for *red*. Homer's use of color plays an important part in the structure of the epic. *Red* is a sign of warning, attention, challenge, and daring, as is quoted of the ships of Odysseus, "twelve ships with bows red painted" (*Iliad* 93.2.638, Lattimore translation). The red signified a warning for all to beware that the maximum of daring strategy could be expected. Might not "red" have had similar significance

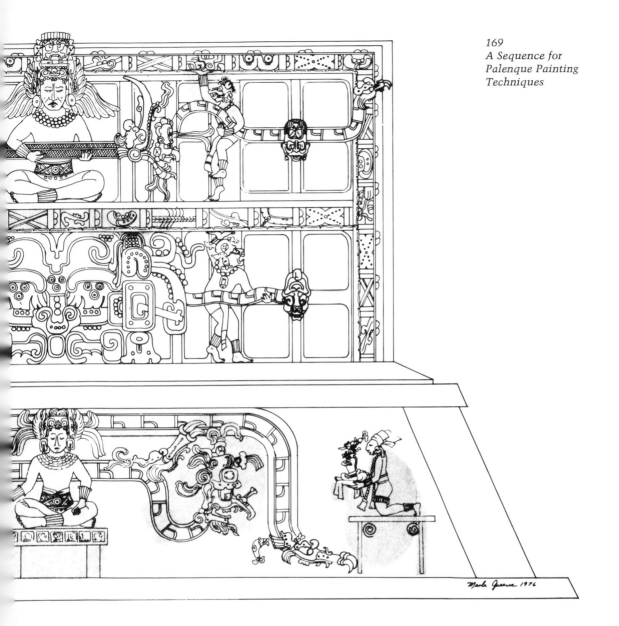

for the Maya—a warning, a challenge, in days when the collapse of a brilliant civilization was approaching?

NOTES

1. This was probably from the first quarter of the seventh century through the middle of the eighth century, as we know that Palenque in its last days was a "city of red."

2. See Table 9-1 for Munsell Color Book notations of a partial list
    of the colors recorded in Palenque painted sculpture.
3. Methods of construction of Palenque's stucco sculpture have been
    discussed previously in Greene Robertson 1975.
4. Pacal was king of Palenque in A.D. 615–683 (Mathews and Schele
    1974).
5. I returned and recorded piers g and i of House A-D at the request of
    INAH Mexico, in the summer of 1975.
6. I made the reconstruction sculptures in 1975 for installation in the
    new Middle American Section of the Florida State Museum,
    University of Florida, Gainesville. National Endowment for the
    Arts grant: S. Jeffrey K. Wilkerson, director. The paintings in
    Plates 9-1 and 9-2 are also in this museum.

Table 9-1. *Munsell Color Book Notes*

Location	Background	Figure	Gods and Other Elements	Border
House A	*10 R 7/4; 10 R 6/6	*10 R 6/6–6/8 7.5 R 5/8–5/10	10 R 7/4 10 R 5/6–6/6 *7.5 BG 6/4–6/10 7.5 BG 5/4 *7.5 YR 6/10	
House D	*10 R 7/4 7.5 R 7/4	10 R 7/4 *10 R 6/6 10 R 4/8 7.5 R 6/6–6/8 7.5 R 5/10	10 R 7/4–7/6 7.5 R 6/8 7.5 R 5/10 7.5 R 4/6 2.5 YR 6/10–4/10 7.5 BG 5/4	10 R 4/10 7.5 R 6/6 7.5 R 5/4–5/8 7.5 BG 6/5 7.5 BG 5/6 7.5 YR 6/10
House C	*10 R 4/8 10 R 3/6 10 R 7/4 *7.5 R 3/6 2.5 B 6/4	10 R 6/6 *7.5 R 3/6	7.5 BG 5/10 *7.5 BG 5/4 *2.5 B 6/4 7.5 R 5/10	7.5 R 5/10
House A-D	*10 R 4/8		*10 R 4/8 10 R 6/10 *2.5 B 6/4 *10 YR 6/10	
Inscriptions piers	10 R 7/4 7.5 R 7/5 7.5 R 3/6	*10 R 6/6	*10 R 6/6 *2.5 B 6/4	

Table 9-1 *continued.*

Location	Background	Figure	Gods and Other Elements	Border
Medallions of House A	Background area	10 R 4/8–5/8 7.5 R 3/8–4/8	Serpent area	2.5 B 4/6
	Cartouche area	7.5 R 6/8–4/8 10 R 4/8 2.5 B 4/6–5/6 7.5 YR 6/10		
House C Dwarf Pier–south face	2.5 YR 4/10 2.5 B 5/6 10 BG 6/4			
House C Narrative Sculpture	10 R 3/10–6/10 2.5 B 5/6 7.5 YR 6/10			
House E Mural	10 R 3/10–3/8 10 R 6/10 7.5 YR 6/10 2.5 B 5/6	2.5 B 8/4 7. B 7/4 7.5 5/6 *10 BG 3/6–5/6		
Walls	*10 R 4/8–5/8 10 R 7/4 10 R 6/4–6/6 10 R 3/10			

Note: Table includes a small fraction of the notations. Munsell notations are not broken down as to individual place of sculpture in this chart, as the entire chart would be too long for permissible space. I am compiling a complete list of color notations of each element and area of color both in the wet season and in the dry season.

10 The Lagartero Figurines
by Susanna M. Ekholm

Several years ago the New World Archaeological Foundation began a program of investigations on the southwestern frontier of the Maya area (Lee 1975). While re-examining the Preclassic site of La Libertad (Lowe 1959), members of the NWAF decided to investigate the report of "stone structures on islands" just across the river. That area, formerly heavily forested and difficult of access, has been extensively cleared by a ten-year-old agricultural *ejido*. The "stone structures on islands," now readily visible, turned out to be a spectacularly situated Maya site that we call Lagartero.

Lagartero is located on the Chiapas-Guatemala border in the Ciénaga de Lagartero, an 8.6-square-kilometer swamp formed by local springs and the backing up of the waters of the Lagartero and San Lucas rivers behind natural travertine barriers (Fig. 10-1). The "swamp" is really a system of swiftly-flowing small rivers and shallow and cenote-like lakes.

The main part of the site is located on islands and peninsulas that project into the Lagartero lakes. Manmade (?) canals, now entirely under water but visible from the air, indicate possibly lower levels for the lakes and different outlines for the shores in ancient times. On the islands and peninsulas large pyramids and low platforms that apparently supported temples, palaces, and humbler buildings, all mostly constructed of perishable materials, are arranged around large plazas and small patios.

EXCAVATIONS

The three-month-long investigations at Lagartero (February–April 1976), in which I was assisted by Deanne Gurr, concentrated on two areas of the island that is the ceremonial center, called Limonal Group. One area was the northwest and perhaps main plaza that apparently functioned as a necropolis from Middle Classic through Postclassic times. The other area was a major Tepeu 1–2 Horizon refuse dump or *basurero* at the south base of Mound 7a, part of a long pyramidal building platform that defines the south side of the northeast plaza.

The Lagartero *basurero*, a 24-by-10-meter zone of concentrated refuse that varied 2.6 meters in depth, produced half a million potsherds, about 2 percent of which, or ten thousand, are polychrome (see preliminary description presented at Forty-second International Congress of Americanists, Paris, 1976, in symposium Maya Cultural Evolution: Highlands and Lowlands), and many other artifacts. Outstanding among the artifacts are the mold-made figurines.

The *basurero* was excavated in two-by-two-meter sections and by twenty-centimeter levels, as no natural stratigraphy could be dis-

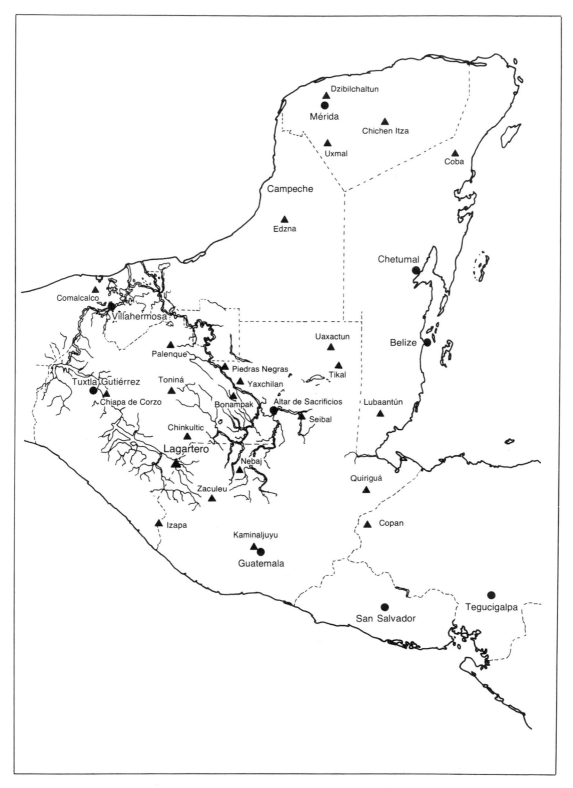

FIGURE 10–1. Map of the general Maya area showing location of Lagartero on Chiapas-Guatemala border.

covered. During excavation most of the figurine fragments could be separated from the mass of potsherds, and these have been partially processed in the laboratory. Almost all the figurines from this refuse situation were unfortunately found headless or bodiless; complete figurines have not yet been reconstructed, and so the descriptions here will be preliminary. The richness of the collection, however is already apparent.

The importance of the figurine collection from Lagartero lies in its size (over five hundred figurines represented), the large number of each variety of figurine, their fair preservation, and some unusual characteristics such as their costume. The great majority, a specific major complex, provide us with a new focus of Maya figurine art, a style previously unrecognized. The homogeneity of this collection corresponds to the extraordinary homogeneity of the pottery vessel collection (this is especially notable in the polychrome pottery) and gives us a glimpse of Maya ceremonial equipment at one point in Maya history on the southwest frontier.

THE FIGURINES

In general, the major Lagartero figurine complex (Figs. 10-2–10-4) fits within the traditions of the Late Classic Maya mold-made figurines. The figurines share traits with both Maya Lowland and Highland examples. They have the stepped haircut, the tall conical hats, the plumed and effigy headdresses, etc. Most of the heads probably fall within Butler's (1935) "Y" type, although we know that that general type is not at all crude and unrealistic, as she characterizes it. However, at Lagartero we have a local style, a particular combination of traits that does not occur in other areas, plus traits specific to Lagartero.

Most of the mold-made human figurines from Lagartero fall within what one can probably call one type of Maya figurine with differences on a varietal level, if I may borrow terms from the classificatory system for Lowland Maya ceramics. The persons shown all seem to be dignitaries of some kind. There are no graceful dancers such as are found in Alta Verapaz. Poses are usually rigid and formal. The mold-made pendants (Fig. 10-5), included here with the figurines, consistently show what are probably shamans and deity representations.

Certain other characteristics of the mold-made figurines are especially outstanding. About 60 percent of the bodies are female. These are not women shown in genre attitudes, but elegant, obviously elite or priestly individuals in highly stylized and presumably meaningful formal poses. The heads, which we have not yet fitted to the bodies, seem generally masculine in aspect, but the faces of female figurines in Maya art usually differ little from those of the males, and I am hopeful that the heads and bodies will be joined together.

Unlike the mold-made figurines from most Maya areas, only a very small percentage of the Lagartero figurines are whistles (Fig. 10-3d); so far only six have evidence of a mouthpiece. When a mouthpiece is present it is on the side of the figurine rather than a third foot-like extension at the back.

Costume and ornament are of greatest importance. To display these fully the Lagartero human seated figurine bodies (80 percent of the total number of bodies) usually were made in three pieces—the backs and many of the bases are mold-made, with designs that continue from the front. Standing figurines are molded in two pieces plus the head.

The heads are mold-made in two pieces, front and back. Decoration, such as turbanlike rolls of cloth, conical hats, earspools, and plumes, are usually added after molding. Heavy appendages were stuck part way between the two halves of the head before they were joined to give extra support.

The largest group of heads (Fig. 10-2a–c), about fifty, have stepped hairdos and turban headdresses. More than half have a row of raised dots down the forehead; these correspond to dots down the forehead and nose of painted figures on the polychrome pottery. Others have a pinch of clay on the nose and another on the forehead. Three have nose plugs; one has filed teeth.

A small group (Fig. 10-2g) of about ten examples have a smile showing teeth and center-parted hair.

The second-largest group of heads (Fig. 10-2d–f, i), about thirty examples, have appliqué strips of hair framing the faces. This group includes more expressions, especially grimaces. Treatment of the forehead is similar to that of the other group.

A fourth and large group (about thirty) look much like the first group except that the turbans and the earspools are included in the mold, as are hairdos on the backs (Fig. 10-2j). Only the tassels on the earspools were added later.

Fifteen heads wear open-mouthed monster mask headdresses (Fig. 10-2h) that were common throughout the Maya area in Tepeu times. The headdresses vary from completely mold-made to completely modeled, and there are combinations of the two.

Small varieties of mold-made heads include those with closed eyes, sunken features, and many others.

Most impressive of the figurine bodies are the seated cross-legged female figurines with their powerful, commanding appearance (Fig. 10-3). The varieties into which I have tentatively divided them are based on costume and gesture.

The variety of seated women that is most common (at least forty examples, and at least twelve are from the same mold) shows them with their hands on their knees (Fig. 10-3a). They wear long *huipils*, probably of cotton gauze, indicated by the many small punctuations. (It should be noted that we found quite a few gauze fabric impressions in the clay; they occur in both plain and basket weave.) On the front and back is the same decoration: a long-nose monster mask with a Chuen-like glyph in its headdress. Across the figure's chest and extending to each shoulder is a water lily. Outstanding is the band of full-face glyphs around the neck of the *huipil*. The figures also wear heavy necklaces with effigy face pendants.

FIGURE 10–2. Figurine heads from the Lagartero *basurero*. All had tall conical hats, plumes, or other ornaments projecting above the turbans and hairdos that are still attached.

e

f

g

h

i

j

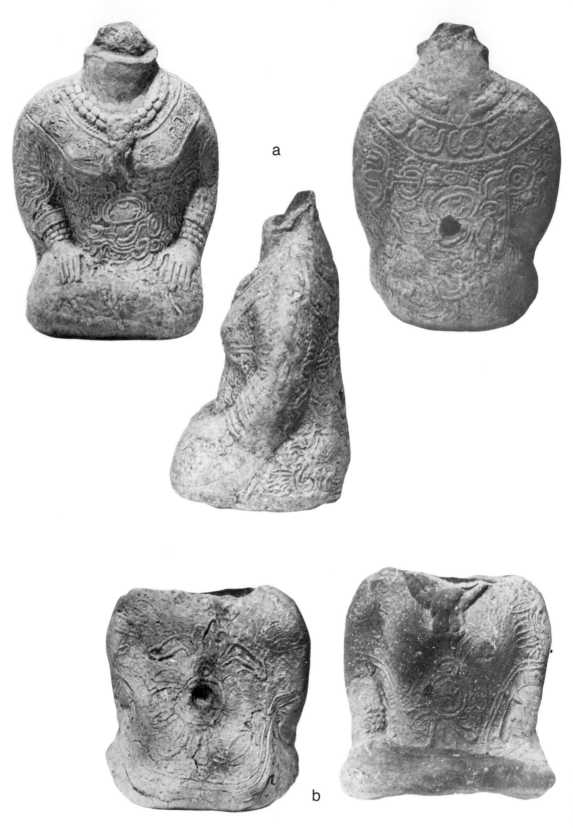

FIGURE 10–3. Seated female mold-made figurine bodies.

c

d

e

f

0   5 cm.

FIGURE 10–4. *a–e*: Seated male mold-made figurine bodies (note the mold-made base showing folded legs in *b*); *f*: standing female figurine body; *g*: standing male figurine body.

c

d

e

f

g

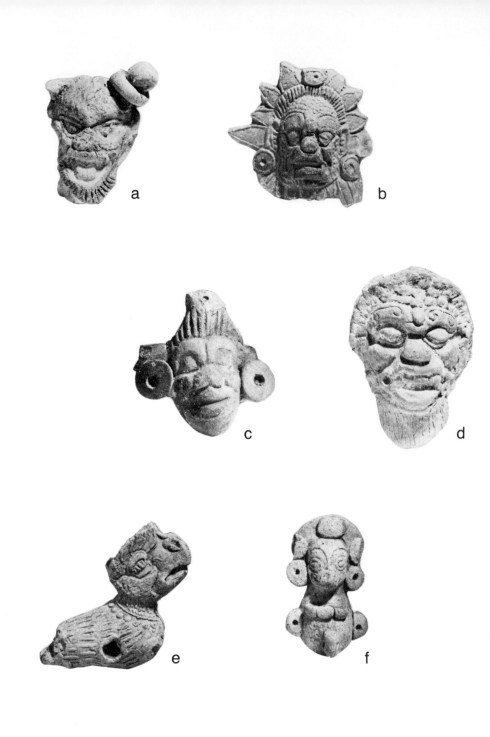

FIGURE 10–5. Mold-made clay pendants.

In another variety of about forty similar figurines (Fig. 10-3b–c) the women wear short *huipils* of gauze. Some have flower designs on the front and back, some have a net design, and some have a combination of the two.

The third variety of women with their hands on their knees wear short jackets or shawls just covering both breasts (Fig. 10-3d). The two examples, quite small figures, were probably both whistles.

Seated women are often shown gesturing elegantly. About twenty-four raise their right hands, the fingers curved (Fig. 10-3e). Nineteen of these wear elaborately decorated shawls like *rebozos*. Three others wear their shawls closed with the corners hanging in points and the *huipil* showing below. One, raising her left hand, has a band of glyphs around the neck of her short *huipil* that is decorated front and back with a monster mask with half-closed eyes. Several wear unusual garments that cover only one breast.

Seated women are also shown gesturing with the left hand, palm outward and fingers extended (Fig. 10-3f). Four of these wear a shawl over a plain, long *huipil* or shawl decorated with circles; these latter are distinctive, however, in that the heads are molded with the bodies —even the earspools and hairdos are molded (Fig. 10-2j).

Other positions cannot yet be described. Three women with jacket-like garments seem to hold both hands at the waist. Four fragments with glyph bands at the neck wear unusual pendants with almost glyphlike faces.

The seated male figurines (Fig. 10-4a–e) are of the same type. They are recognizable by their distinctive garments and their less shapely bodies. They sit in a slightly different position with their feet protruding in front.

The most common man's garment is a short toga or shawllike cloth tied on the left shoulder (about forty) or the right shoulder (about eleven) and passing below the other arm. The designs on these togas and the shape of their edges vary. Ten have a glyph band at the top edge (although these "glyphs" are much more cursive than the ones on the women's garments) and a monster mask on the front and back; the men wear a breechclout that is seen passing between their legs on the molded bases; their right arms are raised across their chests (Fig. 10-4a). A similar toga but with a squared edge and no glyphs is worn by thirty men who raise their left hands across their chests (Fig. 10-4b). Eleven have togas with monster masks in cartouches; they raise their right hands across their chests.

The second typical garment for seated men is a wide decorated cloth or skin worn hanging down in the front only (Fig. 10-4d) over a breechclout that leaves the buttocks naked. In all cases the men sit with both arms encased by the garment. Although the position looks uncomfortable, the figures, with such elaborately decorated clothes, do not seem to be bound prisoners. There appear to be examples of "front capes" (Mahler 1965:590–591) and seem to refute Mahler's suggestion that the representations of these on pottery and in the codices may be side views of a rounded front cloak. Fifteen have monster mask designs on their belts and fringed skirts below. Ten wear triangular garments, some with circle designs, others with monsters.

Three seated men wear fringed jackets, like the Aztec *xicolli*, with flower designs in circles (Fig. 10-4e).

Seven seated males are shown gesturing (Fig. 10-4c). They wear what is probably a deerskin tied behind so that it hangs off the shoulders and covers the figure's front, with the white tail flipped over to make a pendant on the chest; the front has a monster mask in a cartouche. The right hand makes the gesture with the fingers curved that is identical to that of the women.

Standing mold-made female figurines (Fig. 10-4f) are outstanding for their graceful gestures and regal bearing, although these figures are rare. Their costumes are even more elaborate than those of the seated females and are usually shawls over *huipils* that in turn cover one or more skirts. Hands are shown curving up in front of the chest on seven examples, curving down on five examples, one curving up and one curving down on two examples, one pointing up and one pointing down on two examples. Three figurines show the use of fine, long *quexquemitls*.

There are no comparable standing mold-made male figurines. All standing males are possibly shamanlike and may be shown in an act of ritual transformation into an animal. About ten plain ones wear only a breechclout, but they have tails. Others, about fifteen, wear skins or nets and are often grotesquely fat-bellied (Fig. 10-4g).

Much of the original paint—blue, red, and white—remains on the figurines.

There is another group of mold-made clay artifacts that is related to the figurines. These are pendants, presumably to be worn on necklaces. Perhaps they are the pendants that are shown being worn by most of the mold-made figurines. Most of them are simply heads, but they are not broken off of figurines; they are complete as they are, with perforations in the back for suspension.

Eighteen pendants represent what may be shamans (Fig. 10-5). They are bearded grotesque faces; protruding from the head are one round knob or horn and one or two tassels. Even more grotesque faces, often with starlike protrusions, number sixteen. Of twenty-five monsters, six are long-nose creatures. Animals, too, are shown as pendants; they are usually birds, either round-bellied unrealistic ones (twelve examples) or macaws or quetzals (eleven examples).

It is not within the scope of this essay to treat the several hundred animal figurines, most of which are mold-made. It is interesting, however, that about one hundred of the animal figurines represented are dogs. Many dog bones were also found in the *basurero*.

Mold-made and modeled figurines occur together in the Lagartero *basurero*. Modeled figurines are much fewer in number and seem to represent a different class of persons. All are males. They are scantily clad, usually only in loincloths, and some may depict sacrificial victims whose entrails are shown during some form of disembowelment. Other modeled figurines are grotesque, fat, half-animal, and phallic figures. Some animals, too, especially birds, which are usually whistles, are modeled.

What can be said about the Lagartero mold-made figurine complex at this early stage in our analysis?

By the nature of the *basurero*, with its lack of stratigraphy and its homogenous contents, I feel that the refuse in it was deposited within a fairly short time, perhaps even within a single season. Whether it refers to ceremonies that took place on the platforms or was brought in from another part of the ceremonial center we do not know. All of the figurines (and other artifacts) were probably being used at the same time.

It also seems likely that the figurines were manufactured at Lagartero. The pastes are all generally similar. Included in the refuse were about twenty figurine molds. There are many pairs and groups of figurines made in the same mold.

One of the extraordinary facts about the polychrome pottery from the *basurero* is that only about 5 percent of the vessels do not bear glyphs. Of those that do, 90 percent bear only a Chuen-like glyph with various affixes. That is the same glyph as the one shown on the *huipils* of the main group of seated female figurines, and the glyph may be associated especially with Lagartero or its ceremonies.

The elaborate costumes on the Lagartero figurines will merit special attention. Apparently shown are cotton garments with various types of decoration (embroidery, brocade, appliqué, and paint), and the garments are of many types. They indicate a great textile craft specialization and will be studied to identify garments and make comparisons with ethnographic costume and costume shown on Maya stelae and other figurines (Walter F. Morris, Jr., work in preparation). Apparently the Lagartero figurine sculptors took the license of not showing drapery, as that would distort the essential thing, the designs on the fabrics.

The area near Lagartero today is an important cotton-growing zone, and not too distant areas were famous for their cotton production in ancient times. Thomas Gage (J. E. S. Thompson 1958:148) speaks of the production of "cotton-wool" in Copanabastla (Copanaguastla) that was widely traded. Then at Izquintenango, Gage encountered a great trading center, "very rich, by reason of the much cotton-wool in it" (Thompson 1958:161). Izquintenango is about a three-hour walk from Lagartero. The Grijalva Valley until very recently was famous for its fine cotton textiles such as those of the Zoque of Tuxtla Gutiérrez and those of the Tzeltal Maya of San Bartolomé de los Llanos (Venustiano Carranza) (Cordry and Cordry 1941). That this fame possibly extended back to Late Classic times in the eastern part of the valley may be evidenced by the Lagartero figurine costumes.

A major problem when faced with the study of a figurine collection such as this one is the lack of published comparative material. Excavated figurines, usually fragmentary, are rarely published completely. Also, known whole figurines are usually from looted sites and have lost their provenience.

In this respect, however, we have had some luck. In the report on the excavations at Zaculeu, Woodbury and Trik (1953: Figs. 270–277) show some figurine fragments that came from their excavations and from a small mound south of and across the barranca from the Zaculeu ceremonial center, and there is our figurine complex. The heads, while difficult to evaluate exactly, would not be out of place among our figurines. Body fragments shown could be from Lagartero. There are even six examples of our pendants—five grotesque faces and a bird. Here is confirmation of the pendants' relationship with the figurines and some evidence of the areal spread of the entire mold-made complex. Wolfgang Haberland has furnished me with a photograph of a figurine in the Termer Collection in the Museum für Völkerkunde, Hamburg, that was purchased in 1926 and comes from Aguacatan, near Huehuetenango; it could be from the same mold as our male figures wearing short, fringed jackets. This is the only real comparative evidence so far, though, and we must assume that the complex is limited to the southwestern Maya frontier.

Figurines, in spite of their ubiquity and often very illuminating ethnographic detail, remain an enigma. No one has ever been able to say for sure how they were used, and one usually ends up saying, as does Rands (1965) in his summary article on Highland Maya figurines, simply that they were probably used in many ways. This may well be true in the main, but perhaps with finds such as this one at Lagartero we can begin to discuss the function of specific figurine complexes. No figurines (or polychrome pottery) were found in any of the fifty or so burials of the northwest plaza, although many were probably of the same period. The figurines are an exception to Borhegyi's (1965: 35) rule that Highland Late Classic figurines are primarily "offertory or decorative objects" and that "they are never found broken or battered."

The preponderance of female figurines is intriguing. This figurine complex is intimately associated with the polychrome pottery complex with its extensive figure painting. But only males seem to be painted on the pots. The female figurines seem to be more prepossessing and important than the male ones, as if they played a more important role.

We have the tantalizing suggestion that this collection of figurines with such a narrow range of activities shown may represent a small number of individual roles pertaining to a particular ritual or group of rituals such as an end-of-cycle ceremony. The few poses and gestures may also refer to slight variation of class or social status. We are left with the hope of being able to reconstruct in some way some highly formalized ritual.

Ethnohistoric Approaches

11 The Lobil Postclassic Phase in the Southern Interior of the Yucatan Peninsula by Peter D. Harrison

This essay will discuss evidence of a Late Postclassic occupation of significantly large population and wide geographic range in the southern interior of the Yucatan Peninsula. The evidence is largely drawn from field observations in Quintana Roo, Mexico, but is supplemented by examination of previously published field data. At present there are insufficient data at hand to allow any definite tribal identifications for district populations, apart from those discussed by Scholes and Roys (1968) for the Acalan and Tixchel populations. However, archaeological data pertaining to Late Postclassic occupations in southern Quintana Roo are identified as the "Lobil Phase." An attempt is made here to establish the date and physical range of this phase, which probably encompasses more than one tribal population. Some implications of recognition of this phase are discussed.

The new archaeological data derive from a site survey conducted in southwestern Quintana Roo under the auspices of the Royal Ontario Museum (Toronto) during seasons from 1972 to 1974. Previously published preliminary papers have reported some results of this survey (Harrison 1972; 1974a). The locations of sites from which evidence is cited in this essay are shown in Figure 11-1.

EVIDENCE FOR THE LOBIL PHASE IN QUINTANA ROO

The archaeological data of concern here are largely surface remains. The absence of stratigraphy which is inherent in surface situations makes it difficult to determine chronology, if such exists. Evidence from outside the survey area is invoked to help solve this problem.

Four main bodies of data from the survey area are relevant to the discussion. These are: (1) crudely constructed platforms diagnostic of the Lobil Phase, and a pattern of inferred behavior surrounding their construction; (2) foundation remains of simple house structures at ground level; (3) deposits of Late Postclassic censer fragments; and (4) remains of Classic Period architecture buried by the platforms described in (1).

The sample from which evidence is drawn includes eighty-one sites in Quintana Roo examined during the survey. Of these, only 6 percent (five sites) included standing masonry structures. Four of the five sites had only one example each of standing architecture. The remaining structures at these, as well as all other sites, consisted of mounds of earth and loose stone surfaces. At first observation these "mounds"

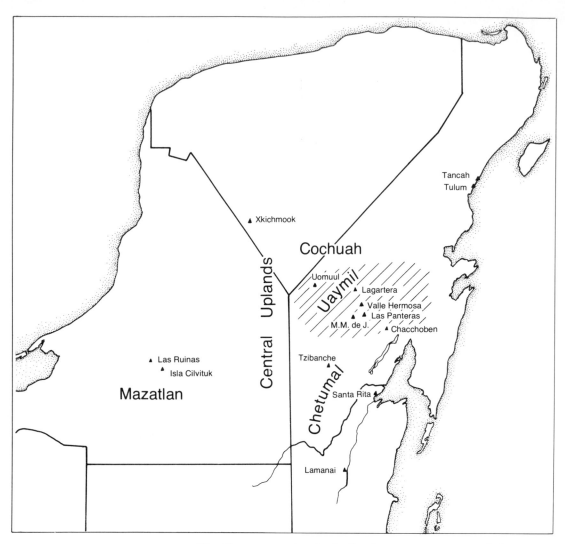

FIGURE 11–1. The Yucatan peninsula, indicating some contact period *cacicazgos*, or provinces, and selected sites within them.

appeared to be the result of natural disintegration, similar in appearance to the collapsed and eroded structures which are familiar throughout the Maya Lowlands. However, closer observation showed that in a majority of cases features of architectural design were still present on the surface of these "mounds." Indications such as step risers still in place, or slightly disturbed; terrace-edging stones *in situ*; and flat summits showed that the existing configurations of the mounds were not natural (Fig. 11-2). A small number of controlled test excavations and a larger number of looters' excavations revealed that masonry architecture of recognizable Classic Period quality lay beneath a significant proportion of the mounds. It can be concluded from the sample evidence that at least a large proportion, if not all, of the Lobil platforms which exceed two meters in height were constructed over Classic Period buildings. Relevant to the behavioral pattern in construction of the platforms is the variability in the treatment of the buried structures as preparation for the final platforms.

The buried structures were differentially modified or partially razed in order to construct the surface platforms. Two examples from controlled excavations are shown in Figures 11-3 and 11-4 from the sites of Las Panteras and Uomuul. In these two examples there are notable differences in the utilization of the earlier structures in accommodation of the later platforms. In the case from Las Panteras, the front (north) wall of the Classic Period building has been razed to a lower level than the rear wall, which is intact up to the lower vault stones. At Uomuul, however, the front (south) wall of the earlier structure has been left intact to a level well above the medial molding of the upper zone. As a result, a much greater quantity of fill was required in front of the buried building at Uomuul in order to produce the desired slope for the final and later platform. The difference in these two examples suggests that the form of a Classic structure had little influence on the form of the platform constructed over it.

This lack of relationship between the forms of buried and overlying structures is more dramatically expressed in another recurring configuration of platforms. In this configuration, abutting platforms of different heights and basal widths are constructed over a single Classic Period building. The higher of the two platform summits is constructed near the roof line of the earlier building, while the lower summit is constructed a little above the floor level of the same earlier building. To produce this Lobil configuration, the Classic Period building has to be differentially razed, preserving part of it almost intact and razing part of it almost totally. Examples of this pattern are found at Structure 15, Las Panteras, Group C; Structure 13, Los Glifos (near Uomuul); and Structure 16 at Uomuul. The pattern was revealed through surface evidence, such as the protruding backs of buried vault stones, and in looters' excavations.

These various examples are cited to establish the fact that, while Classic Period structures were used as a base core for construction of Lobil Phase platforms, there is no continuity of form from the buried to the overlying structures.

This lack of continuity in form marks one break in architectural tradition between the Classic Period structures and the surface platforms. Other markers of a break in tradition are the following: the absence of masonry buildings on top of the late platforms; the crude construction technique in which fill consists of loosely piled rubble, held in place by facing stones. There are indications that these facing stones were reused and probably originated in the partially destroyed Classic Period buildings. They were often set with the unfinished side outward. Finally, the high incidence of low round platforms built in open plaza areas marks another break in continuity with the Classic Period. These platforms are also crudely constructed in a technique similar to that of the larger platforms, but in this case not built over existing structures. A total of sixteen of these round platforms was found at twenty-one sites.

FIGURE 11–2. Surface structure of Lobil Phase at Margarita Maza de Juárez (Quintana Roo, Mexico) with stair risers clearly visible. Examples of this quality of preservation and clarity are rare.

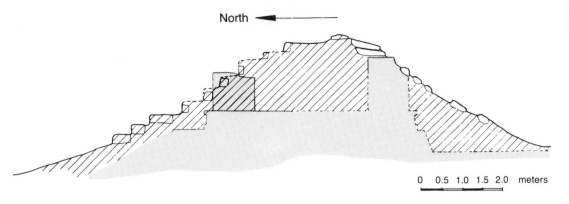

FIGURE 11–3. Schematic section of Structure 14, Las Panteras, Group A (Quintana Roo, Mexico), showing Lobil Phase construction (hatched) overlying Classic Period remains (shaded).

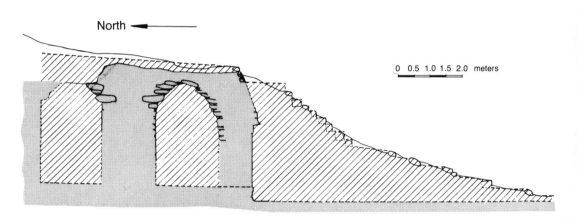

FIGURE 11–4. Schematic section of Structure 1, Uomuul (Quintana Roo, Mexico), showing Lobil Phase construction (hatched) overlying a moderately well preserved Classic Period structure (shaded). Note the difference in Figures 11–3 and 11–4 of the use of a Classic structure as a core base for Lobil construction.

In summary, the architectural works which define the Lobil Phase in southern Quintana Roo include high platforms constructed over partially destroyed Classic buildings, low rectangular platforms, and low round platforms. The last two types are not built over earlier structures.

Another feature of surface evidence requires brief discussion because of its possible relationship to the Lobil Phase. This is the occurrence of simple house foundations, which are found in both rounded and rectangular forms standing at ground level. They are constructed of loosely piled stones of irregular shape. Occasional "dressed" blocks were used to mark corners or door jambs. At Uomuul (see Fig. 11-5), eleven of these occur on ground level, while two others are raised

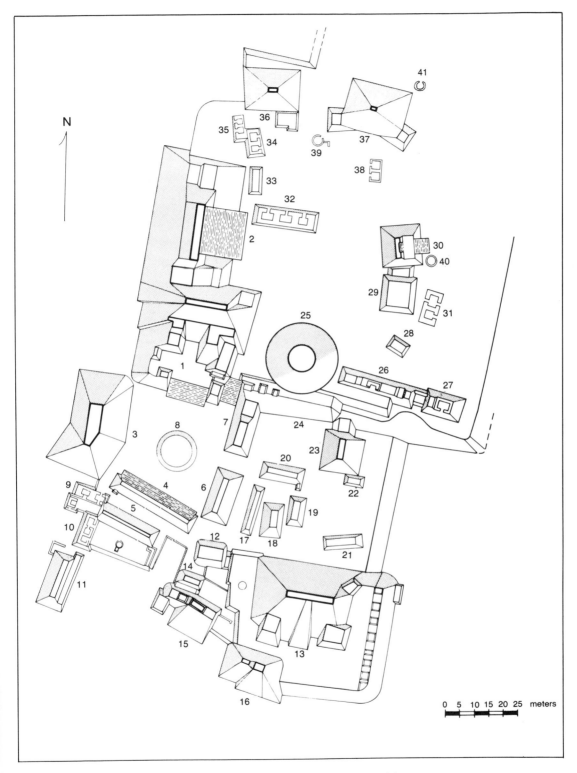

FIGURE 11–5. Map of part of the central zone of the site of Uomuul (Quintana Roo, Mexico).

on low platforms. These foundations are scattered among twenty-eight larger structures within the portion of the site center which was mapped. The house foundations are often in close proximity to the large Lobil platforms. Occasional fragments of manos, metates, and chipped chert tools were found on the surface in association with these foundations at several sites. These surface artifacts are indicators of daily household work activities and aid in identifying the foundations as "houses." The locational distribution suggests that the foundations are not contemporary with the larger Lobil platforms, and are probably later in date. The large platforms are presumed to have had some ceremonial function, so that the extreme proximity of house foundations, sometimes right at the foot of a large platform, does not suggest simultaneous use of the two structure types but rather a sequent reoccupation of the site. If this deduction is correct, then the surface materials represent two Postclassic reoccupations, the latest of which may fall in the Historic Period. An example of a detailed plan of a round house foundation is illustrated in Figure 11-6 from the site of Margarita Maza de Juárez.

The last category of surface evidence comprises deposits of censer fragments. These deposits were located on the summits of large platforms, frequently spilling down the side or back of a platform. In a few incidences (Okcat, Las Panteras, Groups B and C) such deposits were also located on top of, or immediately adjacent to, low platforms in plaza areas. The composition of these deposits is curious. There are many fragments from different censers, but never enough to reassemble one whole vessel. Two obvious interpretations of these deposits are possible. Both the use of the original whole vessels and the deposition of fragments could be the result of Lobil Phase activity. Alternatively, the use of the whole vessels could be associated with the Lobil Phase, while redeposition in the present locations could be related to the occupants of the house foundations, if these are indeed later in date. I am inclined toward this latter explanation. Figure 11-7 shows an example of a censer fragment.

Finally, departing from the surface evidence, reference must be made to the styles of Classic Period architecture in the survey area. The few examples of standing architecture appear to be of earlier date than those Classic structures which were buried by the Lobil Phase. The standing structures are austere in style, possibly of Middle Classic date. This difference from the buried structure *may* be causally related to the fact that they are still standing.

On the other hand, four examples of Classic structures that had been buried by Lobil Phase platforms were seen in controlled excavations. In these cases, the style is closely related to the Central Yucatecan style as defined by Potter (1973). The façade of Structure 1 at Uomuul is illustrated in Figure 11-8 as an example of this style. This particular example is closest to the Río Bec subtype. The geographic spread of the four examples seen convinces me that this was a dominant style in the survey area.

It is still not known how many buildings of the elaborate Central Yucatecan style, like the one illustrated at Uomuul, lie buried and

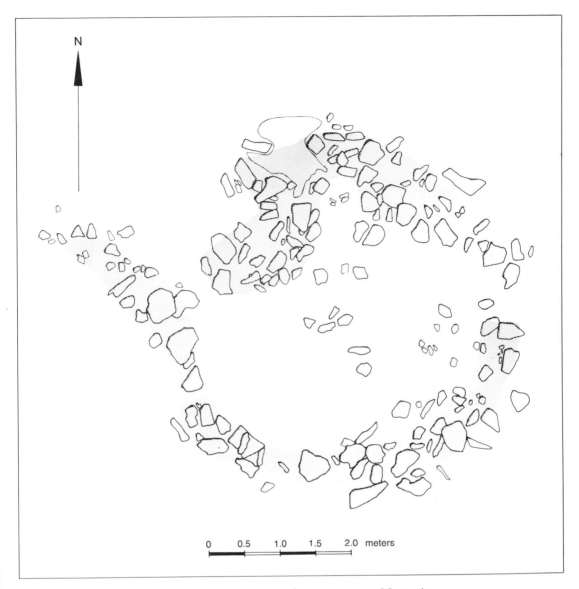

FIGURE 11–6. Plan of house foundation remains of a specimen at Margarita Maza de Juárez (Quintana Roo, Mexico). Shading indicates suggested original location of foundation stones prior to recent disturbance.

partly destroyed in the heartland of southwest Quintana Roo. In fact, the activities of the Lobil Phase in this district may well have obscured the actual center of Central Yucatecan architecture. Sites such as Río Bec, Becan, Hochob, and Xpujil which exemplify *untouched* Central Yucatecan structures are the sites which have received attention on the central uplands. This geographic differential in destruction in ancient times explains, at least in part, why southern Quintana Roo has been neglected for so long. The spectacular Central Yucatecan structures are no longer visible there.

FIGURE 11–7. Fragment of a Late Postclassic anthropomorphic censer with grotesque face and stylized breast.

FIGURE 11–8. Structure 1, Uomuul (Quintana Roo, Mexico). Partially destroyed Classic Period façade in Central Yucatecan style, which was buried by Lobil Phase construction (see Figure 11–4 for section of same structure).

Archaeological Evidence

Because the evidence for the temporal position of the Lobil Phase is drawn from numerous locations outside the survey area, the chronological and spatial parameters must be discussed together.

Recognition of the Lobil Phase in Quintana Roo invites the reexamination of earlier archaeological site reports in the light of this new information. Since the quality of the Lobil Phase construction is so crude that it resembles the natural state of disintegration, it has not often been recognized as a separate stage. Despite this disadvantage it is possible to distinguish data relevant to both temporal and spatial distribution of the phase from detailed descriptions in earlier reports.

The temporal context of the phase can only be determined by working out a broad sequence for the southern peninsula. This sequence is derived from a selection of specific stratigraphic situations and stylistic comparisons from diverse sites, and it involves a variety of categories of evidence. It is a case of a is earlier than b and c at x location, and b is earlier than c and d at y location, while c is earlier than d at z location. The result is a sequence of a-b-c-d.

The first step is to establish that the Lobil Phase relates to Late rather than Early Postclassic.

The differences which mark the break in tradition between Classic architecture and the Lobil "style" of platform already described above can also be cited as evidence of a time gap separating the Classic Period from the appearance of the Lobil Phase. The presence of certain evidence in the form of smashed decorative stucco, ruthless modification of the Classic buildings, and deliberate covering of any decorative façades could suggest religious outrage or revolution. If such were the case, then a time gap might not be involved. However, belying this argument is the apparent lack of skill and knowledge of masonry techniques, even for the construction of solid platforms, let alone masonry buildings on top of these platforms, in the Lobil Phase. The definite discontinuity in technical skill as well as the breaks in tradition strongly indicate a *long* time gap between the Classic constructions and the Lobil overlay. The relatively good state of preservation of constructions which were poorly executed to begin with further indicates a minimal time lapse since their construction and the present. Further archaeological evidence for a time gap is the presence of the Late Postclassic censers, despite the scarcity of other types of known Postclassic ceramics in the survey area.

The chronological sequence at the late end of the Postclassic is complicated by two factors. Spanish contact occurred at different times in the southern peninsula, so that dates of site abandonment vary widely. Furthermore, the same sequence of events and developments did not occur identically in each part of the peninsula. This can be demonstrated from the ethnohistoric record. Nevertheless, a general, overall sequence can be drawn from scattered evidence at various sites and districts in the southern half of the peninsula. All components of a sequence drawn from a broad area are not likely to be represented at any one site or locality. With this geographical variation for cultural events in mind, an overall sequence can be postulated.

In order to construct this Late Postclassic sequence, the specific categories of evidence that are considered here are the following: architectural style, in which beam-and-mortar roofed masonry structures are contrasted with the crude platforms with no superstructure; mural paintings influenced by the Mixtec style, and divided into early and late phases; Late Postclassic redware ceramics; Late Postclassic censers; and simple house foundations. The sequence is pieced together from several sites in southern Quintana Roo; from sites in southwest Campeche; from Tulum and Tancah on the north coast of Quintana Roo; from Santa Rita and Lamanai in northern and north-central Belize.

As far as we now know, the beam-and-mortar architecture as well as the redware ceramics coexisted with both the early and late style of Mixtec-influenced murals. The censers seem to have had a time depth of even greater span, probably originating at Mayapan. They may turn out to represent a long tradition accompanying all other Late Postclassic developments. The only stratigraphic certainty is the later date of the crude platforms in relationship with the late Mixtec murals. These platforms are probably also later than the Late Postclassic redware ceramics. These assessments summarized the specific evidence which is outlined below.

The north coast sites of Tulum and Tancah are involved in the discussion because of the occurrence there of Mixtec-influenced murals and the distinctive coastal architecture. These features serve as a link in the evidence which establishes the Lobil Phase as later in time. This is not to suggest that the Lobil Phase exists on the north coast.

Features comparable to Lobil architecture as well as data which provide a stratigraphic relationship to Tulum and Tancah are found at the site of Santa Rita in northern Belize. Several structures at Santa Rita included a final phase of construction resembling the Lobil Phase, and overlying masonry structures. These structures include Mounds 1, 3, and 4 according to Gann's descriptions (1900:663–665). The relevant evidence is from Mound 1, where the late overlying construction buried an earlier structure containing painted murals.

The Santa Rita murals have been compared with those at Tulum and Tancah (Andrews IV 1943:74–76). Andrews divided the north coast murals into two sequent phases of influence from the Mixtec style as known from the Codex Nuttall. The Santa Rita murals were seen to be closer in style to those of Tancah, and less like the paintings at Tulum. At both north coast sites, the art is associated with beam-and-mortar architecture and redware ceramics.

Although Gann did not note surface stairs and flat summits in the final construction phase at Santa Rita, he clearly established that this final phase was crude but deliberate architecture. The parallel with Lobil architecture is strong. This stratigraphic situation establishes a Lobil-like construction as later than even the latest phase of Mixtec-influenced mural painting. By association, it should also be *later than* beam-and-mortar architecture as well as the late redware ceramics.

Andrews's interest in this sequence was the correlation with similar materials in southwestern Campeche. From here, Andrews described several different kinds of architecture, all of which relate to my proposed sequence. There are occurrences of beam-and-mortar roofed structures (Isla Cilvituk); high platforms with access stairs which had wall foundations built at the summit (Isla Cilvituk, Las Ruinas); low platform mounds with no masonry structures (Las Ruinas, Carrizal); and house foundations at ground level at various sites (Andrews IV 1943:36–38, 42–43, 64, 74). The beam-and-mortar architecture obviously related to the coastal style on the other side of the peninsula. However, the simple low platforms and the higher platforms with wall foundations compare well with the Lobil style in Quintana Roo. The presence in Campeche of stucco decoration and exterior painting also led Andrews to draw a parallel for this evidence with the Santa Rita/Tancah murals. In his concluding sequence for southwest Campeche, Andrews placed the beam-and-mortar structures in his Period II, and other architecture was lumped together in Period III, dated at A.D. 1450–1525 (ibid.:89).

As noted earlier, the house foundations in Quintana Roo are thought to be later in date than the surrounding Lobil platforms, and the same is probably true for southwestern Campeche. In the Campeche evidence, therefore, we find additional comparable data for a phase of construction which is "crude" and postdates beam-and-mortar architecture, as well as for ground-level house foundations. Scholes and Roys independently noted these late types of "ruins" in Campeche (1968: 71–73).

The evidence from Campeche and Santa Rita has been interwoven by Andrews's analysis and compared with the Lobil Phase in Quintana Roo. Also the site of Lamanai further south in Belize has produced relevant evidence. Recent reports from current excavation at this site indicate that there is no Pre-Contact standing architecture. At Lamanai, simple platforms of unimpressive surface appearance have yielded a wealth of artifacts dating to the Late Postclassic (Pendergast 1975). Late Postclassic redware ceramics are strongly represented at Lamanai, but Pendergast believes that he has stratigraphic evidence of the earlier date of these ceramics vis-à-vis the crude Lobil-like architecture which comprises the surface configuration of the mounds (Pendergast, personal communication, 1976). Late Postclassic redwares are very sparsely represented in the survey sample from southern Quintana Roo. Although these redwares are apparently earlier than the Lobil Phase, their relative scarcity in the interior of Quintana Roo requires explanation. Of course there is a major difference in the sampling techniques between a survey with restricted excavation in Quintana Roo and established localized excavation at Lamanai. Nevertheless, the relative absence of the redwares farther north is quite notable. An explanation of this may be derived from the geographical differences in the two areas and their routes of access from the coast, thought to be the source of these redwares. Lamanai has direct access via the New River and also the Hondo River. The interior of Quintana Roo has no such direct access route, despite a shorter physical distance from the presumed source. Apart from this side issue, the present evidence from Lamanai suggests that it was an important center during the Lobil Phase as well as during earlier phases of the Late Postclassic.

The Late Postclassic censers already mentioned have been reported from all the sites under consideration here. Among a variety of forms, a dominant one is the poorly fired, grotesque, anthropomorphic censer as shown in Figure 11-7. In the absence of a sound seriation and because of their surface provenience and nearly universal occurrence, these censers are of little help in attempting to establish a sequence.

The sequence which emerges from the foregoing eclectic data would be as shown in Figure 11-9.

The foregoing discussion has concentrated on evidence which was useful in exploring the temporal parameters of the Lobil Phase. There is additional material from the central uplands or plateau which is useful only in expanding the geographical location of the phase.

The apparent lack of simple mounds with flat summits in the central plateau between the flanklands is deceptive. Such mounds are present, often in the same plaza arrangements in which fine examples of Classic Period standing architecture occur. The case of Chicanna can be cited. Located 2.5 kilometers southwest of Becan, this site is noted for the presence in a single plaza group (Group A) of two subtypes of Central Yucatecan architecture. Structure I on the west side is a clear example of the twin-tower Río Bec subtype, while Structure II on the east side is a classic Chenes subtype (Eaton 1974:133–134). However, the structures on the north and south sides of this same plaza have no standing architecture. The north structure has two distinct elements, the one high and wide, the other long, low, and narrow. Both elements have flat summits and gradual slopes on the plaza side (personal observation). A two-level structure in this form has been described as a recurring pattern of Lobil Phase architecture at several sites in Quintana Roo.

The question of why, on the central plateau, some structures would have been "remodeled," if indeed this is the case at Chicanna, while others were left untouched, must remain unanswered, although the geography of the plateau may be a factor.

To the north, indications of Lobil Phase activity must be secondarily interpreted from the literature. Edward Thompson's report on the site of Xkichmook (Ichmul) described relevant features. Concerning the structures numbered 8, 9, and 10, Thompson reported that "excavation shows them to have been two edifices, but now reduced by time or other destructive agencies to formless masses of ruins" (1898: 222). It is hard to say how much can be read into this description, but it is certainly suggestive of the Lobil style. Thompson also decribes "two raised circular spaces 12 feet in diameter, about a foot high, enclosed by cut stones and filled with rubble" (ibid.:217). This is an excellent description of one of the circular low platforms prevalent at so many of the Lobil Phase sites in Quintana Roo. Fragmented incensarios and "figurines" were also a feature of surface material at

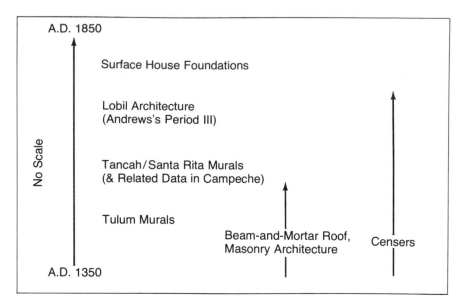

FIGURE 11–9. Chronological sequence for the Postclassic–Colonial Period in eastern Quintana Roo.

Xkichmook. The combination of features compares with the situation further south on the central plateau, where only some structures were "remodeled," and suggests that Lobil Phase activity extended at least as far north as Xkichmook in Yucatan.

Archaeological correlations for late architectural types in southern Quintana Roo have been examined for several surrounding zones. Correlated evidence has indicated that it is likely to date to the late Pre-Conquest, in the late fifteenth and early sixteenth centuries. It is probable that the Lobil Phase in turn predates "house" foundations which are present among Lobil-like ruins both in southern Quintana Roo and in southwest Campeche. These late house foundations could date into the nineteenth century.

Ethnohistoric Evidence

Direct accounts of the *entradas* of Alonso d'Avila to the *cacicazgos* or provinces of Cochuah, Uaymil, and Chetumal in 1531–1533 provide only some small light on the nature of the indigenous populations of the time. These accounts are least helpful where concerned with the locations and characteristics of sites encountered en route. The general movement of the initial *entrada* was from the north of this area and followed a southeastward course with a destination of Lake Bacalar. Avila's route apparently took him through the east central part only of the province of Uaymil, so that there was no contact with the deep interior of southern Quintana Roo by the Spanish until missionaries arrived in the next century. However, it is recorded in Oviedo's account of this *entrada* that before Bacalar was reached, two major towns were passed, respectively called Macanahau and Yumpeten, each having "3,000 houses" (Chamberlain 1948:102–103). No physical description of these "towns" or the nature of their houses was provided, nor a description of the surrounding landscape. However, if the number of houses mentioned was accurate, they indicate a significant population, possibly as high as fifteen thousand inhabitants per town. In the year following the initial contact, the town of Macanahau readily provided Avila with six hundred warriors to move against rebellious towns in Cochuah to the north (ibid:108). This again bespeaks a high indigenous population.

These large towns should be identifiable as sites in the survey area, given their reported large size. On the strength of a "best guess" based on Avila's supposed route, these large towns could correlate with those sites designated as Lagartero, Valle Hermosa, or Chacchoben, all of which lie within the lake belt northwest of Bacalar. The north and south boundaries of the province of Uaymil are reconstructed in Figure 11-1 according to the clues provided by Oviedo (1851–1855, Bk. 14, Ch. 6:415, 416). The archaeological evidence of a sizable and late occupation at the above-named sites is best explained if these sites are the remains of the large occupation encountered by Avila on his expeditions of 1531–1533. The date is also in close agreement with the correlation of the Lobil Phase with Andrews's Period III in Campeche, estimated to extend up to A.D. 1525. The Avila *entradas* were only six to eight years later.

Ethnohistoric references to the interior of Quintana Roo from later centuries are sparse in the extreme, but they include mention of an area of refuge for Christian apostates, and also of peoples who were unfriendly to the Cehache Maya in Campeche (Scholes and Roys 1968: 253, 506). Despite these hints at late intertribal friction between populations of southern Quintana Roo and southern Campeche, a linguistic unity is recorded for these area. A language called Vaimil (Uaymil?) was said to extend from the city of Campeche to Bacalar and south to the mouth of the Ulua River (ibid.:321; Noyes 1932:352). A cultural relationship across the same part of the south peninsula is suggested by the archaeological evidence discussed in the previous section. Similarities in at least some of the Late Postclassic architectural features were noted, as well as the common distribution of the Late Postclassic censer types (Scholes and Roys 1968:320).

During the Post-Contact Period right up to the nineteenth century, the interior of Quintana Roo was characterized by waves of Maya occupation resistant to Spanish culture and domination. These waves apparently occurred in ever decreasing numbers (ibid.:341). These later occupations may be the source of the surface house foundations found scattered among the larger Lobil platforms.

The stronghold of the Lobil Phase appears to have been in the area of the sixteenth-century province of Uaymil. Here are found the sites of Lagartero, Uomuul, Margarita Maza de Juárez, and Las Panteras, where the best-preserved and clearest examples of Lobil architecture exist. Also, within this zone there are no examples of standing architecture. Such examples do occur in what would have been the northern part of the province of Chetumal, where Lobil Phase architecture is found as well. The ethnohistoric as well as archaeological evidence for southern Quintana Roo and northern Belize suggest that the Lobil Phase probably did extend well to the south into Belize. The sixteenth-century province of Chetumal is thought to have reached as far south as the site of Lamanai, and probably as far north as the site of Chaccho-ben.

The brief and admittedly inadequate survey of architectural remains resembling the Lobil Phase showed that the style extends from south central Campeche clear across the peninsula and south into Belize. This distribution agrees remarkably with that outlined for a linguistic unity in the early sixteenth century. The linguistic affiliation extended down to the Ulua River, but to date there is no archaeological indication that a Late Postclassic phase similarly extended this far south.

In summary, the ethnohistoric evidence supports a date for the Lobil Phase which spans the time of Spanish contact, as well as a broad distribution of the phase in the southern peninsula.

CONCLUSIONS

Three bodies of data deriving from surface observations in southern Quintana Roo are indicative of a widespread Late Postclassic occupation or occupations. These are: (1) simple platforms, the larger of which were built over Classic Period structures and form the major component of the Lobil Phase; (2) house foundations at ground level, scattered among the Lobil platforms; and (3) depositions of Late Post-classic censer fragments. Two major interpretations for the chronological ordering of these elements are possible. First, all three could be contemporary in construction and/or use. Second, the platforms and use of censers could be contemporary but earlier than the house foundations and redeposition of the censer fragments.

The second chronological interpretation is favored for two reasons: (1) the distribution of house foundations among large "ceremonial" platforms is an incompatible distribution of functions; and (2) the large population necessary to execute the Lobil Phase constructions is incompatible with the smaller population inferred by the numbers of house foundations.

Ethnohistoric accounts as well as archaeological data from Campeche favor a late-fifteenth–early-sixteenth-century date for the Lobil Phase. This phase is identified with the indigenous population present in the area at the time of Spanish contact. Similarly, the house foundations are correlated with subsequent less populous occupations in this zone as mentioned in seventeenth-century references.

The Lobil Phase in southern Quintana Roo is an archaeological phase and could well correlate with a diversity of tribal identifications. It may be a local manifestation of a much wider population group, one component of which could be the Cehache Maya in the west. The same phase could correlate with other, as yet unnamed tribal groups to the south in Belize, at the same date.

The presence of the Lobil Phase in Quintana Roo is also significant in that it has served to obscure the Classic Period distribution of the

Central Yucatecan style of architecture. This distribution is more than doubled from the previously recognized geographic spread by the addition of a new distributional zone in Quintana Roo, extending as far east as Lake Bacalar and as far north as Uomuul.

ACKNOWLEDGMENTS

For encouragement and support through permission to investigate, gratitude is expressed to the Instituto Nacional de Antropología e Historia, particularly to Arq. Ignacio Marquina and Arq. Eduardo Matos M. The contribution of Norberto González of the Centro Regional del Sureste de INAH by his unfailing good humor and support is greatly appreciated.

The essential financial support was generously provided by the Canada Council, the Richard Ivy Foundation, and the Royal Ontario Museum.

12 Coapa, Chiapas: A Sixteenth-Century Coxoh Maya Village on the Camino Real by Thomas A. Lee, Jr.

INTRODUCTION

One aspect of the New World Archaeological Foundation program of investigation into the history and ecology of human occupation along the uppermost tributaries of the Grijalva River of Chiapas, Mexico, is a direct-historical-approach study of an extinct group of Maya speakers, the Coxoh (Lee 1974; 1975; Lee and Markman 1976a; 1976b). This study has several objectives, not necessarily given here in their order of importance. One primary aim, however, is an attempt to test the practicality of the genetic model as a theoretical base, outlined for the Maya culture specifically by Evon Vogt (1971a).

The genetic model is, as is generally known, a conceptual framework for the study of a segment of culture history which limits its scope to "a group of tribes which are set off from all other groups by sharing a common physical type, possessing common systemic patterns, and speaking genetically related languages" (Romney 1957:36). Further description of the genetic model will not be presented here (but see Vogt 1963; 1971a; 1971b; Romney 1957; and criticism of Sanders 1966 and Price 1974).

Methodologically there is no reason for not limiting the scope of the genetic model, in the beginning, to a single linguistic unit, rather than to the entity of the related group of languages. At least in the beginning, minimal units of analysis and limited variables are the operational base of any sound research program. The Coxoh Colonial Project is the definition, principally through the techniques of archaeology and ethnohistory, of the exact temporal, spatial, and systemic culture parameters of the sixteenth-century through the eighteenth-century Coxoh Maya. The application of linguistic, physical anthropological, and ethnographic methods is also important if the goals of the project are to be reached, and these methods are briefly mentioned below.

From the total description of the extinct Coxoh will be extracted an indigenous, material culture baseline of known linguistic affiliation. This will be a solid anchorpoint from which comparisons and contrasts with earlier Pre-Conquest systemic cultural patterns can be confidently made. The larger, parent project of the foundation is currently concerned with the entire continuum of human occupation in the upper Grijalva River basin and, while we hold no illusions as to how far back linguistically identified attribute, modal, or even whole systemic patterns can be traced, any step beyond the veil of the Conquest is, I think, a big one and most worthwhile.

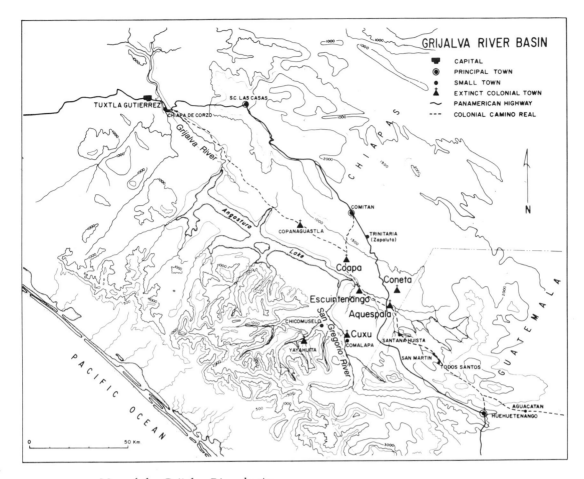

FIGURE 12–1. Map of the Grijalva River basin.

A third objective of this project is the interrelation of the Coxoh and their natural environment. Ecologically, the Coxoh, of course, faced some new problems in the settlement pattern forced on them by the Spanish policy of *reducción y congregación*. The specific dimensions of the environment must be clearly spelled out and closely studied to learn just how they affected, for better or for worse, the development of the colonial communities. The Coxoh also had to face many readjustments necessitated by the utilization of new tools and domestic plants and animals brought by the Spanish. There are already indications in our research that this was a long and costly process for the Coxoh. However, the slowness which characterized the Coxoh acquisition of these new, prestigious, but carefully controlled Spanish elements probably allowed for their relatively unproblematical functional integration into the indigenous economy.

A final purpose of this project is an attempt to understand the process of Coxoh acculturation from an indigenous Maya, presumably Late Classic, base through the Conquest period into a Spanish Colonial *pueblo de indios* (Markman 1970).

The Coxoh were confined to the upper Crijalva River basin along its tributary, the San Gregorio (Fig. 12-1), to the adjacent flanks of the Chiapas Highlands to the north, and to a tip of the Highlands plateau, including a small area around the towns of Comitan and Trinitaria (formerly Zapaluta). Coxoh territory was an area roughly triangular in shape, with the base along the Mexico-Guatemala border and the apex somewhere not too far north of Comitan. The triangle is about thirty-five miles long on the base by forty-five miles to the apex, and it covers roughly 788 square miles.

The Coxoh settlement pattern is a replication of that known for all other Maya groups surrounding the Grijalva River basin, both in Mexico and in Guatemala. That is, each different Maya linguistic group is distributed in a continuous strip from the Lowlands (*tierra caliente*) to the Highlands (*tierra fria*), occupying all microenvironmental zones within the strip. The distribution clearly has sound ecological reasons for its universal acceptance by the indigenous Maya population.

However, the study of the Coxoh ecology will be limited principally to the hot, dry valley surrounding the San Gregorio River and to the cooler upland flanks of the Highlands to the north. This is necessary for two reasons: Comitan and Trinitaria are (1) large, linguistically complex towns, and (2) towns which have physically covered over and subsequently altered, if not altogether destroyed, any original Coxoh community pattern. Therefore, the data from the cooler and wetter end of the environmental continuum are unavailable for consideration. However, in both numbers and area occupied, the Coxoh of the hot country far outstripped their relatives in the Highlands, and a basic description based solely upon them is well justified.

Excepting, then, the Highlands projection, the Coxoh area lies between 540 meters (1,771 feet) and 1,260 meters (4,133 feet) above sea level. The topography can best be characterized as a cul-de-sac with a broad river valley floor walled in by the dramatic rise of the southern slopes of the Chiapas Highlands to the north and the northern flanks of the Cuchumatanes Mountains of Guatemala to the south.

The mean annual temperature of the region ranges from a high of 24° C. (76° F.) to a low of 22° C. (72° F.). The annual mean precipitation is about 1,200 millimeters (47.22 inches) 95 percent of it falling in the summer months (June–September). Under the Koppen classification, modified for Mexico, this area is classified Awl "(w)(i')g (*Cartas de Clima* 1970).

The flora of the Coxoh area is very diverse, ranging from the cool, humid, evergreen forest border at the highest altitudes to the hot, dry, tall tropical forest in the lower altitudes. The dominant species of the evergreen forest are pines and oaks, while ceiba, guajilar, and chicozapote are the most prominent members of the tropical forest. Between these two extremes is a gradation of vegetation beginning with the low brush-chaparral zone just below the evergreen zone, followed by the thorny acacia-mesquite forest zone which interfingers with the high tropical forest. The acacia-mesquite floral zone is confined to hillslopes with poor rocky soil, while the high forest is only found on the valley floor where the alluvium is deep and rich.

A unique microenvironmental zone 2 kilometers (1.2 miles) by 8.6 kilometers (5.6 miles), or 17.2 square kilometers (10.32 square miles), is formed in one flatter part of the San Gregorio River Valley by the highly lime-charged water which covers most of it. This is the beautiful and exotic Lagartero Swamp, a day's walk from either the Chiapas Highlands or the Cuchumatanes Mountains. This dramatically different environmental zone has a floral base of the high forest common to the region as a whole, but it also has an entire gamut of plants which need a constant water supply. These include large sabino trees, certain climbing and running vines, reeds, water lilies, ferns, and many others. The faunal complement of the Lagartero environment has several species that are rarely found elsewhere in the region, including the tree duck, crocodile, and, until recently, the tapir.

ETHNOHISTORY

The Coxoh, soon after their conquest, probably in 1528, were concentrated into five small villages or *pueblos de indios* (Lee and Markman 1976a). Three of these villages were located along the Camino Real, which joined the capital of the Capitanía de Guatemala and Ciudad Real, or San Cristóbal Las Casas, as it is now known. San Cristóbal was the seat of government of the Alcaldía Mayor of Chiapas and was subject to Guatemala throughout the Colonial Period, except for a short time in the very beginning. All five villages were founded on new sites which have no recognizable Pre-Columbian occupation. The villages of Aquespala, Escuintenango, and Coapa were founded on the Camino Real in order to provide service facilities for civil and ecclesiastical authorities and other travelers or merchants. The other two villages, Coneta and Cuxu, are located to the north and south, respectively, well away from the principal routes of Colonial Period communications. These small towns apparently were developed to take advantage of a high Pre-Columbian indigenous population in the area surrounding each and were built in new, previously unoccupied localities.

History of Coapa

The historical and ethnohistorical study of the Coxoh is still in progress and, therefore, our data are still scattered and uneven. We can say that Coapa was founded sometime prior to 1554 (Flores Ruiz 1973: 181), for in that year it had a resident priest. Thirty years later, Friar Ponce spent the night there while passing through the area and found it well populated (Ponce 1948:19–20). In 1591 there was at least one resident Spaniard in Coapa (AGCA A1.57, 1591). Fifteen years later Coapa was administered religiously by Comitan, and, since there were only five priests for nine widely scattered communities, it is not likely that one was a priest residing in Coapa (Remesal 1966, vol. 2:487). By 1660 Coapa had become greatly reduced in size and was a *visita* of Escuintenango, a village having a resident priest. (AGCA A1.39, 1660a; 1660b). Ximénez (1930, vol. 2:199–200) tells us that Coapa was destroyed by pestilence in 1680. A long document containing the search for former Coapa *tributarios* reports less than twenty of the former inhabitants living in towns surrounding Coapa, and all several leagues away. The reasons given for the abandonment of Coapa were bats, mosquitoes, and especially bad water (the last complaint is well attested to by all who lived in our field camp at Coapa and who occasionally had to drink the highly sulfur-charged water).

Coapa had been important to the good functioning of the Camino Real. Without overnight stopping places with a resident population, travelers were forced to sleep out under the stars, a custom apparently abhorred by the Spanish. More important, the lack of people living at the overnight stop now meant that travelers could no longer count on finding food and would be forced to purchase something to carry with them. Nor could travelers any longer obtain burden bearers to go from one town to the next, as had formerly been the custom. Therefore, the abandonment of Coapa left a problem area in the communication system.

After Coapa became extinct there are several documents referring to the need for its resettlement (AGCA A1.23, 1698). Thirty years later a town was founded about one league north of Coapa with Tzeltal Indian families from the 1712 uprising. This town was called Nuestra Señor de la Encarnación, a name which apparently referred indirectly to extinct Coapa and to the reappearance of a formal town in the same general area (Ximénez 1930, vol. 2:199–200). However, this town did not last long. Fifty years later, in 1783, the Alcalde Mayor of Tuxtla was returning from a trip to Guatemala and stayed at the nearby Corral de Piedra ranch, finding it the only place inhabited in the area (Alcalde Mayor 1953:74). Thereafter, the settlement pattern of a few large, widely scattered cattle ranches persisted in the area until the 1940's, when Mujica, a small agrarian colony, was established one league to the west of Coapa.

PHYSICAL ANTHROPOLOGY

The Coapa osteological remains are being studied by Dr. Luis Vargas, physical anthropologists of the Instituto de Investigaciones Antropológicas, UNAM. Through the analysis of both standard anatomical measurements and discrete traits, phenotypic and genotypic characteristics of this community will be determined. An attempt will be made to establish the Coapa physical type and degree of population homogeneity as well as the life expectancy, rate of mortality among age groups, and other aspects of the Coapa demography. These different aspects of the Coapa population will be then compared with data available from the other four Coxoh villages and with nearby modern Maya populations in order to test the following hypothesis: in a relatively stable indigenous situation, language unity does reflect a measurable degree of phenotypic and genotypic unity.

LINGUISTICS

There is a wealth of archival and published evidence that Coxoh was spoken at Coapa, Coneta, Cuxu, Escuintenango, and Aquespala (see AGCA A1.11.3, 1698; A1.24, 1717; Ponce 1948; Feldman 1972; 1973a; 1973b). Coxoh was also spoken at nearby Comitan and Trinitaria (AGCA A1.39, 1659; 1662; Feldman 1972:38; Ximénez 1930, vol. 2: 29), although previously these communities had been identified as solely Tzeltal-speaking towns (Calnek 1970:111–112, 118).

No known speakers of Coxoh exist today, but we are carrying out a specific search for it among older bilingual informants in the area of its ancient distribution. Nothing definite has so far been achieved, but the preliminary results (location of nine locally born bilinguals) are encouraging.

An informant at Colonia San Caralampio reported to me that his now deceased parents were born in Trinitaria and spoke an *idioma* which he says was called "Sectal." He also reported that the speakers of this language could not communicate through it with those from Colonias Cárdenas and Triunfo, who today speak Tojolabal. Otto Schumann and I made a subsequent visit to Trinitaria to follow up this lead, and we interviewed an old *rezador* (shaman, or prayer-maker), Miguel Calvo Calvo, who Schumann says speaks a variety of the Tzeltal language. It seems likely now that "Sectal" and this Tzeltal variant are one and the same. It remains to be seen if "Sectal" and Coxoh are the same or not. At this moment the possibility appears to be a good one.

Kaufman (1974:85) has said that Coxoh is another term for Chicomuceltec. This seems clearly an error, since there are many documents stating that Cabil was spoken at Chicomucelo and at Yayahuita. Cabil may be another name for Chicomuceltec. In the original document written in Chicomuceltec, the inhabitants label themselves as Cotoque (Zimmerman 1966), but Kaufman (1976:102) now says that this label applies to Motozintlec-Tuzantec. The rationale of this argument is still forthcoming.

There are archaeological grounds for arguing that the small area occupied by the Chicomuceltec in the canyons and plains at the foot of the east flanks of the Sierra Madre underwent a ceramic development which began in the Late Classic period and continued on at least to the Conquest. This development was significantly different from that seen either along the Grijalva River or in the San Gregorio River Valley where the Coxoh resided.

Originally, after examining the intermediate and contiguous geographic position of the Coxoh between the Chuj and Jacaltec in Guatemala and the Tojolabal in Chiapas, we suggested that the Coxoh language was probably one or another of these three closely related languages, or something in between (Lee and Markman 1976a). Jocaltec and Chuj/Tojolabal have a glottochronological separation of twenty-one centuries, while Chuj and Tojolabal differ by only sixteen centuries (Kaufman 1974:85). There are ethnohistorical data showing that the Chuj and Jacaltec groups have been in their present position on the north flanks of the Cuchumatanes Mountains and on the adjacent valley floor around the south side of the Lagartero Swamp since the sixteenth century and probably much earlier. The Tojolabal are much more difficult to fix in space due to the fact that they are not well known either ethnographically or ethnohistorically. Nevertheless, they also appear to have been in about their present position in the Chiapas Highlands since the Conquest. The Tojolabal still share a common border with the Chuj between the Cuchumatanes Mountains and the Chiapas Highlands in the Montebello Lakes region. The Tojolabal also still take an annual tithe to San Mateo Ixtatan, an ancient Chuj salt source northeast of Huehuetenango. All this demonstrates that these two groups are still very close culturally as well as linguistically. The two languages surround the Coxoh area on the northeast, east, and southeast sides, but the "Sectal" or Tzeltal variant at Trinitaria now leads me to believe that Coxoh may have been part of the larger Tzeltal language distribution. This is also suggested by the early document described below.

Although several archives were researched for documents written in Coxoh, no definitely known records have been located. There is one early-sixteenth-century document, however, which contains calendrically derived last names of some Coxoh people from Coapa, demonstrating that the Coxoh knew and were using a version of the western Tzeltal-Chuj Maya calendar (Baroco 1970). This document is a rather large book containing two different kinds of information. The first part is a registry of baptisms and marriages performed from 1557 to 1584. The second part is much smaller and consists of the regulations of the Cofradía of the Virgen del Rosario and a list of its members. Baroco was unable to decide whether the document came from Coapa, Comitan, or Copanaguastla, but he finally leaned toward the latter because the book began in the same year Copanaguastla was founded. Baroco might have been more positive if he had not been led astray by following Becerra (1930), who thought Coapa was east of Comitan at Tepancuapan or nearby instead of in its actual location, a few hours' walk up the valley to the south from Copanaguastla.

Another small piece of evidence in this mosaic is the fact that the Virgen del Rosario was an important saint at Copanaguastla, and it was probably for her that the Cofradía regulations were written. This image is locally very famous and still draws large crowds to Socoltenango, where it exists today. In 1645 the last eight families at Copanaguastla were moved to Socoltenango (Ximénez 1930, vol. 2:193), after the former town had been decimated by disease.

A final piece of evidence almost certainly settles the matter of the document's place of origin. One of the priests who signed the first entries of this book is Domingo de Ara, who we know was the author of the Tzeltal dictionary written at Copanaguastla now in the Bancroft Library (1570?). A copy of this work is also available in the Gates collection at Brigham Young University.

In order to make more careful, valid analogies of related contemporary ethnography with the Coxoh archaeological materials, a collaborative ethnoarchaeological project with Brian Hayden of Simon Fraser University is being developed. This project will attempt to study the settlement and community pattern and procurement, tool manufacture and wastage, and tool use and disposal. Special emphasis will be placed on tool kit pattern variations as they reflect different kinds of use-areas (domestic, ceremonial, religious and/or political, workshop, commercial, personal services, etc.).

A Maya linguist will collaborate with the project to furnish the indigenous glosses for terminology at all stages of data recovery and analysis. The linguist will also provide contemporary family structure, status, role, specialization, general functional and social organizational aspects of the material culture and community settlement pattern. Since the exact linguistic relationship of Coxoh is unknown, and there are very few bilingual indigenous people in the immediate Coxoh area, this project will concentrate on the nearest Coxoh neighbors, the Tzeltal, Tojolabal, and Mam villages in Mexico. If the results of the first study justify more research, the project will attempt to pursue similar goals in the Chuj and Jacaltec villages of nearby Guatemala.

COXOH EXCAVATIONS

Coneta was the scene of the first field season of the Coxoh Project in 1975. Almost three months were dedicated to mapping, excavating, and field data collecting there. The preliminary results of the Coneta work have been reported elsewhere (Lee and Markman 1976a).

During the months of February through April 1976, our attention was focused on Coapa, the best preserved Coxoh community. Here Eduardo Martínez, New World Archaeological Foundation topographer, mapped the site at a scale of 1:500 with a contour interval of one-half meter (Fig. 12-2). He was able to record most of the street system throughout the entire town, an area of sixty hectares (150 acres). The public buildings located on the map include a large church-convent complex, a T-shaped chapel, and two large linear secular buildings. These buildings surround a central plaza which contains a low, round, stepped pyramidal cross base in its west end. Other public structures include a barrio chapel, four cross bases at each major entrance to the town, and several quarries. The private, domestic structures recorded on the map include houses, sweatbaths, domestic animal pens, property walls along the streets, and patio division walls within the blocks.

While mapping was being done I was assisted in the excavations by Fausto Ceja, who directed investigation of the T-shaped chapel, two domestic houses, a sweatbath, and part of one of the secular public buildings facing the plaza. My own excavations were directed toward

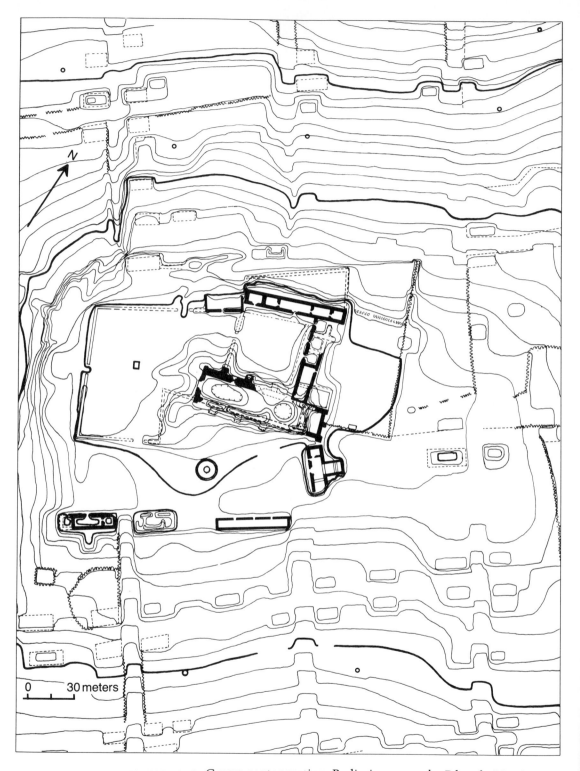

FIGURE 12–2. Coapa: center section. Preliminary map by Eduardo Martínez E.

understanding the church-convent complex with its associated rear patio or *huerta* (orchard), central patio, atrium, and cistern.

217
Coapa, Chiapas

Settlement Pattern

As we have seen above, the location of Coapa can be explained in the overall strategy of the Spanish Colonial communications network. The town is a vital, if not indispensable, service facility. However, a brief discussion of the local particulars of the environment will aid in understanding other aspects of the community's development, history, and demise.

Coapa is located on the highest (but still rather low) ridge on the south side of the Ontela Valley. The ridge has a thin soil mantle and is covered by mixed forest flora midway between the acacia-mesquite zone and the high tropical forest zone. In the valley at the foot of the ridge, about five hundred meters from the center of the town, several small, westerly-trending streams and small springs drain the palm-crowded valley floor. They coalesce into one large stream, which turns south immediately, penetrating the low range of hills on which Coapa stands. Farther south, this stream empties into two deep, round lakes and finally into the Grijalva River. The local water, as indicated earlier, is clear and running but sulfurous. Food cooked in it turns sour. Beans, for instance, never cook soft. Local residents prefer to haul rain water stored in a small, muddy, open reservoir an hour away for cooking and drinking. Water for human consumption would have always been a problem at Coapa, but water for ordinary domestic purposes and for construction during the building phase of the masonry public building was plentiful at the foot of the ridge.

Community Pattern

There are three aspects of the town which characterize its community pattern: layout, orientation, and structural content of the public and domestic domains. Coapa, like most other Spanish-founded towns in the New World, is laid out in a regular grid pattern, with streets six meters wide and blocks sixty-six meters on a side. The streets may not be straight over their entire length nor form blocks that are uniformly square, but the symmetry and regularity are surprising, particularly to one accustomed to Pre-Columbian community patterns. Streets are usually eroded lower than the adjacent patio or lot level. The T-shaped chapel and the two public buildings on the south side of the plaza appear to have been laid out during the original planning and are incorporated into the gridded town plan.

The street system is oriented 44°30' west of true north and at right angles to this. This gives the "east-west" streets a 45°30' east of true north orientation. The T-shaped chapel has this orientation, suggesting that it is the original church of the town, rather than the larger church-convent complex whose ruins are so obvious today. The public buildings on the south side of the plaza, too, seem to coincide with this orientation and probably are of an equally early date. Only the main church-convent complex differs greatly from the town grid orientation. Part of this difference may be caused by the builders' desire to take maximum advantage of the slight rise in the center of the plaza on which the nave is built. But it may also reflect a desire for a more easterly orientation of the main altar than was afforded by the original town orientation.

An identical situation was found at Coneta, where the smaller, more primitively constructed, earlier church was in exact agreement with the orientation of the original town grid system, while the larger, main church-convent was not (Lee and Markman 1976a).

Public Structures

Chronologically the T-shaped masonry chapel appears to be one of the oldest public buildings at Coapa. The chapel façade faces the plaza and aligns with a street running uphill from the southeast. Behind the façade is a single large T-shaped room with a three-step altar which fills the entire end of the room at the end of the T-stem. In the center of the façade is a large, arched doorway flanked by two windows. Deeply incised, pinwheel design motifs decorate the raised band about the door exterior.

On the south side of the plaza is a long, narrow masonry building with three doors leading to a single room. Excavations in this building were inconclusive as to function, but the building appears to be a *posada* or *venta*, a lodging facility for passing travelers. It was the custom for Colonial travelers to sign in the community record book for their lodging and food eaten. At the end of the year, all such accounts were totaled and subtracted from the community tribute due the Crown.

Next to the *posada* in the same block is a second, smaller masonry building with a more complex interior space, divided into at least three rooms. This is believed to have been the seat of the civil government and the jail.

The central town square is dominated by the large masonry single-aisle church and its appended eleven-room L-shaped convent. A small sacristy between the north wall of the nave and the convent is reached from the nave by a door near the main altar. This door also gives access to the convent porch. Behind the main altar is a large, square, deep room which is the same width as the nave. This was originally believed to be a *camarín*, the room behind the altar where the images are dressed and where the ornaments destined for that purpose are kept. But, after testing the room, this seems not to be the case. The function of this room is still problematical, but it may have been for a large water deposit.

Excavations in the front of the nave, just inside the main door, produced eighty-four burials, only one of which was accompanied by any artifacts: a small metal star, with the stitching thread still preserved, was found on a fetal burial. Another fourteen burials were found in

two test excavations in the atrium, also showing no evidence of clothing or adornments.

There are at least four major stages of construction in the church-
convent complex at Coapa. First the nave and the sacristry were built.
Next the sacristy was doubled in size and the deep room behind the
main altar was added. Following this the first five convent rooms
(rooms 2–6) were built adjoining the sacristy. Finally the last six convent rooms (Rooms 1, 7–11) were added, enclosing the patio on the
north side and filling in the corner formed by the sacristy and deep
room.

The sacristy and at least part of the convent were later destroyed
by fire. The sacristy was never used again, and only further work will
aid in deciding if part of the convent and the church nave ever functioned after this fire. There are no archival records of an uprising,
so that we may assume, for the time being, that the fire was caused
accidentally or by lightning. The fire destroyed nearly everything in
the sacristy. Even metal objects, of which there were over four hundred recorded, were subjected to such intense heat that many formed
drops and puddles on the floor. A few recognizable metal objects were
recovered, as well as some small, spike-decorated pottery incense
burners made in the indigenous ceramic tradition.

Beneath the east sacristy window and connecting with an abandoned
room (Room 1), a large trash pile was found. It contained quantities
of the same incense burner type mentioned above, several other re-
storable vessels of the indigenous Coxoh tradition, two metal candle-
wick cutters, and a few vessels of the Spanish glaze tradition. All
had obviously been discarded through the window from the sacristy.

The large round cross base in the plaza may have been the location
of an open-air weekly market. The one structure classified on the basis
of surface observation as an elite residence may well have been just
that, but there is also a possibility that it was a store.

There are public structures outside the community center also.
These include a barrio chapel (orientation 54° east of north) and four
town cross bases at the main entrance to the town. Several quarries,
barrow pits, and other depressions still need to be tested, but they
appear to be reservoirs for retaining rain water.

Domestic Structures

The domestic community at Coapa is comprised of the convent for
the full-time religious practitioners and the numerous individual
house and patio complexes. Each complex includes the house, often
a separate kitchen building, the patio, an open-air work and living
area adjacent to the house partially enclosed informally by the kitch-
en and street fence or formally by a patio wall, and often a sweatbath.
No recognizable storage structures have been located. Corn was probably stored inside the house just as it is today in the area.

Four economic levels within the community have been recognized
according to qualitative characteristics of the houses. The economic

levels probably equate one-to-one with comparable levels of political authority and an intracommunity hierarchy of social prestige and control. Certainly at the top was the convent of the religious practitioners. Just below this were the few elite residences of the community. These, like the convent, were built of stone masonry walls and had true arched doorways. The elite residences, however, were constructed with smaller living spaces, thinner walls, and grass roofs. Part of the convent had a tile roof, but perhaps not when originally built.

After the elite residence class comes a middle class characterized by houses with a special *jacal* wall construction called *corazón de piedra* and grass roofs. The large lower class had houses with normal *jacal*, or pole-and-cornstalk, walls and grass roofs.

There are 336 domestic houses still visible in the community, not counting the convent. Of these, 331 are structures of the lower and middle classes. A total of 83 sweatbaths are also identifiable, giving a ratio of 1:4. On the basis of surface observation, only 5 residences qualify for the elite class.

Portable Material Culture

The description, analysis, and comparison of the Coapa artifacts has only recently begun. In comparison with those of Pre-Columbian communities, the portable material culture inventory of Coapa appears to be most impoverished. Even with the added category of metal, the range of types and variations within artifacts are extremely restricted. This may be due partly to a combination of poor preservation in the shallow Colonial sites and Coapa's short length of occupation. Also, Christianity eliminated many items normally found in connection with the worship and maintenance of native Pre-hispanic religion. Nor was there any longer a need for elite burial and cult offering items. The only indigenous ceramic ceremonial holdover found is the spike-decorated and lime-painted incense burner.

Except for the incense burner type, only domestic functional indigenous forms seem to continue into the Colonial Period. These include the triple-loop-handled water jar, simple silhouette bowls, jars, colanders, and spindle whorls, all of which were made in the polished red and scraped brown indigenous traditions. This is by far the most common pottery in all domestic situations, including the convent. The candleholder is a new form made in the indigenous tradition, and there are probably others.

Glazed pottery of the Spanish tradition is also found in all domestic situations. It is always rare, but even the most humble house excavated had some examples.

The lithics from Coneta have been studied by Brian Hayden (1976a), who also has made a preliminary analysis and interpretation based on our excavated material from Coapa (Hayden 1976b). There is not time here to go into the many provocative ideas his paper raises, but I would like to mention a few of the more interesting aspects of his preliminary results. Coneta and Coapa are very similar in regard to the same broad range of stone-working techniques, and only the materials used tend to vary. Obsidian is present in both communities to about the same degree, suggesting that both had equal access to trade routes in terms of traditional trade items. Inequality of access to another material from sources near San Cristóbal las Casas is indicated by the presence of an as yet unidentified, but characteristic stone in higher frequencies at Coapa, and this seems to be directly related to the latter's position on the Camino Real.

Interpretation of lithic assemblage differences between domestic houses at Coapa suggests that there is one house in which the inhabitants were not involved in routine subsistence activities; elderly occupants or some specialized use of the structure other than residence is indicated. A second house, typically domestic in its total lithic assemblage but with a very high point and cutting flake count, may be the home of a male hunting specialist. Stone implements were always more important at Coapa than scarce, hard-to-come-by metal ones.

Metal is ubiquitous, found in all situations, domestic and public, sacred and secular. Metal, however, is never as plentiful as are lithics. Further excavations must be made to learn if this difference is cultural, functional, or economic. The large quantitative difference at this time appears to be a matter of economics. The most common metal item is the handmade nail with flat head and square cross-section. There are more fragments of pointed tools (knives, chisels, machetes, etc.) at Coapa than at Coneta, and this difference is suggested again to be a result of Coapa's position on a principal Colonial trade route.

Subsistence

Now a few remarks regarding diet. As at Coneta, the single most obvious source of animal protein is a fresh-water gastropod called *jute* (*Pachychilus* sp.), locally available in large quantities in the nearby marsh. Over thirty-seven thousand specimens were analyzed in five eating-mark patterns (patterns of marks on the shells as a result of eating from them) and seven sizes from the twenty-two excavations at Coapa. Four other land and fresh-water gastropods were present, but they are very rare. The *jute* was obviously eaten by everyone, all the time, but until the rest of the faunal material has been analyzed we will be unable to say whether the gastropod represents the most significant source of the total animal protein in the Coapa diet. Cattle and horse bones are present in the collection, as well as chicken and turkey.

As I think is clearly recognized, corn has for several millennia been the subsistence basis for Mesoamerican agriculturists, including, of course, the Coxoh. These same groups also knew and used much of the entire range of subsistence possibilities in their natural environment. A Coxoh example is related by Friar Ponce (1948). He tells of a tree in Coxoh territory called *pit* (*Enterolobium ciclocarpum*), or *guanacaste* as it is now known (also called *pich* in Yucatan), with seeds shaped like beans inside black, half-round pods. These seeds are eaten in time of hunger. Ponce further states that he was told that when these trees bear fruit there is not going to be a good crop of corn, and vice versa. Furthermore, it is believed that if the *pit* near one village bears fruit in combination with a good corn crop, then another village nearby will lack both. Ponce ruins this neat piece of ecological folklore by saying, "It is all a marvelous thing if that's the way it really is."

Chile and beans as well as *pollinas de Castilla* (chickens) and *pollinas de la tierra* (turkeys) figure in the tribute list of 1684 for nearby Escuintenango (AGCA A3.16, 1684), and undoubtedly they were raised then and even earlier at Coapa.

Escuintenango also paid thirteen *mantas* and one *pierna* tribute that same year (ibid.). In 1625, Gage (1946:1) wrote about the great development in cotton growing and weaving at Escuintenango. The *mantas* and *pierna* are, without a doubt, of cotton. (*Mantas* are indigenous cotton cloths of a specific size; *piernas* are literally "legs" but refer to a fraction of a *manta*.) The many spindle whorls found at Coapa indicate that this Coxoh community was also participating in at least the cloth-weaving end of the cotton industry, if not indeed the cultivation of this valuable plant.

DOMINICAN LIFE AT COAPA

It is too early to draw many conclusions about the Coxoh from our work at Coapa. There remains much to do, including at least another field season of excavations. Therefore, I would like to leave you with a picture of Coapa as Friar Ponce's scribe recorded it on their entrance into the town, almost 390 years ago to the day:

> . . . such a good welcome was made the Padre Comisario in that town and with such solemnity, it was as though he were the general of the St. Dominican order. From the entrance of the town to the church, the streets were filled with [floral] arches, and leading us through them were many Indian dancers, cheering him and creating for him a holiday. There was much music of flute, trumpet, and bells. At the church the Indian women formed two lines, one on each side of the route taken by the Padre Comisario. All showed the devotion they have for our habit and state. The *indios principales* and their women crowded around altogether to see the Padre Comisario, and they offered him chickens and eggs; the same was done by the Indian women catechists. (Ponce 1948:19–20)

13 Religious Syncretism in Colonial Yucatan: The Archaeological and Ethnohistorical Evidence from Tancah, Quintana Roo
by Arthur G. Miller and Nancy M. Farriss

Belief systems of the past are among the most difficult phenomena to study. Beliefs are not always consciously articulated, much less recorded, even in supposedly literate societies, and discrepancies often exist between what people profess to believe and what they actually believe.

The problems are compounded when dealing with a subordinate group in a colonial setting, such as the indigenous population of Post-Conquest Mesoamerica, whose traditional beliefs were proscribed by the conquerors. Most of the documents on Colonial Mesoamerica were written by people of an alien culture, that is, Spanish Christianity, who may have known only a part of what the Indians believed—because the Indians deliberately concealed the rest from them—and who may have misinterpreted what evidence they did possess.

One approach is to concentrate on actions rather than dogma, since beliefs are embedded in behavior and perhaps more accurately expressed by behavior than by verbal explanation. However, for Colonial Mesoamerica we are still faced with written sources that, although abundant, are very uneven and possibly misleading. And it is for this reason that a collaboration between history and archaeology can be particularly fruitful. Material evidence can provide essential clues missing from the documentary record—either because the Spanish were unaware of or failed to record them—and help to interpret evidence that may have been distorted through the alien filter of European perceptions.

In this essay we combine both types of evidence in an attempt to shed some light on native responses to Christianity, especially among the Maya of the East Coast of Yucatan during the transitional period of Conquest and the first century of Colonial rule. The archaeological evidence is derived from a Colonial site adjacent to the Pre-Columbian center of Tancah, where surveys were carried out and test pits made in and around the principal structure, an early Spanish-Maya chapel. The documentary evidence consists of unedited manuscript material from the Archivo General de Indias (abbreviated as AGI in the citations) and of contemporary published records and chronicles.

COLONIAL TANCAH

The East Coast of Yucatan is an ideal laboratory in which to study the natural dynamics of Maya-Spanish culture contact, because of the relatively peaceful nature of that contact. Unlike the rest of the peninsula, which suffered a long and often brutal Conquest, Cozumel and the adjacent East Central Coast were brought under Spanish dominion with scarcely any bloodshed. Neither Hernán Cortés during his stopover in 1519 on the way to the Conquest of the Aztec Empire, nor the Adelantado Francisco de Montejo in his first *entrada* of 1527–1529, nor Montejo's nephew in the final phase of the Conquest in 1543 encountered any concerted opposition. Cooperation and sometimes flight were the usual initial reactions, changing into passive resistance or sporadic threats of hostility when Spanish demands became excessive (Chamberlain 1948:15, 35–43, 227–228). Only one overt act of retaliation—the massacre of a group of stragglers left behind on the coast for the march inland—has been recorded (ibid.:58–59). Consequently, the area also escaped the savage military campaigns that devastated the Uaymil-Chetumal province to the south and the severe reprisals in the Cupul province to the west and north after the Great Revolt of 1545–1547.

Perhaps the East Coast Maya had already learned through their long and close contact with foreigners from the Central Mexican Highlands and intermediate areas the policy of passive resistance, a policy that the rest of the Colonial Maya were to develop eventually.

The spiritual conquest of the area, as we shall show later, was if anything more relaxed and perfunctory than the military one, so that the East Coast Maya were relatively free to respond to Christianity on their own terms. In addition, after the Conquest Period the region was isolated enough from the Spanish centers of economic and strategic importance to continue to enjoy a benign neglect from both Church and State.

The relative neglect by the Colonial authorities has resulted in a spottier written record for the East Coast than for areas of more direct concern to the Spanish imperial system. Nevertheless, with the aid of the material evidence, we can reconstruct at least the outlines of the Post-Conquest history of Tancah.

First of all, we can with a fair degree of certainty establish that the Colonial site of Tancah is the Tzama (also written Zama, Çama, and Sama) of the Colonial documents. Tzama has been identified in recent times as Tulum, the Pre-Columbian coastal site four kilometers to the south (Fig. 13-1; Lothrop 1924:13, 64). Roys (1957:146–148) equates the two, while also citing evidence that Tancah rather than Tulum is the more likely site for the Colonial port of Tzama described in the 1579 *Relaciones de Yucatán*. The apparent contradictions in this source can be resolved by a careful look at the local topography: although what is clearly Tulum was described as the landfall for the southern seaward approach to Tzama (RY 1898–1900, vol. 2:200), the entire reef-enclosed bay extends from below Tulum to a point north of Tancah; the opening in front of Tancah is the only plausible entrance for the deep-draught Spanish ships that traded between Honduras and Tzama after the Conquest; and the Tancah portion of the bay is the only safe anchorage (Farriss and Miller 1977) (Fig. 13-2). In addition, Tzama is described in the *Relaciones* as a scattered set-

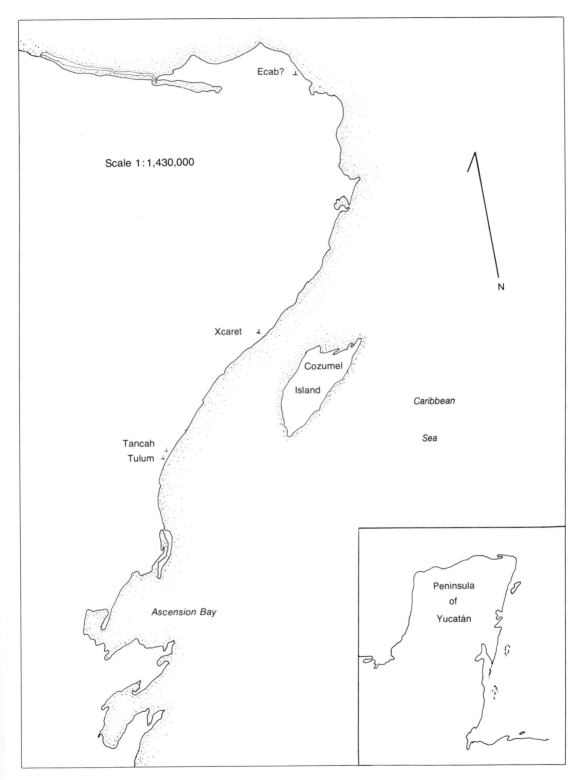

FIGURE 13–1. Map of the East Coast of Yucatan, showing location of Pre-Contact and Post-Contact sites discussed in the text.

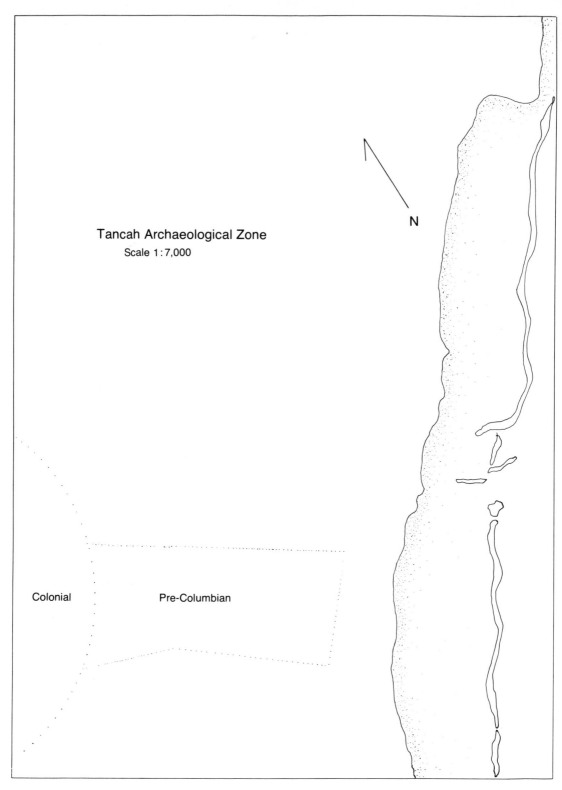

Tancah Archaeological Zone
Scale 1:7,000

N

Colonial

Pre-Columbian

FIGURE 13–2. Map of the Tancah archaeological zone, showing areas of Pre-Columbian and Colonial settlement at Tancah-Tzama.

tlement (RY 1898–1900, vol. 2:197), a pattern that corresponds more closely to what our survey revealed at Tancah than to the compact, walled site of Tulum.

There was clearly Post-Conquest occupation at Tancah. The evidence includes a majolica sherd and the head of a horse carved in coral recovered from the uppermost level of Tancah Structure 44 during the 1974 excavations, and a sixteenth-century Spanish ceramic water jug recovered during an underwater exploration of the cenote cave at Tancah. Although these items could be interpreted merely as proof of a Spanish presence in the general area during early contact, evidence exists of sustained Colonial settlement at the site: in addition to the chapel, there are remains of at least one other Colonial structure, a small rectangular "house" with boulder-built *mampostería* walls and presumably thatched roof, which was possibly a residence for the visiting Catholic priests (RY 1898–1900, vol. 2:199); and the remains of at least four stone walls of Spanish design exist among the housemounds in this sector of the site. A modern attribution for these Spanish-type constructions is highly implausible. Aside from the ceramic evidence for an early dating from test pits in and around the chapel, we know that after Colonial settlement the area was abandoned to pirates, fugitives, and, later, *chicleros*, until the establishment in the present century of a cattle ranch, whose owner found these structures already in place.

Colonial records mention only two Post-Conquest villages on the East Coast between Bacalar, at the base of the peninsula, and Ecab, near Cape Catoche on the northeast tip: Pole, directly across from Cozumel, and Tzama, to the south. Surveys of the area, including our own from Xelha to Ascension Bay, have so far located only two Colonial sites. One of them is at Xcaret, a modern name which seems to correspond to Colonial Pole (Andrews and Andrews 1975:1, 10–12); and the other is at Tancah, which we believe can now be identified as Tzama (Fig. 13-1).

Perhaps the Tancah-Tzama site has previously eluded identification because it is located a kilometer inland from the coast, to the west of Pre-Columbian Tancah (Fig. 13-2). This location is probably not accidental. French and English pirates—often lumped together under the general term *corsarios luteranos*—began to harass the undefended East Coast of Yucatan as early as the 1560's (AGI, Mexico 359, 1565; Patronato 56, 1565) and became more of a menace in succeeding years (AGI, Mexico 359, 1579; Cogolludo 1688, Bk. 6, Ch. 9; Edwards 1957: 149–151). We know that the Colonial settlement at Pole was deliberately situated inland in order to be hidden from the sea (AGI, Mexico 361, 1664), and there is indirect evidence that Tzama, too, especially after it no longer served as a major Colonial port, was located well behind the concealing coastal ridge for protection from the sea raiders (AGI, Mexico 361, 1659). Only *vigías*, or lookouts, were posted on the shore to warn of the approach of enemy shipping, a practice common to the North Coast as well. It is possible that many of the East Coast Maya settlements had moved inland even earlier, some time in the 1520's between the early voyages of exploration and the first actual *entrada* by Montejo in 1527, in order to escape the Spanish shipping that began to frequent the area. Certainly Tulum, so conspicuous on its high seacliff, could well have been abandoned then, and its population could have dispersed or moved a short distance to Tancah; for nothing that could be identified at Tulum appears in the accounts as inhabited after Cortés's 1519 expedition.

The Colonial history of Tzama-Tancah and the central East Coast as a whole is one of continuous decline, almost as severe as in the Uaymil-Chetumal area but without being directly attributable to the ravages of a military campaign. It is likely that the most drastic phase of depopulation preceded the actual Conquest and therefore went largely unrecorded. The area must have been flourishing still in 1519 when Cortés visited it and have declined rapidly thereafter. Otherwise it is hard to understand why Montejo, who had accompanied Cortés and had seen both coasts during the earlier expedition, had bothered to return to the East Coast to launch his Conquest of Yucatan in 1527. The early introduction of contagious disease may well be a major cause for this sharp decline (Edwards 1957:129–132, 143), but it should also be noted that the basis of the area's prosperity, long-distance trade, had been severely shaken during this period by the Spanish Conquest of the Aztec Empire and subsequent campaigns in Central America.

In 1579, when Tzama's population had fallen to 50 tributaries, it was reported that the town at one time had contained "many Indians" (RY 1898–1900, vol. 2:197). This description scarcely tallies with the first colonial census of 1549, which lists only 88 male tributaries for Tzama (AGI, Guatemala 128, 1548–1549:386v.)–or 352 people, if we use Cook and Borah's conversion factor for 1549 of 4.0 (1971–1974, vol. 2:50). But Tzama's population loss between 1543 and 1549 could well have been greater than the slightly more than 50 percent drop estimated for the whole peninsula (ibid., vol. 2:61–65); or the report could refer to some earlier time after initial contact.

It is likely that the Post-Conquest loss was also due, in part, to commercial isolation and not solely to disease and dislocation. For a period after Conquest the East Coast, through Tzama, continued to serve as a link in the trade route, now taken over by the Spanish, between Honduras and the interior of the peninsula. But some time before 1579 the port for eastern Yucatan was shifted to the North Coast sites of Conil and, mainly, Río Lagartos (RY 1898–1900, vol. 2:173, 200; AGI, Mexico 359, 1605). Eventually Campeche became almost the sole port for the entire peninsula, the only one the Spanish could afford to fortify against the corsairs. It became increasingly evident that the other coastal settlements, especially those far from centers of Spanish population, could not be effectively protected, and a decision was made to abandon the entire East Coast down to Bacalar (AGI, Mexico 360, 1638).

The settlements on Cozumel, the most frequent target of raids, were the first to go: in the early 1650's they were resettled in Bolona (Cogolludo 1688, Bk. 4, Ch. 19), which can be traced through colonial records to the modern town of Xcan on the present boundary between Yucatan and Quintana Roo. In 1668 the remnant populations of Pole and Tzama, which by then had declined to one-half the 1579 figure for

Tzama alone—a mere twenty-five tributaries—were moved to Bolona and Chemax, another town further inland, presumably for the same reason (AGI, Mexico 245, 1668). Mention of Pole and Tzama and the two Cozumel villages in later documents (e.g., AGI, Contaduría 920, 1688) might lead investigators to believe that the sites remained inhabited (Roys et al. 1940:10). But, like other resettled communities, these four merely retained their separate identities as *parcialidades*, or subdivisions, of the towns to which they became annexed.

The starting point for Tzama cannot be fixed with the same precision as its terminal date. In many ways Postclassic Tancah simply merged into Colonial Tancah-Tzama, with a possibly gradual shift westward in the settlement pattern (Fig. 13-2). The construction of the chapel can most reasonably be dated to some time shortly after the final *entrada* of 1543, when most of the encomiendas in Yucatan were allocated. Tzama did not become part of an established parish until 1582, but it had been under the general aegis of the Franciscan mission territory of eastern Yucatan, and the *encomenderos* were responsible for church construction even in the absence of resident clergy. Furthermore, the chapel's size suggests a very early Post-Conquest date, before the population had dwindled to a remnant.

THE TANCAH CHAPEL

The Tancah chapel exhibits several Spanish and Maya features in combination (Fig. 13-3). Its most striking architectural characteristic is that it is a Christian form constructed by means of thoroughly Maya building techniques. It is essentially a raised platform, twenty-three by ten meters, capped with a stucco floor. The large boulder fill and the Tulum Red pottery sherds found in the lowest levels of our test pits would suggest a Late Postclassic horizon for the construction of the platform. Were it not for the non-Maya configuration of nave, galilee, and high walls on the east end, defining and protecting the altar area, and the platform's precise magnetic east-west orientation, the complex could easily be taken for one of the many Late Postclassic platforms which occupy the extreme western area of the site of Tancah, where the chapel was found. As Charlton (1972:206) has pointed out for the Valley of Teotihuacan, the transition from Pre-Conquest to Colonial is not immediately apparent in the ceramic sequence. A look at a profile drawing of the chapel's east wall (Fig. 13-4) reveals the use of large boulders set in a matrix of small stones and mortar, typical of the Late Postclassic Maya construction technique (called *mampostería* in the Colonial Period), which we repeatedly found during our 1974 excavation of the Tancah Structure 44 complex.

In plan our chapel is more like the Dzibilchaltun chapel (Folan 1970: Fig. 3), although much smaller, than it is like the Xcaret chapel (Andrews IV 1975: Fig. 39), located some fifty kilometers north of Tancah (Fig. 13-1). Because we found no roof rubble, we assume that the nave was originally enclosed by pole and thatch construction and that the stones of the four steps located on the north side marked the

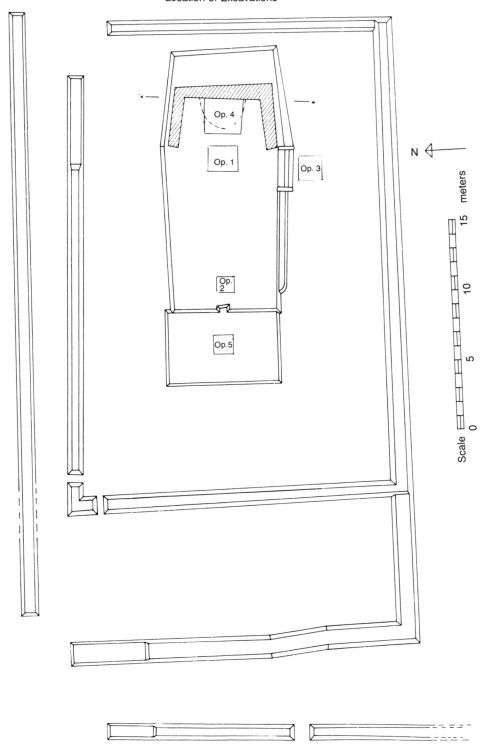

Tancah Structure Z
Location of Excavations

Op. 4

Op. 1

Op. 3

Op.
2

Op.5

N

Scale 0 5 10 15 meters

FIGURE 13–3. Tancah chapel, showing location of test pitting operations. Plan by Arlen F. Chase.

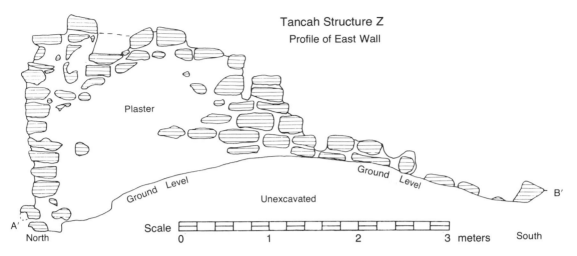

Tancah Structure Z
Profile of East Wall

Plaster

Ground Level

Ground Level

Unexcavated

A' North

Scale

0   1   2   3 meters South

B'

FIGURE 13–4. Elevation of east wall of Tancah chapel. Drawing by Arlen F. Chase.

entrance to the nave. Such an interpretation would explain the function of the narrow niche in the east side of the galilee as a repository for a *santo* or other holy image, which would have faced on to an open galilee and courtyard to the west of it. The most protected area was the altar, enclosed by *mampostería* construction on the east, north, and south sides. The open chapel design, with nave enclosed by pole and thatch or open on the sides with thatch roof only, is typical of early Colonial churches. We have documentary evidence that very few churches in the whole peninsula were made entirely of stone by the end of the sixteenth century (AGI, Mexico 396, 1599).

The chapel proper of galilee, nave, and altar area was bounded by a series of low, dry-laid walls, averaging one meter in height. On the north and west sides are parallel double walls; on the south and east side only single walls are extant. Although this area of Tancah has been used as a cattle ranch since the 1940's, we have direct testimony that none of these walls has been disturbed by cattle or men (José González Avilés 1975, personal communication).

In an unpublished sixteenth-century document (AGI, Mexico 369, 1573), two Franciscan friars report that they led the Maya in a procession around the patio of the church in Cozumel, and Molina Solís gives a description based on Colonial accounts (Molina Solís 1896: 832–835; Chamberlain 1948:319–320) of carefully organized processions into churches and of the practice of segregating the sexes as they entered. We suggest that the dry-laid walls surrounding the Tancah chapel serve the function of organizing processions into the chapel area.

The design of the mazelike walls surrounding the Tancah chapel suggests two processional directions (Fig. 13-3). To enter the chapel without climbing over the walls, the worshipers would have had to proceed through the openings in the walls at the northeast or northwest corners. Entering at the northeast corner, they would most likely have had to walk to the front of the chapel past the open galilee, where there was probably a venerated *santo*, and around to the south side entrance in order to enter the chapel itself; they could have taken a shortcut by going around the apse of the chapel to the south side entrance. However, formal ritual procession would favor a roundabout, frontal approach.

Entering the church yard from the northwest corner, the worshipers would have had to walk between the parallel north walls to get to the northeast corner and go around to the south side in the manner of those entering from the northeast. The two separate roundabout paths, as indicated by the arrangement of low walls, suggest a procession which may have been a practical means of accommodating and segregating into two groups large masses of converts.

The arrangement of these walls can be seen as an organizational device to segregate worshipers according to sex or some other criterion: one group entering by either the northeast or northwest corner and the other group entering by the opposite corner. Although segregation of worshipers by sex was a Spanish custom, we also have documents referring to Colonial Maya processions organized according to village divisions. We do not know whether these divisions may have originally been according to lineage, but we do know that by the sixteenth century they were fundamentally territorial, and that they were also used for village roll calls after Mass on Sundays and holidays (Cogolludo 1688, Bk. 4, Ch. 17).

Our excavation data from the Tancah chapel suggest that there was segregation by sex in the burial pattern we uncovered. Our nineteen burials encountered in the nave and galilee have been identified as male. In the pit next to the nave directly to the south of the staircase (Fig. 13-3: Op. 3) we found a skeleton which Dr. Frank Saul, who carried out our physical anthropological analysis, has identified as female. Although it is premature at this point to suggest that the nave was reserved for burial of men and the church yard for burial of women, the possibility of segregation of the dead by sex cannot be ignored in the light of the presence of ethnohistorical evidence for segregation of the living by sex.

The burials we encountered during the course of our investigation of the Tancah chapel provided insights into the nature of culture contact between Spanish and Maya on the East Coast. Most of the burials were located under the stucco floor of the nave, a practice which is not in itself Spanish, since the Maya buried their dead under the floors of their houses and temples. But the simple east-west dorsal position of most of the burials found, lacking offerings of any kind, clearly points to Christian practice. In all of our test pits inside the platform and next to it, with the significant exception of the altar area, we encountered burials, almost all of which were oriented in accordance with Christian practice. On the basis of our test pits it is not unreasonable to assume that every available space inside and outside the chapel was crammed with dead and that this chapel served as a consecrated burial ground.

Genetically, the physical anthropological evidence suggests a mixture of Spanish and Maya, with possible mestizo identification of the dead. This "mixed bag" of genetic types coincides with the mixed bag of burial practices we encountered and other factors that indicate the practice of religious syncretism in the use of this chapel at Tancah.

Our Operation 1 pit (Fig. 13-3), just underneath the nave's stucco floor, produced two burials (Fig. 13-5; Burials 4 and 5), one of which was virtually complete. The stucco floor of the nave had been opened to accept the body and subsequently repaired with fresh stucco. Skeleton 4 was found lying on its back with hands crossed over the chest, head toward the west, body in an east-west axis. The burial had been placed directly in the center of the eastern part of the nave, suggesting by its position relative importance. Burial 5 was encountered at the same level as Burial 4 and may have been partly disturbed in the process of interring Burial 4. With coccyx and 8 vertebra surviving, it was possible to determine that the orientation of Burial 5 was like that of Burial 4: east-west.

One class of evidence associated with Burial 4 unquestionably links it with Spanish Christian burial practices, if it does not securely identify the burial itself as that of a Spanish Christian. This evidence is in the form of two rusted iron nails found just below the skeleton of Burial 4. It is most probable that these nails were part of a wooden coffin belonging to Burial 4, the wood of which has long since disintegrated. Nailed wooden coffins are of course Spanish, not Maya, burial traits.

Our subsequent test pits in the nave and in the galilee of the chapel and another just in front of the stairs on the south side of the nave produced a total of twenty burials; almost all of them were simple, with no offerings, laid out on their backs in an east-west orientation. There was one significant exception: our Burial 13 in Operation 2 of a flexed figure found with a jade bead in its mouth. This burial appears to have been that of a young adult under eighteen years of age. Although the skull was fragmented, there was evidence of cranial deformation. This flexed burial with jade bead in mouth was most probably a Colonial Maya buried in the same manner as our Postclassic examples encountered in Tancah Structure 44 and serves as an example of the survival of Maya burial practices in the chapel.

Although the skeletal study has not yet been completed, our preliminary observations suggest mestizo and Maya physical types buried in the Tancah chapel. The mestizos were found in more important places near the altar, the Maya further away, most of them buried according to Christian practice, with one clear example following Maya burial customs.

The pit dug in front of the altar of the chapel (Fig. 13-3: Op. 4) produced no skeletons but proved to be the most fascinating and the one that most clearly suggested the presence of religious syncretism in the Tancah chapel. At 125 centimeters in the Operation 4 trench we encountered a foundation cache consisting of a fragmented pottery vessel which J. W. Ball has identified as an example of Tituc Orange Polychrome: Camichin Variety. This offering was centered directly in front of the altar, unmistakably a cache. Although this vessel was found in primary association with the Tancah chapel, the time of manufacture of this ceramic ware does not date the period of construction of this chapel. The discovery of this foundation cache raised two im-

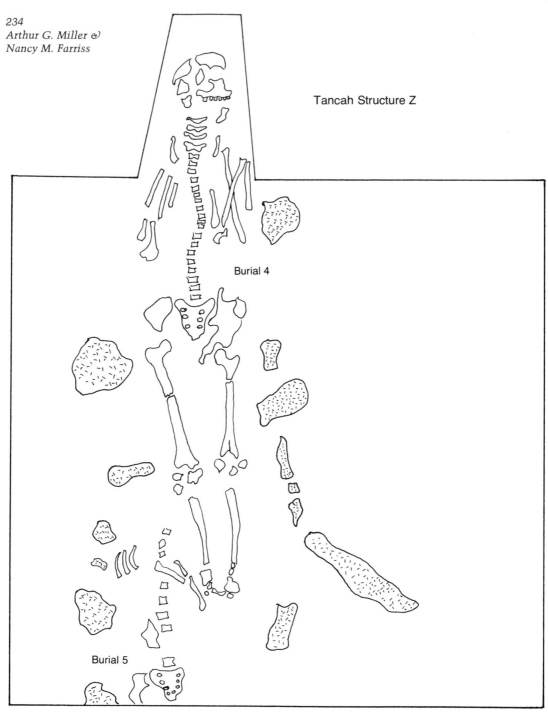

Tancah Structure Z

Burial 4

Burial 5

Operation 1, Level 3

Burials 4 and 5

Scale 1:11.4

N

FIGURE 13–5. Scale drawing of Burials 4 and 5 in Operation 1 of the Tancah chapel test pitting program.

mediate questions: (1) If the vessel pertained to the construction of an early Colonial chapel, how could the A.D. 450–550 time period assigned to this type be explained? (2) The fragmented vessel was badly weathered before interment as a foundation cache; if it was an heirloom—which could possibly explain its occurrence in a later context —one would expect the vessel to have been kept in such a way that it would not have been subjected to such weathering. What accounted for the vessel's extremely weathered state?

The explanation for these questions became clear as a result of careful examination of the four pits excavated into the chapel at bedrock. The analysis of the ceramic content of the pits indicated that the fill used in the construction of the platform derived from an Early Classic dump. Were it not for the Late Postclassic fill techniques of using large boulders on end which we recognized from the Late Postclassic platform at Tancah Structure 44, superficial examination of the cultural material alone would have suggested an Early Classic date for the construction of this platform. Examination of the ceramic lots from the four pits into this platform demonstrated that the lowest level produced Tulum Red Ware sherds, proving that the fill of the Tancah chapel was a secondary deposit representing reverse stratigraphy: an Early Classic midden was the source for the loose fill used in the construction of the Tancah chapel; scattered Late Postclassic sherds were deposited on the surface of this Early Classic dump. As the midden was excavated for use in the Tancah chapel, the uppermost level of the midden, containing the Late Postclassic sherds, was deposited first, forming the lowermost level of the chapel platform fill.

This explains the occurrence of the Late Postclassic sherds at the bottom of our pits of Early Classic fill, but what of the weathered Early Classic foundation cache? We reconstruct its deposition as follows: the fragmented Tituc Orange Polychrome vessel was found by the builders of the Tancah chapel in an Early Classic dump, possibly the same one that produced the Early Classic fill used in the construction of the chapel itself. The fragmented and weathered Early Classic pot may have been recognized by the Colonial Maya builders as an "old" vessel and was buried, probably secretly, as a foundation cache in the manner of a "pagan" cache. The precise circumstances of the foundation cache of the Tancah chapel can never be known for sure. But we do know it must have been laid down during the Late Postclassic–Early Colonial Period as indicated by the Tulum Red Ware sherds from the bottom levels of the chapel pits. The implications of this foundation cache clearly suggest the survival of Pre-Conquest traditions in a Post-Conquest context and is perhaps the most fascinating example of religious syncretism found at Tancah.

MAYA RESPONSES TO CHRISTIANITY

The development of religious syncretism in Mesoamerica is very imperfectly understood, especially for the Maya area. This is not surprising, since most of the evidence for Post-Conquest religious change has remained buried in the archives—or in the ground. Yucatan is considered one of the better-documented regions; yet little is known of the period between Fray Diego de Landa's campaign against idolatry in the early 1560's and the emergence of the cult of the Speaking Cross almost two centuries later (Madsden 1967:382–388; D. E. Thompson 1954).

The usual view of conversion is that it was purely nominal: Christian practices were imposed by force on top of a truncated but otherwise unchanged pagan foundation. The remnants of native religious tradition emerged after a long clandestine existence to mix with certain by then habitual Christian elements to form the syncretic religion of the Modern Maya. Donald Thompson (1954:16) sees an early beginning for the mixing process but still assigns a largely passive or defensive role to the Maya in their confrontation with Christianity.

The documentary and archaeological evidence from Tancah-Tzama and the surrounding area suggest that force may have played a less decisive part in the process of religious syncretism than we have realized. Other written records from the Colonial Period indicate that the Yucatec Maya in general were not always initially hostile to Christianity. A number of accounts by Franciscan friars relate that groups of unconquered Maya beyond the Colonial frontier accepted missionaries, fed and supported them, and even built churches for Christian worship, in the absence of any Spanish military force (AGI, Escribanía de Cámara 308A, 1582–1689). But without corroborating evidence, such as that from the site of Tancah, these accounts could easily be dismissed as tendentious or fanciful.

The uncoercive conditions under which Christianity was introduced to the East Coast of Yucatan are well documented. The first and only recorded attempt at conversion that was backed by any military power was the preaching by Montejo's chaplain in 1527 during the first brief *entrada* (Chamberlain 1948:41). After that, any ecclesiastics who visited the area were on their own: no Spaniards resided closer than Valladolid, several days' journey away through mainly uninhabited wilderness; and after Tancah declined as a port there were few visitors. In fact, the English may have visited the East Coast more often than the Spanish (Edwards 1957:152–155). They certainly had better maps of the area (AGI, Mexico 361, 1664).

The *encomenderos*, whose direct contact with their encomiendas was minimal, were at best indifferent to missionary activity. One of them ordered his people on Cozumel not to support or even heed the cleric who had been sent there by the Bishop of Yucatan in 1570 (Roys et al. 1940:7–10, 24–28). The Franciscans, despite Cogolludo's claim that his order had brought Christianity to Cozumel (1688, Bk. 7, Ch. 1), demonstrated little more missionary zeal than the laity or the secular clergy. In 1549 one of the early friars, Luis de Villalpando, visited the area, but for only three days (Scholes and Adams, eds. 1938, vol. 2:70). And in 1573 two friars who had been sent by the bishop to establish a permanent mission for the East Coast on Cozumel left after two weeks and refused ever to return (AGI, Mexico 369, 1573; Mexico 359, 1575).

Tzama and the other mainland settlement, Pole, received even less attention from the Church than Cozumel. The Bishop of Yucatan made a pastoral visit to the island for three weeks in 1563 (Scholes and Adams, eds. 1938, vol. 2:70), and the hapless cleric who spent six months there at the bishop's insistence in 1570 merely paused in Tzama on the way to perform baptisms (Roys et al. 1940:25). Someone must have supervised the construction of the crude churches in the two coastal villages and on Cozumel, but evangelization and ecclesiastical supervision were at best haphazard. Cozumel received only twice-yearly visits for a few days at a time from some unidentified priest (Scholes and Adams, eds. 1938, vol. 2:91). Tzama (and possibly Pole also), though technically within the Franciscan orbit, was merely a frontier outpost of the distant friary in Valladolid (RY 1898–1900, vol. 2:197–198).

Not until 1582 did the East Coast receive a resident priest, and even then the *cabecera*, or curate's residence, was on Cozumel, with Pole and Tzama as *visita* towns of the parish (AGI, Mexico 359, 1583; Scholes et. 1936–1938, vol. 2:62). Neither of these mainland settlements, particularly Tzama-Tancah, which is even further away from Cozumel than Pole, could have received very close supervision from their curate.

The pagan flavor of some of the Colonial practices discovered at Tancah is thus easy to explain. Without any resident Spaniard in its entire history and with few visitors, lay or ecclesiastical, the Tancah Maya were left largely to their own devices. Colonial supervision was so desultory that they could easily have placed their traditional ceramic offering in front of the altar when constructing the chapel or have buried their dead in a flexed position with a jade bead, without any Spaniard's being the wiser. The chapel was doubtless designed by a Spaniard but probably constructed largely in his absence. As for burials, even in less isolated communities of Colonial Yucatan with resident priests, these ceremonies were usually left to the Maya sacristans to perform anyway, unless the deceased happened to be a Spaniard or a rich Maya willing to pay for a fancy funeral.

The Catholic clergy's ignorance of pagan or syncretic practices was by no means uncommon throughout Colonial Yucatan. What was unique to the East Coast and perhaps other frontier areas was the fact that the clergy there had to tolerate many unorthodox practices they did know about.

The Maya of Cozumel, Pole, and the East Coast in general were considered to be "notorious idolaters" who brazenly worshiped their idols in public (AGI, Mexico 3048, 1585; Cogolludo 1688, Bk. 7, Ch. 1; Scholes and Adams, eds. 1938, vol. 2:91). Even worse, the area persisted as a cult center for the entire peninsula. According to the Spanish governor, writing forty years after the Conquest, Cozumel remained as important a pilgrimage center to the Maya as Jerusalem was to Christians (AGI, Mexico 359, 1584). The Catholic priests there, so far from the centers of Spanish authority, had no power to correct these abuses. Perhaps, as one chronicler complained, they were derelict in their duty. But the same chronicler also suggested that one of these priests had been deliberately drowned by the Maya on a crossing between Cozumel and the mainland, because he had been too zealous in his attempts to extirpate idolatry (Sánchez de Aguilar 1937: 120–121).

It is therefore not difficult to understand how non-Christian practices could have continued. The association of these practices with the Tancah chapel, especially the cache made during its construction, suggests a very early starting date for the process of syncretic merging of Maya and Christian elements. What is more difficult to explain is the existence of some of the Christian elements. It is this archaeological evidence of early Christian practice, in the context of documentary evidence on the desultory character of Spanish supervision and the absence of Spanish coercive power in the area, that challenges the usual view of the purely nominal nature of conversion and the Maya's implacable hostility to Christianity.

Why did the Tancah Maya bother with Christianity at all? The East Coast was a zone of refuge for apostate and pagan Maya, especially around Ascension Bay, a short distance to the south (Ciudad Real 1872, vol. 2:408; Cogolludo 1688, Bk. 8, Ch. 8; Roys et al. 1940:28–29; AGI, Mexico 294, 1604). The Spanish were unable to subdue this area thoroughly, and there was nothing to keep the entire Tancah population from escaping Spanish and Christian influence altogether by moving south. Perhaps some did, but the ones who remained must have done so out of choice.

That choice could have been made because of a sense of attachment to the place or for any other reason unconnected with Christianity, but it must also been out of choice that the residents buried their dead in consecrated Christian ground and performed most of the burials according to Christian practice; for there was no resident priest to oversee such compliance. In that climate the dead must be buried immediately, and it is safe to assume that most of the Tancah chapel burials were made in the absence of any Spanish supervision. Written evidence also suggests that the East Coast Maya, despite adherence to their pagan rituals, valued other Christian cult elements, such as having Mass celebrated and obtaining ornaments for their churches (Roys et al. 1940:26–28).

It is possible that Tancah was reoccupied or at least used after having been officially abandoned, as seems to be the case for Indian Church (Lamanai) in Belize. The Ascension Bay area was still populated by "idolatrous" Indians in 1717, when a government *vigía*, or lookout post, was established at the head of the bay to deter pirates (AGI, Mexico 1017, 1719). This possibility does not, we believe, invalidate our suggestion that religious syncretism there was both early and largely voluntary. The Maya-type burial, being intrusive, could postdate abandonment, but the cache surely does not. As for the Christian-type burials, if some were made after Tancah-Tzama had passed out of the Spanish Colonial system altogether by former inhabitants or other refugees, this simply means that some apostates did not entirely renounce Christian ways, whether these had originally been imposed by force or not.

If we accept that the Maya, even in the absence of coercion, did not invariably reject Christianity, this still does not explain exactly how they responded or why. Obviously we must expect a variety of responses, since Christianity did not impinge on all groups within Maya society and on all aspects of religious experience in the same way and to the same degree. These differences, as well as changes over time and from place to place, must be considered in developing a satisfactory general model that will explain Post-Conquest religious change among the Lowland Maya. Here we are concerned with explaining—as a contribution to the larger inquiry—why the East Coast Maya in particular, inhabiting such a strong Pre-Columbian cult center, should have been receptive at all to an alien religion.

We suggest that the East Coast Maya, or at least some portion of the theologically sophisticated elite, may have accepted Christianity on their own terms, not as a totally alien cult, but as a further development of or new twist to what they already believed. The idea that many if not all the Mesoamerican cultures managed to incorporate some aspects of Christianity into their own systems is far from new. What we wish to emphasize is the possibility that their incorporation started early, as part of an initial response, rather than emerging only gradually (see also Scholes and Roys 1938:605–606).

We also suggest that to speak of a mixture of the two religions caused by "confusion" and "bewilderment" (D. E. Thompson 1954: 12–16, 56ff.) may be valid from a European perspective, in which Christian and pagan concepts are seen as incompatible. But it may not explain the process from a Maya point of view, in which such a combination may represent a perfectly coherent system. Since religious syncretism is not a conscious procedure, and since most innovation is conservative in intent, the Maya probably did not think of themselves as incorporating (much less confusing) new elements so much as developing their own cult along lines already established. Such a process has been suggested to explain more recent syncretic conversions to Christianity in Africa (Horton 1971).

That the Aztecs may have viewed Hernán Cortés as Quetzalcoatl or his emissary who had come to announce the deity's return according to the prophecies is a long established—if not universally accepted—proposition. There is also the possibility that Christ could have been identified in the indigenous mind with Quetzalcoatl or the Maya equivalent, Kukulcan. The Kukulcan cult itself had originally been introduced from Highland Mexico, and the Maya had already achieved a syncretic merger with this alien cult well before the Spanish arrived. The very fact that the East Coast of Yucatan was a strong cult center for Venus, which, as Morning Star of the East, was identified with Kukulcan (Miller 1977), could have made the inhabitants there more receptive to Christian doctrine and ritual rather than less so.

Quetzalcoatl-Kukulcan in the form of Venus was worshiped at various centers on the East Coast, such as Tulum, Tancah, and Xelha. He was the Pre-Columbian deity who was said to have died as a mortal and, as Venus, or Morning Star, was supposed to come again, rising out of the eastern sea after a period in the underworld. The sixteenth-century Spanish friars preaching the essential mystery of the Christian faith—"Christ has died. Christ has risen. Christ will come again."—could well have received a nod of recognition from the Maya. Certainly the concept of resurrection was far from alien to Maya cosmoslogy. And the traditional east-west orientation of Christian churches, including the Tancah chapel, could have been interpreted as further evidence of the Kukulcan-Christ identification.

We cannot say for certain that the East Coast Maya or any other Mesoamerican group accepted Christianity as the fulfillment of the Quetzalcoatl-Kukulcan prophecies. However, there is enough resemblance between the symbolism and dogma of the two cults to help account for the receptivity to Christianity on the East Coast and elsewhere.

As a frontier area the East Coast provided uncommonly open conditions in which the Maya could accept or reject Spanish culture with relative freedom. The archaeological and documentary evidence indicates that they found something of value in the new religion, without at the same time totally renouncing their own traditions. Considerable further research is needed to learn exactly what about Christianity appealed to them and how they formed the creative mix of old and new.

ACKNOWLEDGMENTS

This work formed part of the Tancah-Tulum Archaeological Project field program of 1974 and 1975. We were assisted by Arlen F. Chase, graduate student in anthropology at the University of Pennsylvania, who prepared the plan and the elevation of the Tancah Chapel shown in Figures 13-3 and 13-4.

The principal sponsors of the Tancah-Tulum Archaeological Project are the Center for Pre-Columbian Studies, Dumbarton Oaks, and the Committee for Research and Exploration, National Geographic Society, with additional support from the Brooklyn Institute of Arts and Sciences and the Mexican-Canadian Foundation. The field research was carried out with the authorization and cooperation of the Instituto Nacional de Antropología e Historia, Mexico, and particularly its agency, the Centro Regional del Sureste, Mérida, and its Director, Arq. Norberto González Crespo.

The archival research for this study was made possible by a fellowship for 1975–1976 awarded to coauthor Farriss by the National Endowment for the Humanities.

14 Continuity in Maya Writing: New Readings of Two Passages in the Book of Chilam Balam of Chumayel by Gordon Brotherston

The Maya manuscripts known to the outside world as the Books of Chilam Balam belong to a tradition of literacy which stretches back to the Classic Period of the Maya and which, though diminished, survived even the Caste War of the nineteenth century. The two main links in this tradition have received some attention: first, the transcription into the Roman alphabet, as in the Book of Chilam Balam, of almanacs and other hieroglyphic texts from the three surviving screenfolds of the Postclassic period, known as the Dresden, the Paris, and the Madrid (J. E. S. Thompson 1960; 1972; Alvarez 1974); then, going back in time, the more elusive connections between these screenfolds and the inscriptions at Palenque, Tikal, Copan, and other Classic cities (J. E. S. Thompson 1960; Kubler 1976). Few attempts have been made however to see the Books of Chilam Balam in the larger perspective of Maya literacy as a whole.[1]

The Book of Chilam Balam from the town of Chumayel, Yucatan, gains especially from being put in this perspective. It is the only Book of Chilam Balam to make use of the Long Count place-value arithmetic of the Classic Maya; to reflect at length on Maya history; or to elaborate a Maya philosophy of time. The two principal translators of the Chumayel into a modern European language, A. Médiz Bolio (1930) and Ralph Roys (1933), recognized the special qualities of this among the other Books of Chilam Balam. Yet they were working at a time (the early 1930's) when ignorance of the Classic heritage was even greater than it is now. It had still to be shown, for example, that the Classic hieroglyphic texts deal not just with calendrics and astronomy but with dynastic history as well (see Kelley 1976:213–243). And few then suspected the strong cultural continuity implicit in the Katun Round calendrical tradition, which Munro Edmonson's masterly new version of the Book of Tizimin (1977) now vindicates. In short, hieroglyphic writing, as the expression of a quite specific cosmology and philosophy, could not be appreciated as an indispensable source of Post-Columbian literature in the Chilam Balam tradition.

Two passages which call particularly for reinterpretation in the light of modern knowledge are those on pages 19–21 and 60–63 of the Book of Chilam Balam of Chumayel. The first recounts Maya experience and assesses it morally and philosophically. These pages are much more than the "Memoranda of Yucatan" that Roys calls them, and lead us back to the ancient Maya. The second passage is an example of classic Maya philosophy: it deals with time theory, and with the problem of the "prime mover" in genesis. Each illuminates the other as finely wrought literature. Together, the two pieces are among the richest to be found in Maya writing in the Roman alphabet. They may be dated to the late sixteenth and early seventeenth centuries.

THE MAYA "GOLDEN AGE"

They didn't want to join the foreigners;
  Mat yoltahob u paktob dzulob
Christianity was not their desire;
  ma u kat cristianoilob
they didn't want another tax—
  ma yoltahob u bot patan

Those with their sign in the bird,
  Ah uayom chichob
5 those with their sign in the stone, flat worked stone,
  ah uayom tunob, ah ziniltunob
those with their sign in the jaguar—three emblems—
  ah uayom balamob—ox uayohob
four times four hundred years was the period of their lives
  can bak hab u xul u cuxtalob
plus fifteen score years before that period ended
  catac holhun kal hab yan cataci u xul cuxtalob
because they knew the rhythm of the days in themselves.
  tumen yohelob u ppiz kinob tubaob

10 Whole the moon, whole the year,
  tuliz U   tuliz hab
whole the day, whole the night,
  tuliz kin   tuliz akab
whole the breath when it moved too, whole the blood too
  tuliz ik cu ximbal xan   tuliz kik xan
when they came to their beds, their mats, their thrones;
  tu kuchul tu uayob tu poopoob tu dzamob
rhythm in their reading of the good hours,
  ppiz u canticob yutzil oraob
15 rhythm in their search for the good days,
  ppiz u caxanticob yutzil kin
as they observed the good stars enter their reign,
  la tu ppiz yilicob yocolob utzul ekob tu yahaulil
as they watched the reign of the good stars begin.
  tan u ppix ich ticob yocolob yahaulil utzul ekob.
Everything was good.
  Utz tun tulacal

For they kept sound reason;
  Catun u takbez yalob tu cuxolalob yan
20 there was no sin in the holy faith of their lives,
  manan tun keban tu santo okolalob yan u cuxtalob
there was no sickness, they had no aching bones,
  manan tun chapabal   manan tun chibil bac tiob
they had no high fever, they had no smallpox,

manan tun dzam chacuil tiob   minan tun xpomkakil tiob
they had no burning chest, they had no bellyache,
    minan tun elel tzemil tiob   minan tun ya nakil tiob
they had no chest disease, they had no headache.
    minan tun tzemtzem cimil tiob   minan chibil pol tiob.
25 The course of mankind was ciphered clearly.
    Tzolombil tun u bin uinicilob.

Not what the foreigners arranged when they came here:
    Ma bay tun u mentah dzulob ti uliob lae
then shame and terror were preferred,
    zubtzilil tal zahob ca talob
carnal sophistication in the flowers of Nacxit Xuchit
        and his circle;
    ca cuxhi yol nicte cuxhi tun yol tu nicteob N. X.
        tu nicte u lakob
no more good days were shown to us;
    minan tun yutz kinob yetzahob toon
30 this was the start of the two-day chair, the two-day rule;
    lay u chun cakin xec   cakin ahaulil
this was the start of our sickness also;
    lay ix u chun cimil toon xan
there were no good days for us, no more sound reason.
    manan yutz kin ton xan   minan cuxolal toon
At the end of the loss of our vision and of our shame
        everything will be revealed.
    tu xul ca zatmail ilil y zubtalil etlahom tulacal

There was no great priest, no lord speaker, no lord priest
    minan nohoch can   minan yahau than   minan ahau can
35 with the change of rulers when the foreigners came.
    til lay u hel ahauoob ti uliob lae
The priests they set down here were lewd;
    tzuc cep ah kinil cu talel u mentabal ti telae dzulob
they left their sons here at Mayapan.
    catun tu ppatahob yal u menehob uay Tancah lae

These in turn received their affliction from the foreigners
        called the Itza.
    Lay tun kamicob u numyailob uchci u chibil lae dzulob lae
        he bin ah Itzaobe

The saying is: since the foreigners came three times
    oxtenhii bin uchci dzulob
40 threescore years is the age to get us exempted from tax.
    lay tun tumen oxkal haab yan toon lukzicob ca patan

The trouble was the aggression of those men the Itza;
    tumen uchci u chibilob tumen uinicob ah Itzaob lae
we didn't do it; we pay for it today.
    ma toon ti mentei   toon botic hele lae

But there is an agreement at last to make us
        and the foreigners unanimous.

Heuac consierto yanil yan u xul ca yanac hum olal ton y dzulob
Failing that we have no alternative to war.
Uamae bin yanac toon noh katun

(The Book of Chumayel, pp. 19–21; English translation
by Gordon Brotherston and Ed Dorn)

This first passage concludes and sums up the long opening section
of the Chumayel, which is divided into five chapters by Roys and
into two by Médiz Bolio. Prompted by the arrival of the Spaniards in
Yucatan after 1539, the Maya go into matters of land ownership, dwelling on the problem of whether to enter into agreement (*consierto*)
with the newly arrived foreigners and pay them tribute, or whether
to resist them militarily (lines 43–44). They draw on various authorities, including the Bible and European almanacs and *reportorios* (an
early form of newspaper). The dominant Pre-Columbian sources are
oral compositions of probable Toltec origin and their own written literature, our main concern here. The whole section appears extremely
complex, partly no doubt because of the complexity of the historical
situation the Maya found themselves in, but also because of the wit
and allusiveness with which they describe it, and their anger at the
treachery of fellow Maya (p. 14). Yet two main parties may at once
be distinguished: the Maya and the foreigners. These last include the
Christian Spanish, of course, but also the Itza, who fought unsuccess-
fully against the Spanish, and the shadowy predecessors of the Itza
whose language was not Maya when they arrived in Yucatan. On the
other side, the "Maya" comprise the author himself (who sometimes
uses the first-person singular), his contemporaries (referred to as "we"),
and his ancestors. These last are identified in several ways: as the
builders of the pyramids (p. 15), whose way of life was destroyed like
that of the Egyptians, and as the wise men and priests, whose knowledge is waning and is sorely missed by their modern descendants (pp.
14–15). All play their role in the highly charged concluding pages.

The foreigners correspond to those we have identified and fall into
three groups: Toltec, Itza, and Christian. Indeed, from the Maya point
of view the impression of three invasions is so clear that a joke is made
of it (lines 39–40). Roys supplies the further information you need
to get the point: that the Spaniards exempted old men, the "over-
sixties," from tax or tribute. But his translation does little to bring
out the wit. ("Three times it was, they say, that the foreigners arrived. It was because of this that we were relieved from paying tribute at the age of sixty.") In the vigesimal arithmetic of the Maya
it's more like saying: next time, the fourth invasion, we'll have to be
eighty (fourscore years) to get exempted.

Allusiveness of this order presupposes a highly developed historical
consciousness. True, we are faced with a radical contrast between
Maya and foreign ways in the negative in line 26, the turning point
of the passage. But the foreigners are not all condemned out of hand,
or for the same reason; and they are dealt with separately in chronological order. In the comment "We didn't do it; we pay for it today"
(line 42) there is an ironic reminder that the non-Maya military powers
in Yucatan (the Itza "captains") failed to defend themselves and their

subjects against the Spanish. A word of Spanish origin, *santo* (line 20), is used as a term against which the lewdness of the Toltecs (line 36) may be contrasted. And so on. Confident in their own tradition, the Maya see this or that culture as *they* choose and take from them what *they* find fitting. These are qualities of cultural longevity and resilience which Médiz Bolio's version does not bring out. He suppresses the Toltec name Nacxit Xuchit (line 28), for example; and he reads an obviously Spanish word like *oraob* ('hours', line 14) as an unlikely native form *oxaob* 'the Three'.² All this has the effect of making the Maya in the piece appear victims of the Black Legend, the more innocent and improbable survivors of a very remote Golden Age. And this in turn inevitably gives the impression that they should not be taken too seriously as interpreters of their own experience.

The tendency to underestimate the capacity of the Maya to tell their own history was largely corrected by Roys. He too, however, sometimes exposes the bias implicit in his use of the term *colonial* to refer only to Spanish rule in Yucatan and not to its Toltec and Itza precedents. And in the end he seems little more committed to the Maya point of view than Médiz Bolio. At one point he openly suggests that the narrative is confused, and says this "confusion" is "probably due to the fact that while the writer was referring ostensibly to the Itza, he really had the Spaniards in mind."

According to the Maya text, things began to go wrong not with Cortés or Montejo, nor yet with the Itza, but with Nacxit Xuchit. This is the debased Nahuatl name of the Toltec leader who successfully invaded Yucatan several centuries before the Spaniards (an event recorded in Nahuatl in the "Toltec Elegy," in the *Cantares mexicanos* manuscript). But he was far less respected there than by Maya groups elsewhere, among whom the native tradition of literacy was broken after the "collapse" and who to this extent lost touch with Classic values. So that while Nacxit Xuchit is paid homage, as the imperial dispenser of insignia and status, in the *Popol Vuh* and the *Annals of the Cakchiquels* (works written by the Highland Maya to the south), to the north, in Yucatan, he is said to have initiated a regrettable change in attitudes and behavior. In the Chumayel, he and his companions are accused of causing deathly sickness (*cimil*), where previously there was none. The particular complaints may be deduced negatively from lines 20–24. These are less interesting for themselves, medically, than as symptoms of disease in the body politic as a whole, this body being federal, like the cities of the Classic and the Postclassic Maya, and not subject to a single capital. The close association of politics and medicine among the Yucatecan Maya recurs unambiguously as late as the nineteenth century, in the prefatory note to the medicinal section (pp. 30ff.) of the Book of Chilam Balam of Nah. With its explicit reference to the Caste War (*tu haabil katun*) this note also invokes the remedy foreseen in the Chumayel, in the absence of an agreement: expulsion of the intruder.

Further, the health of Maya society is not just a matter of internal politics, but depends on the sky. The coursing of breath and blood corresponds to astronomical movement. The good days which vanished with the Toltecs' coming were assured by the correct calendrical reading of the reign (*ahaulil*) of good stars. What had been sound and whole was afflicted and eclipsed, *chibil* serving for both meanings. Of course, similar connections between the terrestrial and the celestial may be found in ancient cultures other than the Maya, in Confucianism, for example, and in the astrology of the Babylonian zodiac, which survived in Europe up till the Enlightenment (Cassirer 1963). Among the Maya however, the relationship of earth to sky was formulated in a way peculiar to them, in the Classic Period; and the moral history in the Chumayel is best understood with this in mind.

The main link between pages 19–21 of the Chumayel and the Classic Period is provided by a tradition of texts dealing with speculative history and based on the Katun Round, *u kahlay katunob*, a period of thirteen katuns (a katun consists of twenty tuns, or 360-day years). These texts, with their attendant sequences for the tuns, appear in hieroglyphic form on one side of the Paris screenfold, and fragmentarily in the Dresden (p. 60). In the Chilam Balam corpus they form an important part of the Books of Tizimin, Mani, Oxkutzcab, Kaua, and Chumayel itself, along with descriptions of the Maya federal system of government, based on the katun period, and examination questions asked of candidates for political office (Barrera Vásquez and Rendón 1948; Roys 1949*b* and 1954). The Katun Round texts may readily be seen to be the source, in turn, of plain chronological accounts of the past found in the Books of Chilam Balam, like the Matichu chronicle. And, at the same time, they give shape to personal statements about the future, like the "prophecies" of Chilam Balam himself and other Maya leaders. As for the comprehensive narrative we are concerned with on pages 19–21 of the Chumayel, the influence of the Katun Round texts is even more significant, since here we are faced with cultural history on an epic scale, and because the survivors of the Classic Maya have sometimes tacitly been considered to have had only a cyclic sense of history. (This is an interpretation encouraged by the form of the Katun Round itself: what happens in any one of the thirteen katuns in the past is likely to recur in the same katun in the future.) In the "Golden Age" passage whole phrases do indeed reappear, especially from the older of the two complete surviving Katun Rounds (Series 1), like so many hieroglyphic formulae: "the loss of vision and shame"; "the start of sickness"; "there were no good days for us"; and so on. Similarly, the lewdness of Xuchit (lines 28–29) is described in terms characteristic of the 11 Ahau *nicte* or 'flower' katun. More tellingly still, the parallel between moon and blood (lines 10–12) is stated in traditional vocabulary. In the text for a Katun 13 Ahau (Chumayel, p. 100) we read: *tu lobil kik tu hokol U; tuliz iuil U u chac cuchie tuliz kik'*; here, too, the 'wholeness' of blood (*tuliz kik*) corresponds to that of the moon. The main point is, however, that in the invocation of the past times when "everything was good," all this Katun Round rhetoric is not simply cyclic but is firmly set in an undeniable historical dimension, at once political and philosophical. The "history" of the *u kahlay katunob* has the quality of being based and rooted in time, which was the distinguishing feature, in Mesoamerica, of the "Initial Series" Long Count inscriptions, which record dates counted from the start of the Maya

Era (3113 B.C.). Indeed, the Maya literary tradition itself is here made to indicate its own point of origin and inspirational source in the Classic Period, in times prior to foreign domination.

The "great priests and speakers" who presided over the time when "everything was good" are not expressly identified as ancient Maya, though in context they can hardly be anything else. The paragraphing introduced by Roys makes them identical with those contemporaries of the Maya author who didn't want Christianity or "another tax" (lines 1–3). But they are much more necessary as the subject of lines 4–9, which otherwise are deprived of one. The three signs they bore, bird, stone, and jaguar, remain opaque, though they do coincide strikingly with the three glyphs represented on Monument 13 at La Venta, of uncontested antiquity.[3] The antiquity these ancients are in fact credited with (1,600 ± 300 years) is of the same order as that of the pyramid builders (1,200 ± 300 years), both period counts being consonant with Initial Series chronology.

In any case, these organizers of the Golden Age which preceded foreign invasion can be seen to have had a cosmology and a calendar that are quite specific and exemplified in detail in what is said of them by their Maya descendants. While the ancient rulers knew "the rhythm of the days in themselves" (line 9), the foreigners led by Nacxit Xuchit introduced a "two-day chair" and a "two-day rule." Roys took the phrase ca-kin 'two-day' to mean temporary or short-lived, which it might do. It could more purposefully refer to the leap-year or double-day system of the Toltec calendar, which unlike that of the Classic Maya was annual, not diurnal, following the yearly sun (Apollo, in Greek terms), not the daily sun (Helios). In the Katun Round texts, which derived directly from the Initial Series katun-ending dating convention of the Late Classic at Tikal and elsewhere, there are numerous references to Postclassic ineptitude in calendrical matters (Barrera Vásquez and Rendón 1948:87–89), and to two- or even three-day rulers. The Toltecs lacked or did not insist on the formula which lay at the heart of the Maya Long Count system: one day equals one unit (cf. Castillo 1971). Without this equation, the place-value notation of the Long Count, and hence hieroglyphic writing itself (the distinctive achievement of the Classic Period), would have been impracticable (Brotherston 1976b). Hence when we read that the great priests ensured that "the course of mankind was ciphered clearly" (line 25), we see that the main term, tzolombil, is charged with connotation. Tzol means 'to set in order', or 'count', or 'make clear', and describes exactly the mental processes formulated in the arithmetical logic of hieroglyphic writing.

The usual translation of tzolombil, including Roys's, has been 'orderly', which is not incorrect. But it doesn't alert us sufficiently to the principle of this ordering. According to Diringer (1968), Maya hieroglyphic writing is an exception among the scripts of the planet in that it appeared in the tropics, and all at once, complete in its essentials. This is true, although "Olmec" inscriptions in and near the Maya area, dating from before 300 B.C., clearly anticipate the principles on which Maya literacy was based. Paramount among these is the calendrical use of place-value arithmetic, a feature shared by no other known script besides the Inca quipu system, to which Maya writing is historically doubtless related on these grounds alone.[4] (Over the world as a whole, place-value arithmetic in itself is known elsewhere only from Mesopotamia at a similar or possibly even later date.) By any account the calendrical script of the Maya remains quite exceptional in integrating astronomical and social time, cosmology and history, within the same formal and semiotic system from the very start. Old World notions of celestial and terrestrial correspondence never found expression in a cultural form anything like as succinct and cogent as Maya hieroglyphics (Barthel 1968; Zimmermann 1971). And it is just this quality which is so highly prized in retrospect by the historian-author of the Chumayel, who, with his use of terms like *tzolombil*, points up the importance of Maya calendrical literacy and hence of their numerical "ordered" astronomy.

All available evidence suggests that the Classic Maya astronomers operated within the single space-time dimension of the tropics, the continuum between east and west, and placed exclusive emphasis on ciphers and numbers (Brotherston and Ades 1975; Brotherston 1976a).[5] Because they did not geometricize space or see it in static Euclidean terms, these numbers were never shown to be irrational or made subject to fixed points or lines. The count of numbers, and of days as invariable units, was indeed everything. This affects in turn our reading of the words *ppiz* and *tuliz*, which carry such weight in the account of the days when "everything was good." Roys translates *ppiz* as 'in due measure', which does not bring out the distinction, made by the Greeks after Euclid but not by the Maya, between *metron* and *rhythmos*. Similarly, to have *tuliz* as 'complete', which with 'measure' suggests ideas of proportion as geometrical division foreign to Maya mathematics, goes against the definition of *tuliz* given in the *Vienna Dictionary*: "entera cosa sana, no quebrada ni partida ni comensada" ("a whole, sound thing, not broken or divided or begun"). In Maya numerical logic, completion is better expressed as wholeness, of the basic date unit and its sums and multiples: lunar, menstrual, solar, dynastic, planetary, moral, and so on. Ratio is of things in time, measured from moment to moment, from rest to rest (bed, mat, throne—line 13). The astronomy of the Maya, and the script which conveyed it, may in turn be held responsible for the remarkable concept *cuxolalob* (line 19), preserved in Maya philosophy from the Classic to the Post-Columbian period: a sound or living knowledge, a science that is rational yet animate ("whole" means "hate" or "reality").

In many respects the harmonious way of being, the loss of which is lamented in the Chumayel, resembles our Golden Age. But it does not precede "real" time, as ours tends to do. Just the opposite. Then, people were more thoroughly part of time than they are now. In other words, unlike the old myth elaborated in Hesiod's account of the degenerating ages of the world, and the modern psychological postulate of childhood consciousness, the narrative of the Maya Golden Age does not appeal to some remote and undefined past "in the beginning." The Classic Period of the Maya stands as a term of precise historical reference. There can be no doubt about the political consequences of this fact, though these are not brought out by Roys and are actively neglected in Médiz Bolio's elegiac stanzas.[6] In their reckonings with foreigners the Maya relied on the Classic Period not least as a term of philosophical reference. It is the inspirational source of a way of understanding the cosmos which may be explored in more detail in the passage on pages 60–62 of the Chumayel.

THE "BEGINNING OF TIME" RECOUNTED

It was set out this way by the first sage Melchisedek, the first
     prophet Napuctun, sacerdote, the first priest.
  Bay tzolci yax ah miatz Merchise yax ah bovat
     Napuctun sacerdote yax ah kin
This is the song of how the uinal was realized,
     before the world was.
  lay kay uchci u zihil uinal ti ma to ahac cab cuchie
He started up from his inherent motion alone.
    ca hoppi u ximbal tuba tu hunal
His mother's mother and her mother, his mother's sister
     and his sister-in-law, they all said:
    ca yalah u chich ca yalah u dzenaa ca yalah
     u min ca yalah u muu
5   How shall we say, how shall we see, that man is on the road?
    bal bin c'alab ca bin c'ilab uninc ti be
These are the words they spoke as they moved along,
    where there was no man.
    ca thanob tamuk u ximbalob cuchie minan uinic cuchi

When they arrived in the east they began to say:
    catun kuchiob te ti likine ca hoppi yalicob
Who has been here? These are footprints. Get the
    rhythm of his step.
    mac ti mani uay lae he yocob lae Ppiz ta uoci
So said the Lady of the world,
    ci bin u than u colel cab
10 and our Father, Dios, measured his step.
    cabin u ppizah yoc ca yumil ti D[io]s citbil
This is why the count by footstep of the whole world,
    xoc lah cab oc, was called *lahca oc* '12 Oc'.
    lay u chun yalci xoc lah cab oc lae lahca Oc
This was the order born through 13 Oc,
    lay tzolan zihci tumen oxlahun Oc
when the one foot joined its counter print to make
    the moment of the eastern horizon.
    uchci u nup tanba yoc likciob te ti likine
Then he spoke its name when the day had no name
    ca yalah u kaba ti minan u kaba kin cuchie
15 as he moved along with his mother's mother and her mother,
    his mother's sister and his sister-in-law.
    ximbalnahci y u chiich y u dzenaa y u min y u muu
The uinal born, the day so named, the sky and earth,
    zi uinal zihci kin u kaba zihci caan y luum

the stairway of water, earth, stone, and wood,
    the things of sea and earth realized.
        eb haa luum tunich y che zihci u bal kabnab y luum

1 Chuen, the day he rose to be a day-ity and made the sky and
    earth.
        Hun Chuen u hokzici uba tu kuil u mentci caan y luum
2 Eb, he made the first stairway. It ebbs from heaven's heart,
    Ca Eb u mentci yax eb.   Emci likul tan yol caan
20 the heart of water, before there was earth, stone, and wood.
        tan yol haa, minan luum y tunich y che
3 Ben, the day for making everything, all there is,
    Ox Ben u mentci tulacal bal, hibahun bal
the things of the air, of the sea, of the earth.
    u bal caanob y u bal kaknab y u bal luum
4 Ix, he fixed the tilt of the sky and earth.
    Can Ix uchci u nixpahal caan y luum
5 Men, he made everything.
    Ho Men uchci u meyah tulacal
25 6 Cib, he made the number one candle
    Uac Cib uchci u mentici yax cib
    and there was light in the absence of sun and moon.
        uchci u zazilhal ti minan kin y u.
7 Caban, honey was conceived when we had not a caban.
    Uuc Caban yax zihci cab ti minan toon cuchi
8 Etznab, his hands and feet were set, he sorted
        minutiae on the ground.
    Uaxac Etznab etzlahci u kab y yoc ca u chichaah yokol luum
9 Cauac, the first deliberation of hell.
    Bolon Cauac yax tumtabci metnal
30 10 Ahau, evil men were assigned to hell out of respect for Ds.
    Lahun Ahau uchci u binob u lobil uinicob ti
        metnal tumen Ds Citbil
that they need not be noticed.
    ma chicanac cuchie
11 Imix, he construed stone and wood;
    Buluc Imix uchci u patic tuni y che
he did this within the face of the day.
    lay u mentah ichil kin
12 Ik, occurred the first breath;
    Lahcabil Ik uchci u zihzic ik
35 it was named Ik because there was no death in it.
    Lay u chun u kabatic Ik tumen minan cimil ichil lae
13 Akbal, he poured water on the ground;
    Oxlahun Akbal uchci u chaic haa, ca yakzah luum
this he worked into man.
    Ca u patah ca uinic-hi
1 Kan, he "canned" the first anger because
        of the evil he had created.
    Hunnil Kan u yax mentci u leppel yol tumenal u lobil zihzah
2 Chicchan, he uncovered the evil he saw within the town.

Ca Chicchan uchci u chictahal u lobil hibal
   yilah ichil u uich cahe
40 3 Cimi, he invented death;
   Ox Cimil u tuzci cimil
as it happened the father Ds. invented the first death.
   uchci u tuzci yax cimil ca yumil ti Ds
[4 Manik missing]
5 Lamat, he invented the seven great seas.
   Ho Lamat lay u tuzci uuclam chac haal kaknab
6 Muluc, came the deluge and the submersion of everything
   Uac Muluc uchci u mucchahal kopob tulacal
before the dawning. Then the father Ds. invented the word
   ti mato ahac cabe. Lay uchci yocol u tuz thanil ca yumil ti Ds
45 when there was no word in heaven, when there was
    neither stone nor wood.
   tulacal ti minan tun than ti caan ti minan tunich y che cuchi
Then the twenty deities came to consider themselves
    in summation and said:
   Catun binob u tum tubaob ca yalah tun bayla
Thirteen units plus seven units equals one.
   Oxlahun tuc: uuc tuc, hun
So said the uinal when the word came in, when there
    had been no word,
   Lay yalah ca hok u than ti minan than ti
and this led to the question by the day Ahau, ruler,
   Ca katab u chun tumen yax Ahau kin
50 Why was the meaning of the word not opened to them
    ma ix hepahac u nucul than tiob
so that they could declare themselves?
   uchebal u thanic ubaobe
Then they went to heaven's heart and joined hands.
   Ca binob tan yol caan ca u machaah u kab tuba tanbaobe

   (The Book of Chumayel, pp. 60–62; English translation
   by Gordon Brotherston and Ed Dorn)

This second passage also sums up a whole section of the Chumayel, pages 42–63 (Roys's chapters "The Creation of the World," "Ritual of the Angels," "Song of the Itza," and "Creation of the Uinal"). The dominant concern of this section is with origins: the origin of the physical world and, more important, of time itself. It is said to be written "for Maya men" (p. 42) and attempts to reconcile traditional Maya cosmology with ideas imported by the Christians. From our point of view there is a bewildering mixture of Old and New World thought: Katun Round texts incorporate verses from the Bible; number symbolisms of both traditions, notably of the number seven, are interfused; the Twenty Signs, semiotically essential to Maya and Mesoamerican ritual as a whole, are interspersed among the Latin names of the planets; and the arithmetical astronomy of the Maya is matched with the system of points, lines, and spheres inherited from Ptolemy by medieval Europe. But all is evidently presented for a purpose. In contrast to, say, the *Popul Vuh*, the Chumayel deals with Christian accounts of origins, particularly Genesis, in a highly critical spirit, comparable in America only with that of the histories written in Nahuatl by Chimalpahin. The Yucatecan book engages with the Bible directly, and indirectly via the corpus of medieval Biblical scholarship. The "Damaceno" mentioned on page 58 (and unidentified by Médiz Bolio and Roys) is in fact St. John of Damascus, and the Jeronix on page 50 St. Jerome. The explanation of occult terms like *nilu* 'night', also on page 50, points to Alfonso X of Castile and his use of Arabic science in his *General e grand estoria* of the world.

A helpful guide to this section of the Chumayel is the Maya critique of Old World origin theories found in the Kaua, pages 145–165, and in the Chan Kan, pages 28–33 and 52–62. There, St. John of Damascus is invoked for his application of Aristotelian physics to Genesis and for his summary of the decisions reached by the doctors of the early Church Councils (*consilios de doctores*). Jerome is mentioned too, for his interpretation of Genesis in *Questiones hebraicae*, and so is Alfonso X, albeit as "Alonso," in both books. These texts leave one in no doubt about the seriousness of the intellectual endeavor of the Maya, or about the significance of the problems they presented themselves with. Because the Spaniards were their conquerors the Maya may have remained outside the mainstream of Renaissance thought. And for the most part they could work only with the potted philosophy of the almanacs and *reportorios*, which the Inquisition allowed to circulate in New Spain. But they scoured these sources for answers to questions which as Stephen Toulmin shows in the *Discovery of Time* (Toulmin and Goodfield 1965), have come to seem paramount in the Western tradition only in the modern age.

The culmination of this section of the Chumayel, pages 60–63, "is worth all the labour that can be put on it," to quote Gates (1931), who also objected, fairly, to Roys's heavily Christianizing version.[7] The person said to be responsible for the piece is credited with having set it down clearly (the verb *tzol-* is used) and enjoys both Maya and Christian authority. Napuctun (line 1) is the name of a sage whose role in the Books of Chilam Balam rivals that of their namesake himself: like Chilam Balam he embodies the learning of the past and applies it in Post-Columbian times. Merchise, or Melchisedek, is not just "a pious interpolation into native legend" (Roys); this mention of the priest-king of a civilization more ancient than Abraham (Genesis 14:18) neatly echoes that of the Egyptian pyramid builders noted earlier.

In this Maya genesis the primary force is the uinal, the figure who embodies the Twenty Signs of Mesoamerican cultures (their "patrimonium commune," as Seler put it). As a beginning, the uinal stirs in the absence of all else (lines 2–3). The first proof of his existence is his movement. This movement is inherent and axiomatic; once it is accepted, there is nothing that may not be derived from it. In their engagement with Old World cosmology the Maya enquired persistently into notions of the primum mobile, and carefully assessed the amendments made in the Middle Ages to the Ptolemaic system of spheres. In their own origin theory they avoided the problem of needing to set static space into motion by making movement itself the prime fact of the universe, prior to matter, structure, and even thought.[8]

The first definition of the uinal, now mobile, is kinship. Vertically and laterally he is held by a mesh of feminine beings, themselves in motion. They anticipate his separate existence, yet his birth, consummated in line 16, is not from a material womb but from a place that could as well be external as internal, the outer as much as the inner cosmos. At first he is no more than the footprints on the road foreseen, and then seen, by the women.[9] But his tracks reveal a good deal about him: his presence on the eastern horizon, and that he is indeed a man, *homo erectus*. The common root of *uinal* and *uinic* 'man' in Yucatecan Maya is now generally accepted (though Médiz Bolio's version perpetuates an erroneous derivation of uinal from *U* 'moon' or 'month'). And it is worth emphasizing here because elsewhere in Mesoamerica the Twenty Signs were not so purposively defined and normally belong to the bodies of creatures not so much human as animal or divine. This etymology of the uinal, his precise kinship, and his dual step indicate the importance attached by the Maya to the notion of a specifically *human* rationality. J. E. S. Thompson reads the very concepts *human* and *mankind* as glyphic derivatives of the uinal sign (T521). Consistent with this Maya definition of the uinal is their arithmetization of it (or him), so that his course, like that of mankind (passage 1) becomes "clearly ciphered" even as we follow the text.

In Mesoamerican ritual, the Twenty Signs combine with another such set, the Thirteen Numbers, to form the Sacred Round, 260 different sign-numbers in all. Now a consequence of the Long Count *one-day-equals-one-unit* formula was that, when the Maya incorporated the Sacred Round into their calendar, the Twenty Signs each acquired an unvarying unit value in arithmetic, which was not the case with the Toltec and other calendars. They became the regular day units without which the Classic calendar could not have worked, having the Thirteen Numbers as true coefficients. The score, which functioned as the unit of the second order in the place-value notation of the Long Count, was accordingly expressed as the formula announced by the Twenty Signs themselves in line 47: "thirteen units plus seven units equals one." Only the Maya so subjected the Twenty Signs or uinal "figure" to numerical logic, without which the formal philosophy we now encounter (lines 10–13) could not exist. Yet, though the uinal thus represents and is "made up" of twenty units, he is not merely a vigesimal sum. His charge is not twenty indifferent units but continues to be Twenty Signs of primary significance, whose range of coefficients retain a Pythagorean force. The head and full-body "variants" of the Thirteen Numbers in the inscriptions, for example, testify that the arithmetical logic of the Long Count did not destroy the living identity of its constituent parts. As a primary figure in the Maya cosmos, the uinal bears his charge of signs and numbers in himself, organically. He is "whole" rather than complete, to recall the distinction made earlier.

When the steps of the uinal are first measured, that is, when their intervals and rhythms (*ppiz*) are first consciously registered, the count proper may begin. Order of a specifically Maya kind is instituted (*tzolan zihci*), and the way is prepared for the enumeration of the world by means of the all-important signs and numbers carried within the uinal. "Named" and categorical creation starts with an acutal demonstration of the power of the mind, in the multiple pun in line 11, in the phase *xoc lah cab oc lae lahca oc*. *Xoc* means 'count' (T738); *lahcab* means 'whole world', and *lahca* is the number 12; *oc* is 'foot' or 'footprint' and is the name of one of the Twenty Signs (T765) and therefore, among the Maya, a day name. The verbal agility engages us unawares in the potent internal logic of the uinal and brilliantly overcomes those "paralogistic" problems (as Kant called them) of explaining the "beginning of time." For, from *lahca(b)* Oc we move immediately to 13 Oc, as the other foot comes forward. In the conventions of number and name now unequivocally invoked, such a step is impossible: in the Sacred Round no two consecutive numbers may have the same sign. But by virtue of being unthinkable it aptly corresponds to that moment of stasis shown to be undefinable in the Eleatic paradoxes, when the one foot is exactly even with the other moving past it. This is the moment of the eastern horizon, the space-time edge of the day unit. It is the start position of right with left, of even with odd (12, 13), not ex nihilo (0 to 1). This initial parity is characteristic of Mesoamerican dualism as a whole, earlier exemplified here in the dual mistress-god figure of lines 9–10, and in the very decimal halves of the set of Twenty Signs, which we are to be poised between and which balance each other conceptually. For Oc (Foot) is the tenth sign, the last of the first half, while Chuen (Ape), which follows, begins the second. Defined with a numerical precision peculiar to the Maya, this parity starts the sequence which enumerates the world day by day.

In the sequence of this first uinal, which has its all-important beginning in 13 Oc and runs through to 6 Muluc (twenty day-events in all), the author openly alludes to the Genesis held to be orthodox by the Christian foreigners. In this way we are brought to realize that the Bible has no equivalent to the prior achievement of the mind in the Maya, which had been to find a means of initiating a primary sequence of categories and of thereby setting conscious time in motion. And in the Maya the creation of mere matter and disposition of living creatures, effected so momentously by God in the Bible, appear almost deliberately effortless by comparison, now that the sequence has begun. In the events specified by the twenty days begun by 13 Oc, despite local narrative effects (9 Cauac to 10 Ahau for example), there is sooner the positive denial of anything as question-begging as a material creation "story." Events repeat themselves (3 Ben and 5 Men), or are revoked (6 Muluc goes back on line 17 and on 11 Imix). And the unmistakable Biblical allusions tell against their source, and are in keeping with the undevout abbreviation of God's name in Spanish to *Ds*. Note for example the tone of 10 Ahau, and of 3 Cimi, with its pointed refusal morally to justify human mortality. The only coherence to be celebrated lies in a consciousness of the logic of numbers and signs embodied in the uinal.

The names of the individual signs produce flashes of word-play in which, as before, Maya priorities are affirmed and which, in translation, can be rendered only by analogy. These Twenty Signs were after all fundamental as hieroglyphs not just in the calendar but in the whole corpus of Maya writing. As a "divine" day, 1 Chuen recalls the fact that in the screenfolds the hieroglyph for Chuen was interchangeable with that for the uinal itself. As the "stairway" (which is what *eb* means), 2 Eb uses the uinal's track of footprints to join height and depth, sky and sea. The man of clay or mud created on 13 Akbal refers both to Genesis and to the "sloppy" race of men mentioned in the *Popol Vuh*. 8 Etznab shows "the twenty" to be the properly set (*etzlahci*) digits of hands and feet. A remarkable conceit in 6 Cib makes the candle (*cib*), abhorred in Revelation (18:23 and 22:5) as the source of Babylonian intellectual enlightenment, antedate sun and moon. The event for 11 Imix could be read as 'rocks and trees were created on this day'. However, the verb *patic* means 'to mold', as Gates pointed out when censuring Roys for his monotonous use of 'to create' for no less than seven distinct Maya verbs in this passage. The Motul dictionary gives *inventar* and *fingir* as translations of *patic*. The materials involved, stone and wood, may conventionally evoke the art of painting and carving and hence of writing. 'Within the day' has the inherent meaning of 'in the face of one day' and could thus refer to the formula on which hieroglyphic writing was based (one day equals one unit). So that what looks like a dull echo of God's creation day by day could again be a subtle allusion to Maya cosmology. The closing day of this first uinal, 6 Muluc, with its watery associations, plays on the verb *mucchahal* 'to drown'. In glyphic terms, as 'count' (T513), *muluc* also neatly complements the *xoc* (T738) which introduced 12 and 13 Oc and also means 'count', the two glyphs being interchangeable in calendrical use (especially in conjunction with T679).

Finally, we are reminded once more that the uinal is both twenty signs and twenty units. The formula used to express this second equation, thirteen plus seven equals one (line 47), with its classic precedent in the place-value notation of the Long Count, is applied to the uinal elsewhere in the Books of Chilam Balam. The thirteen corresponds to the cardinal number of the first named day, 13 Oc. In context it also has the effect of making the seven days of Biblical creation appear secondary, along with the sevens of planets, graces, and other Old World sets referred to earlier in this section of the Chumayel (p. 48, for example). All this cannot but raise the question of the relative validity of the Maya account of creation, a question in fact put at the close by the day-sign Ahau. The entrusting of a question of such transcendence to this particular sign can readily be associated with its meaning 'lord' or 'pre-eminence', also palpable in its Toltec equivalent Flower (*xochitl*). Moreover, with the glyph for 'sun' or 'day' (T544, *kin*), which is after all what it and the other nineteen signs are here, the *ahau* glyph (T533) gives the meaning 'east' (in some cases *ahau* may even be interchanged with *kin*). And east is one of the only two "direction" signs surely identified in the Classic texts, west being the other. It is the starting edge of the Maya single space-time dimension, and the place of the uinal's conception, or, better, realization, in both the physical and the intellectual senses.

Their work done, the Twenty Signs join hands in heaven's heart, ritually, just as they are shown doing on the famous Sun Stone of the Aztecs. But before they regather as an unbreakable ring, their spokesman Ahau asks why the word of the Christians, if universally true, was not revealed to them and why they, the Maya party, were not allowed even to put their case or declare themselves (lines 50–51). We find here an astounding faith in universal human intelligence, just as in the phrase in the "Golden Age" passage: "at the end of the loss of our vision . . . everything will be revealed." In turn this phrase echoes, on the one hand, the old Maya doctrine in the *Popul Vuh* about the perfect vision enjoyed by man before his eyes were chipped by the gods, so that he could see only part of reality, and, on the other hand, the Biblical Last or General Judgment, repeatedly mentioned in the Books of Chilam Balam, in which all peoples in the world are assessed before God. As agents of the Maya creation the Twenty Signs of the uinal, in reaffirming their identity, ask that it at least be noticed.

There are many details in the uinal passage which remain obscure, some of them no doubt due to the intricacy of Maya calendrical practices.[10] But more than enough is clear for it to bear comparison with "classic" accounts of origins from other parts of the world. Together with the "Golden Age" passage it certainly vindicates the notion that the Maya tradition strongly survived successive invasions of foreigners in Yucatan. For both pieces make use of specific formal conventions which were first given shape with Maya hieroglyphic literacy itself.

NOTES

1. This may explain the nonchalance with which the Maya are treated in J. Goody's *Literacy in Traditional Societies* (1968), otherwise probably the best general introduction to that subject. See also Garza 1975, León-Portilla 1968, and M. D. Coe 1966. For full details of the Chilam Balam manuscripts, see Gibson and Glass 1975. Those which have been published are listed in the Bibliography. Books of Chilam Balam quoted in the text but unlisted in the Bibliography (the Books of Kaua, Nah, and Chan Kan) are unpublished and untranslated and have been consulted in manuscript copies.
2. For *oraob*, Roys has 'their prayers'.
3. These three emblems merit an article to themselves, since Monument 13 at La Venta, "Olmec" in style, was carved two millennia before the Chumayel was written. The bird and flat-stone emblems are unmistakable in the carving. Joralemon (1971) takes what I see as the jaguar emblem to be a "three petal flower." It much more closely resembles the tripartite sign that emerges characteristically from the mouths of jaguars depicted in the murals at Teotihuacan. The signs at Atetelco are ac-

companied by a speech sign (roar?), and those at Tetitla, west portal, have inset claws. See Figure 14-1.

4. This matter is explored at length by Luxton (1977), to whom I owe this and other suggestions made here, including the idea of the decimal halves of the Twenty Signs and their "walk."

5. These articles of ours rely in part on an established view of Old World, extratropical astronomy now demolished by Otto Neugebauer (1975, vol. 1:3): "From the cuneiform texts we learned that ephemerides had been computed exclusively by means of intricate difference sequences which, often by the superposition of several numerical columns, gave step by step the desired coordinates of the celestial bodies—all this with no attempt of a geometrical representation, which seems to us so necessary for the development of any theory of natural phenomena. It is a historical insight of great significance that the earliest existing mathematical astronomy was governed by numerical techniques, not by geometrical considerations, and, on the other hand, that the development of geometrical explanations is by no means such a 'natural' step as it might seem to us who grew up in the tradition founded by the Greek astronomers of the Hellenistic and Roman period." This being so, the Maya, if better understood, may explain for us forgotten tracts of the pre-Hellenistic world.

6. One of these is engraved at the entrance of Hall 12 of the Museo de Antropología in Mexico City, and reads (in the official guide translation): "All the moons, all the years, all the days, all the winds, run their course and have an end. Living creatures also reach their time of repose" (cf. lines 10–14).

7. This has been superseded by Munro Edmonson's version (1968), which also draws out the qualities of the passage as "song" (line 2) by putting it in binary verse form. This paper has benefited generally from a conversation I had with Edmonson in March 1976.

8. In the Genesis section of the Book of Chan Kan (p. 30) we find the significant phrase: "culic Dios ah tepal yetel primer mobil caan." From the Toltecs, 'holy God' acquires majesty (*ah tepal*),

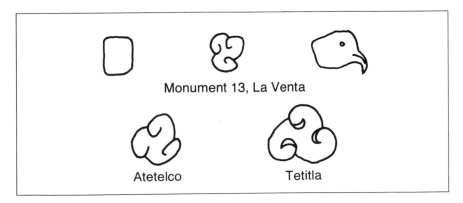

Monument 13, La Venta

Atetelco   Tetitla

FIGURE 14–1. The three emblems.

and in the very vocabulary of the Christians he is credited with being 'the first mover of the sky'.

9. Berlin (1958) has commented upon the frequent association of the uinal with the foot glyph. That the walk of the uinal is bound up with American rituals concerned with true birth after mortal death is suggested by numerous exact parallels to it from civilizations both south and north of the Maya. After the burning of the body in the Winnebago-Sioux funeral, for example, the soul is instructed by a grandmother figure in the following terms: "[on your journey] you will see the footprints of the day on the blue sky before you. These footprints represent the footprints of those who have passed into life again. Step into the places where they have stepped and plant your feet into their footprints, but be careful you do not miss any" (Radin 1970: 105). These footprints are actually shown in a Toltec funeral ritual recorded in the Laud screenfold (pp. 26–25), a chapter which in turn has very close connections with the Visionary's journey depicted in the Navajo "Whirling Logs" sandpainting. This and other formal coherences of a similar order are discussed in my forthcoming book *Image of the New World*. They bear out in specific, formal detail (literary and graphic) the kind of continental "syncretism" argued for in generalized "structural" terms by Lévi-Strauss in his *Mythologiques* (1964–1971).

10. I refer here to the function of 13 Oc as the regulator of the katun (Roys 1949*b*:158); and to the four "Ahtoc" figures mentioned immediately after line 52 and brought up in the Book of Tizimin also in the context of the uinal and of the formula "thirteen plus seven equals one" (f. 33 and f. 38). In the Chumayel the Ahtoc named 4 Chicchan faces the signs which Thompson reads as 'change' (T573). A doubly numbered uinal follows (Chumayel, p. 62):

5 Lahun Kan
6 Buluc Chicchan
  Lahca Cimiy
7 Oxlahun Manik

Here, 11 Chicchan and 12 Cimi share the number 6; 13 Manik is next in line with 7. T573 could thus indicate calendrical adjustment as a "pause" or change in step analogous to that with which the first uinal began, at 13 Oc.

Bibliography

Adams, Richard E. W. 1969. Maya Archaeology, 1958–1968: A Review. *Latin American Research Review*, 4:3–45.

———. 1970. Suggested Classic Period Occupational Specialization in the Southern Maya Lowlands. In *Maya Archaeology*, ed. William R. Bullard, Jr. Papers of the Peabody Museum, 61:487–502. Cambridge, Mass.

———. 1971. *The Ceramics of Altar de Sacrificios*. Papers of the Peabody Museum, 63, no. 1. Cambridge, Mass.

———. 1974. A Trial Estimation of Classic Maya Palace Populations at Uaxactun. In *Mesoamerican Archaeology: New Approaches*, ed. Norman Hammond, pp. 285–296. Austin: University of Texas Press.

———. 1977. Comments on the Glyphic Texts of the "Altar Vase." In *Social Process in Maya Prehistory*, ed. Norman Hammond, pp. 412–420. London and New York: Academic Press.

AGCA (Archivo General de Centro América) A1.11.3, 1698, 5040-212, fol. 101.

———. A1.23, 1698, leg. 1523, fol. 194.

———. A1.24, 1717, 10.226-1582, fol. 181.

———. A1.39, 1659, leg. 1751, fol. 306v.

———. A1.39, 1660*a*, leg. 1751, fol. 343v.

———. A1.39, 1660*b*, leg. 1751, fol. 345.

———. A1.39, 1662, leg. 1751, fol. 442v.

———. A1.57, 1591, leg. 4588, fol. 159.

———. A3.16, 1684, 4547-357.

AGI (Archivo General de Indias, Seville). Contaduría 920. 1688. No. 2 Cuaderno de testimonios de certificaciones dadas por los oficiales reales y alcaldes mayores . . .

———. Escribanía de Cámara 308A. 1582–1689. No. 1. Documentos de la religión de San Francisco . . . , piezas 1, 2, 6, 15, and 16.

———. Guatemala 128. 1548–1549. Tasaciones de los naturales de las provincias de Guatemala y Nicaragua y Yucatán . . .

———. Mexico 245. 1668. Título de encomienda concedida a Antonia de Lara Bonifax. August 13, 1668.

———. Mexico 294. 1604. Probanza de Antonio de Arroyo.

———. Mexico 359. 1565. Información hecha ante el governador . . . sobre el peligro que tiene con los franceses. November 6, 1565.

———. ———. 1575. Governor of Yucatan to King. March 26, 1575.

———. ———. 1579. Governor of Yucatan to King. April 2, 1579.

———. ———. 1583. Decree of Governor and Bishop of Yucatan. July 15, 1583.

———. ———. 1584. Governor of Yucatan to King. March 11, 1584.

———. ———. 1605. Governor of Yucatan to King. September 13, 1605.

———. Mexico 360. 1638. Governor of Yucatan to King. July 10, 1638.

———. Mexico 361. 1659. Documentos sobre la pérdida del galeón Santiago . . .

———. ———. 1664. Documentos sobre el robo del patache y navío de azogues pour los ingleses . . .

———. Mexico 369. 1573. Relación del viaje de Fray Gregorio de Fuenteovejuna y Fray Hernando Sopuerta a Cozumel. August 15, 1573.

———. ———. 1599. Bishop of Yucatan to King. July 15, 1599.

———. Mexico 1017. 1719. Cabildo of Mérida to King. October 7, 1719.

———. Mexico 3048. 1585. Governor of Yucatan to King. April 16, 1585.

————. Patronato 56. 1565. No. 4, Ramo 2. Probanza de Juan de Contreras.

Alcalde Mayor. 1953. Diario de viaje del Alcalde Mayor de Tuxtla, 1783–1789. *Boletín*, 2. Archivo General del Estado (Chiapas).

Alvarez, M. C. 1974. *Textos coloniales del Libro de Chilam Balam de Chumayel y textos glíficos del Códice de Dresde.* Mexico City: UNAM.

Anderson, A. H., and H. J. Cook. 1944. *Archaeological Finds near Douglas, British Honduras.* CIW Notes on Middle American Archaeology and Ethnology, 40. Cambridge, Mass.

Andrews, E. Wyllys IV. 1943. *The Archaeology of Southwestern Campeche.* CIW Contributions to American Anthropology and History, 40; bound in CIW Publication 546:1–100. Washington, D.C.

Andrews, E. Wyllys IV, and Anthony P. Andrews. 1975. *A Preliminary Study of the Ruins of Xcaret, Quintana Roo, Mexico.* MARI Publication 40. New Orleans.

Andrews, E. Wyllys IV, and Irwin Rovner. 1973. Archaeological Evidence on Social Stratification and Commerce in the Northern Maya Lowlands: Two Masons' Tool Kits from Muna and Dzibilchaltun, Yucatan. In *Archaeological Investigations on the Yucatan Peninsula.* MARI Publication 31:81–102. New Orleans.

Andrews, E. Wyllys V. 1976. Review of *Maya Cities: Placemaking and Urbanization*, by George F. Andrews (Norman: University of Oklahoma Press, 1975). *American Antiquity*, 41:241–243.

Angel, J. Lawrence. 1972. Ecology and Population in the Eastern Mediterranean. *World Archaeology*, 4:88–105.

Annals of the Cakchiquels. 1953. Ed. A. Recinos and D. Goetz. Norman: University of Oklahoma Press.

Ara, D. de. 1570? Bocabulario Lengu Tzeldal. MS in Bancroft Library, University of California, Berkeley (MS no. M-M 479, f. 325).

Archivo General de Centro América. *See* AGCA.

Archivo General de Indias. *See* AGI.

Armillas, Pedro. 1971. Gardens on Swamps. *Science*, 174:653–661.

Ball, Joseph W. 1974*a*. A Coordinate Approach to Northern Maya Prehistory: A.D. 700–1200. *American Antiquity*, 39:85–93.

————. 1974*b*. A Teotihuacan-Style Cache from the Maya Lowlands. *Archaeology*, 27:2–9.

————. 1977. *The Archaeological Ceramics of Becan, Campeche, Mexico.* MARI Publication 43. New Orleans.

Bandelier, Adolphe F. 1877. On the Art of War and Mode of Warfare of the Ancient Mexicans. In *Peabody Museum of American Archaeology and Ethnology Reports*, 2:95–161. Cambridge, Mass.

————. 1878. On the Distribution and Tenure of Lands, and the Customs with Respect to Inheritance, among the Ancient Mexicans. In *Peabody Museum of American Archaeology and Ethnology Reports*, 2:385–448. Cambridge, Mass.

————. 1880. On the Social Organization and Mode of Government of the Ancient Mexicans. In *Peabody Museum of American Archaeology and Ethnology, Twelfth Annual Report*, 2:557–669. Cambridge, Mass.

————. 1884. Report of an Archaeological Tour in Mexico, in 1881. In *Papers, Archaeological Institute of America, American Series*, 2. Boston: Cupples, Upham and Company.

Baroco, J. V. 1970. Notas sobre los nombres calendáricos durante el siglo XVI. In *Ensayos de antropología en la zona central de Chiapas*, ed. Norman A. McQuown and Julian Pitt-Rivers. Instituto Nacional Indigenista, Colección de Antropología Social, 8:135–148. Mexico City.

Barrera, A., A. Gómez-Pompa, and C. Vásquez-Yanes. 1977. El manejo de las selvas por los mayas: Sus implicaciones silvícolas y agrícolas. *Biotica*, 2:47–61.

Barrera Vásquez, Alfredo. 1951. La historia de los mayas de Yucatán a través de sus proprias crónicas. In *The Civilizations of Ancient America: Selected Papers of the 29th International Congress of Americanists*, ed. Sol Tax, pp. 119–122. Chicago: University of Chicago Press.

Barrera Vásquez, Alfredo, and Sylvanus G. Morley. 1949. *The Maya Chronicles*. CIW Contributions to American Anthropology and History, 48; bound in CIW Publication 585. Washington, D.C.

Barrera Vásquez, Alfredo, and Silvia Rendón. 1948. *El libro de los libros de Chilam Balam*. Mexico City: Fondo de Cultura Económica.

Barthel, Thomas S. 1968. Writing Systems. In *Current Trends in Linguistics*, 4, *Ibero-American and Caribbean Linguistics*, ed. T. A. Sebeok, pp. 275–301. The Hague and Paris.

Bateson, Gregory. 1972. Pathologies of Epistemology. In *Steps to an Ecology of Mind*, ed. idem, pp. 478–487. New York: Ballantine.

Becerra, Marcos E. 1930. *Nombres geográficos indígenas del Estado de Chiapas*. Tuxtla Gutiérrez: Imprenta del Gobierno.

Becker, Marshall Joseph. 1971. *The Identification of a Second Plaza Plan at Tikal, Guatemala, and Its Implications for Ancient Maya Social Complexity*. Ph.D. dissertation, University of Pennsylvania. Ann Arbor: University Microfilms.

———. 1973*a*. Archaeological Evidence for Occupational Specialization among the Classic Period Maya at Tikal, Guatemala. *American Antiquity*, 38:396–406.

———. 1973*b*. The Evidence for Complex Exchange Systems among the Ancient Maya. *American Antiquity*, 38:222–223.

———. 1975. Moieties in Ancient Mesoamerica: Inferences on Teotihuacan Social Structure Derived from the Evidence of Mural Paintings and Other Archaeological Data. Paper presented at the XIV Mesa Redonda de la Sociedad Mexicana de Antropología, Tegucigalpa.

Beltrán de Santa José María, Pedro. 1746. *Arte del idioma maya, reducido a sucintas reglas y semilexicón yucateco*. Mérida: J. D. Espinosa.

Benzoni, Girolano. 1857. *History of the New World*, trans. W. H. Smythe. London: Hakluyt Society, 21.

Berlin, Heinrich. 1958. El glifo "emblema" en las inscripciones mayas. *Journal de la Société des Américanistes*, 47:111–119.

Bernal, Ignacio. 1966. Teotihuacán: ¿Capital de imperio? *Revista Mexicana de Estudios Antropológicos*, 20:95–110.

Blanton, Richard E. 1972*a*. Prehispanic Adaptation in the Ixtapalapa Region, Mexico. *Science*, 175:1317–1326.

———. 1972*b*. *Prehispanic Settlement Patterns of the Ixtapalapa Peninsula Region, Mexico*. Occasional Papers in Anthropology, 6. University Park: Pennsylvania State University, Department of Anthropology.

Blom, Frans. 1932. *Commerce, Trade and Monetary Units of the Maya*. MARI Publication 4, no. 14. New Orleans.

———. 1946. Apuntes sobre los ingenieros mayas. *Irrigación en México*, 27: 5–16.

Bodde, Derk. 1956. Feudalism in China. In *Feudalism in History*, ed. Rushton Coulborn, pp. 49–92. Princeton: Princeton University Press.

Borhegyi, Stephan F. de. 1956*a*. The Development of Folk and Complex Cultures in the Southern Maya Area. *American Antiquity*, 21:343–356.

———. 1956*b*. Settlement Patterns in the Guatemala Highlands: Past and Present. In *Prehistoric Settlement Patterns in the New World*, ed. Gordon R. Willey, pp. 101–106. New York: Viking Fund, Publication 23.

————. 1965. Archaeological Synthesis of the Guatemalan Highlands. In *Handbook of Middle American Indians*, 2:3–58. Austin: University of Texas Press.

Bowditch, Charles P. 1901. On the Age of Maya Ruins. *American Anthropologist*, 3:697–700.

Bowra, C. M. 1971. *Periclean Athens*. Harmondsworth: Penguin.

Bradbury, J. 1974. Pollen Evidence at San Antonio Rio Hondo. Paper presented at the 73rd Meeting of the American Anthropological Association, Mexico City.

Brainerd, George W. 1954. *The Maya Civilization*. Los Angeles: Southwestern Museum.

————. 1958. *The Archaeological Ceramics of Yucatan*. University of California, Anthropological Records, no. 19. Berkeley: University of California Press.

Brasseur de Bourbourg, Charles E. 1869–1870. *Manuscript Troano*. Estudes sur le systême graphique et la langue des Mayas. 2 vols. Paris: Imprimerie Impériale.

Brinton, Daniel Garrison, ed. and trans. 1882. *The Maya Chronicles*. Philadelphia: D. G. Brinton.

Bronson, Bennet. 1968. Vacant Terrain. MS on file with the Tikal Project of the University Museum, Philadelphia.

Brotherston, Gordon. 1976a. Mesoamerican Description of Space, II: Signs for Direction. *Ibero-Amerikanisches Archiv*, 2:39–62.

————. 1976b. Time and Script in Mesoamerica. *Indiana*, 3:9–30.

————. 1977. *The Emergence of the Latin-American Novel*. Cambridge: Cambridge University Press.

————. 1978. *The New World in Its Own Image*. London.

Brotherston, Gordon, and D. Ades. 1975. Mesoamerican Description of Space, I: Myths, Stars and Maps, Architecture. *Ibero-Amerikanisches Archiv*, 1:279–305.

Brunhouse, Robert L. 1971. *Sylvanus G. Morley and the World of the Ancient Mayas*. Norman: University of Oklahoma Press.

————. 1975. *Pursuit of the Ancient Maya: Some Archaeologists of Yesterday*. Albuquerque: University of New Mexico Press.

Bullard, William R., Jr. 1960. Maya Settlement Pattern in Northeastern Peten, Guatemala. *American Antiquity*, 25:355–372.

————. 1964. Settlement Pattern and Social Structure in the Southern Maya Lowlands during the Classic Period. In *Actas y Memorias, XXXV Congreso Internacional de Americanistas, México, 1962*, 1:279–287. Mexico City.

————. 1965. *Stratigraphic Excavations at San Estevan, Northern British Honduras*. Art and Archaeology Occasional Paper, 9. Toronto: Royal Ontario Museum.

Bunzel, Ruth. 1952. *Chichicastenango: A Guatemalan Village*. Seattle: University of Washington Press.

Butler, M. 1935. A Study of Maya Mouldmade Figurines. *American Anthropologist*, 37:363–372.

Calnek, Edward E. 1970. Los pueblos indígenas de las tierras altas. In *Ensayos antropológicas en la zona central de chiapas*, ed. Norman A. McQuown and Julian Pitt-Rivers. Instituto Nacional Indigenista, Colección de Antropología Social, 8:105–133. Mexico City.

Carneiro, Robert L. 1970. A Theory of the Origin of the State. *Science*, 169: 733–738.

Carr, R. F., and J. E. Hazard. 1961. *Map of the Ruins of Tikal, El Peten, Guate-

mala. Museum Monograph, University Museum, University of Pennsylvania. *Tikal Report*, no. 11. Philadelphia.

Cartas de Clima. 1970. Mexico City: Secretaría de la Presidencia, Dirección de Planeación, and Instituto de Geografía, UNAM.

Caso, Alfonso. 1967. *Los calendarios prehispánicos*. Mexico City: UNAM, Instituto de Investigaciones Históricas.

Cassirer, Ernst. 1963. *The Individual and the Cosmos in Renaissance Philosophy*. Oxford: Oxford University Press.

Castillo, V. M. 1971. El bisiesto náhuatl. *Estudios de Cultura Náhuatl*, 9:75–99.

Chamberlain, R. S. 1948. *The Conquest and Colonization of Yucatan, 1517–1550*. CIW Publication 582. Washington, D.C.

Chang, K.-C. 1958. Study of the Neolithic Social Grouping: Examples from the New World. *American Anthropologist*, 60:298–334.

Chapman, A. C. 1957. Port of Trade Enclaves in Aztec and Maya Civilization. In *Trade and Market in the Early Empires*, ed. K. Polanyi, C. M. Arensberg, and H. W. Pearson. New York: Free Press.

Charlton, T. H. 1972. *Post-Conquest Developments in the Teotihuacan Valley, Mexico: Part 1, Excavations*. Report 5. Iowa City: Office of the State Archaeologist.

Charnay, Désiré. 1887. *The Ancient Cities of the New World*. Trans. J. Gonino and H. S. Conant. New York: Harper and Brothers.

Chase, Stuart. 1931. *Mexico: A Study of Two Americas*. New York: Literary Guild.

Cheek, Charles. 1976. Teotihuacan Influences at Kaminaljuyu. Paper presented at the XIV Mesa Redonda de la Sociedad Mexicana de Antropología, Tegucigalpa.

———. n.d. Analysis and Composition of the Middle Classic Burials [of Kaminaljuyu]. MS, Department of Anthropology, University of Tulsa.

Chimalpahin, D. 1963. *Das Geschichtswerk von . . .* , ed. Günter Zimmermann. Hamburg: Museum für Völkerkunde und Vorgeschichte.

Chumayel, Book of. 1913. Facsimile, ed. G. B. Gordon. Philadelphia: University Museum.

Church, G. E. 1900. The Ruined Cities of Central America. *Geographical Journal*, 15:392–394.

Ciudad Real, Antonio de. 1872. Relación de las cosas que sucedieron al R. P. Comisario General Fray Alonso Ponce . . . [orig. 1588]. In *Colección de documentos inéditos para la historia de España*, 57–58. Madrid.

Clarke, David L. 1968. *Analytical Archaeology*. London: Methuen.

Clegern, Wayne M. 1962. Maudslay's Central America: A Strategic View in 1887. In *Studies in Middle American Economics*. MARI Publication 29:73–94. New Orleans.

Coe, Michael D. 1961. *La Victoria: An Early Site on the Pacific Coast of Guatemala*. Papers of the Peabody Museum, 53. Cambridge, Mass.

———. 1965. A Model of Ancient Community Structure in the Maya Lowlands. *Southwestern Journal of Anthropology*, 21:97–114.

———. 1966. *The Maya*. London: Thames and Hudson.

———. 1973. *The Maya Scribe and His World*. New York: Grolier Club.

———. 1975a. *Classic Maya Pottery at Dumbarton Oaks*. Washington, D.C.: Dumbarton Oaks, Trustees for Harvard University.

———. 1975b. Death and the Ancient Maya. In *Death and the Afterlife in Pre-Columbian America*, ed. Elizabeth P. Benson, pp. 87–104. Washington, D.C.: Dumbarton Oaks, Trustees for Harvard University.

———. 1976. Matthew Williams Stirling, 1896–1975. *American Antiquity*, 41:67–73.

Coe, Michael D. and Kent V. Flannery. 1967. *Early Cultures and Human Ecology in South Coastal Guatemala*. Smithsonian Contributions to Anthropology, 3. Washington, D.C.: Smithsonian Institution.

Coe, William R. 1957. Environmental Limitations on Maya Culture: A Re-examination. *American Anthropologist*, 59:328–335.

———. 1959. *Piedras Negras Archaeology: Artifacts, Caches, and Burials*. Museum Monograph, University Museum, University of Pennsylvania. Philadelphia.

———. 1965a. Tikal, Guatemala, and Emergent Maya Civilization. *Science*, 147:1401–1419.

———. 1965b. Tikal. *Expedition* 8, no. 1:5–56.

———. 1967. *Tikal: A Handbook of the Ancient Maya Ruins*. Philadelphia: The University Museum.

———. 1972. Cultural Contact between the Lowland Maya and Teotihuacán as Seen from Tikal, Peten, Guatemala. In *Teotihuacán: XI Mesa Redonda*, pp. 257–271. México City: Sociedad Mexicana de Antropología.

Coe, William R., and Michael D. Coe. 1956. Excavations at Nohoch Ek, British Honduras. *American Antiquity*, 21:370–382.

Coggins, Clemency Chase. 1975. *Painting and Drawing Styles at Tikal: An Historical and Iconographic Reconstruction*. Ph.D. dissertation, Harvard University. Ann Arbor: University Microfilms.

———. 1976a. What Happened at A.D. 550? or, Was There a Middle Classic Period at Tikal? Paper presented at the Second Cambridge Symposium on Recent Research in Mesoamerican Archaeology, Cambridge, August 1976.

———. 1976b. Teotihuacan at Tikal in the Early Classic Period. Paper presented at the XLII Congrês International des Américanistes, Paris, September 1976.

———. 1976c. New Legislation to Control the International Traffic in Antiquities. *Archaeology*, 29:14–15.

———. 1977. Quetzalcoatl: Precious Twin. Paper presented at a seminar, Columbia University.

Cogolludo, D. L. de. 1688. *Historia de Yucatan*. Madrid.

Cook, S. F., and W. Borah. 1971–1974. *Essays in Population History: Mexico and the Caribbean*. Berkeley: University of California Press.

Cordry, D. B., and D. M. Cordry. 1941. *Costumes and Weaving of the Zoque Indians of Chiapas, Mexico*. Southwest Museum Papers, 15. Los Angeles.

Cowgill, George L. 1974. Quantitative Studies of Urbanization at Teotihuacan. In *Mesoamerican Archaeology: New Approaches*, ed. Norman Hammond, pp. 363–396. Austin: University of Texas Press.

———. 1975a. On Causes and Consequences of Ancient and Modern Population Changes. *American Anthropologist*, 77:505–525.

———. 1975b. Population Pressure as a Non-Explanation. In *Population Studies in Archaeology and Biological Anthropology: A Symposium*, ed. Alan C. Swedlund. Society for American Archaeology, Memoir 30:127–131. Washington, D.C.

Cowgill, U. M., and G. E. Hutchinson. 1963. Ecological and Geochemical Archaeology in the Southern Maya Lowlands. *Southwestern Journal of Anthropology*, 19:267–286.

Creel, Herrlee G. 1964. The Beginnings of Bureaucracy in China: The Origin of the *Hsien*. *Journal of Asian Studies*, 28:155–183.

———. 1970. *The Origin of Statecraft in China, 1: The Western Chou Empire*. Chicago: University of Chicago Press.

Culbert, T. Patrick. 1973. Introduction: A Prologue to Classic Maya Culture and the Problem of Its Collapse. In *The Classic Maya Collapse*, ed. idem, pp. 3–20. Albuquerque: University of New Mexico Press.

———. 1974. *The Lost Civilization: The Story of the Classic Maya*. New York: Harper and Row.

———. 1977. Maya Development and Collapse: An Economic Perspective. In *Social Process in Maya Prehistory*, ed. Norman Hammond, pp. 509–530. London and New York: Academic Press.

Culbert, T. Patrick, ed. *The Classic Maya Collapse*. Albuquerque: University of New Mexico Press.

Dahlin, Bruce H. 1974. Preliminary Findings of the Albion Island Settlement Pattern Survey. Paper presented at the 73rd Meeting of the American Anthropological Association, Mexico City.

———. 1976. *An Anthropologist Looks at the Pyramids: A Late Classic Revitalization Movement at Tikal, Guatemala*. Ph.D. dissertation, Temple University.

———. 1977. The Chalchuapa Figurine Industry. In *The Prehistory of Chalchuapa, El Salvador*, ed. Robert J. Sharer, 2. Philadelphia: University Museum, University of Pennsylvania.

Dieseldorff, Erwin P. 1926–1933. *Kunst und Religion der Mayavölker*. 3 vols. Sonderabdruck aus *Zeitschrift für Ethnologie*. Berlin.

Diringer, D. 1968. *The Alphabet*, 1. London: Hutchinson.

Donkin, R. A. 1970. Pre-Columbian Field Implements and Their Distribution in the Highlands of Middle and South America. *Anthropos*, 65:505–529.

Drewitt, Robert Bruce. 1967. *Irrigation and Agriculture in the Valley of Teotihuacán*. Ph.D. dissertation, University of California, Berkeley.

Drucker, D. R. 1974. *Renovating a Reconstruction: The Ciudadela at Teotihuacan, Mexico: Construction Sequence, Layout, and Possible Uses of the Structure*. Ph.D. dissertation, University of Rochester.

Dumond, D. E. 1972. Demographic Aspects of the Classic Period in Puebla-Tlaxcala. *Southwestern Journal of Anthropology*, 28:101–130.

Easby, E. K. 1968. *Pre-Columbian Jade from Costa Rica*. New York: Andre Emmerich.

Eaton, Jack D. 1972. A Report on Excavations at Chicanna, Campeche, Mexico. *Cerámica de Cultura Maya et al.*, 8:42–61.

———. 1974. Chicanna: An Elite Center in the Rio Bec Region. In *Preliminary Reports on Archaeological Investigations in the Rio Bec Area, Campeche, Mexico*, comp. Richard E. W. Adams. In *Archaeological Investigations on the Yucatan Peninsula*. MARI Publication 31:133–138. New Orleans.

Eberhard, W. 1969. *A History of China*. 3d ed. Berkeley: University of California Press.

Edmonson, M. 1968. *La literatura maya*. Verhandlungen des XXXVIII Internationalen Amerikanisten Kongresses, Stuttgart, 1968.

Edwards, C. R. 1957. Quintana Roo: Mexico's Empty Quarter. M.A. thesis, University of California, Berkeley.

Ehret, Christopher. 1976. Linguistic Evidence and Its Correlation with Archaeology. *World Archaeology*, 8:5–18.

Ekholm, G. F. 1949. Middle America. In News and Notes. *American Antiquity*, 15:77.

Farriss, Nancy M., and Arthur G. Miller. 1977. Maritime Culture Contact of the Maya. *Journal of Nautical Archaeology and Underwater Exploration*, 6, no. 2:141–151.

Feldman, Lawrence H. 1971. *A Tumpline Economy: Production and Distri-*

bution Systems of Early Central-East Guatemala. Ph.D. dissertation, University of Pennsylvania.

———. 1972. A Note on the Past Geography of Southern Chiapas Languages. International Journal of American Linguistics, 38:57–58.

———. 1973a. Languages of the Chiapas Coast and Interior in the Colonial Period, 1525–1820. In Contributions of the University of California Archaeological Research Facility, 18:77–85. Berkeley.

———. 1973b. Chiapas in 1774. In Contributions of the University of California Archaeological Research Facility, 18:105–135. Berkeley.

Flannery, Kent V. 1968. Archaeological Systems Theory and Early Mesoamerica. In Anthropological Archaeology in the Americas, ed. Betty J. Meggers, pp. 67–87. Washington, D.C.: Anthropological Society of Washington.

———. 1972. The Cultural Evolution of Civilization. In Annual Review of Ecology and Systematics, 3:399–426.

Flores Ruiz, Eduardo. 1973. Investigaciones históricas sobre Chiapas. Mexico City.

Folan, W. J. 1970. The Open Chapel of Dzibilchaltun, Yucatan. In Archaeological Studies in Middle America. MARI Publication 26:181–199. New Orleans.

Ford, Richard I., and Joel N. Elias. 1972. Teotihuacan Paleoethnobotany. Paper presented at the Annual Meeting of the Society for American Archaeology, Bal Harbour.

Gage, Thomas. 1946. The English-American: A New Survey of the West Indies, 1648, ed. A. P. Newton. Reprint of 1928 New York ed. Guatemala City: El Patio.

Gann, T. W. F. 1900. Mounds in Northern British Honduras. Nineteenth Report [1897–1898] of the Bureau of American Ethnology, Part 2, pp. 655–692. Washington, D.C.: Smithsonian Institution.

———. 1918. The Maya Indians of Southern Yucatan and Northern British Honduras. Bureau of American Ethnology Bulletin 64. Washington, D.C.: Smithsonian Institution.

———. 1927. Maya Cities. London: Duckworth.

Gann, T. W. F., and M. Gann. 1939. Archaeological Investigations in the Corozal District of British Honduras. Bureau of American Ethnology Bulletin 123:1–66. Washington, D.C.: Smithsonian Institution.

Gann, T. W. F. and J. Eric S. Thompson. 1931. The History of the Maya from the Earliest Times to the Present Day. New York: C. Scribner's Sons.

García Cook, Angel. 1974. Una secuencia cultural para Tlaxcala. In Proyecto Puebla-Tlaxcala: Comunicaciones 10:5–22. Puebla: Fundación Alemana para la Investigación Científica.

Garza, M. de la. 1975. La conciencia histórica de los antiguos mayas. Mexico City: UNAM.

Gates, William E. 1931. J. E. S. Thompson: Archaeology of the Cayo District, Review. Maya Society Quarterly, 1:37–44. Baltimore.

Georgiou, H. S., and M. J. Becker. 1974. An American Archaeologist in Crete: Richard B. Seager. Amaltheia (Hagios Nikolaos, Crete), 18–19(January): 74–114.

Gibson, Charles, and John B. Glass. 1975. A Census of Middle American Prose Manuscripts in the Native Historical Tradition. In Handbook of Middle American Indians, 15:322–400. Austin: University of Texas Press.

Gomme, A. W. 1933. The Population of Athens in the Fifth and Fourth Centuries B.C. Chicago: Argonaut.

Goody, J. 1968. Literacy in Traditional Societies. Cambridge: Cambridge University Press.

Graham, Ian. 1967. *Archaeological Explorations in El Peten, Guatemala.* MARI Publication 33. New Orleans.

———. 1975. *Corpus of Maya Hieroglyphic Inscriptions*, 2, part 1. Cambridge, Mass.: Peabody Museum, Harvard University.

———. 1976. John Eric Sidney Thompson: 1898–1975. *American Anthropologist*, 78:317–320.

Graham, John A. 1972. *The Hieroglyphic Inscriptions and Monumental Art of Altar de Sacrificios.* Papers of the Peabody Museum, 64, no. 2. Cambridge, Mass.

———. 1973. Aspects of Non-Classic Presences in the Inscriptions and Sculptural Art of Seibal. In *The Classic Maya Collapse*, ed. T. Patrick Culbert, pp. 207–219. Albuquerque: University of New Mexico Press.

Green, E. L. 1973. Location Analysis of Prehistoric Maya Sites in Northern British Honduras. *American Antiquity*, 38:279–293.

Greene, Merle. 1962. Homer's Use of Color in the Iliad. MS.

Greene, Merle, R. L. Rands, and J. A. Graham. 1972. *Maya Sculpture from the Southern Lowlands, the Highlands, and the Pacific Piedmont.* Berkeley: Lederer Street and Zeus.

Greene Robertson, Merle. 1975. Stucco Techniques Employed by Ancient Sculptors of the Palenque Piers. In *Actas y Memorias del XLI Congreso Internacional de Americanistas*, 1:449–472. Mexico City.

———. 1977. Painting Practices and Their Change through Time of the Palenque Stucco Sculptors. In *Social Process in Maya Prehistory*, ed. Norman Hammond, pp. 297–326. London and New York: Academic Press.

Greene Robertson, Merle, Marjorie S. F. Scandizzo, and J. R. Scandizzo. 1976. Physical Deformities in the Ruling Lineage of Palenque and the Dynastic Implications. In *The Art, Iconography, and Dynastic History of Palenque, Part III*, ed. Merle Greene Robertson. Pebble Beach: Robert Louis Stevenson School.

Guillemin, G. F. 1968. Development and Function of the Tikal Ceremonial Center. *Ethnos*, 33:1–35.

Hammond, Norman. 1972. The Planning of a Maya Ceremonial Center. *Scientific American*, 226, no. 5:82–91.

———. 1974. The Distribution of Late Classic Maya Major Ceremonial Centers in the Central Area. In *Mesoamerican Archaeology: New Approaches*, ed. Norman Hammond, pp. 313–334. Austin: University of Texas Press.

———. 1975. Introduction. In *Archaeology in Northern Belize, 1974/5 Interim Report of the British Museum–Cambridge University Corozal Project*, ed. idem, pp. 6–14. Cambridge: Centre of Latin American Studies.

———. 1977. Ex Oriente Lux: A View from Belize. In *The Origins of Maya Civilization*, ed. Richard E. W. Adams, pp. 45–79. Albuquerque: University of New Mexico Press.

———. In press. Holmul and Nohmul: A Comparison and Assessment of Two Maya Lowland Protoclassic sites. In *Actes de la XLII Congrès International des Américanistes, Paris, September 1976.*

Harrison, Peter D. 1968. Form and Function in a Maya "Palace" Group. In *Verhandlungen des XXXVIII. Internationalen Amerikanistenkongresses*, 1:165–172. Stuttgart-Munich.

———. 1970. *The Central Acropolis, Tikal, Guatemala: A Preliminary Study of the Functions of Its Structural Components during the Late Classic Period.* Ph.D. dissertation, University of Pennsylvania.

———. 1974a. Precolumbian Settlement Distributions and External Relationships in Southern Quintana Roo, Part 1: Architecture. In *Atti degli*

XL Congresso Internazionale degli Americanisti, 1:479–486. Rome.

———. 1974*b*. *Archaeology in Southwestern Quintana Roo: Interim Report of Uaymil Survey Project*. Paper presented at XLI Congreso Internacional de Americanistas, Mexico City. Mimeograph. Available from author.

Harrison, Peter D., and B. L. Turner II, eds. 1978. *Prehispanic Maya Agriculture*. Albuquerque: University of New Mexico Press.

Haviland, William A. 1965. Prehistoric Settlement at Tikal, Guatemala. *Expedition*, 7, no. 3:14–23.

———. 1966*a*. Review of Willey et al. 1965, Prehistoric Maya Settlement in the Belize Valley. *American Antiquity*, 31:592–593.

———. 1966*b*. Maya Settlement Patterns: A Critical Review. In *Archaeological Studies in Middle America*. MARI Publication 26:21–47. New Orleans.

———. 1967. Stature at Tikal, Guatemala: Implications for Ancient Maya Demography and Social Organization. *American Antiquity*, 32:316–325.

———. 1968. Ancient Lowland Maya Social Organization. In *Archaeological Studies in Middle America*. MARI Publication 26:93–117. New Orleans.

———. 1970. Tikal, Guatemala, and Mesoamerican Urbanism. *World Archaeology*, 2:186–198.

———. 1975. *The Ancient Maya and the Evolution of Urban Society*. Museum of Anthropology, University of Northern Colorado, Miscellaneous Series, No. 37.

Haviland, William A., and William R. Coe. 1965. Tikal, Guatemala: Physical and Social Composition. MS.

Hayden, Brian. 1976*a*. Coxoh Early Colonial Lithics: Coneta, Chiapas. MS.

———. 1976*b*. Preliminary Report of the Coapa Lithics. MS.

Hester, J. A. 1952. Agriculture, Economy, and Population Density of the Maya. In *CIW Yearbook* 51(1951–1952):266–271. Washington, D.C.

———. 1953. Agriculture, Economy, and Population Density of the Maya. In *CIW Yearbook* 52(1952–1953):288–292. Washington, D.C.

———. 1954. Maya Agriculture. In *CIW Yearbook* 53(1953–1954):297–298. Washington, D.C.

Hester, James J. 1976. *Introduction to Archaeology*. New York: Holt, Rinehart and Winston.

Heyden, D. 1975. An Interpretation of the Cave underneath the Pyramid of the Sun in Teotihuacan, Mexico. *American Antiquity*, 40:131–147.

Hickling, C. F. 1961. *Inland Tropical Fisheries*. London: Longman.

———. 1968. *The Farming of Fish*. New York: Pergamon.

Holmes, William Henry. 1895–1897. *Archaeological Studies among the Ancient Cities of Mexico*. Field Columbian Museum, Anthropological Series 1, no. 1. Chicago.

Hopkins, J. W. III. 1968. Prehispanic Agricultural Terraces in Mexico. M.A. thesis, University of Chicago.

Horton, R. 1971. African Conversion. *Africa*, 41:85–108.

Houston, Margaret, and Judith Carson Wainer. 1971. Pottery-making Tools from the Valley and Coast of Oaxaca. *Bulletin of Oaxaca Studies*, 36: 1–8.

Hsu, Cho-yun. 1965. *Ancient China in Transition: An Analysis of Social Mobility, 722–222 B.C.* Stanford: Stanford University Press.

Jacobs, Jane. 1969. *The Economy of Cities*. New York: Random House.

Jones, Christopher. 1969. *The Twin Pyramid Group Pattern: A Classic Maya*

Architectural Assemblage at Tikal, Guatemala. Ph.D. dissertation, University of Pennsylvania.

———. 1977. Inauguration Dates of Three Late Classic Rulers of Tikal, Guatemala. *American Antiquity*, 42:28–60.

Joralemon, P. D. 1971. *A Study of Olmec Iconography.* Studies in Pre-Columbian Art and Archaeology, 7. Washington, D.C.: Dumbarton Oaks, Trustees for Harvard University.

Joyce, T. A. 1926. Report on the Investigations at Lubaantun, British Honduras, in 1926. *Journal of the Royal Anthropological Institute*, 56: 207–230.

Kaufman, Terrence. 1974. *Idiomas de Mesoamérica.* Seminario de Integración Social Guatemalteca, Cuaderno 33. Guatemala City.

———. 1976. Archaeological and Linguistic Correlations in Maya Land and Associated Areas of Mesoamerica. *World Archaeology*, 8:101–118.

Keen, Benjamin. 1971. *The Aztec Image in Western Thought.* New Brunswick, N.J.: Rutgers University Press.

Kelley, David Humiston. 1962a. Glyphic Evidence for a Dynastic Sequence at Quirigua, Guatemala. *American Antiquity*, 27:323–335.

———. 1962b. A History of the Decipherment of Maya Script. *Anthropological Linguistics*, 4, no. 8:1–48.

———. 1976. *Deciphering the Maya Script.* Austin: University of Texas Press.

Kidder, Alfred V. 1947. *The Artifacts of Uaxactun, Guatemala.* CIW Publication 576. Washington, D.C.

———. 1950. Introduction. In *Uaxactun, Guatemala, 1931–1937*, by A. Ledyard Smith. CIW Publication 588. Washington, D.C.

Kidder, Alfred V., Jesse D. Jennings, and Edwin M. Shook. 1946. *Excavations at Kaminaljuyu, Guatemala.* CIW Publication 561. Washington, D.C.

Kirchoff, Paul. 1943. Mesoamérica: Sus límites geográficos, composición étnica, y caracteres culturales. *Acta Americana*, 1.

Kluckhohn, C. 1940. The Conceptual Structure in Middle American Studies. In *The Maya and Their Neighbors*, ed. C. L. Hay et al., pp. 41–51. New York: Appleton-Century.

Kraus, Henry. 1967. *The Living Theater of Medieval Art.* Bloomington: Indiana University Press.

Krotser, Paula H., and G. R. Krotser. 1973. The Life Style of El Tajín. *American Antiquity*, 38:199–205.

Kubler, George A. 1967. *The Iconography of the Art of Teotihuacan.* Studies in Pre-Columbian Art and Archaeology, 4. Washington, D.C.: Dumbarton Oaks, Trustees for Harvard University.

———. 1969. *Studies in Classic Maya Iconography.* Connecticut Academy of Arts and Science, Memoir 18. New Haven.

———. 1972a. Jaguars in the Valley of Mexico. In *The Cult of the Feline: A Conference on Pre-Columbian Iconography (1970)*, pp. 19–49. Washington, D.C.: Dumbarton Oaks, Trustees for Harvard University.

———. 1972b. La evidencia intrínseca y la analogía ethnológica en el estudio de las religiones mesoamericanas. In *Religion en Mesoamérica, XII Mesa Redonda.* Mexico City: Sociedad Mexicana de Antropología.

———. 1976. Mythological Dates at Palenque and the Ring Numbers in the Dresden Codex. In *The Art, Iconography, and Dynastic History of Palenque, Part III*, ed. Merle Greene Robertson, pp. 225–230. Pebble Beach: Robert Louis Stevenson School.

Kuhn, Thomas S. 1962. *The Structure of Scientific Revolutions.* Chicago: University of Chicago Press.

Kurjack, Edward B. 1974. *Prehistoric Lowland Maya Community and Social*

Organization—A Case Study at Dzibilchaltun, Yucatan, Mexico. MARI Publication 38. New Orleans.

Landa, Diego de. 1864. *Relation des choses de Yucatan de Diego de Landa . . . accompagné de documents divers historiques et chronologiques . . .*, ed. C. E. Brasseur de Bourbourg. Paris: A. Durand.

Large, E. G. 1975. Cotton: A Basic Resource for the Classic Maya of the Southern Lowlands. Paper presented at the 74th Meeting of the American Anthropological Association, San Francisco.

Lattimore, R., trans. 1962. *The Iliad of Homer.* Chicago: University of Chicago Press.

Le Clézio, J. M. G. 1976. *Les Prophéties du Chilam Balam.* Paris: Nouvelle Revue Française.

Lee, Thomas A., Jr. 1974. Preliminary Report of the 2nd and Final Reconnaissance Season of the Upper Grijalva Basic Maya Project, January–May 1974. MS filed with Departamento de Monumentos Prehispánicos INAH. Mexico City.

————. 1975. The Upper Grijalva Basin: A Preliminary Report of a New Maya Archaeological Project. In *Balance y perspectiva de la Antropología de Mesoamérica y del Norte de México.* XIII Mesa Redonda, 2:35–47. Mexico City: Sociedad Mexicana de Antropología.

Lee, Thomas A., Jr., and Sidney D. Markman. 1976a. The Coxoh Colonial Project and Coneta, Chiapas, Mexico: A Provincial Maya Village under the Spanish Conquest. Paper presented to the 9th Meeting of the Society for Historical Archaeology, Philadelphia.

————. 1976b. Colonial Coxoh Acculturation: A Necrotic Archaeological Ethnohistoric Model. Paper presented at XLII Congrès International des Américanistes, Paris.

León-Portilla, Miguel. 1968. *Tiempo y realidad en el pensamiento Maya.* Mexico City.

Lévi-Strauss, Claude. 1964–1971. *Mythologiques.* 4 vols. Paris.

Linton, R. 1940. Crops, Soils, and Culture in America. In *The Maya and Their Neighbors*, ed. C. L. Hay et al., pp. 32–40. New York: Appleton-Century.

Litvak King, Jaime. 1970. Xochicalco en la caída del Clásico, una hipótesis. *Anales de Antropología*, 7:133–144.

Longyear, J. M. III. 1952. *Copan Ceramics.* CIW Publication 597. Washington, D.C.

Lorenzo, José L., ed. 1968. *Materiales para la arqueología de Teotihuacán.* INAH, Serie Investigaciones, 17. Mexico City.

Lothrop, S. K. 1924. *Tulum: An Archaeological Study of the East Coast of Yucatan.* CIW Publication 335. Washington, D.C.

Lounsbury, Floyd G. 1973. On the Derivation and Reading of the "Ben-Ich" Prefix. In *Mesoamerican Writing Systems*, ed. Elizabeth P. Benson, pp. 99–143. Washington, D.C.: Dumbarton Oaks, Trustees for Harvard University.

Lowe, G. W. 1959. *Archaeological Exploration of the Upper Grijalva River, Chiapas, Mexico.* New World Archaeological Foundation Papers, 2. Orinda, Utah.

Lundell, Cyrus L. 1940. The 1936 Michigan-Carnegie Botanical Expedition to British Honduras. CIW Publication 522:1–58. Washington, D.C.

Luxton, R. 1977. *The Hidden Continent of the Maya and the Quechua.* Ph.D. dissertation, University of Essex.

McBryde, F. W. 1934. Sololá: A Guatemalan Town and Cakchiquel Market-Center. In *Studies in Middle America.* MARI Publication 5:45–152. New Orleans.

McClung de Tapia, Emily S. 1976. Palaeoethnobotanical Investigation at
    Teotihuacán, Mexico. Paper presented at 41st Meeting of the Society
    for American Archaeology, St. Louis.
Madsen, William. 1967. Religious Syncretism. In *Handbook of Middle Ameri-
    can Indians*, 6:369–391. Austin: University of Texas Press.
Mahler, Joy. 1965. Garments and Textiles of the Maya Lowlands. In *Hand-
    book of Middle American Indians*, 3:581–593. Austin: University of
    Texas Press.
Maler, T. 1901–1903. *Researches in the Central Portion of the Usumacintla
    Valley*. Memoirs of the Peabody Museum, 2, nos. 1 and 2. Cambridge,
    Mass.
———. 1908a. *Explorations of the Upper Usumacintla and Adjacent Regions*.
    Memoirs of the Peabody Museum, 4, no. 1. Cambridge, Mass.
———. 1908b. *Explorations in the Department of Peten, Guatemala, and
    Adjacent Regions*. Memoirs of the Peabody Museum, 4, nos. 2 and 3.
    Cambridge, Mass.
———. 1911. *Explorations in the Department of Peten, Guatemala: Tikal*.
    Memoirs of the Peabody Museum, 5, no. 1. Cambridge, Mass.
Mani, Book of. 1949. In *Códice Pérez*. Mérida: Liga de Acción Social.
Marcus, Joyce. 1973. Territorial Organization of the Lowland Classic Maya.
    Science, 180:911–916.
———. 1974. The Iconography of Power among the Classic Maya. *World
    Archaeology*, 6:83–94.
———. 1976. *Emblem and State in the Classic Maya Lowlands: An Epigra-
    phic Approach to Territorial Organization*. Washington, D.C.: Dum-
    barton Oaks, Trustees for Harvard University.
Markman, Sidney D. 1970. Pueblos de Españoles and pueblos de Indios in
    Colonial Central America. In *Verhandlungen des XXXVIII. Interna-
    tionalen Amerkanisten congresses, Stuttgart 1968*, 4. Stuttgart.
Mason, J. A. 1938. Observations on the Present Status and Problems of Mid-
    dle American Archaeology, Part II. *American Antiquity*, 3:300–317.
Mathews, Peter, and Linda Schele. 1974. Lords of Palenque: The Glyphic
    Evidence. In *Primera Mesa Redonda de Palenque, Part I*, ed. Merle
    Greene Robertson, pp. 63–76. Pebble Beach: Robert Louis Stevenson
    School.
Maudslay, A. P. 1886. Exploration of the Ruins and Site of Copan, Central
    America. *Proceedings of the Royal Geographical Society*, 8, no. 9:569–
    594.
———. 1889–1902. *Biologia Centrali-Americana: Archaeology*. London:
    Dulau.
Means, Philip A. 1917. *History of the Spanish Conquest of Yucatan and of
    the Itzas*. Memoirs of the Peabody Museum, 7. Cambridge, Mass.
Médiz Bolio, A. 1930. *El libro de Chilam Balam de Chumayel*. Mérida.
Merwin, R. E., and G. C. Vaillant. 1932. *The Ruins of Holmul, Guatemala*.
    Memoirs of the Peabody Museum, 3, no. 2. Cambridge, Mass.
Miles, S. W. 1957. Maya Settlement Patterns: A Problem for Ethnology and
    Archaeology. *Southwestern Journal of Anthropology*, 13:239–248.
———. 1958. An Urban Type: Extended Boundary Towns. *Southwestern Jour-
    nal of Anthropology*, 14:339–351.
Miller, Arthur G. 1972. Maya Influence in Some Teotihuacan Paintings. Paper
    presented at a Seminar on Maya Art at Tulane University.
———. 1973. *The Mural Painting of Teotihuacan*. Washington, D.C.: Dum-
    barton Oaks, Trustees for Harvard University.
———. 1977. The Maya and the Sea: Trade and Cult at Tancah and Tulum,
    Quintana Roo, Mexico. In *The Sea in the Pre-Columbian World*, ed.

Elizabeth P. Benson, pp. 97–138. Washington, D.C.: Dumbarton Oaks, Trustees for Harvard University.

Millon, René F. 1955. *When Money Grew on Trees: A Study of Cacao in Ancient Mesoamerica*. Ph.D. dissertation, Columbia University.

———. 1966. El problema de integración en la sociedad teotihuacán. In *Teotihuacán, XI Mesa Redonda*, 1:149–155. Mexico City: Sociedad Mexicana de Antropología.

———. 1970. Teotihuacán: Completion of Map of Giant Ancient City in the Valley of Mexico. *Science*, 170:1077–1082.

———. 1973. *The Teotihuacán Map: Text. Urbanization at Teotihuacán, Mexico*, 1, part 1. Austin: University of Texas Press.

———. 1974. The Study of Urbanism at Teotihuacan, Mexico. In *Mesoamerican Archaeology: New Approaches*, ed. Norman Hammond, pp. 335–362. Austin: University of Texas Press.

———. 1976. Social Relations in Ancient Teotihuacán. In *The Valley of Mexico: Studies in Pre-Hispanic Ecology and Society*, ed. Eric R. Wolf, pp. 205–248. Albuquerque: University of New Mexico Press.

Millon, René F., Clara Hall, and May Diaz. 1962. Conflict in the Modern Teotihuacán Irrigation System. *Comparative Studies in Society and History*, 4:495–524.

Moholy-Nagy, Hattula. 1975. Obsidian at Tikal, Guatemala. In *Actas y Memorias, XLI Congreso Internacional de Americanistas, México, 1974*, 1:511–518. Mexico City.

Molina Solís, J. F. 1896. *Historia del descubrimiento y conquista de Yucatán*. Mérida.

Molloy, John P., and William L. Rathje. 1974. Sexploitation among the Late Classic Maya. In *Mesoamerican Archaeology: New Approaches*, ed. Norman Hammond, pp. 431–444. Austin: University of Texas Press.

Morley, Sylvanus G. 1910. A Group of Related Structures at Uxmal, Mexico. *American Journal of Archaeology*, 14:1–18.

———. 1915. *An Introduction to the Study of the Maya Hieroglyphs*. Bureau of American Ethnology Bulletin 57. Washington, D.C.: Smithsonian Institution.

———. 1920. *The Inscriptions at Copan*. CIW Publication 219. Washington, D.C.

———. 1924. Archaeology. In *CIW Yearbook*, 22:267–273.

———. 1937–1938. *The Inscriptions of Peten*. 5 vols. CIW Publication 437. Washington, D.C.

———. 1946. *The Ancient Maya*. Stanford: Stanford University Press.

———. 1956. *The Ancient Maya*. 3d ed., revised by George W. Brainerd. Stanford: Stanford University Press.

Motul, Diccionario de. 1929. Ed. J. Martínez Hernández. Mérida: Talleres de la Compañía Tipográfica Yucateca.

Muller, Florencia. 1973. La extensión arqueológica de Cholula a través del tiempo. In *Proyecto Puebla-Tlaxcala, Comunicaciones*, 8:19–22. Puebla: Fundación Alemana para Investigaciones Científicas.

Munsell Book of Color. 1976. Baltimore: Munsell.

Neugebauer, Otto. 1975. *A History of Ancient Mathematical Astronomy*. Berlin and New York: Springer.

Noyes, E. 1932. Fray Alonso Ponce in Yucatan, 1588. In *Middle American Papers*. MARI Publication 4:297–372. New Orleans.

Ochse, J. J., M. J. Soule, Jr., M. J. Dijkman, and C. Wehlburg. 1961. *Tropical and Subtropical Agriculture*, 1. New York: Macmillan.

Olivé N., Julio Cesár, and Beatriz Barbá A. 1957. Sobre la desintegración de las culturas clásicas. *Anales del Instituto Nacional de Antropología e Historia*, 9:57–72.

Olson, Gerald W. 1969. *Descriptions and Data on Soils of Tikal, El Peten, Guatemala, Central America.* Agronomy Mimeograph 69-2. Ithaca: Cornell University Department of Agronomy.

Orozco y Berra, Manuel. 1880. *Historia antigua y de la conquista de México.* 4 vols. Mexico City: Tip. de G. A. Esteva. (Reissued 1960.)

Oviedo y Valdés, G. F. de. 1851–1855. *Historia general y natural de las Indias, islas y tierra-firme del Mar Oceano.* Madrid.

Ower, L. H. 1927. Features of British Honduras. *Geographical Journal*, 70: 373–386.

Palerm, A., and E. R. Wolf. 1957. Ecological Potential and Cultural Development in Mesoamerica. In *Pan American Union Studies in Human Ecology.* Social Science Monograph 3:1–38. Washington D.C.

Parsons, E. C. 1936. *Mitla: Town of the Souls.* Chicago: University of Chicago Press.

Parsons, Lee A. 1967–1969. *Bilbao, Guatemala: An Archaeological Study of the Pacific Coast Cotzumalhuapa Region.* Milwaukee Public Museum Publications in Anthropology, 11–12. Milwaukee.

———. 1974. *Pre-Columbian America: The Art and Archaeology of South, Central, and Middle America.* Milwaukee: Milwaukee Public Museum.

Parsons, Lee A., and Barbara J. Price. 1971. Mesoamerican Trade and Its Role in the Emergence of Civilization. In *Observations on the Emergence of Civilization in Mesoamerica*, ed. R. F. Heizer and John A. Graham. Contributions of the University of California Archaeological Research Facility, 11:169–195. Berkeley.

Parsons, Jeffrey R. 1968. Teotihuacan, Mexico, and Its Impact on Regional Demography. *Science*, 162:872–877.

———. 1971. *Prehistoric Settlement Patterns in the Texcoco Region, Mexico.* University of Michigan Museum of Anthropology, Memoir 3. Ann Arbor.

———. 1972. Archaeological Settlement Patterns. In *Annual Review of Anthropology*, 1, ed. B. J. Siegel. Palo Alto: Annual Reviews, Inc.

———. 1974. The Development of a Prehistoric Complex Society: A Regional Perspective from the Valley of Mexico. *Journal of Field Archaeology*, 1:81–108.

Pasztory, E. 1972. *The Murals of Tepantitla, Teotihuacan.* Ph.D. dissertation, Columbia University.

Pendergast, David M. 1969. *Altun Ha, British Honduras [Belize]: The Sun God's Tomb.* Royal Ontario Museum, Art and Archaeology Occasional Paper 19. Toronto.

———. 1971. Evidence of Early Teotihuacan–Lowland Maya Contact at Altun Ha. *American Antiquity*, 36:455–460.

———. 1975. The Church in the Jungle. *Rotunda*, 8, no. 2:32–40.

Pendergast, David M., ed. 1967. *Palenque: The Walker-Caddy Expedition to the Ancient Maya City, 1839–1840.* Norman: University of Oklahoma Press.

Pennington, T. D., and J. Sarukhan. 1968. *Manual para la identificación de campo de los principales árboles tropicales de México.* Mexico City: Instituto Nacional de Investigaciones Forestales, Secretaría de Agricultura y Ganadería.

Péret, B. 1955. *Livre du Chilam Balam de Chumayel.* (French translation of Médiz Bolio 1930.) Paris: Ed. de Noël.

Ponce, Fray Alonso. 1948. *Viaje a Chiapas, 1586, Antología.* Cuadernos de Chiapas, 14. Tuxtla Gutiérrez: Gobierno Constitucional del Estado.

Popol Vuh. 1971. Trans. and ed. Munro S. Edmonson, as *The Book of Counsel: The Popol Vuh of the Quiché Maya of Guatemala*. MARI Publication 35. New Orleans.

Potter, D. F. 1973. *Maya Architectural Style in Central Yucatan*. Ph.D. dissertation, Tulane University.

Price, Barbara J. 1974. The Burden of the *Cargo*: Ethnographical Models and Archaeological Inference. In *Mesoamerican Archaeology: New Approaches*, ed. Norman Hammond, pp. 445–465. Austin: University of Texas Press.

Pring, Duncan C. 1975. Summary of the Ceramic Sequence in Northern Belize. In *Archaeology in Northern Belize, 1974/5 Interim Report of the British Museum–Cambridge University Corozal Project*, ed. Norman Hammond, pp. 116–127. Cambridge: Centre of Latin American Studies.

Proskouriakoff, Tatiana. 1950. *A Study of Classic Maya Sculpture*. CIW Publication 593. Washington, D.C.

———. 1960. Historical Implications of a Pattern of Dates at Piedras Negras, Guatemala. *American Antiquity*, 25:454–475.

———. n.d. A History of the Lowland Maya from Their Texts. MS.

Puleston, Dennis E. 1974. Intersite Areas in the Vicinity of Tikal and Uaxactun. In *Mesoamerican Archaeology: New Approaches*, ed. Norman Hammond, pp. 303–311. Austin: University of Texas Press.

———. 1976. An Epistemological Pathology and the Collapse, or, Why the Maya Kept the Short Count. Paper presented at the Second Cambridge Symposium on Recent Research in Mesoamerican Archaeology, Cambridge, August 1976. (Published in this volume.)

———. 1977. The Art and Archaeology of Hydraulic Agriculture in the Maya Lowlands. In *Social Process in Maya Prehistory*, ed. Norman Hammond, pp. 449–467. London and New York: Academic Press.

Puleston, Dennis E., and D. W. Callender, Jr. 1967. Defensive Earthworks at Tikal. *Expedition* 9:46–48.

Quirarte, Jacinto. 1972. Murals and Vase Paintings of the Southern Lowlands: Central Zone. Paper presented at a Seminar on Maya Art at Tulane University.

———. 1973. Mayan and Teotihuacan Traits in Classic Maya Vase Painting of the Peten. Paper presented at the IX International Congress of Anthropological and Ethnological Sciences, Chicago.

———. 1974. Terrestrial/Celestial Polymorphs as Narrative Frames in the Art of Izapa and Palenque. In *Primera Mesa Redonda de Palenque, Part I*, ed. Merle Greene Robertson. Pebble Beach: Robert Louis Stevenson School.

———. 1976. The Underworld Jaguar in Maya Vase Painting: An Iconographic Study. *New Mexico Studies in the Fine Arts*, 1:20–25.

———. 1978. Actual and Implied Visual Space in Maya Vase Painting: A Study of Double Images and Two-Headed Compound Creatures. In *Studies in Ancient Mesoamerica*, ed. John A. Graham, 3:27–28. Contributions of the University of California Archaeological Research Facility, no. 36 (January). Berkeley.

Radin, P. 1970. *The Winnebago Tribe*. Lincoln: University of Nebraska Press.

Rands, Robert L. 1965. Classic and Postclassic Pottery Figurines of the Guatemalan Highlands. In *Handbook of Middle American Indians*, 2:156–162. Austin: University of Texas Press.

———. 1974. A Chronological Framework for Palenque. In *Primera Mesa Redonda de Palenque, Part I*, ed. Merle Greene Robertson. Pebble Beach: Robert Louis Stevenson School.

Rathje, William L. 1970. Socio-political Implications of Lowland Maya

Burials: Methodology and Tentative Hypotheses. *World Archaeology*, 1:359–374.

———. 1971. The Origin and Development of Lowland Maya Civilization. *American Antiquity*, 36:275–285.

———. 1973. Classic Maya Development and Denouement: A Research Design. In *The Classic Maya Collapse*, ed. T. Patrick Culbert, pp. 405–454. Albuquerque: University of New Mexico Press.

Redfield, Robert. 1941. *The Folk Culture of Yucatan*. Chicago: University of Chicago Press.

———. 1953. *The Primitive World and Its Transformations*. Ithaca: Cornell University Press.

———. 1956. *Peasant Society and Culture: An Anthropological Approach to Civilization*. Chicago: University of Chicago Press.

Redfield, R., and A. Villa Rojas. 1934. Chan Kom, a Maya Village. CIW Publication 448.

Relaciones de Yucatán. 1898–1900. In *Colección de documentos inéditos relativos al descubrimiento, conquista, y organización de las antiguas posesiones de Ultramar*, 11 and 13. Madrid.

Remesal, Fray Antonio. 1966. *Historia general de las Indias Occidentales y particular de la Gobernación de Chiapa y Guatemala*. Biblioteca de Autores Españoles, 175 and 189. Madrid.

Rice, D. S. 1974. *The Archaeology of British Honduras: A Review and Synthesis*. University of Northern Colorado Museum of Anthropology, Occasional Publications in Anthropology, Archaeology Series, 6. Greely.

———. 1976. Population Growth and Subsistence Decision-Making in the Yaxhá-Sacnab Region, Peten, Guatemala. Paper presented at XLII Congrès International des Américanistes, Paris, September 1976.

Ricketson, Oliver G., and E. B. Ricketson. 1937. *Uaxactun, Guatemala: Group E, 1926–1931*. CIW Publication 477. Washington, D.C.

Rogge, A. E. 1976. A Look at Academic Anthropology: Through a Graph Darkly. *American Anthropologist*, 78:829–843.

Romney, A. 1957. The Genetic Model and Uto-Aztecan Time Perspective. *Davidson Journal of Anthropology*, 3, no. 2:35–41.

Rovner, Irwin. 1975. The Cyclical Rise of Maya Lithic Trade Spheres. Paper presented at the 40th Meeting of the Society for American Archaeology, Dallas.

Roys, Ralph L. 1933. *The Book of Chilam Balam of Chumayel*. CIW Publication 438. Washington, D.C. (Reprinted in 1967 by University of Oklahoma Press, Norman.)

———. 1943. *The Indian Background of Colonial Yucatan*. CIW Publication 548. Washington, D.C. (Reprinted in 1972 by University of Oklahoma Press, Norman.)

———. 1949a. *Guide to the Codex Pío Pérez*. CIW Contributions to American Anthropology and History, 49; bound in CIW Publication 585:87–106. Washington, D.C.

———. 1949b. *The Prophecies for the Maya Tuns or Years in the Books of Chilam Balam of Tizimin and Mani*. CIW Contributions to Anthropology and History, 51; bound in CIW Publication 585:153–186. Washington, D.C.

———. 1954. *The Maya Katun Prophecies of the Books of Chilam Balam, Series I*. CIW Contributions to American Anthropology and History, 57; bound in CIW Publication 606:1–60. Washington, D.C.

———. 1957. *Political Geography of the Yucatan Maya*. CIW Publication 613. Washington, D.C.

———. 1967. Reprint of Roys 1933. Norman: University of Oklahoma Press.

————. 1972. Reprint of Roys 1943. Norman: University of Oklahoma Press.

Roys, Ralph L., F. V. Scholes, and E. B. Adams. 1940. *Report and Census of the Indians of Cozumel, 1570.* CIW Contributions to American Anthropology and History, 30; bound in CIW Publication 523:1–30. Washington, D.C.

Ruppert, Karl, and J. H. Denison. 1943. *Archaeological Reconnaissance in Campeche, Quintana Roo, and Peten.* CIW Publication 543. Washington, D.C.

Ruppert, Karl, J. Eric S. Thompson, and Tatiana Proskouriakoff. 1955. *Bonampak, Chiapas, Mexico.* CIW Publication 602. Washington, D.C.

RY. See *Relaciones de Yucatán.*

Sabloff, Jeremy A. 1973. Major Themes in the Past Hypotheses of the Maya Collapse. In *The Classic Maya Collapse,* ed. T. Patrick Culbert, pp. 35–40. Albuquerque: University of New Mexico Press.

————. 1975. *Excavations at Seibal: Ceramics.* Memoirs of the Peabody Museum, 13, no. 2. Cambridge, Mass.

Sabloff, Jeremy A., William L. Rathje, David A. Freidel, Judith G. Connor, and Paula L. W. Sabloff. 1974. Trade and Power in Postclassic Yucatan: Initial Observations. In *Mesoamerican Archaeology: New Approaches,* ed. Norman Hammond, pp. 397–416. Austin: University of Texas Press.

Sanchez, P. A., and S. W. Buol. 1975. Soils of the Tropics and the World Food Crisis. *Science,* 188:598–603.

Sánchez de Aguilar, P. 1937. *Informe contra idolorum cultures del obispado de Yucatán.* (Written ca. 1615.) 3d ed. Mérida.

Sanders, William T. 1965. *The Cultural Ecology of the Teotihuacán Valley.* University Park: Pennsylvania State University, Department of Sociology and Anthropology.

————. 1966. Review of *Desarrollo cultural de los mayas,* ed. Evon Z. Vogt and Alberto Ruz Lhuillier. *American Anthropologist,* 68:1068–1071.

————. 1973. The Cultural Ecology of the Lowland Maya: A Reevaluation. In *The Classic Maya Collapse,* ed. T. Patrick Culbert, pp. 325–365. Albuquerque: University of New Mexico Press.

Sanders, William T., A. Kovar, T. Charlton, and R. A. Diehl. 1970. *The Teotihuacán Valley Project, Final Report, Volume 1.* University Park: Pennsylvania State University, Department of Anthropology.

Sanders, William T., and J. Marino. 1970. *New World Prehistory: Archaeology of the American Indian.* Englewood Cliffs, N.J.: Prentice-Hall.

Sanders, William T., and Barbara J. Price. 1968. *Mesoamerica: The Evolution of a Civilization.* New York: Random House.

Satterthwaite, Linton, Jr. 1936a. An Unusual Type of Building in the Maya Old Empire. *Maya Research* 3, no. 1:62–73. New Orleans.

————. 1936b. Notes on the Work of the Fourth and Fifth University Museum Expeditions to Piedras Negras, Peten, Guatemala. *Maya Research* 3, no. 1:74–91. New Orleans.

————. 1937a. Identification of Maya Temple Buildings at Piedras Negras. In *Twenty-fifth Anniversary Studies,* 1, ed. D. S. Davidson. Philadelphia Anthropological Society.

————. 1937b. Thrones at Piedras Negras. *Bulletin of the University of Pennsylvania Museum,* 7:18–23.

————. 1944. *Piedras Negras Archaeology: Architecture, Part IV, Ball Courts.* Philadelphia: University Museum, University of Pennsylvania.

————. 1951. Reconnaissance in British Honduras. *Bulletin of the University of Pennsylvania Museum,* 16:21–37.

————. 1954. *Piedras Negras Archaeology: Architecture, Part VI, no. 5, The Plazuela of Str. V-1.* Philadelphia: University Museum, University of Pennsylvania.

———. 1958. Five Newly Discovered Carved Monuments at Tikal and New Data on Four Others. Museum Monograph, University Museum, University of Pennsylvania. *Tikal Report*, no. 4:85–150.

Saul, Frank P. 1973. Disease in the Maya Area: The Pre-Columbian Evidence. In *The Classic Maya Collapse*, ed. T. Patrick Culbert, pp. 301–324. Albuquerque: University of New Mexico Press.

Schele, Linda. 1976. Accession Iconography of Chan-Bahlum in the Group of the Cross at Palenque. In *The Art, Iconography, and Dynastic History of Palenque, Part III*, ed. Merle Greene Robertson. Pebble Beach: Robert Louis Stevenson School.

Scholes, F. V., ed. 1936–1938. *Documentos para la historia de Yucatán*. Mérida.

Scholes, F. V., and E. B. Adams, eds. 1938. *Don Diego de Quijada, Alcalde Major de Yucatán, 1561–1565*. Mexico City.

Scholes, F. V., and Ralph L. Roys. 1938. *Fray Diego de Landa and the Problem of Idolatry in Yucatan*. CIW Contributions to American Anthropology and History; bound in CIW Publication 501:585–620. Washington, D.C.

———. 1968. *The Maya Chontal Indians of Acalan Tixchel: A Contribution to the History and Ethnography of the Yucatan Peninsula*. 2d ed. Norman: University of Oklahoma Press.

Schorr, T. S. 1973. The Structure, Purpose, and Social Organization of Pre-Columbian "Ridged Field" Systems. Paper presented at 72nd Meeting of the American Anthropological Association, New Orleans.

Sears, W. H. 1961. The Study of Social and Religious Systems in North American Archaeology. *Current Anthropology*, 2:223–246.

Seler, Edward. 1902–1923. *Gesammelte Abhandlungen*. 5 vols. Berlin: Mann. (Reprint.)

Sharer, Robert J. 1968. *Preclassic Archaeological Investigations at Chalchuapa, El Salvador: The El Trapiche Mound Group*. Ph.D. dissertation, University of Pennsylvania.

———. 1969. Chalchuapa: Investigations at a Highland Maya Ceremonial Center. *Expedition*, 11:36–38.

———. 1974. The Prehistory of the Southeastern Maya Periphery. *Current Anthropology*, 15:165–187

———. 1975. Review of *The Ceramics of Altar de Sacrificios*, by Richard E. W. Adams. *American Journal of Archaeology*.

Sharer, Robert J., ed. 1977. *The Prehistory of Chalchuapa, El Salvador*. Philadelphia: University Museum, University of Pennsylvania.

Sharer, Robert J., and J. C. Gifford. 1970. Preclassic Ceramics from Chalchuapa, El Salvador, and Their Relationships with the Maya Lowlands. *American Antiquity*, 35:165–187.

Sheets, Payson D. 1971. An Ancient Natural Disaster. *Expedition*, 14, no. 1: 24–31.

———. 1975. *Ilopango Volcano and the Maya Protoclassic: A Report of the 1975 Field Session of the Protoclassic Project in El Salvador*. Mimeograph. Boulder: Department of Anthropology, University of Colorado.

———. 1976. *Ilopango Volcano and the Maya Protoclassic: A Report of the 1975 Field Season of the Protoclassic Project in El Salvador*. Carbondale: University of Southern Illinois Museum of Anthropology.

Shook, Edwin M., and Tatiana Proskouriakoff. 1956. Settlement Patterns in Mesoamerica and the Sequence in the Guatemalan Highlands. In *Prehistoric Settlement Patterns in the New World*, ed. Gordon R. Willey, pp. 93–100. Viking Fund, Publication 23. New York.

Shook, Edwin M., and R. E. Smith. 1950. Descubrimientos arqueológicos en Poptún. *Antropología e Historia de Guatemala*, 2, no. 2.

Siemens, A. H., and Dennis E. Puleston. 1972. Ridged Fields and Associated Features in Southern Campeche: New Perspectives on the Lowland Maya. *American Antiquity*, 37:228–239.

Simmons, C. S., J. M. Taranto T., and J. H. Pinto Z. 1958. *Clasificación de reconocimiento de los suelos de la República de Guatemala*. Guatemala City: Editorial de Ministerio de Educación Pública.

Sjoberg, G. 1955. The Preindustrial City. *American Journal of Sociology*, 1: 438–445.

———. 1960. *The Preindustrial City: Past and Present*. Glencoe, Ill.: Free Press.

Smith, A. Ledyard. 1934. *Two Recent Ceramic Finds at Uaxactun*. CIW Contributions to American Anthropology and History; bound in CIW Publication 436:1–25. Washington, D.C.

———. 1950. *Uaxactun, Guatemala, 1931–1937*. CIW Publication 588. Washington, D.C.

Smith, A. Ledyard, Richard E. W. Adams, Gordon R. Willey, and J. Ladd. 1963. *Altar de Sacrificios, 1963: Fifth and Terminal Preliminary Report*. Cambridge, Mass.: Peabody Museum, Harvard University. Mimeograph.

Smith, A. Ledyard, and Alfred V. Kidder. 1951. *Excavations at Nebaj, Guatemala*. CIW Publication 594. Washington, D.C.

Smith, Robert Eliot. 1955. *Ceramic Sequence at Uaxactun, Guatemala*. MARI Publication 20. New Orleans.

Snow, Dean R. 1969. Ceramic Sequence and Settlement Location in Pre-Hispanic Tlaxcala. *American Antiquity*, 34:131–145.

Sodi, D. I. 1961. Como nació el Uinal. *Estudios de Cultura Maya*, 1:211–219.

Spence, Michael E. 1967. The Obsidian Industry of Teotihuacan. *American Antiquity*, 32:507–514.

———. 1975. The Development of the Teotihuacan Obsidian Production System. MS, on file, Department of Anthropology, Western Ontario University. London, Ontario.

Spencer, J. E., and G. Hale. 1961. The Origin, Nature, and Distribution of Agricultural Terracing. *Pacific Viewpoint*, 2:1–40.

Spinden, Herbert J. 1913. *A Study of Maya Art: Its Subject Matter and Historical Development*. Memoirs of the Peabody Museum, 6. Cambridge, Mass.

Starbuck, David R. 1975. *Man-Animal Relationships in Pre-Columbian Central Mexico*. Ph.D. dissertation, Yale University.

Steggerda, Morris. 1941. *The Maya Indians of Yucatan*. CIW Publication 531. Washington, D.C.

Stephens, John L. 1843. *Incidents of Travel in Yucatan*. 2 vols. New York: Harper and Brothers. (Dover Publications, unabridged, 1963.)

Steward, Julian H. 1955. *Theory of Culture Change*. Urbana: University of Illinois Press.

Stirling, M. W. 1961. The Olmecs, Artists in Jade. In *Essays in Pre-Columbian Art and Archaeology*, ed. S. K. Lothrop et al. Cambridge, Mass.: Harvard University Press.

Stoltman, James B. In press. *Lithic Artifacts from a Complex Society: The Chipped Stone Tools of Becan, Campeche, Mexico*. MARI Publication. New Orleans.

Stone, D. Z. 1972. *Pre-Columbian Man Finds Central America: The Archaeological Bridge*. Cambridge, Mass.: Peabody Museum Press.

Stuart, G., J. C. Scheffler, E. B. Kurjack, and J. W. Collier. 1965. *Map of Dzibilchaltun, Yucatan, Mexico*. New Orleans: MARI.

Tax, Sol. 1937. The Municipios of the Midwestern Highlands of Guatemala. *American Anthropologist*, 39: 423–444.

———. 1953. *Penny Capitalism: A Guatemalan Indian Economy*. Washington, D.C.: U.S. Government Printing Office.

Taylor, W. W. 1948. *A Study of Archaeology*. Memoirs of the American Anthropological Association, 69.

Terkel, Studs. 1970. *Hard Times: An Oral History of the Great Depression*. New York: Pantheon.

Thomas, Cyrus. 1899. Maudslay's Archaeological Work in Central America. *American Anthropologist*, 1:552–562.

Thompson, Donald E. 1954. Maya Paganism and Christianity. In *Nativism and Syncretism*. MARI 19:5–36. New Orleans.

Thompson, Edward H. 1886. Archaeological Research in Yucatan. *Proceedings of the American Antiquarian Society*, n.s. 4:248–254.

———. 1892. The Ancient Structures of Yucatan Not Communal Dwellings. *Proceedings of the American Antiquarian Society*, n.s. 8:262–269.

———. 1895. Ancient Tombs of Palenque. *Proceedings of the American Antiquarian Society*, 10:418–421.

———. 1938. *The High Priest's Grave, Chichen Itza, Yucatan, Mexico*. Prepared for publication, with notes and introduction, by J. Eric S. Thompson. Field Museum of Natural History, Anthropological Series, 27, no. 1:1–64. Chicago.

Thompson, Edward H., and G. Dorsey. 1898. *Ruins of Xkichmook, Yucatan*. Field Columbian Museum Publication 28; Anthropology Series, 2, no. 3. Chicago.

Thompson, J. Eric S. 1927. *The Civilization of the Mayas*. Field Museum of Natural History, Anthropology Leaflet 25. Chicago.

———. 1931. *Archaeological Investigations in the Southern Cayo District, British Honduras*. Field Museum of Natural History, Publication 274; Anthropological Series 17, no. 3. Chicago.

———. 1939. *Excavations at San José, British Honduras*. CIW Publication 506. Washington, D.C.

———. 1941. *Dating of Certain Inscriptions of Non-Maya Origin*. CIW Division of Historical Research, Theoretical Approaches to Problems, 1. Cambridge, Mass.

———. 1942. 4th ed. of Thompson 1927.

———. 1943. Pitfalls and Stimuli in the Interpretation of History through Loan Words. In *Philological and Documentary Studies*. MARI Publication 11:17–28. New Orleans.

———. 1945. A Survey of the Northern Maya Area. *American Antiquity*, 11: 2–24.

———. 1948. *An Archaeological Reconnaissance in the Cotzumalhuapa Region, Escuintla, Guatemala*. CIW Contributions to American Anthropology and History, 44; bound in CIW Publication 574. Washington, D.C.

———. 1954a. *The Rise and Fall of Maya Civilization*. Norman: University of Oklahoma Press.

———. 1954b. *A Presumed Residence of the Nobility of Mayapan*. CIW Division of Historical Research, Current Reports, 2, no. 19. Cambridge, Mass.

———. 1956. *Notes on the Use of Cacao in Middle America*. CIW Division of Historical Research, Notes in Middle American Archaeology and Ethnology, 128. Cambridge, Mass.

———. 1960. *Maya Hieroglyphic Writing: Introduction*. 2d ed. Norman: University of Oklahoma Press.

———. 1962. *A Catalog of Maya Hieroglyphs*. Norman: University of Oklahoma Press.

———. 1966. Merchant Gods of Middle America. In *Summa antropológica en homenaje al Ingeniero Roberto J. Weitlaner*, ed. A. Pompa y Pompa, pp. 159–172. Mexico City.

———. 1967. *The Rise and Fall of Maya Civilization*. 2d ed. Norman: University of Oklahoma Press.

———. 1970. *Maya History and Religion*. Norman: University of Oklahoma Press.

———. 1972. *A Commentary on the Dresden Codex, a Maya Hieroglyphic Book*. Memoirs of the American Philosophical Society, 93. Philadelphia.

———. 1974. "Canals" of the Rio Candelaria Basin, Campeche, Mexico. In *Mesoamerican Archaeology: New Approaches*, ed. Norman Hammond, pp. 297–302. Austin: University of Texas Press.

Thompson, J. Eric S., ed. 1958. *Thomas Gage's Travels in the New World*. Norman: University of Oklahoma Press.

Thompson, J. Eric S., H. E. D. Pollock, and J. Charlot. 1932. *A Preliminary Study of the Ruins of Cobá, Quintana Roo, Mexico*. CIW Publication 424. Washington, D.C.

Tizimin, Book of. 1977. Ed. Munro S. Edmonson. New Orleans.

Toulmin, Stephen, and J. Goodfield. 1965. *The Discovery of Time*. London: Hutchinson.

Tourtellot, Gair. 1970. The Peripheries of Seibal. In *Maya Archaeology*, ed. William R. Bullard, part 4, no. 3. Papers of the Peabody Museum, 61: 405–415. Cambridge, Mass.

Tozzer, Alfred M. 1910. *Animal Figures in the Maya Codices*. Papers of the Peabody Museum, vol. 4, no. 3. Cambridge, Mass.

———. 1911. *A Preliminary Study of the Prehistoric Ruins of Tikal, Guatemala*. Memoirs of the Peabody Museum, 2. Cambridge, Mass.

———. 1937. Prehistory in Middle America. *Hispanic American Historical Review*, 17:151–159.

———. 1957. *Chichén Itzá and Its Cenote of Sacrifice: A Comparative Study of Contemporaneous Maya and Toltec*. Memoirs of the Peabody Museum, 11–12. Cambridge, Mass.

Tozzer, Alfred M., trans. and ed. 1941. *Landa's Relación de las cosas de Yucatán*. Papers of the Peabody Museum, 18. Cambridge, Mass.

Tschopik, H. 1950. An Andean Ceramic Tradition in Historical Perspective. *American Antiquity*, 15:196–213.

Tsukada, M., and E. S. Deevey, Jr. 1967. Pollen Analysis from Four Lakes in the Southern Maya Area of Guatemala and El Salvador. In *Quaternary Paleoecology*, ed. E. J. Cushing and H. E. Wright, pp. 303–332. New Haven: Yale University Press.

Turner, B. L. II. 1974a. *Prehistoric Intensive Agriculture in the Mayan Lowlands: New Evidence from the Río Bec Region*. Ph.D. dissertation, University of Wisconsin, Madison.

———. 1976. Prehistoric Population Density in the Maya Lowlands: New Evidence for Old Approaches. *Geographical Review*, 66:73–82.

Urquhart, D. H. 1961. *Cocoa*. 2d ed. New York: John Wiley and Sons.

Vaillant, G. C. 1941. *The Aztecs of Mexico*. Garden City: Doubleday, Doran and Co.

Van Hall, C. J. 1914. *Cacao*. London: Macmillan.

Vienna Dictionary, or *Bocabulario de Mayathan*. 1972. Ed. E. Menguin. Graz: Akademische Druck-Verlag.

Vogt, Evon Z. 1961. Some Aspects of Zinacantan Settlement Pattern and Ceremonial Organization. *Estudios de Cultura Maya*, 1:131–145.

———. 1963. Courses of Regional Scope. In *The Teaching of Anthropology*, ed. David G. Mandelbaum, Gabriel W. Lasker, and Ethel M. Albert. American Anthropological Association Memoir 94, 1:183–190.

———. 1964a. Ancient Maya Concepts in Contemporary Zinacantan Religion. In *VI Congrès International des Sciences Anthropologiques et Ethnologiques, Paris 1960*, part 1, 2:497–502. Paris.

———. 1964b. The Genetic Model and Maya Cultural Development. In *Desarrollo cultural de los mayas*, ed. idem and Alberto Ruz Lhuillier. 1st ed. Mexico City: Centro de Estudios Mayas, UNAM.

———. 1965. Structural and Conceptual Replication in Zinacantan Culture. *American Anthropologist*, 67:342–353.

———. 1969. *Zinacantan: A Maya Community in the Highlands of Chiapas*. Cambridge, Mass.: Harvard University Press.

———. 1971a. The Genetic Model and Maya Cultural Development. In *Desarrollo cultural de los mayas*, ed. idem and Alberto Ruz Lhuillier. 2d ed. Mexico City: Centro de Estudios Mayas, UNAM.

———. 1971b. Summary and Appraisal. In *Desarrollo cultural de los mayas*, ed. idem and Alberto Ruz Lhuillier. 2d ed. Mexico City: Centro de Estudios Mayas, UNAM.

Vogt, Evon Z., and F. Cancian. 1970. Social Integration and the Classic Maya: Some Problems in Haviland's Argument. *American Antiquity*, 35:101–102.

Volz, F. E. 1975. Volcanic Twilights from the Fuego Eruption. *Science*, 189: 48–50.

Voorhies, B. 1972. Settlement Patterns in Two Regions of the Southern Maya Lowlands. *American Antiquity*, 37:115–126.

Wadell, H. 1938. Physical-Geological Features of Peten, Guatemala. In *The Inscriptions of Peten*, by Sylvanus G. Morley, 4, Appendix 1. CIW Publication 437, 4:336–348. Washington, D.C.

Wagley, C. 1941. *Economies of a Guatemalan Village*. American Anthropological Association Memoir 53.

Waldeck, Jean-Frédéric M. de. 1938. *Voyage pittoresque et archéologique dans la province d'Yucatan et aux ruines d'Itzalanes*. Paris: Dufour.

Wauchope, Robert. 1934. *House Mounds of Uaxactun, Guatemala*. CIW Publication 436. Washington, D.C.

———. 1965. *They Found the Buried Cities: Exploration and Excavation in the American Tropics*. Chicago: University of Chicago Press.

Webb, Malcolm C. 1964. *The Postclassic Decline of the Peten Maya: An Interpretation in Light of a General Theory of State Society*. Ph.D. dissertation, University of Michigan.

———. 1973. The Peten Maya Decline Viewed in the Perspective of State Formation. In *The Classic Maya Collapse*, ed. T. Patrick Culbert, pp. 307–404. Albuquerque: University of New Mexico Press.

Webster, David. 1977. Warfare and the Evolution of Maya Civilization. In *The Origins of Maya Civilization*, ed. Richard E. W. Adams, pp. 335–372. Albuquerque: University of New Mexico Press.

Weitz, Charles. 1976. *Resource Manual for "Physical Anthropology and Archaeology" (Clifford J. Jolly and Fred Plog)*. New York: Alfred A. Knopf.

Wexler, H. 1952. Volcanoes and World Climate. *Scientific American*.

Wilken, G. C. 1971. Food-Producing Systems Available to the Ancient Maya. *American Antiquity*, 36:432–448.

———. 1972. Microclimate Management by Traditional Farmers. *The Geographical Review*, 62:544–560.

Willey, Gordon R. 1953. *Prehistoric Settlement Patterns in the Virú Valley, Perú*. Bureau of American Ethnology Bulletin 155. Washington, D.C.: Smithsonian Institution.

———. 1956a. Introduction. In *Prehistoric Settlement Patterns in the New World*, ed. Gordon R. Willey, pp. 1–2. Viking Fund Publication 23. New York.

———. 1956b. Problems Concerning Prehistoric Settlement Patterns in the Maya Lowlands. In *Prehistoric Settlement Patterns in the New World*, ed. Gordon R. Willey, pp. 107–114. Viking Fund Publication 23. New York.

———. 1956c. The Structure of Ancient Maya Society: Evidence from the Southern Lowlands. *American Anthropologist*, 58:777–782.

———. 1974a. Precolumbian Urbanism: The Central Mexican Highlands and the Lowland Maya. In *The Rise and Fall of Civilizations*, ed. J. A. Sabloff and C. C. Lamberg-Karlovsky, pp. 134–144. Menlo Park: Cummings.

———. 1974b. The Classic Maya Hiatus: A Rehearsal for the Collapse? In *Mesoamerican Archaeology: New Approaches*, ed. Norman Hammond, pp. 417–430. Austin: University of Texas Press.

———. 1976. Sir Eric Thompson [1898–1975]. *Archaeology*, 29:57.

———. 1977. The Rise of Maya Civilization: A Summary View. In *The Origins of Maya Civilization*, ed. Richard E. W. Adams. Albuquerque: University of New Mexico Press.

Willey, Gordon R., and William R. Bullard, Jr. 1956. The Melhado Site: A House Mound Group in British Honduras. *American Antiquity*, 22:29–44.

———. 1965. Prehistoric Settlement Patterns in the Maya Lowlands. In *Handbook of Middle American Indians*, 2:360–377. Austin: University of Texas Press.

Willey, Gordon R., William R. Bullard, Jr., and John B. Glass. 1955. The Maya Community of Prehistoric Times. *Archaeology*, 8:18–25.

Willey, Gordon R., William R. Bullard, Jr., John B. Glass, and J. C. Gifford. 1965. *Prehistoric Maya Settlement in the Belize Valley*. Papers of the Peabody Museum, 54. Cambridge, Mass.

Willey, Gordon R., T. Patrick Culbert, and Richard E. W. Adams. 1967. Maya Lowland Ceramics: A Report from the 1965 Guatemala City Conference. *American Antiquity*, 32:289–315.

Willey, Gordon R., and J. C. Gifford. 1961. Pottery of the Holmul I Style from Barton Ramie. In *Essays in Pre-Columbian Art and Archaeology*, ed. S. K. Lothrop et al., pp. 152–170. Cambridge, Mass.: Harvard University Press.

Willey, Gordon R., and D. B. Shimkin 1971. The Collapse of Classic Maya Civilization in the Southern Lowlands: A Symposium Summary Statement. *Southwestern Journal of Anthropology*, 27:1–18.

———. 1973. The Maya Collapse: A Summary View. In *The Classic Maya Collapse*, ed. T. Patrick Culbert, pp. 457–502. Albuquerque: University of New Mexico Press.

Willey, Gordon R., and A. Ledyard Smith. 1963. New Discoveries at Altar de Sacrificios, Guatemala. *Archaeology*, 16:83–89.

———. 1969. The *Ruins of Altar de Sacrificios, Department of Peten, Guatemala: An Introduction*. Papers of the Peabody Museum, 62, no. 1. Cambridge, Mass.

Willey, Gordon R., A. Ledyard Smith, G. Tourtellot III, and Ian Graham. 1975. *Excavations at Seibal, Department of Peten, Guatemala: Introduction:*

The Site and Its Setting. Memoirs of the Peabody Museum, 13, no. 1. Cambridge, Mass.

Wing, Elizabeth S., and Norman Hammond. 1974. Fish Remains in Archaeology: A Comment on Casteel. *American Antiquity*, 39:133–134.

Winick, C., ed. 1964. *Dictionary of Anthropology*. Patterson, N.J.: Littlefield, Adams and Co.

Wisdom, C. 1940. *The Chorti Indians of Guatemala*. Chicago: University of Chicago Press.

Wolf, E. R. 1959. *Sons of the Shaking Earth*. Chicago: University of Chicago Press.

Woodbury, R. B., and A. S. Trik. 1953. *The Ruins of Zaculeu, Guatemala*. Richmond: William Byrd Press.

Wright, A. C. S. 1962. Comment: Some Terrace Systems of the Western Hemisphere and Pacific Islands. *Pacific Viewpoint*, 3:97–101.

Wright, A. C. S., D. H. Romney, R. H. Arbuckle, and V. E. Vial. 1959. *Land in British Honduras*. Colonial Research Publication 24. London: HMSO.

Ximénez, Fray Francisco. 1930. *Historia de la Provincia de San Vicente de Chiapa y Guatemala*, 2. Sociedad de Geografía e Historia, Biblioteca "Goathemala," 2. Guatemala City.

Zimmerman, Günter. 1966. El cotoque, la lengua mayense de Chicomucelo. In *Traducciones mesoamericanistas*, 1:27–71. Mexico City: Sociedad Mexicana de Antropología.

———. 1971. La escritura jeroglífica en la historia cultural de los mayas. In *Desarrollo cultural de los mayas*, ed. Evon Z. Vogt and Alberto Ruz Lhuillier, 2d ed., pp. 243–256. Mexico City: Centro de Estudios Mayas, UNAM.

General Index

Author Index